GABRIEL I.H. WILLIAMS

CORRUPTION *is* DESTROYING AFRICA

The Case of Liberia

Order this book online at www.trafford.com
or email orders@trafford.com

Most Trafford titles are also available at major online book retailers.

Print information available on the last page.

ISBN: 978-1-4907-9571-3 (sc)
ISBN: 978-1-4907-9570-6 (e)

Library of Congress Control Number: 2019908086

Our mission is to efficiently provide the world's finest, most comprehensive book publishing service, enabling every author to experience
success. To find out how to publish your book, your way, and have it available worldwide, visit us online at www.trafford.com

Trafford rev. 09/20/2019

Trafford
PUBLISHING®   www.trafford.com

North America & international
toll-free: 1 888 232 4444 (USA & Canada)
fax: 812 355 4082

Corruption is Destroying Africa

The Case of Liberia

Gabriel I.H. Williams

The Caption of the Photo on the Cover:

A glowing evening sunset on the Atlantic Ocean in Liberia, endowed with natural resources and beauty but empoverished. (Courtesy, Nee Allison and Alvin Allison)

CONTENTS

ACKNOWLEDGMENTS

Let me begin by declaring, praise God from whom all blessings flow, for it is for His mercy and grace that I am alive and have a purpose in life.

I am grateful to all those who have supported me in whatever way possible, especially during the course of this publication. Deserving notable mention among the many wonderful people are the following:

I am grateful to my wife, Neiko Irene Williams, who bore with my shortcomings and material disadvantage for the benefit our family. As now late Archbishop George D. Browne of the Episcopal Church of Liberia acknowledged in his autobiography, a good wife is hard to find, and I thank God for her.

I am grateful to the Reverend Emmanuel Z. Bowier, a former Liberian minister of Information and diplomat, whose mentorship was very critical during my respective tenure as assistant minister and deputy minister at the Ministry of Information, Cultural Affairs, and Tourism at the beginning of the Sirleaf administration. There are accounts related to the Reverend Bowier in this book.

I am also grateful to Dr. D. Elwood Dunn—a retired political science professor, eminent international scholar, and author—for his mentorship during the course of this book project. Dr. Dunn was particularly instrumental in the availability of materials regarding Liberia's role in Africa, as you will read in the book.

I owe a debt of gratitude to Mr. William Ponder, an economist and prolific writer, who edited the original manuscript for this book before the focus was changed. I thank the Lord for his contributions.

Much gratitude is also in order for Mr. Joe S. Kappia, a journalist and teacher, who edited most of the manuscript for this book. A senior media colleague, I am grateful to Joe for his friendship and strong professional support. Joe's professional relationship with me started from my days as a reporter in training at the *Daily Observer* newspaper in Monrovia, where he was the features editor, as also reflected in the book.

During my tenure as a diplomat at the Embassy of Liberia in the United States, I have been blessed to work with many amazing people, past and present, who have positively contributed to the success of my diplomatic service. I am grateful for their friendship and moral support.

Among those for notable mention are the following: Ambassador Jeremiah C. Sulunteh, former deputy chief of mission and now ambassador Jeff G. Dowana, Mrs. Cecelia Harmon-Rogers, Mrs. Nancy Stewart Nwabunnia, Ms. Decontee Clements, Ms. Haibatu Pussah, Ms. Vickie Ward, Mrs. Sophia T. Mawlue, Mr. Edmond K. Neblett, Mrs. Kathleen Demmah, Mr. Elmore Hanky Delaney, Mrs. Nyanda Finda Davis, Mr.

Josiah Domah, Mrs. Muna Wallace-Wah, Ms. Maryann Perry, Mr. Ernest Bowier, Mr. Dolaikeh Quoimie, Ms. Nimalka Joseph, Mr. Upul Jagoda, and Mr. Rohan Abeysinghe.

I wish to also acknowledge various individuals who have provided moral support to my family over the years. These include Dr. Donald S. E. Taylor and Mrs. Esther Taylor for the many years of goodwill toward my family. Dr. Taylor is professor emeritus of communication studies and former assistant vice president for Academic Affairs at California State University, Sacramento (CSUS). Dr. Taylor and his wife are prominent members of the African community in Sacramento. Meanwhile, Mr. Quilly Boyoue, commonly known as Cousin Quilly, and Mother Cecelia Tor have been strong supporters of my family.

Also worthy of commendation are Mr. and Mrs. Gerald F. B. and Roberta Cooper for their contributions toward humanitarian causes in Liberia; immigration attorney Patricia Minikon of the Minikon Law Office in Maryland, United States of America, for supporting humanitarian causes; engineer James J. Johnson, for leaving his promising career in California and returning to Liberia to help develop the country's modern infrastructure, including the newly constructed ELWA Hospital in Monrovia; Dr. Paul Kim, an optometrist in Sacramento, California, for about twenty years of professional service to my family and for his friendship; Flomo B. Washington, a former Liberian government official and senior citizen of the Liberian community in Sacramento, who has been like a father figure to many in the Liberian community; Mr. Charles W.S. Russell, Sr., for his support during my high school days; Ms. Nee Allison, former president of the Liberian Community Association in the Washington DC, Maryland and Virginia metro area; and immigration attorney Varney Taylor of the Taylor Law Firm in Washington DC for his support in legal matters.

I pay homage to the Reverend Joseph Richards-Dedegah, who has been a teacher for more than forty years, molding minds in rural Liberia. Among his contributions to education, cousin Richards-Dedegah served as the principal of Pillar of Fire Mission, a Christian boarding school in Rivercess County operated by the Pillar of Fire Church in the United States. He also served for several years as principal of the Neegbah Public Junior High School in Neegbah, Rivercess, our home village, where I was born. He rose through the ranks to become bishop of the Pillar of Fire Church in Liberia, a position he held for two years. When I was in junior high or middle school, cousin Joseph and his wife, Mrs. Nancy Richards-Dedegah, agreed to have me live with them so that I could continue my education at Pillar of Fire Mission. However, I did not attend Pillar of Fire Mission.

I pay tribute to the late Augustine Nyepan Wolo, commonly known as Gus Wolo, a well-known and beloved Liberian member of the African community in the Sacramento, California area. He was a unifier, bringing people together through social activities. Gus, who passed suddenly in 2018, will always be missed for his care and compassion for others. I also pay tribute to the late Doeba P. Bropleh, former president of the Association of Citizens and Friends of Liberia (ACFLi), the Liberian community association in Sacramento, who is similarly remembered for his invaluable services to the community and humanity. I also celebrate the memory of my late first cousin, Colonel Mark B. Saulwah, who died suddenly in Monrovia in May 2019. A retired member of the disbanded Armed Forces of Liberia following the end of Liberia's civil war, Mark was a colonel actively serving in the Liberia Immigration Service (LIS) during his sudden death from an apparent heat condition. He contributed to Liberia's post-war security sector reforms and also served as a lead investigator with the Truth and Reconciliation Commission (TRC) during the TRC's war-related investigations and hearings in Liberia. He will be always missed for his love and care for family and others.

Before concluding, it is with a sense of deep gratitude to the State of California and the City of Sacramento for affording my family and me a beautiful place of refuge, since we resettled there in the 1990s during the civil war in Liberia. Thank God for His Blessings, because there have been meaningful and fulfilling relationships the Lord has enabled us to establish along the way in the Golden State. I am grateful for our Church Family at Trinity Cathedral in Sacramento, the head church for the Episcopal Church of Northern California. My three children were baptized and confirmed at Trinity by now retired Bishop Jerry Lamb during the tenure of the dynamic Dean Donald Brown, also retired, who embraced my young family and supported us so much during the period of readjustment in a new society. While there have been clergy changes at Trinity over the years, we bless the Lord for the continued presence of the Reverend Canon Lynell Walker, who has remained engaged with my family. Canon Lynell is an amazing priest, who has been actively involved in the lives of my children.

I am well appreciative of the Liberian community in Sacramento, for the strong spirit of togetherness, especially during times of crisis. The University of California, Davis (UC Davis) also deserves a special commendation, as it was the UC Davis Immigration Legal Aid Clinic that provided free immigration legal service to my wife and me when I fled Liberia during the civil war. My daughter Yarvoh was an infant when we used to visit UC Davis campus for our immigration appointments. How notable that in June 2019, Yarvoh received the degree of Bachelor of Science with a major in Psychology with an Emphasis in Biology from UC Davis, a world-class university.

It is also fitting to acknowledge a few other individuals for the friendship and love that they share with my family. These include the following: Mr. Richard and Mrs. Maimah Barclay Cunningham, Mr. Willie and Mrs. Blessing Iyasarie, Mr. Agabus and Mrs. Leanette Adorkor Dahn, Mr. David and Mrs. Elizabeth Moore, Mr. Dickson and Mrs. Kormassah Kollie George, Ms. Evelyn Vongon, Mr. Trokon and Mrs. Elizabeth Richards, Mr. Kolleh and Mrs. Wohma King, Ms. Jennifer Thompson, Mr. Mwah Polson, Apostle MacDonald Jaa, Minister Tim and Mrs. Minor Tor Wulah, Ms. Evelyn Mende, Mr. Silvest Morris, Ms. Christina Bindu Hunter, Mr. Ben Nmah, and one of my favorite friends, Alex Dee.

Finally, bless the Lord for spiritual leaders who have provided spiritual guidance for me to be grounded in the things of God. Those include the Reverend Canon John T. W. Harmon, rector and pastor of Trinity Episcopal Church in Washington DC (my church home away from home), as well as Apostle Seth Baah and his wife, Minister Priscilla Baah, of Dominion Chapel, Full Gospel Ministries in Gaithersburg, Maryland. Apostle Baah is a famous Ghanaian gospel musician. The impact of his gospel music is felt across Africa, Europe, United States, and other parts of the world.

Words are inadequate to express gratitude for what the Lord has done and continues to do for me and my family. When God is with us, who can be against us?

A NOTE TO READERS

In 2009, British Broadcasting Corporation (BBC) world affairs correspondent Mark Doyle took a journey across Africa to ask people the question "Why is Africa poor?" for a BBC radio documentary series. During his journey, which took him to South Sudan, Liberia, Nigeria, and Kenya, people explored the impact that both non-Africans and Africans had had on why Africa is poor.

In a report regarding his journey, Doyle said, "I was asked to investigate why it is that the vast majority of African countries are clustered at or near the bottom of the United Nations Development Index—in other words they have a pretty appalling standard of living" ("Why Is the African Continent Poor?," BBC News, August 24, 2009, http://news.bbc.co.uk/2/hi/africa/8215083.stm).

The effects of colonialism and civil wars were among some of the major problems identified by those from diverse backgrounds who were interviewed on the question why Africa is poor. Nevertheless, there was one notable answer that was pretty much a chorus as to why Africa is poor, and that was corruption.

"Every African I met, who was not actually in government, blamed corrupt African leaders for their plight," Doyle stated in his report. He quoted a fisherman on the shores of Lake Victoria who complained that "the gap between the rich and the poor in Africa is still growing." He added, "Our leaders, they just want to keep on being rich. And they don't want to pay taxes."

Also interviewed for the documentary series was President Ellen Johnson Sirleaf, who was then Liberia's and Africa's first democratically elected female president. In January 2018, following two successive terms of office covering a period of twelve years, President Sirleaf was succeeded by George Manneh Weah, a retired global soccer icon.

In her interview for the documentary series, President Sirleaf said she had underestimated the level of corruption in Liberia when she took office. "Maybe I should have sacked the whole government when I came to power," she said.

"Africa is not poor," President Sirleaf added, "it is poorly managed."

The BBC survey and the interview with President Sirleaf, as reported, are instructive and informative relative to how corruption is a major source of bad governance, widespread poverty, and instability in Africa. It is in view of the foregoing that this book is titled *Corruption Is Destroying Africa: The Case of Liberia*. This is part of my quest to understand in a larger scheme of things why Liberia or Africa continues to be poor in the midst of abundant natural resources.

This book is intended to contribute to the ongoing discourse about Liberia or Africa that has often left people perplexed. According to a 2013 World Bank report, Africa has 30 percent of the world's minerals and proven oil reserves equivalent to 10 percent of global stock. How is it that Africa, which has such enormous mineral and oil wealth, is the poorest continent in the world?

A similar question would suffice for Liberia, which became independent since 1847 and has been a sovereign nation for over 170 years, but it is ranked as one of the poorest countries in the world. This is irrespective of the fact that the country is endowed with abundant natural resources. Accordingly, I herewith submit that Africa or Liberia is not poor but poorly managed and that corruption is a major source of bad governance, widespread poverty, and instability on the continent.

While spending the 2017 Christmas holidays with my family in Sacramento, California, during which I also worked on this book, it was interesting, as always, to get the perspectives of my wife, Neiko Irene Williams, and children on global issues, especially relating to Liberia and Africa or people of color.

My son, whom I would not name because he serves in the US military, was born in Liberia before the start of that country's civil war in 1989, which was why he was brought to the United States as a juvenile. A sergeant in the US military as of this publication, his early upbringing in Liberia, where he has revisited, has helped to shape his perspectives regarding Liberia, Africa, and people of color.

Yarvoh Williams, my daughter, was born in California in the 1990s, after Neiko and I were blessed by the grace of God to resettle and get married in one of the most beautiful and developed parts of the world when we fled from the state of terror in our homeland. Yarvoh, who has visited Liberia and is also being nurtured with African values, graduated on June 15, 2019 from the University of California at Davis (UC Davis), where she earned the degree of Bachelor of Science with a major in Psychology with an Emphasis in Biology, commonly called psychobiology or biopsychology. As of this publication, she is preparing for enrollment in medical school.

It was during one of those family discussions, while we were trying to wrap our minds around some of the challenges confronting Africa, that Yarvoh recommended to me and later assisted me to access online a copy and reviews of the book *Why Nations Fail: The Origin of Power, Prosperity, and Poverty*. She thought that I would find the book insightful in my quest to understanding why Liberia and Africa as a whole have continued to lag behind the rest of the world in progress.

Indeed, the book is an eye-opener on why some nations fail and why others succeed, which also explains why some countries are poor and other are prosperous. *Why Nations Fail* was first published in 2012 by Turkish American economist Daron Acemoglu from the Massachusetts Institute of Technology and British political scientist James A. Robinson from the University of Chicago.

The book applies insights from institutional economics, development economics, and economic history to understand why nations develop differently, with some succeeding in the accumulation of power and prosperity and others failing. The authors also try to examine which factors are responsible for the political and economic success or failure of states.

The authors use as an example the Korean Peninsula, which is divided into two countries: the Democratic People's Republic of Korea (DPRK) (commonly known as North Korea) and South Korea. Since they were divided in 1953, both countries' economies have diverged completely, with South Korea becoming one of the richest countries in Asia, while North Korea remains among the poorest.

To illustrate their point as to which part of the Korean Peninsula is rich or poor, the authors encourage readers to look at the peninsula at night, and the answer would be obvious: South Korea has a lot of light or electricity, while North Korea is mostly dark. A plausible explanation for North Korea being in darkness is because North Koreans do not have access to the types of technologies like electricity and power that the South Koreans do, and that enormously restricts their economic potential.

It is the considered opinion of the authors that the difference between rich countries and poor countries is that poor countries like North Korea tend to have much worse technology than rich countries. They also note that poor countries have much less educated people, much less healthy people who live shorter lives, and have much worse public services and infrastructure.

I would like to further illustrate the above point from an African context by interjecting my personal experience with a comparison of the Ghanaian capital, Accra, and the Liberian capital, Monrovia. In 2011, I boarded a flight from the United States to Liberia via Brussels, Belgium, and Accra, which was the last stop before Monrovia. The flight out of Accra to Monrovia was during the night.

When the plane took off and flew over Accra, passengers could see lights across the city below—a spectacular view, which was a reflection of Ghana's progress in modernization. About two hours later, the plane landed in Monrovia, which was mostly dark. As the pilot announced that we had landed in Monrovia, which was recovering from a destructive civil war, one of the two passengers seated in front of me looked through the window and said to the other, "The place is so dark you can hardly see anything. I can't believe this is Monrovia. It's like a village."

Since the end of Liberia's civil war up to this publication, many Liberians who can afford the cost often travel to Ghana for advanced medical treatment, while Liberia's health care system has remained in a state of dysfunction. The rate of hypertension among Liberians appears to be at a crisis level. Because of the lack of adequate medical care, many able-bodied men and women, young and old, are being struck down by stroke and heart attack at alarming proportions. The impact of the deadly Ebola Virus Disease epidemic, which spread to several West African countries with Liberia the worst affected, reflects the terribly poor state of Liberia's health system.

In *Why Nations Fail*, the authors argue that most of the resources in poor countries that could be used for infrastructural development and improvement in the living conditions of the people are wasted.

They also argue that poor countries and rich countries are organized in different ways. The organization in rich countries creates incentives and opportunities for people, while most poor countries are organized in ways that block incentives and opportunities, and that creates poverty.

Authors Acemoglu and Robinson support their thesis by comparing country case studies. They identify many of the countries that are similar in the above-mentioned factors but become more or less prosperous because of different political and institutional choices. These examples include the United States, which is more prosperous than its neighbor Mexico to the south, as well as several African countries like Zimbabwe and the Democratic Republic of the Congo (DRC), which are among the poorest countries in the world, although they are highly endowed with natural resources.

For example, among a wealth of other metals, the DRC is known to have more than half of the world's cobalt, an essential ingredient in the batteries that power mobile phones and electric cars. According to Reuters News Agency, the DRC is Africa's top copper producer and mines more than 60 percent of the world's cobalt. The DRC, which is also regarded to be one of the world's richest countries in natural resources, has continued to languish as one of the poorest countries in Africa and the world.

Thus, Acemoglu and Robinson's major thesis is that economic prosperity depends above all on the inclusiveness of political and economic institutions. They note that institutions are "inclusive" when many people have a say in political decision-making, as opposed to cases where a small group of people control political institutions and are unwilling to change. The authors argue that inclusive institutions promote economic prosperity because they provide an incentive structure that allows talents and creative ideas to be rewarded.

In contrast, the authors describe "extractive" institutions as ones that permit the elite to rule over and exploit others, extracting wealth from those who are not in the elite. Nations with a history of extractive institutions have not prospered, they argue, because entrepreneurs and citizens have fewer incentives to invest and innovate.

Like many other African countries, Liberia, which is recovering as a failed state following nearly fifteen years of brutal and devastating civil wars, has continued to exhibit the symptoms that are responsible for why a country is poor.

The Story of the Foolish and Wise Builders

In Matthew 7:24 of the Holy Bible, our Lord Jesus Christ tells an interesting parable of the wise and foolish builders. In that account, there was a wise man who built his house on a rock. "The rain came down, the streams rose, and the winds blew and beat against that house; yet it did not fall, because it had its foundation on the rock." On the hand, the foolish man built his house on sand. "The rain came down, the streams rose, and the winds blew and beat against that house, and it fell with a great crash."

The biblical tale of the house built on sand that fell with a great crash is akin to what happened to Liberia. The country was built on a faulty foundation, where an elite minority discriminated against and exploited the vast majority the population for over 130 years. Even though the constitution and system of government of Africa's oldest independent republic was modeled on the US system of government to ensure checks and balances, the rule of law, and accountability, these were nothing more than mere concepts on paper and in name. In real life, while the constitution and laws of the land gathered dust on bookshelves, the rule of men prevailed over the rule of law and democratic governance. State institutions like the national legislature and the judiciary, which are supposed to serve as checks and balances with the executive branch of the government, were weak at best and dysfunctional at worst.

Successive Liberian leaders failed to fully utilize the opportunities that have existed, including the period of economic boom, to ensure infrastructural development and economic growth. Besides the capital, Monrovia, and a few other cities, most parts of Liberia lack electricity and pipe-borne water. Health and educational facilities are limited or inaccessible to people in many rural parts even though the people were forced and sometimes abused to pay taxes to their government that failed to provide basic services for them.

Across the continent, many African leaders have flagrantly violated the laws and constitutions of their respective countries by hanging on to power for decades amid widespread corruption to the detriment of those countries and their peoples. Forcing despots out of power have often led to violence, bloodshed, destruction, and economic hardship for the defenseless masses.

For Liberia or Africa to ensure sustainable growth and development, there is a need for leaders with broad-minded wisdom, courage, and vision to bring about the much-desired transformation.

PREFACE

In August 2006, about seven months after the government of Liberia and Africa's first democratically elected president—Madam Ellen Johnson Sirleaf—assumed power in Liberia, I represented the government at a two-week program, which was the Third Seminar for African Press Officials, sponsored by the State Council Information Office of the People's Republic of China. The seminar brought together government press officials from various African countries and China in order to develop strong media partnership and coordination in information exchange and dissemination. The program was aimed at how China and Africa could better work together to counter some of the many negative reports in the Western media regarding the People's Republic of China and African countries.

The seminar took place about three months following my relocation to Liberia from the United States, where I had lived in exile for a decade after fleeing Liberia's brutal and barbaric civil war due to death threats. I was fortunate to be among a small group of Liberians of diverse professional backgrounds recruited from abroad by the new president to serve in various capacities in the government, which hit the ground running in terms of instituting aggressive reforms to rebuild the war-torn country.

As the Assistant Minister for Information Services at the Ministry of Information, Culture Affairs, and Tourism (MICAT), my responsibilities included devising communication strategies and providing leadership in the planning and execution of public information dissemination and also serving as a prominent government spokesman. MICAT is the official state agency responsible to regulate the media and disseminate government information to the general public, as well as provide oversight for tourism and cultural activities in Liberia.

The program—which enabled the African press officials to travel to several parts of that beautiful, vast, and most populated country in the world (including its capital, Beijing)—was attended by ministers, deputy and assistant ministers, as well as directors of information or communications from more than a dozen African countries, which included Cape Verde, Ethiopia, Eritrea, Ghana, Guinea, Guinea-Bissau, Sierra Leone, Mozambique, Namibia, Kenya, Botswana, Lesotho, Libya, Uganda, Zambia, and Zimbabwe.

The program began in the city of Shenzhen, one of the most industrialized areas in the world, which is separated from Hong Kong by the Shenzhen River. As we shuttled from one part to the other of that beautiful, awe-inspiring city, we learned that Shenzhen was an underdeveloped market town with not more than thirty thousand inhabitants until the city was designated as China's first special economic zone (SEZ) around 1979 or 1980.

Since then, Shenzhen has become one of the leading financial centers in China, home to the Shenzhen Stock Exchange and headquarters of several Chinese multinational high-tech companies. According to the 2017

World Population Review, the town that was once home to just thirty thousand residents has grown to a metropolis that boasts an urban population of over ten million in 2016. During our visit, we learned that the city was inhabited by a predominately young population, attracted by the high-tech industry.

As we toured world-class industrial facilities and other places of interest around the city, the conversations among us, the African delegates, became increasingly focused on how Africa continues to lag behind the rest of the world, like the continent of Asia or China as a country, due to lack of strong visionary leadership that would focus on reforms and infrastructural development that are geared toward improvement in the conditions of the people.

It was clear to us that China, which until the 1970s was similarly as poor and underdeveloped as many parts of Africa, was able to attain the level of progress that marveled us because the country's leadership was able to successfully tap into the country's natural and human resources. From the briefings that we attended at various places, we learned a bit about policies and programs, including economic programs, instituted by the Chinese leadership that have generated major trickle-down effects in terms of the empowerment and improvement of the lives of ordinary Chinese citizens.

While we talked and discussed about the economic and technological power that Africa could become, considering the continent's abundant natural resources, one African colleague made a sad comment that struck me and has remained vividly in my memory, especially whenever reflecting on the seemingly endless problems that have hindered Liberia's and Africa's progress. With a look of disappointment, he shook his head and said, "My heart bleeds for Africa!" There was a momentary silence on the bus in the wake of his comment.

In their book *Why Nations Fail*, authors Daron Acemoglu and James Robinson argue that even though the People's Republic of China has a centralized political system under the Chinese Communist Party, the country's economic growth was jump-started with the introduction in the 1980s of inclusive economic institutions in the rural economy that spread to the industrial sector. This was intended to create incentives and opportunities.

According to the authors, in the 1970s, China was an incredibly poor and technologically backward economy, which started moving economic institutions in the more inclusive direction during the leadership of Chairman Deng Xiaoping. The authors note that moving toward a more inclusive economy spurred the very rapid economic growth and technological advancement of China.

Africa needs leaders who will think and act like Deng Xiaoping in terms of creating the enabling environment to develop inclusive economic institutions that would have trickle-down effects on the vast mass of the population, empower the people, and lead to economic growth.

Africa Yearns for Visionary Leaders

The level of development or progress in any country is measured by the vision of its leaders and the productivity of its people. This is true, for example, of countries like Ghana and Rwanda, which are attaining appreciable progress due to visionary leadership, and countries like Liberia and the Democratic Republic of the Congo

(DRC), which have struggled through conflicts and are among the poorest countries in the world largely because of corrupt leadership.

In the Holy Bible, Proverbs 29:18 (KJV) states, "Where there is no vision the people perish . . ." Africa cannot move forward without leaders with the vision to empower the people to bring out their innovation and entrepreneurship. The need to focus on entrepreneurship and capital investment as the engine for sustainable growth and development in Africa cannot be overemphasized. The Chinese understand this principle that sustainable development comes through empowerment of the people by instituting visionary policies and programs to yield benefits that will percolate or trickle down to the people.

According to the Economic and Social Council of the United Nations, as of 2014, thirty-four out of fifty countries classified as "least developed countries" are in Africa. The nagging question surrounding this puzzling state of affairs is, why is it that many African countries, even though endowed with abundant natural resources, continue to be so poor? Simple answers to the question include corruption and other manifestations of poor governance.

Given these challenges, it goes without saying that Africa has been faced with a crisis of governance. And this is why the poverty rate on the continent has continued to remain very high. Install systems of good governance—such as proper management of public resources, adherence to the rule of law, and adequate provision of basic services—and the livelihood of the masses would improve. Empower the people through education, skills training, and job opportunities; and you will find people being lifted out of power because of the trickle-down effects of the economic benefits. You can also be assured of a continent with high prospects for accelerated economic growth when there is value added to Africa's abundant natural resources through the establishment of local industries. Similarly, hunger would be eliminated in Africa when African countries institute robust agricultural programs to boost food production.

What separates the African people from people in North America, Europe, or Asia is not necessarily race or religion, but opportunity and the lack thereof.

In order for Africa to measure up and equally compete with the rest of the developed world, science and technological innovations are critical to the continent's growth. Hence, the need to build Africa's capacity through science and technology cannot be overemphasized.

Let me, however, hasten to indicate that this publication by no means seeks to create an impression that it is all gloom and doom in Africa. It is pleasing to note that despite the challenges, progress has been steady in several African countries, such as Namibia, Ghana, and Rwanda, where there have been encouraging leadership efforts to strengthen democracy and the rule of law, create economic opportunities, build capacity through education, skills training, employment, and other incentives to empower the people.

As then US president Barack Obama declared while attending the Global Entrepreneurship Summit during his historic visit to Kenya on July 25, 2015, "Africa is on the move, Africa is one of the fastest growing regions in the world" ("Obama Says 'Africa is on the move,'" AFP, July 25, 2015).

Indeed, Africa is on the move. President Obama was on point when he said that people are being lifted out of poverty, incomes are up, the middle class is growing, and young people are harnessing technology to change the way Africa is doing business.

Nevertheless, while the continent is on the move and many are being lifted out of poverty, majority of Africans have been feeing left behind, stuck in the mud of limited opportunity and poverty, so to speak. *The benefits of the economic gains have yet to trickle down* fast enough to the masses, who are mostly the less fortunate. It is that feeling of hopelessness and destitution that have in recent years driven tens of thousands of Africans, mostly young people, including unaccompanied minors, from various parts of the continent to risk their lives attempting to cross the Mediterranean Sea into Europe in rickety boats. Feeling dispossessed and desperate for a better future, thousands of unfortunate migrants and refugees have perished in the Sahara and drowned at sea trying to make the treacherous journey to Europe.

The Need to Involve Diaspora Africans in Africa's Development

With the reported rise of nationalism and right-wing extremist political activities based on racism and other acts of discrimination in Europe, the United States, and other parts of the world, Africans and people of color and African descent have come under attack in these places. Reports abound of how African families have been uprooted, shattered, humiliated, and reduced to poverty due to challenges related to immigration policies being instituted in recent years. If the enabling environment existed in African countries where Africans in the diaspora could return home and live with the quality of life they enjoy abroad, many of them may not choose to remain abroad and continue to suffer humiliation.

Many accomplished or prosperous Africans in the diaspora usually express how they yearn to return home with their knowledge and resources to give back to their people, but they are hindered or discouraged by the systems of bad governance at home. At a time Africa has been faced with a crisis of unemployment among young people, the hundreds of millions of dollars in remittances from Africans in the diaspora to families and other causes back home have helped to sustain the economies of those countries. Thanks to the remittances, millions of families in various parts of Africa, among them the poorest, are able to keep a roof over their heads and provide food, medical care, and education to their children, among others.

It is also about time African countries adopt liberal immigration policies and programs to create the enabling environment that would encourage more African Americans and people of African descent in Europe and other parts of the world to easily immigrate to Africa and settle in any country as they wish. African Americans are the most advanced and prosperous among the people of African descent in the world. The transfer of knowledge and resources to Africa by people of African descent in the diaspora would be mutually beneficial in terms of empowerment of the people as well as connectivity of people, better understanding, and expansion of African American businesses in the African markets. We must seek to overcome the ignorance and break the artificial barriers that divide us as a people.

This is why there can be no question that Africa will truly rise when there is adherence to good governance and the rule of law, combined with economic benefits that would percolate or trickle down to the ordinary people. Africa will surely rise when young Africans have access to quality education with a focus on science and technological innovations that would enable them to compete globally, aspire to the best of their possibilities, and enjoy the benefits of a decent modern living condition.

An Urgent Need for African Empowerment

As then president Obama indicated in his 2010 State of the Union address, "In the twenty-first century, the best anti-poverty program around is a world-class education." There is a need for educational programs that would also focus on entrepreneurship as well as apprenticeship training for the less educated. These programs, alongside robust agricultural ventures to boost food production, would be in the right direction to lift Africans out of poverty. That is what would help empower the people and create the momentum for Africa to move faster or leap ahead in development.

Africa does not necessarily need aid and handouts from the outside world. What Africans need most is the opportunity to aspire to the best of their human potentials and capabilities so as to enable them to be lifted from the valley of despair toward the mountain of hope and opportunity, where they would be empowered to fully compete globally.

Mr. James E. Cooper, a forward-thinking dear friend of mine who is an entrepreneur in the rubber business in Liberia, shared with me on social media a quote attributed to President Paul Kagame of Rwanda, who has emerged to be regarded as one of Africa's farsighted and innovative leaders. President Kagame is quoting as saying, "I would rather argue, that we need to mobilize the right mind-set, rather than more funding. After all, in Africa, we have everything we need, in real terms. Whatever is lacking, we have the means to acquire. And yet we remain mentally married to the idea that nothing can get moving, without external finance . . ."

Speaking at the 2018 Oxford Africa Conference at Oxford University, England, President Nana Addo Dankwa Akufo-Addo of Ghana, who is also emerging as one of Africa's farsighted and eloquent leaders, articulated a similar thought regarding Africa. According to President Akufo-Addo, Africa is endowed with immense natural resources—every mineral mankind requires to run a modern economy—and that the continent is in possession of 30 percent of the earth's remaining mineral resources. Unfortunately, he noted, Africans are poor amid huge infrastructural deficit because of the economic structure based on the exportation of Africa's natural resources, importation of manufactured products from abroad, and dependence on foreign aid. He emphasized the need to create the enabling economic environment in Africa to add value to the continent's natural resources, which would generate more employment and economic prosperity for the African people.

President Akufo-Addo intoned that Africa must be developed and become known for prosperity and opportunities rather than poverty and despair. He added that Africa cannot afford a slow period of growth because so much time has been lost; and the continent's dynamic, restless young population, who demand and deserve the best in the world, are not in the mood to wait for the dividends from a slow progress, as their trek across the Sahara Desert has vividly illustrated.

Indeed, it is about time that Africa, one of the world's most endowed continents with natural resources, concentrates more on the establishment of light and heavy manufacturing industries to add value to the natural resources so as to generate more employment and revenue and empower the people. This is the only way the economic benefits will have trickle-down effects on the entire population, including the less fortunate living in conditions of poverty. The traditional focus on the exportation of natural resources out of Africa has seriously undermined the progress of the continent and reduced African countries to nothing more than recipients of foreign aid.

As an example of what Africa needs to consolidate economic gains, Mr. Cooper, who is chief executive officer (CEO) of the Cooper Rubber Farm Processing Plant in Bomi County, Liberia, has been struggling to establish the first rubber manufacturing industry in the country, with a focus on manufacturing vehicle tires, gloves, and other latex products for sanitary and medical purposes and others. As the company expands its operations, more people, who are mostly based in that rural part of Liberia, have opportunity for skills development and employment.

It may be interesting to note that since Firestone Natural Rubber Company (headquartered in Akron, Ohio, United States) began operation in Liberia in 1926 and was once the world's largest rubber plantation, Liberia has not been able to boast of a single rubber processing plant to produce even gloves. The raw material, like virtually all natural resources of the country, is exported abroad.

To ensure sustainable peace and progress, efforts must be directed at adding value to Africa's natural resources and containing the cancer of corruption and other vestiges of bad governance that have long kept African countries and the African people from reaching their full potentials.

Since my China trip, I have served in other capacities over the past twelve years of the Sirleaf administration, such as the Deputy Minister for Public Affairs at the Ministry of Information and finally assuming a diplomatic post at the Embassy of the Republic of Liberia in the United States. During this period of public service, I have experienced what is achievable in terms of progress under a leadership that has a vision and subscribes to the tenets of good governance and the rule of law. I have also sadly experienced how bad governance, as manifested by corruption and other vices, has interrupted or stalled progress.

There can be no contradiction that bad governance and a lack of visionary leadership are a major source of poverty and underdevelopment in Liberia and Africa in general. There can also be no question that visionary leadership is critical for Africa's development.

While using Liberia as the context for this publication, I hasten to note that it is also an attempt to delve into issues that are crosscutting in African countries, such as common problems related to inadequate or poor infrastructure and public services, high unemployment, corruption, and mismanagement of public resources, among others, which have negatively impacted the quality of life of the people across the continent.

From the Liberian experience, I hope those familiar with the African reality would see some of the common threads of how poor governance, as exemplified by corruption, is the main culprit for the underdevelopment, instability, bloodshed, destruction, and poverty in Africa. There can be no question that the last major hurdle to Africa's breakthrough is corruption.

As Dr. Kwame Nkrumah, legendary Pan-Africanist and first president of Ghana, once said, "Africa is rich and not poor. It is Africans who are poor, not Africa."

As indicated earlier, over the past twelve years in public service, I have experienced a country that showed significant progress during a period when the resources were being properly managed; and I have also experienced progress being stalled in the national rebuilding process due to the mismanagement of public resources.

Because of Madam President's effective leadership during her first term and thanks to the very strong support from international partners, war-torn Liberia achieved impressive growth and development and became one of Africa's fastest-growing economies. For example, in 2010, Liberia was one of the twelve fastest-growing economies in the world, with a projected growth rate of 7.53 percent, according to the Economy Watch news outlet.

This notable achievement, as you will read in this book, was because of the implementation of policies and programs in keeping with the principles of good governance. Under the guidance of the international community, accountability in the management of public resources was put in place. As a result, corruption was under control, and the country achieved surplus in its foreign reserves.

On the other hand, as Liberians assumed full control of the administration of financial matters when the direct involvement of international partners ended, the country began to stray away from adherence to the principles of good governance. Even though the president, a proven competent leader, was backed by a leadership team comprising some of the brightest minds and highly experienced administrators, failure to adhere to the requirements of good governance undermined Liberia's progress. Accordingly, corruption became the order of the day as the president basically acknowledged losing the war on corruption in the twilight of her administration.

Reporting on the state of the nation in her last annual message to the Joint Session of the National Legislature on January 23, 2017, President Sirleaf said, "We have not fully met the anti-corruption pledge that we made in 2006. It is not because of the lack of political will to do so, but because of the intractability of dependency and dishonesty cultivated from years of depravation and poor governance." During her inauguration in 2006, President Sirleaf had declared war on corruption as public enemy number one, which must be contained in order to accelerate national progress.

While Liberia was grappling with a serious economic crisis blamed largely on corruption and a decline in global commodity prices that negatively affected the country, President Sirleaf turned over the affairs of Liberia to newly elected president George Manneh Weah, a global soccer legend. The inauguration, which took place on January 22, 2018, was a historic moment in Liberia because it was the first time in more than seventy years for a peaceful transition from an incumbent administration to a newly elected government.

On January 29, 2018, in his first state of the nation address to the Joint Session of the National Legislature upon assuming office, President Weah announced that his government inherited a country that was broke. President Weah said, "Our economy is broken, our government is broke, our currency is in freefall, inflation is rising, unemployment is at an unprecedented high, and our foreign reserves are at an all-time low."

In the absence of proper utilization of the country's resources, Liberia's progress has been gravely hindered, and the government's efforts to ensure poverty reduction have yet to achieve the desired results.

Nevertheless, one of the positive things for which Madam President will be remembered is for ensuring twelve years of uninterrupted peace and for the promotion of freedom of speech and of the press during her tenure. Underscoring efforts her government had made to maintain the peace in fragile Liberia in her last address to the Joint Session of the National Legislature on January 23, 2017, President Sirleaf said, "We have young people who have never known war or civil conflict. We have young people who have not had to run, hide or cower in their homes. We have thousands of children back in school. We have farmers who have returned to their villages, refugees and professionals who are returning home. This peace is our greatest triumph."

This book project was undertaken for a period of six years, beginning in 2013, one year after the start of the second term of President Ellen Johnson Sirleaf, Liberia's and Africa's first democratically elected female president. The initial focus of the book was to tell the success story of a country that was experiencing major reforms and commendable transformation since the international intervention under the auspices of the United Nations (UN) to end the bloody and destructive civil war that reduced Liberia to a failed and pariah state.

Despite some shortcomings, the first term of Madam President was mostly successful in getting war-torn Liberia back on the road to recovery. Liberia's economy became one of the fastest growing in the world as the country regained its place as a respectable member of the international community, as well as a rare success story in international partnership under the auspices of the UN.

However, at the time she left office in 2018, the gains that had been made in postwar Liberia were threatened to be reversed because the country was literally consumed by corruption, which is the source of bad governance, poverty, and instability in Liberia and in Africa, as you will read throughout this book. The aftermath of the deadly Ebola pandemic, characterized by Liberia's economic decline, compelled the need to reconsider the original focus of the book, which was to highlight Liberia as a postwar success, a country that was building upon the gains made in good governance and infrastructural development to lift its citizens out of poverty and empower them.

I first changed the focus of the book following the outbreak of the Ebola Virus Disease (EVD) epidemic in several West African countries, of which Liberia was worst affected. I had determined that focusing on the Ebola pandemic would highlight the extreme poverty, limited or none existent health infrastructure, and weak governance, which intensified the deadly impact of the disease, especially in Liberia.

However, I decided against the use of the Ebola pandemic as the book's main theme, thanks to the advice from my media colleague and friend for thirty years, Mr. Bill Berkeley, an American journalist with more than a decade reporting on African affairs for The Atlantic Monthly, The New Republic, the New York Times Magazine and The Washington Post. After a review of some of my manuscript, he advised that I shoud not focus only on the Ebola crisis because the world's attention would be drawn to other developments and public interest would wane once the Ebola pandemic was contained in West Africa.

An investigative reporter with The New York Times, Berkeley is the author of the book, Liberia: A Promised Betrayed: A Report on Human Rights, published in 1986 by the U.S.-based Lawyers' Committee for Human Rights. I was a young journalist becoming actively involved in the ongoing advocacy and struggle for free speech and democratic governance in Liberia when Bill came to the country to conduct investigation for the book, which provides extensive details of the widespread human rights abuses during the despotic regime of

Samuel Doe. After the book was published, the Doe regime banned its distribution in Liberia, while General Charles Julu, a notorious perpetrator singled out for perpetrating some egregious acts of brutality, threatened that he could not guarantee Berkeley's safety if he returned to Liberia. In the wake of threats from the regime because of the book, I wrote Bill a letter to alert him of these developments. He never returned to Liberia until 1992 during the civil war, following Doe's death and the collapse of his brutal regime. Berkeley's visit was part of another investigation for his most recent book, The Graves Are Not Yet Full: Race, Tribe and Power in the Heart of Africa, published in 2001. The book examines racial or ethnic conflicts in Africa, with a focus on Liberia, Democratic Republic of Congo (previously known as Zaire), South Africa, Sudan, Uganda and Rwanda. Mr. Berkeley also teaches writing at Columbia University's graduate school of International and Public Affairs.

Meanwhile, as corruption became widespread and uncontrollable in Liberia, the focus of the book was finally changed to reflect this prevailing reality, highlighting corruption as the cancer that is eating at Liberia's and Africa's vitals. There is no question that corruption is destroying Liberia or Africa and that there can be no meaningful progress until this vice is contained.

Even though the book was originally scheduled to be published in 2018 following the end of the Sirleaf administration, the publication was delayed until 2019 for technical reasons.

I beseech you, therefore, to join me through these pages, which seek to highlight some of the reasons for Liberia's and Africa's underdevelopment. There are similarities in why many Africans have been impoverished and disempowered in a country or a continent endowed with abundant natural resources. Liberians are a resilient people, and I can certainly make similar claim for peoples in other parts of Africa. However, many Africans are not able to realize their full potentials due to a lack of opportunities resulting from poor governance.

Let us start with the Liberian story, beginning with the founding of the country in 1822 by ex-slaves and freeborn blacks from the United States who were repatriated to Africa, their ancestral homeland.

CHAPTER ONE
The Founding of Liberia

I was born in Liberia, a small, but beautiful country with abundant natural resources located on the Atlantic coast of West Africa, bordering Sierra Leone to its west, Guinea to its north, the Ivory Coast (also known as Côte d'Ivoire) on the east, and the Atlantic Ocean to its south. Liberia's population is estimated at more than 4.5 million as of the date of this publication. The climate is tropical with two main seasons. The dry season begins from November to April, and the wet season from May to October. English is the official language, spoken alongside some thirty indigenous languages.

My home village, Neegbah, located in Rivercess County on southeastern Liberia, is within an area situated across the Cestos River from Cestos City, capital of Rivercess County, just about a couple of miles from the estuary, which is the area where the Cestos River joins the Atlantic Ocean. The view of the area, which has not been affected by human activities, is spectacular and breathtaking; and it bears close resemblance to the San Francisco Bay Area in California. This is why San Francisco is one of my most favorite cities in the world, and whenever I visit there, I feel a connection to the place of my birth in Liberia.

A beautiful wood carving depicting the map of the Republic of Liberia

I was born in traditional royal families on my mother's and father's sides. Neegbah was the home of my mother, Yarvoh, where I was fortunate to see my grandmother reign as queen before she died in the early 1980s. She was called Brumkan, which literally means "queen." She was known to be such a powerful and no-nonsense leader that she commanded the respect of everyone, including the men, in our clan. My family quarter in Neegbah was known as Badaykay, meaning "the barracks," because it was a defensive fortress against enemy invasion back in those days, long before I was conceived.

It may be interesting to note that my maternal family, known as the Geh Zor family, is involved in a traditional practice that could raise eyebrows during this modern era. In keeping with our traditional practice, those who belong to the Geh Zor lineage are not buried when they die. Following the burial rituals, during which the deceased is adorned with certain traditional attires, including leopard teeth as a mark of high honor, the body is then deposited on an island on the Cestos River. The island where the bodies of the dead are deposited is called Zeo.

The practice of depositing bodies on the island continues to this day even though it is no longer mandatory, but optional, based on the wishes of the person who died or the immediate family of the deceased. The prevailing necessity to bury the dead rather than deposit it on the island is largely due to the spread of Christianity and modern influence among the indigenous population.

Surrounded by beautiful sandy grassland, Neegbah is only accessible by canoe and boat ride from Cestos City, which is the official residence of the county superintendent and the county administration. Bordering Cestos City is an ancient forest, which has been recognized as a UNESCO heritage site. Because of the sacred nature of the forest to the indigenous population, traditional laws forbid humans from using blade to cut any stump or tree within the ancient forest. Another old landmark in Cestos City is what used to be a small domestic airstrip that accommodated smaller planes. The airport was also used for commercial flights by the national carrier Air Liberia and Weasua Air Transport, among others, until the civil crises, which resulted in the destruction of facilities at the airstrip.

I remember my first plane ride in my early teenage years aboard a Cessna flight from Monrovia to Cestos City with my aunt, Konwree, who was a resident in Neegbah. She was taking me back home to spend time with her and my grandmother Bromkahn. That was my first return to my home village since my father took my younger sister, Mai, and me from the village immediately following the death of our mother, Yarvoh, from childbirth. We were each younger than ten years old when our family was destroyed because of the death of our mother.

The Cestos River, after which Rivercess is named, is navigable, as is the case with many of the rivers that run through Liberia and empty into the Atlantic Ocean. Before modern means of transportation like land vehicles and airplanes, the most convenient means of transportation was by canoe and boat, which navigated the river channels and the Atlantic Ocean conveying goods and passengers.

Many rivers in Liberia, like the Junk River in Margibi County (photographed), are navigable and run into the ocean (photo courtesy of the author).

My father, Tommy, who was also known as Teah, was a carpenter and mason by trade. He generated extra income by serving as a crew member for some of the commercial boats that transported goods and passengers from Rivercess to mostly the port city of Buchanan and the national capital, Monrovia.

Even though Rivercess is well endowed with natural resources such as diamonds, gold, timber, fisheries and other seafood, vast agricultural land areas, not to mention tourism potentials, it has been one of the most economically depressed and underdeveloped parts of Liberia. It was not until after the end of the civil war that Cestos City, the Rivercess County capital, was connected by motor road.

Like my friend James Cooper, whom I referenced in the Preface, often said, "Open the roads, and people will follow." The delay in constructing roads in Rivercess and most of southeastern Liberia has been a major factor for that part of the country's underdevelopment, as compared with other areas like Bong, Nimba, and Lofa counties, for example, which benefitted from road networks several decades ago.

Rivercess is a replica of Liberia, which is very rich in natural resources but has been rated as one of the poorest countries in Africa and in the world. Equally so, Liberia is a replica of Africa, which is one of the world's richest continents in natural resources but is the poorest in terms of limited infrastructural development and poor living conditions of the overwhelming majority of the people.

Liberia, which lies on the southwestern corner of the "bulge" of West Africa, is the African continent's thirty-ninth-largest country out of fifty-four countries, covering an area of forty-three thousand square miles. Liberia is blessed with a 360-mile coastline of white sandy beaches lined with palm and coconut trees along the Atlantic coast. The country is also blessed with mountain ranges, lakes, waterfalls, and 43 percent of the rain forest in West Africa, with unique plant and animal spices, including the pygmy hippopotamus, which was first discovered in Liberia.

An impressive view of the Atlantic Ocean near the shore

Liberia is blessed with 360 miles of Atlantic coastline.

A view of Liberia's sandy beach in need of development

Liberia's wildlife includes many types of monkeys, fifteen varieties of snakes, elephants, buffaloes, antelopes and duikers, three types of crocodiles, as well as many predators of the leopard group, among others. The country is also blessed with a variety of birdlife. Of all the birds, the most plentiful and the one most often seen is the common bulbul, also known as pepper bird. It is not surprising that it should have provided Liberia with its nickname, the Land of the Pepper Bird (*Background to Liberia*, published by the Ministry of Information, Culture Affairs, and Tourism, 1979, page 40).

Liberia has two seasons: rainy and dry seasons. The rainy season is from May to October, and the dry season runs from November to April.

As another example of Liberia as a potential tourism haven, the country has been recognized to have one of the best surfing waters in the world, in addition to its biodiversity. US-based global television network CNN (Cable News Network) has reported that one of the world's best surfing areas, which is now attracting tourists from around the world, is located in Robertsport, the capital of Grand Cape Mount County. The picturesque city lies on the shore of the magnificent Lake Piso, which measures some forty square miles, and is recognized as a national "beauty spot" for great tourism. "Fairly shallow, it abounds with tropical fish of many sorts and sizes, and is surrounded by beautiful sandy beaches and palm trees. Used by the Allies during the Second World War as a major seaplane base, it is ideal for speed-boating, and is earmarked for tourist development" (*Background to Liberia*, pages 20–21).

The challenge has been how to create the enabling environment to develop the infrastructure that would attract more tourists and more tourism dollars to sustain the local economy and help improve the living conditions of local residents. With the requisite support, some of the young Liberian surfers who started the sport of surfing following the end of the civil war in Liberia, as featured in the CNN report, could emerge to compete globally and be empowered to help develop the surfing tourism industry.

Those young surfers could be potential world champions when given the opportunity to excel in the sport to the best of their abilities. An example of how young Liberian athletes have demonstrated the ability to compete and win at the global level is George Manneh Weah, the current president of Liberia. Even though he grew up in poverty in a slum in Monrovia, when he got an opportunity as a soccer player, he excelled to be ranked as the world's number one soccer star, earning millions before his retirement from the sport. President Weah exemplifies the importance of giving every young African child an opportunity to aspire to the best of their abilities because you never know what he or she might become.

Young surfers are heading to the ocean in Liberia, which is recognized to have one of the best surfing waters in the world (Courtesy, Naquetta Ricks, Liberian Surfing Federation.)

The abundance of Liberia's beautiful scenery have yet to be exposed to the outside world due to lack of infrastructural development (Courtesy, Nee Allison)

A partial view of the magnificent Lake Piso, which measures some 40 miles with breathtaking scenery (Courtesy, Mohamedu F. Jones, donated to the Liberian Embassy, U.S.)

Liberia's vast Atlantic coastline and body of ocean also have huge potential for a lucrative fishing industry as the country once had a thriving fishing industry and exported fish and other seafood to some parts of Africa and the world, including Japan. The country, whose per capita income was equivalent to that of Japan in the 1970s, has been a major maritime power with thousands of ships around the world flying its flag of convenience.

Endowed with abundant natural resources, Liberia was once one of the world's leading exporters of iron ore. The country's natural resources include diamonds, rubber, timber, gold, coffee, cocoa, and oil palm. Firestone Rubber Plantation, once the world's largest rubber plantation, is located in Liberia, from where the raw material of latex is exported abroad to produce the Firestone tires. In 2002, oil became a new discovery in the country; and several American companies, including Chevron and Exxon Mobile, established partnerships with Liberia in the oil sector.

The country once operated its own national airline, Air Liberia, which made domestic and international flights. It also exported to neighboring countries and beyond manufactured products such as toiletries, flour, cement, tennis shoes, and some rubber products, among others.

Notwithstanding the economic progress the country made, the benefits did not percolate to the ordinary people. The economic benefits did not have enough trickle-down effects on the majority of the population, who have languished in poverty and deprivation, and this was a major root cause of Liberia's underdevelopment and recent civil crises.

The population of Liberia includes people of local ethnic origin, descendants of Africans who returned from various parts of the Americas in the early 1800s to found a free country in the continent of their ancestors, and descendants of recaptured slaves on the high seas who were brought ashore and set free in Liberia. The population also includes settlers from the Middle East, Asia, Europe, and United States, among others. Constituting an overwhelming majority of the population are the seventeen major ethnic groups that speak different languages. Some of the ethnic languages, such as the Vai and Bassa, have written alphabets and printed materials.

According to the 2008 Liberian census, 85.5 percent of the Liberian population practices Christianity while Muslims comprise 12.2 percent of the population ("Liberia: Man, 21, Suffers 'Religious Persecution' for Joining Christianity," *FrontPage Africa*, March 13, 2019).

In the book *Background to Liberia*, published in the 1970s by the Ministry of Information, Cultural Affairs, and Tourism (MICAT), it is noted that "a large proportion of Liberians can claim affiliation with more than one tribe, intermarriage having been very common for some time, especially in the cities, and becoming more so; similarly, of the settlers who arrived with no tribal affinities, there are few who do not have the blood of one or more of the Liberian tribes in their veins and who do not identify with a tribal group" (*Background to Liberia*, page 53).

Despite the close blood and ethnic bonds connecting the people, as reflected above, Liberia was a country divided by class and ethnicity. It was this unresolved past that conspired to destroy a country that has every potential to be a beautiful place for everyone to live.

The following is a brief historical account regarding how the Republic of Liberia came about and why the country is struggling in the process of rebuilding following years of civil upheaval.

Brief Historical Highlights

The modern state of Liberia was founded in 1822 by the American Colonization Society (ACS), a philanthropic organization, to settle ex-slaves and freeborn blacks from the United States, who are now referred to as African Americans. The country was founded as a land of freedom and liberty for people of African descent from around the globe during a period when black people endured slavery and colonial subjugation around the world. During that year, the first group of repatriates from America landed in that part of West Africa and founded a settlement that would evolve to become the Republic of Liberia.

The ACS was supported by such prominent American leaders as senators Henry Clay and Daniel Webster, as well as presidents Thomas Jefferson, James Madison, and James Monroe, who worked toward the creation of a colony in Africa for free blacks and manumitted slaves, along the lines of an earlier British effort at Sierra Leone ("The ACS and the Establishment of the Liberian Colony, 1816–1847," introduction, *Historical Dictionary of Liberia*, second edition, page 3).

In addition to those antislavery religious entities that also supported the repatriation of African Americans to Africa, other American leaders who supported the ACS included Francis Scott Key, who authored the American national anthem, "The Star-Sparkled Banner," and Justice Bushrod Washington, nephew of George Washington, first president of the United States. It was in recognition of their respective roles in the founding of Liberia that many places in the country are named after some American leaders, states, and places. For example, Liberia's capital Monrovia was named for James Monroe, the fifth president of the United States, under whose administration Liberia was founded. Meanwhile, Bushrod Island, a borough of Monrovia, is named for Bushrod Washington. Monrovia was originally called Christopolis (City of Christ), reflecting the strong influence of Christianity in the country's foundation.

According to historical accounts, the ACS was a mixture of people who had different agendas. There were antislave activists, such as the Quakers, who supported the repatriation of freed blacks to Africa so as to enable them to enjoy equality, justice, and the freedom that was denied them in America. On the other hand were former slave owners who supported the repatriation of freed blacks from America out of fear that a growing population of the emancipation of blacks could lead to revolt against the establishment. In the 1700s, revolt by slaves in Haiti, who overthrew their French master and took over the country, had generated fear regarding the possibility of such an occurrence in America.

Some slave owners decided to emancipate their slaves on condition that the slaves and their families would leave the United States to start anew in Africa. American states that were regarded as slave states encouraged the formation of colonization societies to get rid of the free African American population. For example, Maryland, Virginia, and Mississippi established colonies in what is present-day Liberia for former slaves and free blacks. These colonization societies operated independent of the ACS (chronology, *Culture and Customs of Liberia*, page xvi). Today, there are places in Liberia named after places in America from whence the settlers came.

In 2017, while serving as a diplomat at the Embassy of Liberia in the United States, I had the opportunity to visit the very beautiful historic campus of the prestigious University of Virginia (UVA) in Charlottesville, Virginia, as a member of the delegation of President Ellen Johnson Sirleaf. As part of the activities during her visit to the United States at that time, President Sirleaf attended the commencement convocation of her granddaughter, who was graduating with a master of business administration (MBA) degree from the Darden School of Business of the University of Virginia, which is reputed to be among the world's ten best graduate business schools.

While interacting with university officials and staff during a tour of the breathtaking campus of UVA, which was established by Thomas Jefferson, a Founding Father of the United States, I heard the story of a former slave who was connected to Liberia who helped to build UVA. The story exemplifies how slaves were offered freedom on condition that they leave America to settle in Africa, and they were even given free passage by ship.

In 1833, a prominent Virginia resident and slave owner, John Hartwell Cocke, who was one of the first members of the governing Board of Visitors of the now-renowned University of Virginia, emancipated an enslaved man named Peyton Skipwith, along with his wife and five children, with the caveat that they be transported to Liberia. According to historical accounts, Skipwith, who became a literate man and a skilled mason, was apprentice to two white stonemasons responsible for the building of Cocke's home. While in Liberia, Skipwith and his family kept in regular contact with their former slave master, who served as vice president of the ACS, through a series of letters describing the conditions of the early colonists in Liberia.

In recognition of his labor and sacrifices in helping to build the UVA, the university, in 2017, dedicated a new $6 million Skipwith Hall, which is built at or near the quarry where Skipwith and others quarried stone for the school, according to a report by the *Washington Post* ("Enslaved Man Who Helped Build U-VA. Has a Building Named for Him," April 14, 2017). As someone noted, the Skipwith story is also an example of how America was built on the backs, blood, and sweat of slaves.

The UVA must be applauded for this initiative to honor the memory of a slave who sacrificed sweat and blood and, even more, to help build what is now a world-class university, which is making tremendous contributions to the advancement of mankind. We cannot undo the evil past, but we can certainly use the painful examples of the past to make the future better for all of God's children.

A year following my visit to UVA, I was honored to represent the Embassy of Liberia near Washington at the dedicatory ceremony of a historical marker in memory of Ms. Margaret Mercer, an educator and abolitionist. Ms. Mercer, who worked for the freedom and dignity of all people, educated children of slaves and ex-slaves. She also arranged and financed the repatriation of many former slaves from the United States to Liberia in the 1830s.

The historical marker stands on the grounds of St. David's Episcopal Church and School in Ashburn, Virginia. According to historical accounts, Ms. Mercer gave the land on which St. David's Church and School is built to the Episcopal Church. Even though she was from a very wealthy and influential family of her time and her father was a slave owner, Ms. Mercer dedicated her life to the cause of others, including the enslaved and underprivileged, even at personal risks. Today we celebrate her for daring to make a difference in the cause of humanity in the face of personal danger and sacrifices.

As a result of Ms. Mercer's courage and hard work, there have been long-standing historical ties between the Republic of Liberia and St. David's Episcopal Church and School. These ties are the chains that connect us as humans despite our racial, ethnic, religious, or any other superficial differences. As a result of the connections, St. David's can boast among its membership an impressive number of Liberian Americans, who are also prominent members of the Liberian diaspora.

An example of the special ties between Liberia and St. David's is the critical support that the church has provided to sustain Bromley Mission, a boarding school for girls, operated by the Episcopal Church of Liberia in the western part of the country. Like every part of Liberia, Bromley Mission, which has produced many women leaders in Liberia for decades, was closed and destroyed during the war. Thanks to St. David's, through the instrumentality of its members of Liberian descent, as well as other Episcopalians and alumni, the Episcopal Church of Liberia was able to reopen Bromley after the war in order to continue to provide quality education for girls.

Another example of St. David's ties to Liberia was the Very Reverend Dr. Emmanuel W. Johnson, former dean of Trinity Cathedral in Monrovia and former president of Cuttington University College in Liberia, now Cuttington University. He served for sixteen years as priest associate, spiritual leader, and mentor at St. David's until his death in March 2018. After he relocated to the United States in the wake of the Liberian civil war, the Reverend Dr. Johnson also served as dean of Academic Support Services and chaplain of Voorhees College in Denmark, South Carolina, from 1992 to 2003.

Now late Rev. Dr. Emmanuel W. Johnson being decorated by directive of then president Sirleaf at a 2014 Liberian embassy event in Washington by then ambassador Jeremiah Sulunteh (L) and then deputy foreign minister Elias Shoniyin.

Following his funeral at the Washington National Cathedral in Washington DC, the Very Reverend Dr. Johnson, who was in his ninety-fourth year, was laid to rest at a cemetery on the grounds of St. David's Episcopal Church and School, where many prominent citizens of Virginia are also buried.

The historic Washington National Cathedral is the mother church for the Episcopal Diocese of Washington, currently under the stewardship of Bishop Mariann Edgar Budde. It is also the home church for the presiding bishop of the Episcopal Church of the United States, who is the overall leader of the Episcopal Church in the United States. The current presiding bishop of the Episcopal Church of the United States is the Most Reverend Michael Curry. Archbishop Curry, known for his pulpit-pounding and animated preaching, is the first African American presiding bishop and primate of the Episcopal Church of the United States, which is part of the worldwide Anglican Communion.

For those not familiar with church history, it may be fitting to note that the Episcopal Church and the Anglican Church are one and the same with two different names, depending on where you are. For example, the church that is called the Anglican Church in the United Kingdom and territories with strong British influence is the same church that is called the Episcopal Church in the United States and areas within America's sphere of influence.

While there is the Episcopal Church in Liberia because of the American connection, Liberia's next-door neighbor Sierra Leone and countries like Ghana, Nigeria, and Kenya, among others, have the Anglican Church because of the British colonial connections. The worldwide Anglican Communion is headed by the archbishop of Canterbury in the United Kingdom. The current archbishop of Canterbury is the Most Reverend Justin Welby, who was enthroned in 2013.

According to the *Historical Dictionary of Liberia*, the Episcopal Church of Liberia was established in 1836 under the direction of the Domestic and Foreign Missionary Society of the United States of America. The affairs of the Episcopal Church of Liberia was run by American missionary leaders or bishops until 1970, when George Daniel Browne was elected and consecrated as the first Liberian-born bishop of the Episcopal Church of Liberia.

Even though it is reported from his background that he endured a difficult childhood due to poverty, Browne was able to surmount the odds to earn a BS in education and a bachelor of divinity from Cuttington. He later matriculated at the Virginia Theological Seminary in the United States, where he earned a master's degree in sacred theology (STM) in 1964. He was ordained a priest in 1963. At the young age of thirty-seven, he ascended to become the first Liberian-born bishop of the Episcopal Church of Liberia.

Bishop Browne was an eminent civic-minded religious leader on the Liberian national scene. A veteran teacher, counselor, and a powerful preacher, Bishop Browne was appointed a member of the National Constitution Commission, established in 1981 by the military regime to draft a new constitution for Liberia, which was part of the process to return the country to civilian rule. This was after the bloody military coup in 1980, during which the president was assassinated and the constitution of the Republic of Liberia was suspended, as you will read later in this chapter. Like Bishop Browne, the commission, which prepared the original draft of the constitution for Liberia's second republic, included prominent citizens of diverse backgrounds from across the country.

In addition to overseeing the growth of the church in Liberia, Bishop Browne's accomplishments also included getting the Episcopal Church of Liberia into a close partnership with the Anglican Church in the West African region and beyond. Before then, the Episcopal Church in Liberia was only closely engaged with the Episcopal Church in the United States. As a manifestation of his leadership in the region, he was enthroned at Trinity Cathedral in Monrovia in 1982 as the first Liberian archbishop of the Church of the Province of West Africa (CPWA).

According to *The Autobiography of George D. Browne*, during his tenure, the Church of the Province of West Africa had a population of over thirty-five million covering eleven dioceses and a missionary area in six African countries. He was the tenth bishop of Liberia and sixth archbishop of the Province of West Africa, posts in which he served well until his death in 1993 at the age of sixty.

It is pleasing to note that in 2019, another bishop of the Episcopal Church of Liberia, the Most Reverend Jonathan B. B. Hart, was consecrated at the Trinity Cathedral in Monrovia as the eleventh primate and the metropolitan archbishop of the Church of the Province of West Africa, which has covered seventeen dioceses. He succeeded the primate and metropolitan archbishop of the CPWA, the Most Reverend Professor Daniel Yinkah Sarfo of the Anglican Diocese of Kumasi, Ghana.

It is fitting to also interject that it was due to the vision and hard work of Dean Emmanuel Johnson that the Liberian Episcopal Community in the United States (LECUSA) was established in 2006 in Reston, Virginia. LECUSA was organized with the aim to strengthen relationships among Episcopalians of Liberian descent residing in the United States, render pastoral care to US-based Liberian Episcopalians, pull individual and collective resources, and solicit assistance for the benefit of the church and people of the Episcopal Church of Liberia, among others. LECUSA's annual convention, which is rotated from one state to another, brings together a large number of Episcopalians of Liberian descent and friends of the Episcopal Church of Liberia, comprising members of the clergy and laity. The organization's leadership is composed of the clergy and laity.

I am an Episcopalian who was baptized and confirmed by Archbishop Browne at Trinity Cathedral in Monrovia, under the spiritual guidance of Dean Johnson. While in the United States, I have been affiliated with LECUSA for a few years. In 2014, my church home in Washington DC, Trinity Episcopal Church, led by the Reverend Canon John T. W. Harmon, rector and pastor, hosted the LECUSA convention. Father Harmon was born in Maryland County, Liberia, a coastal area with breathtaking scenery.

The membership of Trinity Church, which is noted to be one of the most affluent predominantly African American congregations within the Episcopal Church of the United States, also includes Nigerians, Ghanaians, Sierra Leoneans, Liberians, as well as people from various parts of the Caribbean.

Serving as the keynote speaker at the 2014 LECUSA Convention dinner, which was characterized by a presentation of awards and Liberian cultural entertainment, was Mr. Juan A. Williams, a well-known and highly respected American journalist and political analyst for Fox News. Mr. Williams, who is an author and a former senior news analyst for National Public Radio (NPR), is also a writer for internationally renowned newspapers such as the *Washington Post*, the *New York Times*, and the *Wall Street Journal*, among others.

In his keynote address at the well-attended LECUSA event, Mr. Williams, who is also a member of Trinity Episcopal Church in Washington DC, focused on the importance of identity. Irrespective of origin, whether an individual is a Liberian, an American, or another nationality, we are all the children of God, he said.

Mr. Williams indicated that members of LECUSA must "work with a sense of higher purpose, as you strive to fit in as an immigrant community." Considering the growing immigrant population in the life of the Church in the United States and the role of immigrant missionaries, such as Liberian priests serving in various places around America, he said the time is now for the immigrant community like LECUSA to assert itself.

"You need to have a new conception of who you are in America," he said, noting that "the immigrant community is playing an important role in the life of the American Church."

The noted American journalist observed that even though Christianity was taken to Africa by European and American missionaries, the trend has reversed as a growing number of Africans are now serving in missionary capacities in Europe and America. He added that while Christianity is declining in Europe and the United States, there is a rapid growth in the spread of Christianity across the African continent.

It is in view of these developments, he said, that Africans must be more assertive in the life of the global church so that the people of Africa and of African descent would reap the full benefits from Africa's engagements.

Alongside the plenary session, another section of the LECUSA conference that also generated some fruits for thought was the lecture on Liberian history by Dr. C. Patrick Burrowes, who was then associate professor of communications at Penn State University at Harrisburg, Pennsylvania. Dr. Burrowes had conference attendees intoned to his spirited lecture, titled "The Kola Forest and the Salty Sea."

Some members of the clergy at the 2019 LECUSA Convention in Atlanta, Georgia (courtesy of LECUSA social media platform)

In his lecture, Dr. Burrowes spoke about the interconnectedness of Liberia's ethnic groups and how they lived together in harmony over the centuries. He expressed regret that misconceptions have undermined the unity of the Liberian people.

Dr. Burrowes lamented that Liberian society will continue to face serious challenges in the process of reconstruction "if we lose sight of the non-material aspects" of the rebuilding process, which regards the need to positively orientate the mind-set of the people. As examples from Liberia's recent history of civil upheaval have shown, Dr. Burrowes warned, "We risk all those material things being destroyed if we do not work on the state of mind of our people by providing them with accurate historical information."

Professor Burrowes noted that the first step to recovering the history of Liberia is to tackle stereotypes. He added that there are many stereotypes that have bred disunity among the Liberian people, hence the need for proper education to mold the minds of people in the right way.

In 2016, Dr. Burrowes published a very well researched and an educational and informative book titled *Between the Kola Forest and the Salty Sea: A History of the Liberian People before 1800*. In 2018, he became vice president for Academic Affairs at Cuttington University in Liberia, the oldest private coeducational four-year-degree-awarding institution in sub-Saharan Africa, founded in 1889 under the auspices of the Episcopal Church of Liberia, with support from the Episcopal Church of the United States.

As you will read in this chapter and subsequent chapters, Liberia was like a melting pot where people from around the world, especially people of color, were welcome to settle, integrate, and seek their own fortune. Dr. Burrowes is an example of the melting pot that Liberia was. In his book *Between the Kola Forest and the Salty Sea*, Dr. Burrowes narrates that he was born in Monrovia, Liberia, to Jamaican parents who settled in Liberia from Jamaica, influenced by the "Africa first" ideas of Jamaica's illustrious Marcus Garvey.

Born in 1887 in Jamaica, Garvey was a black nationalist and leader of the Pan-African movement, which sought to unify and connect people of African descent worldwide. Known to be a charismatic figure and a dramatic public speaker, Garvey founded the United Negro Improvement Association (UNIA), which became a worldwide organization of millions, with headquarters in New York.

In a historic move to empower people of African descent and enable them to compete globally, Garvey's UNIA launched the Black Star Line shipping company, among other business ventures. In the 1920s, Garvey also began a strong engagement with the government of Liberia, Africa's first independent republic, to use the country for the creation of a Pan-African empire that would work for the upliftment, redemption, and empowerment of people of African descent all over the world, as well as for the decolonization of the African continent. During that period, almost the entire continent of Africa was under colonial subjugation, except for Liberia and Ethiopia, an empire that had existed from ancient times, as reflected even in the Holy Bible.

Through Garvey's engagement with the president and other leaders of the Liberian government, the UNIA committed to provide financial support to Liberia, which was in financial distress, as well as for the building of infrastructure and institutions that would compete with the best in the world. The UNIA plan was aimed at positioning Liberia as a major commercial and industrial commonwealth under the stewardship of people of color. To undertake this ambitious project, the UNIA started the recruitment of professionals of African descent from diverse career backgrounds in the United States and the Caribbean to have them resettled in Liberia.

According to historical accounts, President Charles D. B. King welcomed the UNIA to Liberia and invited the organization to establish its headquarters in the country. Needless to say, this bold initiative generated the concerns of France and Britain, the colonial powers that were in control of countries neighboring or near Liberia. Because of his outspoken activism for black empowerment in the United States, Garvey had also gotten on the radar of J. Edgar Hoover of the Federal Bureau of Investigation (FBI), who viewed him as a danger to the American society. Hoover recognized that Garvey had the ability to stir up domestic unrest in the United States.

A series of events that followed led to Garvey's "back to Africa" plan being aborted, as well as his imprisonment and deportation from the United States. With pressure mounted from the United States, Britain, and France, which was also buttressed by financial inducement from the United States, the Liberian government terminated their cooperation with the UNIA in its plan to settle what were called New World Negroes in Liberia.

The land that the Liberian government had allocated to be used by the UNIA was then offered to American business tycoon Harvey Firestone, owner of the Firestone Tire and Rubber Company based in Akron, Ohio.

In 1926, Liberia signed an agreement with Firestone for the lease of one million acres of land for ninety-nine years at the rate of eight cents an acre (*Historical Dictionary of Liberia*, second edition, page 134).

This led to the establishment of the Firestone Rubber Plantation in Liberia, which was once the world's largest rubber plantation. Liberia has since dropped to second place, having been surpassed by Malaysia.

On the US front, after a period of FBI investigation, Garvey was arrested in 1922 for mail fraud in connection with the sale of stock in the Black Star Line shipping company, which had now failed. He was sent to prison and later deported to Jamaica. In 1935, he moved permanently to London, where he died in 1940.

Garvey's vision to unite Africa and people of African descent was championed by many Pan-African leaders who emerged after him, including Kwame Nkrumah, who led Ghana to independence from British colonial rule. However, during the 1963 formation of the Organization of African Unity (OAU), following the independence of many African countries from colonial domination, Liberia led the charge in defeating an effort spearheaded by Nkrumah to establish an organization for the creation of a United States of Africa.

Just as Liberian leaders were known to have aborted the Garvey plan for a united Africa partly due to external pressure, the country's position against the establishment of a United States of Africa during the formation of the OAU was also attributed to influence by external powers and other factors. A growing recognition of the need for a united Africa explains why Dr. Nkrumah is being widely recognized for his role in the founding of the OAU than, say, the staunchly antisocialist and pro-Western former president William V. S. Tubman of Liberia, as you will read in chapters 12 and 13 of this book.

Meanwhile, even though Firestone has operated in Liberia since 1926, the country has yet to boast of a single manufacturing plant to produce rubber materials, even latex gloves, as of this publication.

The accounts reflected above have been added to the historical highlights to broaden the understanding of the reader and to reflect the oneness and interconnectedness of people, irrespective of geographic or cultural differences.

Back to the accounts on Liberia's history, on July 26, 1847, Liberia declared her independence, thus becoming Africa's first republic and, after Haiti, the second black independent republic in the world. Liberia's declaration of independence signaled to the world that the black man was capable of self-governance. The country grew with the characteristics of the American bureaucracy. The 1847 Constitution of the Republic of Liberia, which was drafted at Harvard University in the United States, was modeled on the Constitution of the United States, with three branches of government—namely, the legislative, judiciary, and executive. The country's national flag of red, white, and blue with one star, called the Lone Star, bears close resemblance to the American flag, which has fifty stars.

The Declaration of Independence was signed in the edifice of the Providence Baptist Church in Monrovia. According to the *Historical Dictionary of Liberia*, the Baptists established the first church in 1822, the Providence Baptist Church, which was built in 1824 under the leadership of Lott Cary (Carey), a missionary and vice agent of the colony of Liberia. Born a slave in Virginia, Cary purchased his freedom in Virginia in 1813 and studied to become a minister.

The original Providence Baptist Church building, where the Declaration of Independence was signed, survived the massive destruction of the civil war and remains standing as of this publication.

The preamble of the 1847 Declaration of Independence speaks volumes of the dehumanizing conditions the settlers endured in America. It reads thus:

We the people of the Republic of Liberia were originally the inhabitants of the United States of America. In some parts of that country, we were debarred by law from all the rights and privileges of man—in other parts, public sentiment more powerful than law frowned us down.

We were everywhere shut out from all civil office. We were excluded from all participation in the government. We were taxed without our consent. We were compelled to contribute to resources of a country which gave us no protection. We were made a separate and distinct class and against us every avenue to improvement was officially closed.

Strangers from all lands of a different color from ours were preferred before us. We uttered our complaints but they were unattended to, or only met by alleging the peculiar institutions of the country. All hope of a favorable change in our country was thus wholly extinguished in our bosoms, and we looked with anxiety abroad for some asylum from the deep degradation.

The western coast of Africa was the place selected by American benevolence and philanthropy for our future home. Removed beyond those influences, it was hoped we would be enabled to enjoy those rights and privileges and exercise and improve those faculties, which the God of nature has given us in common with the rest of mankind. ("Liberia at 171: What Have We to Show?," Liberian Observer, July 25, 2018)

Following Liberia's independence, more blacks from the United States immigrated to the country. For example, in 1878, there was a mass immigration of black people from South Carolina to Liberia, which was called the Liberian exodus. According to the *South Carolina Encyclopedia*, black leaders in South Carolina—including Richard Harvey Cain, Harrison Bouey, George Curtis, and the Reverend B. F. Porter—responded to the interest in black immigration by incorporating the Liberian Exodus Joint Stock Steamship Company in the spring of 1877, naming Porter as its president.

The return of the Democratic Party to power in South Carolina in 1876 and the campaign of violence that accompanied it raised the anxiety of African Americans in the state and interest in the possibility of immigration. Similar feelings toward immigration could be found across the South, where blacks endured political weakness, restrictions on their civil rights, and difficulties in finding gainful employment, as reflected previously in the preamble of Liberia's Declaration of Independence.

In South Carolina, interest in immigration became focused on Liberia, founded by the American Colonization Society (ACS). The ACS, which did not have enough funds to transport the swelling numbers of black immigrants, welcomed the formation of the Charleston-based company and lent it moral support and advice.

Even though the company lacked the necessary funds for a Liberian voyage, Reverend Porter bowed to pressure from hundreds of prospective passengers and hastily acquired a vessel, a clipper ship named the *Azor*. In March 1878, the *Azor* set sail for Liberia with 206 immigrants. After a forty-two-day voyage, during which immigrants endured delays, deaths, and unforeseen expenses in Sierra Leone, they arrived in Liberia short of money and supply.

According to the *South Carolina Encyclopedia*, news of the disastrous voyage discouraged hundreds of black South Carolinians who were waiting in Charleston for passage to Liberia. Some of the *Azor* immigrants returned to South Carolina disappointed, but others who stayed enjoyed success in Liberia. By the early 1890s, reports appeared claiming that several of the leading political and business figures in Liberia had come from South Carolina, including C. L. Parsons, chief justice of the Liberian Supreme Court; Clements Irons, who constructed the first steamship in Liberia in 1888; and the Reverend David Frazier, a member of the Liberian Senate.

There are other historical accounts that one of the *Azor*'s passengers, Daniel Frank Tolbert, was the grandfather of William R. Tolbert Jr., who became the twentieth president of the Republic of Liberia. Mr. Daniel Tolbert originated from a town called Ninety Six in Greenwood County, South Carolina. As you will read later in this chapter, President Tolbert was assassinated in 1980 in a military coup staged by noncommissioned officers of the Armed Forces of Liberia, bringing a violent end to a 133-year rule of the tiny elite Americo-Liberian ruling class. His elder brother Frank E. Tolbert, then president pro tempore of the Liberian Senate, and the president's own son, A. Benedict Tolbert, who was a member of the House of Representatives, were also killed following the bloody military takeover.

In an effort to keep alive and promote the special historical ties subsisting between the Republic of Liberia and the state of South Carolina, some churches and organizations in South Carolina have endeavored to undertake programs in this regard. For example, the Allison Creek Presbyterian Church in York, South Carolina, and the Brookland Baptist Church in West Columbia, South Carolina, have been involved in activities to promote the ties between Liberia and South Carolina. Allison Creek Presbyterian Church has started an annual festival to highlight the relationship.

According to Mr. Joseph James, a passionate member of the South Carolina African American Heritage Commission (SCAAHC) involved in the endeavor to promote the historic ties between the state and the African nation, the SCAAHC has established the South Carolina–Liberia Connection Initiatives to explore, document, and bring attention to the many historical connections between Liberia and South Carolina. It has recommended that the South Carolina Commission for Minority Affairs explore mutually beneficial, social, and economic relations with Liberia. It is also recommended that South Carolina churches support interpersonal, religious, and missionary work in Liberia.

Meanwhile, during the period of Liberia's founding, the American settlers, who came to be known as Americo-Liberians, retained the dress code, manners, and religion of the American South. They adopted American values, speech, and dress; and they built houses that reflected the architectural taste of Georgia, the Carolinas, and Maryland. For example, men wore tailcoats and tall hats while women were attired in colonial-style gowns and hats. There are places in Liberia named Maryland, Virginia, Louisiana, New Georgia, Lexington, Greenville, Mississippi, and Hartford, among others, which are named after areas from which the settlers originated. Negro spirituals and folk music from the days of slavery in America were among the regular hymns sung at church services and events while American music dominated the entertainment scenes.

Since independence, ten of Liberia's past presidents were born in the United States, beginning with the first president, Joseph Jenkins Roberts, who was born in Norfolk, Virginia. That Liberia was a country where people of color from around the world could enjoy freedom and equal opportunity was reflected by the fact that one other Liberian president was born in Sierra Leone and another in the Caribbean nation of Barbados.

With citizenship since 1847 having been limited by law to people of African descent, Liberians consist of various admixtures of Africans indigenous to the area: descendants of Igbo and Congolese who were settled there after being liberated from slave ships in the nineteenth century and black immigrants from the United States, the Caribbean, and other parts of Africa (introduction, *Culture and Customs of Liberia*, page 1).

The irony was that while members of the settler class enjoyed freedom and aspired to the fullness of their capabilities, the government did not grant suffrage to Liberia's indigenous population until 1946. As a manifestation of the fact that indigenous Liberians were not recognized as citizens of Liberia, they were also not allowed to own property or vote until they were granted suffrage during the administration of President William V. S. Tubman.

Despite the tragic history that underpinned their repatriation to the unknown shores of Africa to establish a country where they would enjoy freedom and human dignity, the ruling settler class instituted policies of discrimination and other acts of injustice to keep the indigenous population, which made up about 85 percent of the population, to endure neglect and poverty. They settled in Liberia with the plantation mentality of the master-servant relationship. This time, they were now the masters, while the indigenous people were reduced to a life of servitude.

The Christian religion was a central part of life of the settlers as one of the reasons noted for Liberia's founding was to Christianize Africa, which was then regarded by Westerners as the Dark Continent inhabited by heathens. The signing of the Declaration of Independence in a church, as noted earlier in this chapter, signified that Liberia's founding was grounded in the Judeo-Christian tradition, which submits that a people once taken away and kept in bondage and slavery have returned to their ancestral homeland in freedom due to the power of redemption and salvation of Almighty God.

However, when they came to Africa bearing the Bible, the American settlers also brought with them some of the vestiges of slavery by creating a class system in which they regarded themselves superior and civilized unlike the indigenous inhabitants, who were treated as primitive and inferior. Even within the settler ruling class, there was a time in Liberian history when the proximity to power was based on how fair the color of one's skin was, as the country's earliest leaders were light in complexion. This practice of leadership—based not on credibility and competence, but on familial, ethnic, or social connections—is also a common practice in various parts of Africa, where people enjoy power and privileges based on family or ethnicity.

Even though Liberia was seen as a beacon of hope on the African continent and a land of freedom and liberty for people of color from around the world for over a century, the Americo-Liberians discriminated against the indigenous population they met in the area now called Liberia. The Americo-Liberians maintained a kind of a feudal oligarchy, exclusively controlling political power and the wealth of the country for 133 years.

Despite the suppression of its indigenous population, Liberia enjoyed substantial economic growth and development from the 1950s to 1970s; and it was during that period that Liberia was regarded as one of the most peaceful and prosperous countries in Africa, as well as a continental leader on global African issues. That was the period most Liberians from that era regard as "the good old days," for which there is a desperate yearning.

For example, President William V. S. Tubman, Liberia's nineteenth president, whose tenure spanned from 1944 to 1971, is regarded as the father of modern Liberia. His Open Door Policy attracted major foreign investment, which led to considerable modernization of the economy and social institutions. The country also experienced considerable infrastructural development. According to the *Historical Dictionary of Liberia*, by the mid-1960s, the Tubman administration registered twenty-five major foreign investors, whereas it met one (Firestone) when it came to office. At the same time, a total of approximately $1 billion worth of investment had been made (*Historical Dictionary of Liberia*, second edition, page 254).

President Tubman also instituted policies to foster national unity and broaden political participation. On the international scene, he was a leader of continental Africa who played a very critical role in the formation of the Organization of African Unity (OAU), renamed the African Union (AU), as you will read in chapter 12. As of this publication, Liberia and Tubman's contributions to the African cause during newly independent Africa's search for identity in the new world order appear to be largely forgotten.

Tubman is also remembered by critics as an autocratic leader who suppressed political dissent to hold on to power for twenty-seven years until his death in 1971. He was succeeded by William R. Tolbert Jr., who was the late Tubman's vice president for nineteen years.

Liberia's Descent into Mindless Bloodshed and Destruction

Upon ascending to the presidency, Tolbert set out to institute wide-ranging reforms that put Liberia on a course of rapid infrastructural development. During his tenure, he worked toward progress in national unity and integration. He created opportunities for more young people of indigenous backgrounds throughout the country to enjoy the benefit of education through the opening of more schools in rural areas and poor urban communities, as well as the provision of scholarships. Although he was a product of the ruling minority elite class that controlled exclusive political and economic power in Liberia for over a century, he encouraged diversity and broader participation of the citizenry in the political and economic life of the country.

Under his Total Involvement for Higher Heights national policy, Tolbert—a successful farmer himself—aggressively instituted agricultural policies and programs aimed at making Liberia sufficient in food production. His administration also focused on ensuring quality and accessible education and skills training for the young people, whom he called his "precious jewels." Tolbert also promoted the cultures and traditions of Liberia's ethnic groups, using those values as a means to promote unity among the people. Through his customary safari suits and other African attires, Tolbert's examples encouraged Liberians to begin to publicly embrace and celebrate their cultural backgrounds and also to appreciate that there was nothing shameful in speaking an ethnic language or wearing African attire, as was the case back then.

Nevertheless, Tolbert's critics accused him of nepotism, corruption, and not instituting political reforms fast enough to create the enabling environment for free and fair democratic activities. An increasingly vocal opposition, empowered by the atmosphere of freedom created under Tolbert's administration, demanded immediate change in the political order. On the other hand, many of the "old guards" within the ruling establishment were bitterly opposed to Tolbert's reforms, fearing it could spell their doom. Tolbert was then caught between a rock and a hard place—between the long-suppressed mass of the population demanding for change and the "old guards" clinging on to power who resisted the call for a peaceful change.

The "old guards" were so consumed by their narrow desire to maintain control at all costs that they failed to recognize that the vast mass of the population was desperate for change in the political order. As tensions mounted, the government instituted heavy-handed measures to suppress dissent. For example, on April 14, 1979, mass protests at the government's proposal to increase the price of rice from $22 per 100 pounds to $30 erupted into violence, resulting in considerable loss of life and property. Many opposition leaders and activists, including student leaders, endured harassment, arrest and detention, and torture.

Former US president John F. Kennedy famously said, "Those who make peaceful revolution impossible will make violent revolution inevitable." That was basically how Liberia disintegrated into chaos because powerful elements within the minority ruling elite class refused to see the glaring sign and hear the increasingly loud drumbeats to change peacefully or perish in violence. And perish they did because they stubbornly refused to change for the common good.

Vice President W. R. Tolbert shakes hands with First Lady Antoinette Tubman at a ceremony while President
W. V. S. Tubman and Mrs. Victoria Tolbert look on (courtesy of Nancy Stewart Nwabunnia)

Notwithstanding the progress that Liberia had made, many of the benefits from the economic boom did not trickle down fast enough to the vast mass of the population at the lower end of the economic ladder. In the 1970s, a deteriorating global economic situation had its effects on Liberia's economic conditions, causing further sociopolitical decline. The economic and political disparities, which characterized more than a century of bad governance by the minority ruling class, created very deep fault lines under the veneer of peace and stability in the country. Tolbert's reforms were too late to create the desired positive impact on the lives of the vast mass of the population to avert a national catastrophe.

This is why most of the international community watched in shock and disbelief when Liberia, a country that was the embodiment of peace and hope, was plunged into nearly three decades of instability, bloodshed, and destruction.

Liberia's descent into mindless bloodshed and destruction, characterized by nearly fifteen years of civil war, began on Saturday, April 12, 1980, when seventeen noncommissioned officers of the Armed Forces of Liberia (AFL) attacked the Executive Mansion, the beautiful seaside official presidential residence in Monrovia and staged a bloody military coup. President Tolbert, sixty-six, who was reportedly in bed with his wife at the time of the coup, was assassinated when the attackers stormed the sixth floor of the presidential residence.

Following the brutal murder of President Tolbert, there was massive arrest of former officials of the deposed government. Many senior officials of the deposed administration were tried by a kangaroo military tribunal, where the accused did not have the opportunity of legal representation to defend themselves against the charges of treason, rampant corruption, and gross abuse of power, among others.

On April 22, 1980, thirteen senior officials of the Tolbert government who were tried by the tribunal were tied to stakes and publicly executed by a firing squad on the beach next to the Barclay Training Center military barracks in Monrovia. The barbaric executions were broadcast on national television in Liberia. According to a BBC News account of the tragic event, journalists who had been taken to the barracks to watch the executions said they were cruel and messy. "They said four men were forced to watch the others die before being shot themselves as there were only nine stakes" ("1980: Deposed Ministers Executed in Liberia," BBC: On This Day, April 22, 1980).

Those publicly executed on a beach in Monrovia included the speaker of the House of Representatives, Richard A. Henries; the chief justice of the Supreme Court of Liberia, James A. A. Pierre; the senate pro tempore Frank Tolbert, as mentioned earlier; and the foreign minister, C. Cecil Dennis, then regarded as one of Africa's eminent diplomats on the global stage.

Other senior government officials who were executed included E. Reginald Townsend, national chairman of the ruling True Whig Party (TWP); P. Clarence Parker II, chairman of the National Investment Commission (NIC) and vice chairman of the TWP; Joseph J. Chesson Sr., minister of justice; Cyril A. Bright Sr., minister of planning and economic affairs; John W. Sherman, minister commerce and industry; Frank Stewart, director of the budget; James T. Philips, former minister of finance; and Charles D. King, member of the House of Representatives of Nimba County.

President Tolbert and his executed officials, along with more than two dozen other government officials who had also been killed in the wake of the coup, were buried in a mass grave in Monrovia. There are other accounts that President Tolbert's body was removed from the mass grave and reburied separately. Tolbert's son, the eloquent Adolphus Benedict Tolbert, who was a member of the House of Representatives before the coup, was seized upon orders of the military rulers from the French embassy near Monrovia, in violation of international laws regarding the inviolability of diplomatic premises; and he was reportedly buried alive.

President Tolbert was chairman of the Organization of African Unity (OAU) at the time he was overthrown. The April 14, 1980, edition of the *Washington Post* described the late Tolbert as a leader who had gained a reputation as a force of progressive change and development in his own country and as a conciliator in Africa at large. For example, a week before his death, according to the *Washington Post*, Tolbert had submitted a peace plan to warring factions in Chad. Tolbert's other forays into international relations, according to the *Post*, had included efforts to help mediate between factions fighting for control in the old Spanish Sahara and meetings in Monrovia with South African officials concerning the future of Namibia.

The *Washington Post* story indicated that even though Tolbert emphasized Liberia's "special relationship" with the United States, he also established diplomatic relations with the Soviet Union and other Eastern bloc countries. President Tolbert said that Liberia would "waltz to no foreign rhythm of flirtatious expedience but would dance instead, with steadfast grace, to African drums of age-long passions" ("Liberia's W. R. Tolbert Was Leader of Progressive Change," *Washington Post*, April 14, 1980).

As reported by the *Post*, among the changes that occurred in Liberia during his presidency, Tolbert, who had been vice president for twenty years, dismissed corrupt officials, encouraged greater freedom of press, and lowered the voting age to eighteen. The *Post* report also stated that Tolbert inaugurated a social security fund and unemployment compensation and pushed for the construction of schools and medical facilities. The *Post* report also stated that Tolbert's economic policy for Liberia included increased attention to agriculture in an effort to lessen Liberia's reliance on food imports, exploitation of lumber, and pressure on foreign exporters of iron ore and to hire and train more Africans.

Tolbert's leadership on the African and international scenes, including international factors that may have contributed to his downfall, are also discussed in chapter 12 of this book. I was a teenager in the tenth grade when the bloody coup d'état occurred in Liberia. At the time a resident in a section of Monrovia's downtown district, I ran to the barracks along with some neighborhood friends after news spread about the executions. I never saw the bodies, but there was widespread jubilation among most indigenous Liberians, who chanted the slogan "Country woman born soldier! Congo woman born rogue!" This was a reference that native women gave birth to the soldiers who had liberated their people from the subjugation of the now-vanquished Congo or Americo-Liberian ruling elite. I remember that the sky turned dark like a storm was gathering to take place immediately following the executions.

The seventeen enlisted men of the AFL, who were of indigenous stock, were led by Master Sergeant Samuel Kanyon Doe, then twenty-eight years old. Members of the People's Redemption Council (PRC) were generally functionally literate as Doe was barely a high school graduate while some of them could hardly read and write. The civilian members of the new regime, who were mostly intellectuals and political and rights activists, were those who assumed the burden of steering the affairs of the country.

The civilian appointees in the new government were mostly progressive individuals who kept the Tolbert government under heavy pressure for reforms, leading to the violent military takeover. In Liberia, those who were in the vanguard advocating for social justice, equality, and democratic governance were known as the progressives. Some of them were in detention for their political activities when the coup occurred. Those released from detention included Mr. Gabriel Baccus Matthews, leader of the opposition United People's Party (UPP), who spearheaded the April 14, 1979, demonstration against the increase in the price of rice, which turned bloody. Straight out of prison, he was taken to the Executive Mansion, where he and other "progressive leaders" joined the coup makers to form the new government. Matthews was appointed the minister of foreign affairs.

The PRC regime charged officials of the deposed government with rampant corruption, high treason, and gross violation of human rights. Among the grievances cited by the soldiers for the brutal overthrow of the government was discrimination against indigenous Liberians by the minority Americo-Liberian ruling class. The military rulers suspended the 1847 Liberian Constitution and ruled by decrees promulgated by the junta. For example, one of the infamous decrees called Decree 88A criminalized freedom of speech and of the press, among other restrictions on basic civil rights during that time. That meant anyone who said anything that was regarded to be against the head of state or other regime officials could be arrested and penalized.

Master Sergeant Doe was declared commander in chief (CIC) of the Armed Forces of Liberia, chairman of the PRC, and head of state of the Republic of Liberia. Other prominent leaders of the ruling PRC junta were Major General Thomas Weh Syen, co-chairman of the PRC and vice head of state; Brigadier General J. Nicholas Podier Jr., speaker of the PRC; and Brigadier General Thomas Quiwonkpa, senior member of the PRC and commanding general of the AFL.

It may be interesting to note that when journalists foresee problems, even at considerable personal risks, they do raise alarm that something is taking root that might have grave consequences for any society or country. It was in keeping with the role of the press that the *Washington Post* was, perhaps, the earliest international news organ to raise alarm that Liberia was heading in the wrong direction following the military takeover.

The April 27, 1980, edition of the *Washington Post* titled "Liberia's Sergeants Take Turn toward Authoritarian Rule" states the following: "Once touted as Africa's oldest democratic republic, Liberia has shifted into a troubled phase of its current 'revolution.'" The *Post* article states that the suspension of the continent's oldest constitution and the formal imposition of martial law point to a dramatic change in course from that originally set by a cadre of civilians who were trying to direct the new military regime.

The bloody takeover was greeted with a popular euphoria as the vast mass of the Liberian population, who were of indigenous descent, welcomed the change to bring about the equality of all Liberians and equal access to opportunities. Hopeful that a new day had dawned to lift Liberia and all Liberians, jubilant crowds celebrated for days in a carnival affair.

Nevertheless, given the wave of killings and abuse of human rights perpetrated by the PRC regime, it was only a matter of time before it started to become clear that the regime was dragging the country down toward total anarchy and bloodshed.

Although the military junta had justified its takeover to bring about equality and justice and to end rampant corruption and abuse of power, which the previous government and ruling class were accused of, the new rulers soon began to exhibit far more extreme acts of brutality and plunder of public resources. State-sanctioned violence and murders to eliminate real or perceived enemies became commonplace while the mismanagement and corruption of public resources became rampant at an unprecedented level.

As a result of bloody infighting within the ruling military junta itself, almost all of the junta members were purged from power or killed, as Commander in Chief Doe sought to consolidate power and hang on at all costs. For example, each of the prominent leaders of the PRC named in one of the above paragraphs was killed under different circumstances in the bloody contest for power.

Most of the progressives who were appointed at the beginning of Doe's regime were also relieved from the government or purged from political activities. Despite the impressive academic credentials of most of the civilian members of the new military regime, many of them did not have the work or administrative experience required to administer the affairs of a country. Accordingly, as Liberia struggled to find a constructive direction, the influence of the progressives in the government was undermined. This was also partly due to infighting within the ranks of the progressives.

Eventually, nearly all of the progressives were thrown out of the government. Some suffered imprisonment for allegedly plotting to overthrow Doe—developments that led to many of them, along with other Liberians, being forced into exile. Nevertheless, many Liberians would blame the progressives for creating the combustible atmosphere that led to the coup and for their failure to set the country in the right direction, when they took leadership following the violent change in government.

As Commander in Chief Doe consolidated power, he surrounded himself with remnants of the "old guards" from the deposed political order as well as from his ethnic group. The "old guards" were more familiar with the affairs of government and the crafts of statesmanship. Members of Doe's Krahn ethnic group were placed in strategic positions of the government, especially in the military and paramilitary forces. Some of the "old guards" devised strategies that enabled Doe to eliminate his comrades and others within the ruling junta while his fellow ethnic members in the military and security agencies were used to suppress dissent and opposition.

Legendary journalist Kenneth Y. Best, my professional mentor, once shared with me something he was told when he was a young man coming of age. An elderly man told him something to the effect of the following: "If you want to see the true color (nature) of an African, give him power." This expression appears to be so true in the case of the PRC members. Although the soldiers seemed to be well-intentioned when they took over, once they tasted "sweet power," with all the influence and wealth that come along with it, they simply reversed course. Instead of creating the enabling environment to bring about democratic governance as promised, the soldiers instituted draconian measures to consolidate power. As the saying goes, power corrupts, and absolute power corrupts absolutely.

By 1985, the PRC regime had executed eighty persons for political reasons and detained over six hundred without trial, usually in connection with one alleged plot or another ("Liberia since 1980," *Historical Dictionary of Liberia*, second edition, page 8).

After years of struggle to bring about the rule of law and democratic governance, Liberians went to the polls in October 1985 to elect a president and members of the legislature. The four presidential candidates included military ruler Samuel Doe. Following the election, a preliminary count in the presence of representatives of various parties gave 63 percent of the vote to Jackson F. Doe (no relation to Samuel Doe), standard bearer of the Liberia Action Party (LAP). That count was nullified by the regime, and tabulation was turned over to a fifty-member, which awarded the election to Samuel Doe ("Liberia since 1980").

The rigging of the 1985 election amid the brutal suppression of dissent created the combustible conditions for the 1985 attempted coup led by General Thomas G. Quiwonkpa. The coup was successfully suppressed, followed by a massive retaliatory violence against real or imagined supports of Quiwonkpa. More accounts of Quiwonkpa's abortive coup and its bloody aftermath are reflected in chapter 7.

Despite the brutal, dictatorial nature of the Doe regime, the United States supplied more aid to Liberia during the tenure of the military government than to all of the previous civilian governments combined since Liberia's founding. American aid, which had never exceeded more than $20 million per annum prior to 1980, topped $91 million in 1985, with military aid increasing from $1.4 million to $14 million annually.

As the number of Liberians forced to flee from the country into exile increased, the threats against the Doe regime intensified. In the wake of the rigging of the election and the brutal suppression of dissent, many within the opposition circle and the wider Liberian society were convinced that a peaceful change in Liberia under Doe was not possible.

Eventually, the brutal and dictatorial nature of Doe's regime brought about the armed rebellion, which led to the collapse of his regime, his capture, and his brutal murder by rebels. The armed rebellion that plunged Liberia into full-scale civil upheavals started on December 24, 1989, when a small band of Libyan-trained armed men, claiming allegiance to the National Patriotic Front of Liberia (NPFL), an organization hitherto unknown to the outside world and to most Liberians, launched an attack on Liberia from neighboring Ivory Coast. The NPFL was led by Charles Taylor, a fugitive from justice who escaped from prison in the United States to stage his armed insurrection with the backing of Colonel Muammar Gaddafi, the then mercurial leader of Libya.

Following the 1980 coup, Mr. Taylor was appointed managing director of the General Services Agency, the government procurement agency. He served in that capacity for about three years, and thereafter was appointed deputy minister of commerce. But he fled the country for the United States after he was implicated in a plot to overthrow Doe's regime. Shortly after that, he was accused by the Doe regime of embezzling $900,000 of government funds. Liberia instituted extradition proceedings against Mr. Taylor, and he was arrested and imprisoned in 1984 in Boston, Massachusetts.

It has been a mystery as to how Mr. Taylor actually got out of prison. There are accounts that he broke jail, fled from the United States, and eventually went to West Africa, where he proceeded to spearhead his insurgency. In his testimony during his war crimes trial at the International Court for Sierra Leone in The Hague, Mr. Taylor said he was escorted out of prison and set free by some individuals, but he did not break jail as had been widely reported.

Regional and International Interventions to End Bloodshed

What started as an armed insurgency to force Doe's regime out of power plunged Liberia in a full-scale civil war. Taylor's insurgency was simply the spark that was needed to engulf the entire Liberia in an inferno of death and destruction. The barbarity and massive destruction of the war alarmed other West African countries that, along with Liberia, are members of the Economic Community of West African States (ECOWAS), a subregional body. In a frantic effort to contain the bloodshed, ECOWAS organized a military intervention force called the ECOWAS Monitoring Group (ECOMOG). Led by regional power Nigeria, ECOMOG, which was supported by the United States, also comprised troops from Ghana, Guinea, Sierra Leone, the Gambia, and Senegal, among others. Mr. Taylor vehemently opposed ECOMOG, whose creation he regarded as an attempt to prevent him from taking power.

While visiting the headquarters of ECOMOG at the Freeport of Monrovia on September 9, 1990, Doe was captured by General Prince Yormie Johnson, leader of the Independent National Patriotic Front of Liberia (INPFL), amid a hail of gunfire. The INPFL broke away from the NPFL due to differences between Johnson and Charles Taylor, leader of the main NPFL rebel group. Johnson, regarded as a soldier's soldier who received his military training in both Liberia and the United States, was a bodyguard to General Quiwonkpa at the time the once-powerful general fell out of favor with Doe and was forced to flee into exile. Johnson and other known Quiwonkpa supporters who escaped Doe's dragnet also fled into exile, from where they plotted the armed insurgency.

When Johnson announced the split within the NPFL and the formation of the INPFL in early 1990, he said Taylor was a misfit who was exploiting the popular disaffection toward Doe for power grab and self-aggrandizement and that Taylor would be a more destructive dictator than Doe. Accordingly, he vowed to fight to the bitter end to prevent Taylor from capturing the Executive Mansion to declare himself president. He also vowed that he would be the one to capture and remove Doe from power. He succeeded in capturing Doe and preventing Taylor from occupying the Executive Mansion through use of force.

After he was captured at the port, Doe was driven in the hood of Johnson's jeep to the INPFL headquarters, located in the township of Caldwell outside Monrovia. At the INPFL base, he was tortured to death by Johnson and his comrades in arms.

Doe led Liberia from 1980 to 1985, initially under military rule. From 1986 to his death in 1990, he civilianized his military regime by dropping his military uniforms in favor of business suits, when he took on the title of president after rigging the 1985 presidential election. Although Liberia had supposedly returned to civilian rule in January 1986, Doe's so-called civilian government exhibited the characteristics of the brutal and barbaric military regime that he previously led.

Even though the 1980 coup interrupted Liberia's peace and progress, it had a positive impact in terms of shattering the superiority complex members of the deposed America-Liberian minority ruling class had over the majority of indigenous Liberians, who were treated as inferior and discriminated against. As a manifestation of the sense of equality that prevailed after the coup, some Liberians of indigenous backgrounds changed their Western names to indigenous names while African attires and cultural activities became more acceptable and fashionable in affluent Liberian societies.

A female friend who was displaced in the Caldwell community during the early period of the civil war provided some refreshing accounts regarding Doe's death. She said that following news that Doe's dead body was on display at the Island Clinic, which was not far from Caldwell, she was among the crowd that visited the clinic, where she saw Doe's naked body with her own eyes.

According to her, the body, which was reportedly embalmed with a heavy dose of formaldehyde, was kept on display until Charles Taylor's rebels attacked an area near the clinic, as rumors spread that Taylor's forces had attacked in order to get to the clinic to seize Doe's body. Taylor appeared desperate to take possession of Doe's body in order to deceive his mass of drugged child soldiers and other fighters into believing that he was the one who actually captured Doe. This was intended to further cement his claim to the presidency by virtue of being the one who successfully led the insurgency against Doe.

Johnson had put the body on display to convinced Liberians beyond all reasonable doubt that Doe was truly dead, something that seemed unbelievable to most Liberians from the beginning. During the course of his reign, Doe had publicly boasted that bullets and blades could not penetrate his body. This was in reference to his possession of certain magical powers based on juju that would enable his body to become bulletproof and protect him against gun and blade attacks. It was widely believe that he also possessed magical powers to vanish or disappear from an area in the wake of an attack. These falsehoods, which are common in many parts of Africa, were peddled to project the power and control of the leader; and they were widely believed by the people because of traditional practices.

Unfortunately for Doe, those magical or juju powers that he had boasted of in the past did not work when he was captured by Johnson, during which his legs were riddled with bullets. With a can of beer in his hand, Johnson and his comrades in arms are on a widely circulated video in which Doe is interrogated and tortured, and he screams for his mother as one of his ears is being cut off with a bayonet. At a time when Doe undoubtedly needed them most, the magic and juju did not work to save him.

According to my female eyewitness, who was in Caldwell at the time of Doe's death, when Johnson and his forces heard that Taylor's forces had attacked to seize Doe's body, Johnson ordered the body taken from the clinic and buried in Caldwell. She said Doe's body was buried standing in the grave. She said she heard from some of Johnson's fighters that they decided to bury Doe standing so that in the event where Taylor's forces were to attack the area, the body would be hastily dug up from the grave and taken away. She said she saw Doe's embalmed body, which was dug up from the grave. She recalled that the body looked like a dried meat, with the skin on the forehead pulled back, and that both legs were dislocated as a result of the body being buried standing in the grave.

She said she also heard from some of Johnson's fighters that Doe's body was dug up and burnt after an oracle or juju person prophesied to Johnson that the war would not end as long as Doe's body remained buried.

This eyewitness also provided refreshing accounts regarding the killing of Mrs. Angeline Watta Allison, wife of General Gray D. Allison, the once-powerful minister of defense during the Doe regime. She recalled how Mrs. Allison was allegedly killed upon orders of Prince Johnson.

In 1989, General and Mrs. Allison fell from grace to grass after they were accused of murder in what was seen to be a plot concocted to eliminate the once-feared defense minister. He was brought down in a plot allegedly concocted by his enemies within the Doe regime, who felt threatened by his power. Having served as defense minister since 1983, General Allison, regarded as a soldier's soldier who trained in the United States and the United Kingdom, was widely seen to be the most powerful individual in Liberia, second only to Head of State Doe himself.

Allison's enemies within Doe's inner circle convinced the seemingly paranoid dictator that the general was plotting to overthrow him. Doe, who did not hesitate to eliminate anyone that threatened his grip on power, reportedly decided to move swiftly against his longest-serving defense minister.

Accordingly, General Allison and his wife, Mrs. Watta Allison, were arrested and accused of the ritualistic killing of a man identified as J. Melvin Pyne, a police officer, whose decapitated body was found lying across a railroad track near the Allisons' residence in the township of Caldwell. Government prosecutors alleged that Allison was made to believe that he needed a portion of human blood and body to perform juju, a fetish or ritual intended to derive supernatural powers. According to the prosecutors, the portion was then to be used to kill Doe and overthrow his government.

Following Allison's arrest and dismissal, he was charged and convicted of murder and unspecified political offenses. Accordingly, he was banished to the notorious Belleh Yallah prison, where he was discovered by rebel forces in 1990 and killed (*Historical Dictionary of Liberia*, second edition, page 17).

Testifying before Liberia's Truth and Reconciliation Commission (TRC) in 2008, General Armah Youlo, former assistant director of the National Security Agency during the Doe regime who was a leader of one of the armed factions during the civil war, said everyone in the Doe government was afraid of General Allison, including President Doe himself. He noted that General Allison had enemies in high places, which led to a conspiracy for his downfall. According to Youlo, Allison was a man who could intimidate anybody, so everyone was really afraid of him. However, he said, he did not believe that Allison was involved in a plot to overthrow Doe.

There have been speculations that the downfall of Allison, who was banished to Belle Yella a few months before the outbreak of the civil war, was also orchestrated by Doe's enemies to create cracks within the security structure and weaken the regime in anticipation of the launch of Charles Taylor's armed rebellion. There were those who believed that Taylor's armed insurgency against the Doe regime may not have succeeded if General Allison had been at the helm of the Defense Ministry.

Allison became a victim of the vicious process he and his likes used over the years to rise to power and maintain a grip on power by eliminating others, including otherwise-well-meaning citizens, who were falsely implicated in one plot or another. He was known as one of the brutal officials of the Doe regime.

For example, in 1984, with the endorsement of Commander in Chief Doe, General Allison ordered heavily armed soldiers to invade the main campus of the University of Liberia in Monrovia, where students were peacefully protesting the arrest and detention of several of their professors, along with political activists and others. The detainees, who were mostly outspoken critics of the Doe regime, were accused of plotting to overthrow the regime.

The army attack on the student protesters left several dead, many women raped, and over one hundred injured (introduction, *Historical Dictionary of Liberia*, second edition, page 8).

More accounts regarding the fall of General and Mrs. Allison and how they were killed during the civil war are discussed in chapter 4. This includes my own accounts of how the once-powerful general ordered me to be publicly stripped naked, manhandled, and detained for no justifiable reason other than for doing my duties as a journalist.

It may be interesting to also note that Dr. H. Boima Fahnbulleh Jr., a prominent Liberian politician and internationally respected Pan-Africanist, spoke of how he was almost implicated in a murder plot that was being concocted by the Doe regime to eliminate him.

Following the 1980 military coup, Dr. Fahnbulleh was appointed minister of education and later minister of foreign affairs in the Doe regime. A 1972 graduate of the once-prestigious Fourah Bay College in Freetown, Sierra Leone, he holds a master's degree in political science from Howard University and a PhD in international politics from George Washington University, both in Washington DC. He was an assistant professor of Political Science at the University of Liberia when the 1980 coup occurred.

Very eloquent and not afraid to speak his mind, Dr. Fahnbulleh was never found to be associated with corruption, and he did not hesitate to criticize the regime for the reemergence of the very vices that brought about the 1980 coup. Eventually, he had a falling-out with Head of State Doe over policy differences, and he left the government while serving as minister of foreign affairs. Fahnbulleh was one of the leaders of the progressive movement who were appointed to cabinet and other senior positions in the PRC regime following the coup.

Testifying during the TRC hearing in 2008, Dr. Fahnbulleh said that after he left the government due to policy differences with Doe, he did not shy away from continuing to speak openly regarding the state of affairs in the country. As a result of the foregoing, the regime allegedly concocted a plot to eliminate him.

According to Dr. Fahnbulleh, while he was in bed at home one night, he received a call from then National Security Agency director Sylvester Moses, who spoke in code that he was sending someone to meet with him. Fahnbulleh said Moses sent one his agents to inform him that a plot was afoot to kill someone and throw the body in his (Fahnbulleh's) yard and that the government would use this as grounds to have him arrested and executed for murder. The agent said when the body is dropped in Fahnbulleh's yard, the regime would get a few people to testify against him. Following the tip-off, he left the country shortly after and went into exile.

Tall in stature with an imposing personality, Dr. Fahnbulleh and many other prominent Liberians who were exiled during the Doe regime returned to Liberia following Doe's death, the deployment of the West African peacekeeping force called ECOMOG, and the formation of the Interim Government of National Unity (IGNU).

The IGNU was formed in August 1990 in the Gambian capital, Banjul, under the auspices of the ECOWAS, the fifteen-nation subregional bloc, of which Liberia played a leadership role in its founding in 1975. The then president of the Gambia, Sir Dawda Jawara, was chairman of ECOWAS who presided over the ECOWAS Standing Mediation Committee meetings in August 1990 in Banjul, where the historic decision was made by ECOWAS to send a peacekeeping force to Liberia.

ECOWAS was initially organized to promote economic and social cooperation within the West African subregion, which has a population estimated to be more than three hundred million as of this publication.

As events in Liberia quickly unraveled and the country descended into more carnage and destruction, it became apparent to leaders within the subregion that the crisis in Liberia had the potential to spill over into neighboring countries and eventually destabilize the entire subregion. The leaders recognized then that there was no way to forge ahead collectively for sustainable economic progress in the midst of instability within the subregion.

It was in view of the foregoing that while the rest of the world looked away as Liberia descended into the abyss, ECOWAS countries, led by Nigeria, decided to intervene to put an end to the mindless bloodshed and destruction that had consumed the country. Ghana, Guinea, Sierra Leone, and the Gambia also provided troops for the original ECOMOG forces that were deployed in Liberia under the command of Major General Arnold Quainoo of Ghana as force commander.

The ECOWAS countries also adopted the ECOWAS Peace Plan for Liberia in order to bring about a negotiated settlement to the civil war. The peace plan called for the establishment of an interim government to include the warring factions, political parties, and interest groups and that said government will not be headed by leaders of any of the warring factions in the conflict. This was intended to prevent any of the factional leaders from taking power by force of arms, as well as to create the enabling environment for the restoration of peace and security in the country for the holding of democratic elections.

In keeping with the ECOWAS Peace Plan for Liberia, Dr. Amos Claudius Sawyer was chosen by the various political parties and interest groups assembled in the Gambia in August 1990, along with Prince Johnson's INPFL armed faction, as president of the Interim Government of National Unity. He was interim president through 1994, and his tenure was followed by several other interim government arrangements as the search for a peaceful end to the civil war continued for nearly fifteen years.

A 1966 product of the University of Liberia, Sawyer received his MA (1970) and PhD (1973) degrees in political science from Northwestern University in the United States. He served as dean of Liberia College and director of the Institute of Research at the University of Liberia. In 1981, he was appointed by the PRC regime as chairman of the National Constitution Drafting Commission, which drafted the constitution of Liberia's second republic that came into effect in January 1986 (introduction, *Historical Dictionary of Liberia*).

Dr. Sawyer was one of the most prominent leaders of the progressive movement, advocating for democratic governance and the rule of law in Liberia. He was a leading member of the Movement for Justice in Africa (MOJA), a Pan-Africanist organization that advocated for political, social, and economic change in Liberia and Africa as a whole.

MOJA was founded in 1973 through the initiative of Dr. Togba Nah Tipoteh, an economist and one of Liberia's most prominent politicians. He was born Rudolph Nah Roberts of indigenous Liberian parentage, but he changed his name to Togba Nah Tipoteh to reflect his true indigenous identity. This was at a time that the use of Western names was most preferable to that of an indigenous name, which was stigmatized as inferior. He earned his MA from Ohio State University (1964) and his PhD from the University of California, Los Angeles, and the University of Nebraska (1969).

Following his return to Liberia, Dr. Tipoteh served as associate professor and chairman of Department of Economics, University of Liberia, as well as budget advisor to the government. During that period, he played a major role in developing widespread awareness of the real potential for change in Liberia. As a consequence, the contradictions and inadequacies of the sociopolitical system were exposed, thus spurring others to action demanding change. On the African front, MOJA—which was actively involved in the struggle against colonialism, apartheid, and other injustices in Africa—was headquartered in Monrovia with branches in Nigeria, Ghana, Zambia, Algeria, Mauritius, Kenya, and the Gambia (introduction, *Historical Dictionary of Liberia*).

As one of the prominent leaders of the progressive movement that led the advocacy for democratic change in Liberia, Dr. Tipoteh was appointed the minister of planning and economic Affairs in the PRC regime following the 1980 coup. However, less than two years after the PRC regime came to power, Tipoteh was forced to abandon his post and move into exile, where he accused the regime of human rights violations. The regime also accused him of involvement in a plot to overthrow Doe.

Meanwhile, after the approval of the Liberian Constitution and the military regime lifted the ban on political activities to allow for general and presidential elections, Dr. Sawyer declared his intention to run for the presidency. He and his supporters founded the Liberian People's Party (LPP). However, he and the party were banned from participation in the 1985 elections, which were rigged by Doe.

In 1984, Dr. Sawyer was among several individuals arrested and imprisoned by the Doe regime for their alleged involvement in a "socialist plot" to overthrow the regime. It was while demanding for the release of Dr. Sawyer and the other detainees by protesting students on the campus of the University of Liberia that General Allison ordered soldiers to open fire on the unarmed students. As earlier reported, several students were known to have been killed and about a hundred wounded as a result of the attack on the university campus.

So it was that as the war raged in Liberia, NPFL leader Charles Taylor, who had occupied about 95 percent of the country outside the capital Monrovia, denounced the ECOWAS Peace Plan, which called for the deployment of a peacekeeping force and the establishment of a power-sharing transition government to stabilize the country and create the enabling conditions for the holding of free and fair democratic elections under international supervision.

Taylor, who was poised to seize the capital, saw the deployment of the peacekeeping force and the establishment of an interim government as an attempt by the Nigerian government, with the backing of the United States and other powers, to prevent him from becoming president. He vowed to fight to the bitter end to keep, what he called, the foreign invaders out of Liberia.

The United States had backed the ECOWAS intervention in order to forestall a military victory by Taylor's NPFL, which was known to have kept the people in areas occupied by the rebel movement in conditions of subjugation.

In support of Taylor, several Francophone, or French-speaking countries that are members of ECOWAS, were also strongly opposed to the deployment of ECOMOG, whose troops were predominantly from Anglophone, or English-speaking, countries. Guinea was the only Francophone country that was part of the five nations that originally comprised ECOMOG.

The leaders of Côte d'Ivoire, which borders Liberia, and Burkina Faso were very strong supporters of Taylor's armed insurgency to overthrow Doe. Through then president Blaise Compaoré of Burkina Faso, Libya provided training, military, and financial support to Taylor's NPFL while Burkinabe mercenaries, along with mercenaries from other West African countries, were also recruited and used to back Taylor's armed rebellion.

President Félix Houphouët-Boigny of the Ivory Coast, or Côte d'Ivoire, provided critical support toward Taylor's rebellion. On Christmas Eve 1989, a group of about two hundred armed rebels crossed the border from Côte d'Ivoire to launch the insurgency against Doe. The Ivorian leader's support for the NPFL rebellion was apparently in retaliation against Doe for the 1980 coup in Liberia.

President Houphouët-Boigny was a close friend of the late president William R. Tolbert, whose son, Adolphus Benedict Tolbert, was married to President Houphouët-Boigny's goddaughter. As he dealt with the shock of his close friend's assassination, President Houphouët-Boigny reportedly pleaded with the new military leaders in Liberia to spare the life of his son-in-law, Representative A. Benedict Tolbert, who was then hiding at the French embassy in Monrovia. As noted earlier in this chapter, Representative Tolbert was seized from the French embassy by regime security forces and killed.

As a result of this development, an anguished President Houphouët-Boigny reportedly vowed retribution against Doe for the killing of his dear friend and son-in-law. That opportunity to retaliate against Doe presented itself with Taylor's armed rebellion, which was given financial, military, diplomatic, and other support necessary to successfully execute the rebellion.

President Houphouët-Boigny was also known to have a beef with what he considered to be Nigeria's dominance of the subregion. He openly supported the Biafra secessionist movement, which led to the Nigerian Civil War from 1967 to 1970. The Ivory Coast was one of only four African countries that recognized the breakaway Biafra, which, if successful, could have led to the breakup of the Federal Republic of Nigeria.

The other African countries that recognized Biafra were Zambia, Gabon, and Tanzania. After the secessionists were defeated, General Odumegwu Ojukwu, who was the leader of the secessionist Biafra nation, was granted asylum in the Ivory Coast ("Ojukwu Is Given Asylum in Ivory Coast," *New York Times*, January 24, 1970).

An avowed antisocialist, the Ivorian leader, who was in power for over thirty years, was known to have been involved in the destabilization of some African countries that were deemed to be socialist oriented. For example, he was known to be involved in the overthrow and assassination of Captain Thomas Sankara, head of state of Burkina Faso. Sankara was assassinated by his vice head of state, Blaise Compaoré, who declared himself head of state of the impoverished West African country.

According to historical accounts, in 1983, President Houphouët-Boigny financed the military coup that brought Sankara and his close friend Compaoré to power as head of state and vice head of state, respectively. Nevertheless, Sankara became more of a socialist firebrand, much to the chagrin of the pro-Western Ivorian leader, who was regarded as dean of Francophone West Africa and the overall trustee of French strategic and economic interests in West Africa.

After seizing power upon assassinating his comrade and friend in 1987, Compaoré became a close ally of President Houphouët-Boigny. He also became a son-in-law to the legendary Ivorian leader when he wedded the widow of A. Benedict Tolbert, who was killed in the Liberian coup in 1980, as reported earlier.

Liberian exiled dissidents, including Prince Johnson, who later emerged as NPFL combatants were reportedly involved in the overthrow and assassination of Captain Sankara, a popular Pan-African leader, who was mostly regarded by the Burkinabe people and Africans across the continent and beyond as a change agent. This was how, as an apparent payback, Compaoré played a pivotal role in the NPFL rebellion to eliminate the Doe regime. He was the middleman between President Houphouët-Boigny and Libyan dictator Muammar Gaddafi, who provided training and other relevant military support that enabled the NPFL to launch its military incursion from the Ivory Coast. Compaoré also provided the NPFL with Burkinabe mercenaries, who gained notoriety for their brutality during the Liberian civil war.

As an apparent token of appreciation for Compaoré's contribution to the NPFL, Taylor reportedly looted the main hydroelectric dam in Liberia, which provided electricity to many parts of the country; and he gave the hydro equipment to Burkina Faso as a gift. Taylor's forces also looted the radio and television transmission equipment of the main state broadcaster, the Liberia Broadcasting System (LBS), and he used the equipment to set up his own LBS at the NPFL headquarters in the central Liberian city of Gbarnga, Bong County.

Because of the looting and damage to the main electric grid, the entire city of Monrovia still does not have electricity as of this publication, not to talk about the rest of the country. Since the end of the war, the lack of electricity has been a major hindrance to the pace of progress, considering the fact that rapid industrialization is not possible without the availability of electric power.

Following their deployment in Liberia, the country was also looted extensively by the West African peacekeeping forces, who shipped the loot to their respective countries. They looted everything from air conditioners to vehicles, refrigerators, and earth-moving and industrial equipment, to name a few. Copper wire on the light poles down to modern bathroom toilets were stripped and shipped away. There is a certain neighboring country that was known to have gained some level of development from Liberia's loot.

Before dragging down the path of self-destruction, Liberia was regarded to be well-off compared with some of the peacekeeping countries, whose nationals came to Liberia mostly for economic opportunities. Some of the peacekeeping soldiers expressed that they could not understand why Liberians were fighting because Liberia was seen to be much better off than where some of them hailed from.

So it was that amid the regional differences, on August 24, 1990, ECOMOG forces from the various countries that had assembled in neighboring Sierra Leone landed in Liberia under heavy fire from Taylor's NPFL fighters. The NPFL fought desperately to seize the port from Johnson's INPFL and prevent the peacekeepers from landing there. The southwestern suburb of Monrovia, where the port is located, was occupied by Johnson's INPFL forces, which supported the deployment of ECOMOG.

During that period, I was hiding out along with my fiancée, Neiko Irene Foeday, at the residence of an American diplomat friend close to the US embassy in Monrovia. From our hideout overlooking the Atlantic Ocean, we could see Nigerian naval vessels firing in the direction of Taylor's NPFL forces on the outskirts of Monrovia, causing flares or fireballs amid loud explosions. Neiko and I got married after we fled to the United States. We were among several Liberian activists and politicians who had taken refuge at the homes of several American diplomats' and this was how, thanks be to God, we were saved from being killed by state security agents.

Among those at the residence with us were Mr. Lamini A. Waritay, a well-respected mass communications professional, and Mr. Blamo Nelson, a strategic thinker and planner who conceived and designed the model for relief food distribution throughout Liberia, which was adapted internationally. Mr. Nelson was an executive of the opposition United People's Party (UPP), a progressive-oriented party. Mr. Waritay, who was co-chair of the Department of Mass Communications at the University of Liberia, was the immediate past president and advisor of the Press Union of Liberia (PUL), of which I was the secretary-general. The PUL was one of Liberia's leading organizations advocating for human rights and democratic governance in the country, a cause that was fraught with danger.

Waritay and I were among those declared wanted dead or alive after Doe's security forces set out to hunt down those who were alleged to be ringleaders of a demonstration that took place in early 1990, during which tens of thousands of Liberians from all walks of life paraded the streets of Monrovia to present a petition to the national legislature. The petition sought for Doe's impeachment in keeping with the Liberian Constitution because his regime was seen to have lost total control as the country descended into the abyss. The escalation of the conflict had led to the virtual collapse of civil administration. The president was increasingly isolated as nearly all of his senior officials and advisors deserted him and fled into exile.

The petition was never presented as heavily armed government troops opened fire on unarmed demonstrators, which was the beginning of the complete breakdown of law and order in Monrovia. Mr. Waritay and I represented the PUL as part of the coalition of civil society organizations, including the student and labor movements, which prepared the petition for presentation to the legislature.

Taylor's resistance to ECOMOG was because then Nigerian head of state General Ibrahim Badamasi Babangida was known to be a very close friend of Doe, who idolized the Nigerian leader and publicly referred to him as his "big brother," an African term for someone honored or respected for their seniority. As a manifestation of his reverence for the Nigerian military leader, Doe named a graduate school at the University of Liberia the Ibrahim B. Babangida Graduate School of International Relations while the highway linking Monrovia to the Sierra Leone border was also named the Babangida Highway.

At the onset of the civil war, Babangida initially offered to back Doe militarily, something for which he was resoundingly denounced by Taylor, who threatened to fight against any Nigerian troops that would set foot on Liberian soil. It was therefore in an apparent effort to deflect concerns that Nigeria was planning to intervene militarily on behalf of Doe by using the peacekeeping force that a Ghanaian, General Quainoo, was selected as force commander of ECOMOG.

During that period, President Doe was holed up in the heavily fortified Executive Mansion in Monrovia, which was defended by remnants of the Armed Forces of Liberia, comprising mostly of members of his ethnic group. Although he welcomed the deployment of the ECOWAS peacekeeping force, Doe also condemned the formation of an interim government in exile while he, the sitting president, was still in power at the mansion. Doe, like Taylor, argued that the formation of an interim government in exile not only violated the Liberian Constitution, but that it was also treasonable, considering that he, the legitimate president, was still in power.

The quiet atmosphere of the beautiful Sunday afternoon of September 9, 1990, was interrupted by bursts of gunfire from the direction of the Freeport of Monrovia, where Commander in Chief Doe was attacked and captured by Johnson and his INPFL fighters. Doe had left his fortified Executive Mansion to meet for the first time with General Quainoo at the ECOMOG base, which was located at the port.

Upon hearing that President Doe had gone to the port, Johnson and his men attacked the ECOMOG headquarters, shot and seized Doe, and took him away to the INPFL base. Almost all of those who accompanied the president to the port were cut down in a hail of bullets from Johnson and his men. Doe's security could not fight back because they were reportedly disarmed upon arrival at the ECOMOG headquarters, while Johnson and his forces did not surrender their weapons when they arrived.

A senior INPFL commander, once a good friend of mine who participated in the assault to capture Doe, narrated accounts of how General Quainoo fled from the office where he was meeting with the Liberian leader in the wake of the attack. He said that some of Doe's security officers covered him with their bodies when Johnson and his men stormed the office, seized him, and took off with their captive. It was while being interrogated at Johnson's base that Doe was tortured to death.

Owing to his apparent failure to prevent Johnson's INPFL from capturing President Doe at the ECOMOG headquarters, General Quainoo was immediately replaced. From that period until the end of ECOMOG's mandate in Liberia, Nigerian generals were appointed to head the peacekeeping force.

In retaliation for the intervention of the Nigeria-led peacekeeping force, Taylor ordered the arrest and confinement of thousands of mostly Nigerians and nationals from other countries that contributed to ECOMOG in NPFL-occupied territory. He threatened that for every Liberian killed from Nigerian military action in Liberia, a Nigerian in NPFL custody would also be killed. As a result of the foregoing, scores of Nigerians and other nationals who were held hostage by Taylor's NPFL were reportedly killed.

Among the hostages killed by the NPFL were two Nigerian journalists, Tayo Awotunsin and Krees Imobibie, who disappeared in August 1990 while they were reporting on the civil war. Mr. Awotunsin was a member of the *Champion* chain of newspapers, and Mr. Imobibie was the political editor of the *Guardian*, a daily newspaper.

The NPFL leader also threatened Sierra Leone for allowing its territory to be used as a beachhead for ECOMOG deployment in Liberia. The threat became a reality when in 1991, NPFL-backed Sierra Leonean rebels self-styled the Revolutionary United Front (RUF) and invaded Sierra Leone from Liberia, leading to a civil war that lasted for eleven years. The RUF, led by Corporal Foday Sankoh, who was known to have been dishonorably discharged from the Sierra Leone Armed Forces and imprisoned for several years for engaging in mutiny, gained global notoriety for amputating the limbs of their victims. The brutal and barbaric act of amputating the limbs of defenseless people were intended to instill fear and terror to keep the people under subjugation. The Sierra Leone Civil War, which ended in 2002, resulted in an estimated fifty thousand people killed and over half a million people displaced in neighboring countries.

Sankoh was among a number of so-called revolutionary dissidents from various West African countries who were known to have trained in Libya with Taylor's NPFL, and they were involved in the Liberian civil war as NPFL combatants. The invasion of Sierra Leone confirmed the fear of West African leaders that the Liberian civil war could spill over into neighboring countries and eventually destabilize the subregion. And they were on the mark.

The Ivory Coast, or Côte d'Ivoire, then one of the most developed and peaceful countries in Africa, was also plunged in a civil war following the 1993 death of President Houphouët-Boigny, who ruled for over three decades since the country gained independence from France. Taylor was implicated in the Ivorian conflict while Liberian mercenaries—ex-combatants from the Liberian civil war—reportedly fought on opposing sides in the Ivorian civil war, which began in 2002. President Houphouët-Boigny's destabilizing activities, especially in Liberia and Burkina Faso, would drag the Ivory Coast in a civil war following his demise. Neighboring Guinea also experienced Liberian-related armed insurgencies that almost led to a full-scale civil war in that country.

So it was that the Liberian civil war, which started simply as an armed insurgency to depose President Doe, became an equal-opportunity crisis of regional proportions that pitted Anglophone West Africa against Francophone West Africa.

Meanwhile, following Doe's death in September 1990, the country disintegrated into ethnic and factional bloodshed of unprecedented and unimaginable proportions. Many armed factions emerged and occupied various parts of the country in the bloody contest for state power.

After years of hostilities, a cease-fire agreement was reached among the warring parties, allowing for elections in 1997, which was won by Mr. Taylor, the preeminent warlord. During that election, a popular chant by voters was "He killed my ma, he killed my pa, but I will vote for him," referring to Taylor, who the voters feared would continue the war if he was not elected president.

The country under President Taylor soon became a massive criminal enterprise and subsequently degenerated into a failed state. Renewed civil war in Liberia and Taylor's indictment by the UN-backed Special Court for Sierra Leone (SCSL) for his role in arming Sierra Leone's rebel Revolutionary United Front (RUF) in exchange for looted diamonds led to his fall from power, and he was forced into exile in Nigeria in August 2003.

Civil Wars End with Taylor's Removal from Power and Exile

Following Mr. Taylor's departure from power and the signing of an internationally brokered peace accord by Liberia's warring factions and other parties in Accra, Ghana, in 2003, the United Nations Mission in Liberia (UNMIL) was established on September 19, 2003, based upon UN Security Council Resolution 1509. This followed a series of fifteen failed peace agreements during the course of the fourteen years of conflict. African countries, led by Nigeria, spent hundreds of millions of dollars and lost hundreds of lives in the effort to restore peace during the previously failed peace accords.

In October 2003, UNMIL peacekeepers were deployed in Liberia, which reached a strength of up to sixteen thousand military personnel, including police officers, and a civilian component for the provision of leadership, support, and expertise in the area of administration. They were well equipped to carry out the mission's mandate, which included the protection of the civilian population, reform of justice and security institutions, human rights promotion and protection, and public information.

Dr. Kofi Atta Annan, who served as the seventh secretary-general of the UN from 1997 to 2006, played a very critical role in building the international coalition under the auspices of the UN to bring an end to Liberia's civil upheaval. As the bloodshed intensified in Liberia, the secretary-general had strongly advocated for the deployment of an international force to stop the fighting between rebel forces and troops loyal to then president Taylor.

Following UNMIL's deployment, Dr. Annan, a blessed son of Ghana and the first black secretary-general of the UN, did what was possible to ensure that Liberia received the necessary financial, diplomatic, and other support necessary for sustainable peace and reconstruction.

In February 2004, a few months following UNMIL's deployment in Liberia, the United Nations Development Group (UNDG) organized an international donors' conference, cosponsored by the United States, the World Bank, and the UN. Representatives from 110 countries and forty-five organizations attended the conference, during which more than US$500 million was pledged for Liberia's reconstruction. Dr. Annan indicated during that conference that Liberia had arrived at a moment of hope (UN press release online, February 6, 2014).

Also according to the UN press release, then secretary of state Colin Powell, who represented the United States at the donors' conference, announced that the US Congress had appropriated an additional US$200 million in humanitarian and reconstruction aid and another US$245 million for UN Peacekeeping operations in Liberia. The US administration of President George W. Bush and Congress were a blessing to Liberia for providing strong support to the peace-building and reconstruction processes. In addition to President Bush himself, God bless Secretary Powell and then national security advisor to the president Dr. Condoleezza Rice, who were among the strong voices in favor of Liberia. Dr. Rice also succeeded retired General Powell as secretary of state, and during her tenure, US policy toward Liberia was on the front burner.

Because of its holistic posture, from the date of authorization on September 19, 2003 to the end of its mandate on March 30, 2018, covering a period of almost 15 years, UNMIL can, without hesitation, be recorded as one of the most successful peacekeeping missions in the historical annals of the UN.

UNMIL's success in Liberia cannot be overemphasized. The peacekeeping mission secured for all Liberians an undisputed, uninterrupted peace for nearly two decades and can be measured with the following results: the disarmament and demobilization of more than a hundred thousand combatants, including child soldiers from various armed factions, and the creation of an atmosphere of peace and security, ushering in the enabling environment for the holding of three successive general and presidential elections.

The integrated UN Country Team in Liberia played a very critical leadership role in the reintegration of war-affected populations, the restructuring of the security services, the extension of state authority throughout the country, and the restoration of basic services, such as health and education, among others. UNMIL's presence also provided employment opportunities for thousands of local professionals of diverse backgrounds.

As noted above, the atmosphere of peace and security created by UNMIL ushered in the enabling environment for the Liberian people to engage in free democratic political activities without falling prey to intimidation and violence. The first election brought about the 2006 inauguration of Madam Ellen Johnson Sirleaf, Liberia's and Africa's first democratically elected female president.

A graduate of Harvard University's Kennedy School of Government, where she obtained a master's degree in public administration in 1971, Madam Sirleaf assumed the Liberian presidency with a very impressive record of national and international experience. Various prominent positions she held included Liberia's minister of finance, president of the Liberian Bank for Development and Investment (LBDI), vice president of Citicorp's Africa regional office in Nairobi in Kenya, and senior loan officer of the World Bank in Washington DC. In 1992, she joined the United Nations Development Programme (UNDP) as assistant administrator and director of its Regional Bureau for Africa with the rank of assistant secretary-general of the United Nations.

Madam Sirleaf's election and inauguration as Africa's first female democratically elected president created an atmosphere of high hope and optimism at home and abroad. The sentiment among the international community was one of goodwill and confidence in the new government's agenda of reconstruction and development. Madam President also served a second and final term, which ended in early 2018.

The third general and presidential elections, following the end of the civil war, brought about the January 22, 2018, inauguration of former international soccer icon George Manneh Weah as president of the Republic of Liberia. The inauguration, attended by tens of thousands of Liberians who jam-packed the Samuel Kanyon Doe Sports Stadium in Monrovia, as well as an array of African leaders and a host of high-profile international dignitaries, witnessed for the first time in more than seventy years a peaceful transfer of power from one living president to another.

In July 2006, less than six months before the end of his tenure at the UN, Secretary-General Annan paid a three-day visit to Liberia, during which he reaffirmed the pledge of continued UN support for war-ravaged Liberia. While he called on the government and every one of Liberians to take collective responsibility in nation building, the secretary-general particularly urged the international community to stay engaged to help consolidate the achievements Liberia had made in the area of peace and recovery.

During the course of his visit, Secretary-General Annan held talks with President Ellen Johnson Sirleaf, members of the cabinet, and the UN Country Team, as well as addressed the Joint Session of the National Legislature of Liberia. Dr. Annan stressed the importance of good governance and the rule of law and the need to fight the scourge of corruption. He understood that corruption is a major source of bad governance, poverty, and instability.

As a mark of appreciation for his invaluable contributions toward peace in Liberia, President Sirleaf conferred on Secretary-General Annan the Grand Order of the Most Venerable Order of the Knighthood of the Pioneers of the Republic of Liberia, the country's most prestigious civilian award. Conferring the honor, President Sirleaf said the event was an occasion for quiet and sober reflection and for gratitude and appreciation. She lauded Dr. Annan, who was accompanied by his wife, Nane, for his exceptional contributions to the nation. The president said the secretary-general's "singular and selfless act of thoughtfulness has given Liberia a rebirth" ("Highest Honor for Kofi Annan," *UNMIL Focus*, June–August 2006).

Paying tribute to his exemplary life, President Sirleaf described Dr. Annan as one of the world's greatest leaders in the past sixty years. The president said it was Liberia's turn, "in our own small way, to thank Annan by giving him the highest award in the country" ("Highest Honour for Kofi Annan").

My personal encounter with Dr. Annan was during his visit to Liberia, when he first arrived at the Executive Mansion, the beautiful seaside presidential palace, to be received by President Sirleaf. Beaming with smile, he appeared like such a gentle person, someone that any stranger, especially a little child, could run to and hug without fear of being rebuffed. His dignity and grace were enhanced by the way he easily interacted with others of diverse backgrounds despite his high status. He had such a calm and peaceful disposition. His voice was calm and reassuring. I recall those days when the secretary-general was frequently featured on UNMIL Radio, the UN-operated station that is now named ECOWAS Radio. Besides the enlightenment on whatever matters he addressed, I simply enjoyed listening to him or watching him on television because of his pronunciation and poise.

As a manifestation of Liberia's gratitude for Dr. Annan's contributions to Liberia, the Kofi Annan Center for Conflict Transformation was inaugurated at the University of Liberia in October 2006. The illustrious son of Ghana and Africa died in August 2018 at the age of eighty.

The Weah Presidency

The first election brought about the 2006 inauguration of Madam Ellen Johnson Sirleaf, Liberia's and Africa's first democratically elected female president. Her vice president was Mr. Joseph Nyumah Boakai, a veteran politician and public figure who previously served as minister of agriculture during the regime of Samuel K. Doe. In 2011, Madam Sirleaf was reelected to a second six-year term.

The third postwar presidential election resulted in the January 22, 2018, inauguration of Mr. George Manneh Weah, a retired global soccer icon. Weah's inauguration witnessed for the first time in more than seventy years a peaceful transfer of power from one living president to another in Liberia. Mr. Weah won a landslide victory for the presidency against incumbent vice president Boakai in a presidential runoff.

In the first two elections in 2005 and 2011, Mr. Weah ran unsuccessfully as president and vice president, respectively, against Madam Sirleaf. Not deterred by his failure to capture the presidency, Mr. Weah later contested for a senatorial seat for Montserrado County, Liberia's most populated region, which includes Monrovia. Having won a landslide senatorial victory, Mr. Weah was serving as senator for Montserrado

County in the national legislature when he once again contested for the presidency in 2017, eventually becoming victorious.

Born in 1966, Weah, the former internationally acclaimed professional soccer legend turned politician, grew up in poverty in a Monrovia slum community. Due to deprivation of the necessities of life, young George did not have the foundation of a quality early education, which is very critical for the professional development and success of an individual.

Despite the odds stacked against him, Mr. Weah was able to pull himself by his bootstraps, so to speak, to change his life conditions for the better and to make a difference in the lives of others. In media interviews, Mr. Weah has attributed his rise from poverty to prosperity to a focused mind, determination to succeed, hard work, and trust in God.

Current Liberian president George M. Weah (dressed in white) being accompanied
by former president Ellen Johnson Sirleaf at a ceremony

During my seventh-grade literature class at the Seventh Day Adventist (SDA) Mission High School in Buchanan, Grand Bassa County, I learned one of my lifelong favorite quotes, which aptly applies to Mr. Weah. The quote is from Louis Pasteur, the legendary French scientist who rose from a poor background to become a renowned scientist and a wealthy individual. I learned in my literature class that more than a century ago, when asked how he made it from rags to riches, Pasteur was quoted as saying, "Chance favors the prepared mind."

Mr. Weah's popularity with a vast mass of the Liberian population, which catapulted him to the presidency, is attributed to the love and concern he has demonstrated for the welfare of his people. He is widely regarded as someone who never forgot his roots.

Liberians scattered around the world as a result of the brutal civil war would recall that George Weah was like the brightest star connected to a country that had gone dark due to the appalling and mind-boggling state of death and destruction.

For example, on August 1, 2017, the *News* newspaper in Monrovia published an article written by D. Zeogar Wilson, former goalkeeper of Liberia's national soccer team, the Lone Star, who has been associated with Mr. Weah for many years. In his article, Mr. Wilson, who was also a goalkeeper of the Mighty Barrolle, my favorite national soccer club, wrote the following account:

With all the bad news headlined around the world, there was something positive taking place about Liberia that the bad news had overshadowed: George Oppong Manneh Weah. George was making headlines in Monaco, France as a young and upcoming soccer star from Liberia. George pondered for days and months on what he could do to portray a positive image of his motherland, Liberia. He watched on television the displacement of his countrymen, he saw the death and destruction to his country and was in total disbelief of what was happening. Through his struggle to find a course of action he could take, two stood up. One was what he could do to assist his fellow compatriots who were displaced in refugee camps in La Côte D'Ivoire, Ghana and Guinea.

The second was what he could do regarding the National Soccer Team's continental engagements. George remembered that our late President, William R. Tolbert, Jr., used the 1979 Six Nations Tournament to foster peace between Senegal and the Gambia. He came to a quick realization that he could do something to portray a positive image of Liberia to help diffuse the negative image as a result of the civil war.

Many Liberians in the refugee camps in these countries can attest to the level of assistance they received from the generosity of George and I need not delve into that further. George's love for the game of soccer cannot be overstated. He is compassionate and loves the sport without question. George quickly made contact with FIFA (Federation of International Football Association) and CAF (Confederation of African Football) to find out what he could do to facilitate Liberia's participation in continental competitions. As those discussions progressed, both institutions made George aware that Liberia was indebted in back dues prior to the civil war and the amount had increased since the conflict. Being the patriot he is, Ambassador Weah decided to put his country in good standing with both FIFA and CAF thereby clearing the way for Liberia to participate in continental competitions by paying over two hundred thousand ($200,000) of his personal funds. ("George Weah—the Patriot I Know," *News*, August 1, 2017)

Mr. Wilson, who also served as acting minister of youth and sports in a transitional government during the civil war, said that in order for Liberia to prepare and participate in the African Cup of Nations and FIFA competitions for the World Cup in 1996, Mr. Weah expended hundreds of thousands of dollars of personal funds. Following Mr. Weah's election to the presidency, Mr. Wilson was appointed minister of youth and sports.

Having won a strong popular mandate from Liberians to assume the presidency, the challenge for President Weah was to institute the necessary policies and programs to ensure the success of his government's Pro-Poor Agenda for Prosperity and Development, launched in October 2018. In order for President Weah to fully take advantage of the opportunities thrust upon him to transform Liberia and establish a commendable legacy, the need for him to surround himself with individuals who are sufficiently competent with high integrity to deliver in the interest of the people cannot be overemphasized.

It is my hope that the Lone Star national soccer team of Liberia would participate in the World Cup during the tenure of President Weah. The possibilities for the development of sports in Liberia could not be more promising than now, given the president's influence and connections in the sports world.

Mr. Weah's vice president is Mrs. Jewel C. Howard Taylor, the ex-wife of former president Charles Taylor. Beautiful and intellectually bright, Madam Taylor was in her second term as senior senator of Bong County, Liberia's second-most-populous region, when she and her colleague Senator Weah were elected as vice president and president, respectively.

Madam Taylor, who holds a master's degree in professional banking and two bachelors in banking and economics, also has extensive administrative experience. Prior to becoming First Lady, Mrs. Taylor served as deputy governor of the National Bank of Liberia, renamed the Central Bank of Liberia, among others. The Central Bank of Liberia is Liberia's equivalent of the US Federal Reserve.

Despite her accomplishments, Mrs. Taylor has been struggling to come out of the shadow of her ex-husband's legacy. Owing to the stigma, she was not given much of a fighting chance by many when she initially declared her intention to contest for the Bong County senatorial seat during the 2005 general and presidential elections. After a period of peaceful campaign, Liberians went to the polls and elected their leaders through a democratic process. Surprisingly, Mrs. Taylor won majority of the votes in Bong to become senior senator of the county. She was among a few members of the legislature from 2005 who won reelection, as a manifestation of the people's approval of her leadership in the county. It was while serving her second term that she and her fellow senator George Weah teamed up and successfully contested the 2017 presidential election.

There is a need for Mrs. Taylor to be judged on the content of her character and not necessarily based on the fact that she was married to the now-convicted and imprisoned ex-warlord turned president. She should be given the benefit of the doubt and be made to account for her own conduct. She should not continue to suffer from the perception of guilt by association.

Meanwhile, in March 2006, former president Taylor, who was indicted for war crimes and crimes against humanity while in office, was eventually arrested in Nigeria and taken to The Hague. Held in prison, he was prosecuted and convicted on eleven charges, including terrorism, rape, murder, and the use of child soldiers by rebel groups in Sierra Leone during that country's 1991–2002 civil war, in which some fifty thousand people died. He is serving a fifty-year sentence in a prison in the United Kingdom because of the conviction ("Ex-Liberia President Charles Taylor to Stay in UK Prison," BBC online, March 25, 2015).

Bad Governance Undermines Liberia's and Africa's Progress

Even though there are unique historical circumstances regarding Liberia's founding, the story of the country is similar to that of many countries in Africa and perhaps other parts of the world. For example, after gaining independence following decades under colonial rule, during which millions of Africans were dehumanized and massacred under colonial subjugation, most of the liberation leaders who took over the leadership of newly independent African states have committed some of the worst crimes against humanity against their own people. Corruption and mismanagement of public resources have been the order of the day. As a result, many African countries have been mired in poverty, underdevelopment, and instability due to lack of visionary leadership and bad governance. Dictatorial rule, corruption, and poverty are parts of the main ingredients that have fueled instability, bloodshed, and destruction in Liberia and in other parts of Africa and the world in general.

While Africa, the world's second-largest continent, is regarded as one of the richest in natural resources on earth, it is the least developed; and its people have been mostly impoverished and disempowered due to what is regarded to be very limited visionary leadership and opportunities. A striking example is the Democratic Republic of the Congo (DRC), Africa's largest country in territory and reputed to be the world's richest country in natural resources. Sadly, it is common knowledge, as reflected by public records, that the DRC is ranked as one of the poorest and most unstable countries in the world.

As quoted in the introduction, in the Holy Bible, the Proverbs 29:18 (KJV) states, "Where there is no vision the people perish . . ."

So it is that as a broken country like Liberia continues on the painful process of recovery, the need for visionary leadership cannot be overemphasized. There is a need for leadership that would institute the kind of aggressive reforms so as to ensure that economic benefits have trickle-down effects, especially on those at the bottom of the economic scale. For Liberia to enjoy sustainable peace and accelerated progress in its postwar reconstruction, the reconstruction programs must be focused on improving the lives of the people through access to quality services, such as housing, transportation, electricity, water and sanitation, health, and education, among others.

There is a need to institute a new economic policy that would focus on adding value to Liberia's natural resources by promoting local manufacturing to generate more employment and revenues rather than simply exporting our raw materials, as the case has been. Efforts must be made for the economic benefits to also percolate to the impoverished population. These initiatives, along with robust agriculture programs to boost food production, would help lift the population out of poverty.

Recommending Official State Burial for President Tolbert

As Liberia recovers from the vestiges of the war, there is no question that the country is at a crossroads seeking for a way between reconciliation and ensuring accountability for war and economic crimes. There is a growing public call and demand for the establishment of a war and economic crimes court as a means to bring the culture of impunity in Liberia to an end.

As Liberians also grapple with the very delicate issues of national reconciliation, I respectfully request that the Liberian people appeal to and prevail on the government of the day to exhume and officially rebury the remains of President William R. Tolbert and accord him all of the honors befitting a former president of the Republic of Liberia. A monument could also be erected at the mass grave where those former officials were buried, with each of their names and titles engraved on the tombstones. I ask that all charges brought against Tolbert and his officials by the PRC be dropped and that the affected officials' convictions pronounced by the kangaroo military tribunal that tried them be overturned. This, I believe, is in the spirit of national reconciliation and unity.

It may be interesting to note that there is a growing awareness among majority of Liberians that Tolbert was one of the best presidents Liberia ever had, especially during the course of the past several decades. Simply put, ask any Liberian who lived before the outbreak of violence in the 1980s this question: "Is Liberia better off now than it was during Tolbert's administration?" I can guarantee that the answer will be a near-unanimous *No*, if not completely unanimous. While Tolbert had his failures and weaknesses, there is increasing recognition among more Liberians that the country's progress was aborted by the military takeover.

Corruption, nepotism, and other charges for which Tolbert and his officials were brutally killed have worsened. As a result of poor governance, Liberia has been rated as one of the poorest and most corrupt countries in the world. There can be no question that the painful state of affairs of Liberia will not change until Liberians are able to end the culture of impunity and create the enabling conditions for reconciliation in the country.

I suppose the thoughts articulated above also resonate with other parts of Africa. I, therefore, underscore that in order to ensure accelerated progress in Africa, African governments must take appropriate actions and practical measures to ensure accountability and the rule of law, as well as create opportunities for the people to aspire to the best of their potentials.

CHAPTER TWO
Answering the Call to Service

While soundly asleep one early Saturday morning in February 2006, I was abruptly awaken by the ring of the telephone in my bedroom at around 3:00 a.m. This was a call from the Liberian capital, Monrovia, which was eight hours ahead in time from Sacramento, the capital of the state of California, where I had lived in exile for a decade after fleeing Liberia's brutal and devastating civil war.

"Hello, Gabriel. How are you doing? I have been asked to contact you because the incoming minister of information, Honorable Johnny McClain, said he has called your number several times without being able to get you. The reason for the call is that you've been recommended to serve as the deputy minister for technical services at MICAT."

The call came from Dr. C. William Allen, then outgoing minister of the Ministry of Information, Culture Affairs, and Tourism (MICAT) in the Liberia National Transitional Government (LNTG), which had left power in the wake of the inauguration of Madam Ellen Johnson Sirleaf as Liberia's and Africa's first democratically elected female president on January 16, 2006. Established in August 2003 after Liberian warring factions and other parties signed the Comprehensive Peace Agreement (CPA) in Accra, Ghana, ending the country's nearly-fifteen-year brutal civil war, the LNTG was the power-sharing government, dominated by representatives of armed factions that were involved in the civil wars. The power-sharing government also included representatives of political parties and civil society organizations.

In the new government that was being formed by President Sirleaf, Dr. Allen was appointed director general of the Civil Service Agency (CSA) while Mr. Johnny A. McClain replaced Dr. Allen as minister at MICAT. Before returning to Liberia to serve in government, Dr. Allen had served as an associate professor at Virginia State University in Petersburg, Virginia, where he taught journalism and mass communications. A journalist, author, and former president of the Press Union of Liberia (the national organization of journalists), Dr. Allen also taught at the University of South Carolina Upstate in Spartanburg, Xavier University of Louisiana in New Orleans, and the University of Liberia.

It was McClain's second time to serve as the minister of Information, Cultural Affairs and Tourism, commonly known as MICAT. Small in stature and not more than five feet tall, Mr. McClain is soft-spoken, also very fluent in French, and an internationally seasoned media expert. He first served as minister of information during the administration of President William R. Tolbert in the late 1970s, a period during which I was a teenager in junior high or middle school. When President Tolbert was assassinated during the bloody 1980 military coup led by Master Sergeant Samuel K. Doe, Mr. McClain was arrested along with other officials and those considered to have been closely associated with the deposed government. He was almost executed along with thirteen senior officials of the deposed government, who were publicly shot on the beach a few days following the coup. He was imprisoned for several months, and following his release, he left Liberia and lived abroad for decades. He had moved back to Liberia to reside following his retirement as an Africa executive for the United Nations Educational, Scientific and Cultural Organization (UNESCO).

Madam Sirleaf also served in Tolbert's cabinet as minister of finance when the putsch occurred. According to Mr. McClain, he and Madam Sirleaf were among the young members of the cabinet of President Tolbert, widely recognized as a leader who provided opportunities for and promoted young people during his administration. As Liberia's first female finance minister, Madam Sirleaf was among three ministers of the deposed government who were not detained following the 1980 coup.

Following her inauguration, President Sirleaf asked Mr. McClain, her former colleague and longtime friend, to head the Ministry of Information, Culture Affairs and Tourism, with a mandate to reform MICAT, which, during Liberia's recent history, was used as an instrument of state terrorism to suppress freedom of speech and of the press. Mr. McClain then set out to identify a few individuals who had distinguished themselves in media leadership for the president to appoint to key deputy and assistant minister posts at MICAT.

It was during a search process that involved consultations with some of the very prominent media personalities in the country that I was considered to fill one of the posts at MICAT. I was completely unaware of what was unfolding in Monrovia before Dr. Allen's call awoke me that very early morning to inform me of my preferment.

"I'm very delighted and honored to have been chosen from among many competent Liberians to be offered such a position of importance in the government of President Sirleaf," I responded to Dr. Allen. "However, I'm not sure if I would like to work at that ministry," I added. I told him that I did not think I was prepared to serve at the Ministry of Information, the primary government agency charged with the responsibility to disseminate government information and regulate activities of the media and journalists.

I recalled that over the past years, especially during the respective brutal and barbaric regimes of military ruler Samuel K. Doe and rebel leader turned president Charles Taylor, the Information Ministry was used to arbitrarily ban or vandalize media establishments, as well as terrorize or imprison journalists. Under those two regimes, freedom of speech and of the press was criminalized, an offense for which political opponents and rights activists and journalists were regularly harassed, imprisoned, and tortured; and many of them were murdered in cold blood.

I had served as a journalist for a decade in Liberia before fleeing the country to the United States in late 1993 due to death threats. During the first four years of the Liberian civil war, which began on December 24, 1989, I was managing editor of the country's then-leading independent daily newspaper, the *Inquirer*. I had also served for six years in the leadership of the Press Union of Liberia (PUL), the national organization of journalists that was at the forefront in advocating for democratic governance during the Doe and Taylor regimes. I was secretary-general of the PUL when the civil war started and subsequently became acting president during the early years of the war, before fleeing into exile due to death threats.

During my respective tenures as leader of the PUL and editor of the *Inquirer*, I did not hesitate to use the leadership "pulpit" and the editorial pages of the newspaper in the cause to draw public attention to the state of death and destruction that prevailed in Liberia. This was even as the Information Ministry defended actions of the regimes of the day to criminalize freedom of speech and of the press.

This is why I told Dr. Allen that I found it difficult to accept a position at the Information Ministry, which was seen as an agency that was used as an instrument of state terror to suppress free speech. It was my considered opinion that taking a job that could make me to enforce draconian laws or obey unjust laws, such as the antimedia laws, would undermine the democratic values for which I had stood over the years and for which so much sacrifice had been made by the people, including the blood of many rights activists.

Another critical issue I raised with Allen was how an individual could sustain himself and his family working for a government that was starting off with a national budget that was just a puny US$80 million, considering the enormous challenges of rebuilding a country that was almost completely ruined due to more than two decades of civil upheaval. The general Liberian population was in a state of desperation, and the provision of every basic service was a priority.

As Allen and I talked, my mind also drifted to the once-beautiful Information Ministry building, located on Capitol Hill in Monrovia, which was soon to be my office. Like the rest of the infrastructure throughout the country, the MICAT building was badly damaged with virtually all of its doors, windows, roof, and furniture, as well as communications equipment, destroyed or looted. During a period of the war, the building was abandoned; and MICAT's offices were relocated to a building, about a couple of miles away, that once housed the ministry's printing press.

There was no electricity for general public consumption in the entire country because the hydroelectric dam and other generating facilities were completely destroyed or looted. There was also no pipe-borne water as water treatment plants were equally destroyed or looted. Even though the guns had been silent since the 2003 cease-fire, there were many reported deaths attributed to diseases that are otherwise preventable and treatable, such as malaria and diarrhea, which were exacerbated by the alarming unsanitary conditions that prevailed.

The government of President Ellen Johnson Sirleaf had inherited a country in shambles, with a collapsed economy, dysfunctional institutions, displaced people, destroyed infrastructure, and very few basic services. With more than 250,000 people dead during the years of civil wars, the Liberian people were in the state of hopelessness and had learned to live through mere survival.

After patiently listening to my reaction, Allen said he agreed with the sentiments and concerns I expressed regarding the Information Ministry and the other matters that I raised. However, he added, it was in line with President Sirleaf's desire to institute major reforms throughout the government—including the Information Ministry—and that reform-minded individuals like myself were being brought on board to help spearhead the reform agenda in various agencies of the government so as to move our country forward from a failed state.

Dr. Allen, who has been one of my mentors over the years, reminded me of how Madam Sirleaf, one of Liberia's most prominent internationally known political activists, was also terrorized, imprisoned, and exiled in the past for advocating for the rule of law and democratic governance. More importantly, Madam Sirleaf, a Harvard-trained economist, ascended to the Liberian presidency very qualified with a wealth of national and international experience.

He then said something that struck me and brought about my complete change of heart. This is what Allen said: "I'm in agreement with just about everything you said, Gabriel. But remember that President Sirleaf's administration presents a very real opportunity to bring about the transformation of our country we all have been struggling to achieve." He said if I maintained my lack of interest in the job because of all the concerns raised, that was up to me. "Other people will be given the responsibility you don't want," he stated. However, he added, if the responsibility was given to another individual who may not be able to perform up to expectation or if they begin to "screw up," then it would be disingenuous for me to sit on the fence and criticize when things are not going well in the country.

Allen indicated that it was because of my proven record as a change agent that I was being picked to help aggressively spearhead the necessary reforms and bring about the desired change at the Information Ministry. My mandate was to help ensure that freedom of speech and of the press became a reality in Liberia during the six-year tenure of the Sirleaf administration.

"You really got me on that. I think I will accept the responsibility," I told Allen.

"Now that we are in agreement," Allen continued, "when I get off the phone with you, Minister McClain will call on behalf of the president to formally offer you the job. All you have to do is to first express that you accept the job. Once that is done, you can inform the minister about the concerns that you have. I have no doubt that you both would be on the same page regarding what needs to be done at the Information Ministry."

My First Taste of Liberia's Backroom Political Power Play

About fifteen minutes after I got off the phone with Dr. Allen, Minister McClain called and congratulated me that the president was pleased to nominate me as deputy minister for technical services at the MICAT. During the course of the conversation, I broached Minister McClain about my concerns as earlier expressed. In response, he said this was precisely why he wanted me to be on his team at the MICAT. He said, "We have never met, and I don't know you. But in nearly every consultation I have had trying to help the president put a media team together at the MICAT, you have been highly recommended as one of the best members of the team. I look forward to working with you as together, we can institute the necessary reforms at the MICAT that would enable the government to ensure freedom of speech and of the press in Liberia."

Minister McClain then informed me that a press statement from the president's office announcing the appointment will be issued before the end of that day. However, the press statement from the president's office announced my appointment as assistant minister for information services and not deputy minister for technical services, as was previously understood. A confidant of the president who was a friend of mine called from the Executive Mansion, the official presidential residence, to congratulate me on my appointment as assistant minister. I had received a copy of the press statement from the office of the press secretary to the president, which was e-mailed to me. I was taken aback but did not say anything otherwise to the lady from the president's office who had called to congratulate me.

When I telephoned Minister McClain to inquire about the confusion, he expressed that he too was taken aback and disappointed when he heard the news broadcast because he was not informed about a change in position before the press statement from the president's office was released. In the press release, my dear friend and colleague Elizabeth Hoff was named deputy minister for technical services, and I was named as the assistant minister for information services.

Liz, as Minister Hoff is affectionately known, and I go a long way as friends and colleagues from our days as reporters in the field covering news assignments. She was a reporter for the government-owned *New Liberian* newspaper, which is published under the auspices of MICAT. Meanwhile, I was a reporter for the independent newspaper *Daily Observer*. She would also move on to serve as news editor of the independent newspaper the *News*. Liz had been associated with the Information Ministry since her childhood. Her father, now late Mr. Bill Frank Enoanyi, was an eminent journalist and author who settled in Liberia from Cameroon. He served as director of public affairs at MICAT, among others. While she was in school, Liz was a cadet at MICAT. At the time of her appointment by President Sirleaf, she was serving as the first female president of the Press Union of Liberia, a position she resigned to assume her new responsibility in government.

Be that as it may, Liz and I enjoyed a very cordial working relationship during our respective tenures at MICAT. Well experienced in the planning and execution of training workshops and other media-related programs, there could not have been a more qualified person for that office. Together, we were able to work with other professionals on the government's communication policies and programs. We did not always agree on everything, but we worked together as a team and as professional journalists who respected one another.

Honorable Gabriel Williams being received by a senior Chinese Communist Party official and cabinet minister in the Great Hall of the People in Beijing, China, during a visit in 2006 (courtesy of the Chinese government press)

It would be found out subsequently that a top official at the Ministry of State for Presidential Affairs, which is the administrative arm of the Office of the President, had manipulated the appointment process.

From the very beginning of the government, one of the president's most prominent advisors emerged to openly show a dislike for McClain's leadership at MICAT, something that was seen to have eventually contributed to McClain's standing being undermined in the eyes of the president. There appeared to have been a beef between McClain and this individual going back to their days at MICAT, when McClain was a senior official. Letting out steam about the situation many times, Mr. McClain said that the individual who was now opposing him was among a group of a few young men he recruited, trained to become journalists, and employed as cadets in the 1970s. He just could not understand why this individual was trying to undermine him.

Minister McClain is a pioneer in the establishment of the Ministry of Information, Culture Affairs, and Tourism (MICAT). According to the *Historical Dictionary of Liberia*, Mr. McClain began his journalism career as a reporter with the Department of Information and Culture Affairs (now MICAT) in the early 1960s. He served as secretary-general of the Press Union of Liberia, as well as assistant minister and deputy minister, respectively, at MICAT. After he was elevated as minister of MICAT in 1979, the brutal military coup overthrowing the government of President William R. Tolbert took place in 1980. He was imprisoned and almost killed along with the thirteen government officials who were publicly executed following the military takeover. He left the country following his release from detention.

It was after twenty-six years that Mr. McClain returned to head MICAT upon the request of his friend, then newly elected president Sirleaf. She and McClain were among the youngest cabinet ministers in the deposed government of President Tolbert.

In my telephone conversation with Minister McClain at the time the Executive Mansion press statement about my appointment was released, I had told him without hesitation that it was because of the questionable manner in which many officials conducted the affairs of government that had long tainted the public image of the government in Liberia and kept most well-meaning Liberians from being actively involved in public service. In light of that situation, I said, I was beginning to give my involvement with the government a second thought.

Minister McClain had apologized for the confusion and said it would not be good for me to back away since the announcement had already been made, noting that he was hopeful that I would be promoted in due course. Dr. Allen also advised that I should stay the course. "I want you to see this position as putting your foot in the door," said Allen. "Given your history of hard work, I have no doubt that the sky will be the limit with respect to promotion."

Allen's prediction would prove right as I was elevated to the post of deputy minister for public affairs less than a year upon serving as an assistant minister. During my tenure at the MICAT, I was able to demonstrate that it was not so much about promotion or position as much as it was about using the opportunity to serve to make a difference for the common good. I have always expressed that it is not a position or title that brings honor to a person, but that respect and honor are earned from how you conduct yourself.

Following my promotion to deputy minister, young enterprising broadcast journalist Abu Kamara succeeded me as assistant minister for information services. Handsome, talkative, hardworking, and up-front in his approach, Abu—as he is affectionately known—was the news director at Truth FM radio and Real TV when he joined us at MICAT. As professional journalists who were members of the MICAT cabinet, Abu, Liz, and I worked together really well as a team.

The Practice of Peddling Government Positions

After her inauguration, the president was confronted with her first major challenge of forming a government that was to basically hit the ground running because the Liberian people were desperately in need of basic services, such as health, education, food and water, security, employment, and electricity, among others. However, due to limited manpower in the country caused by a massive brain drain as a result of the wars, organizing the new government proved difficult for the president.

The pressure of filling vacancies, nevertheless, provided an opportunity for some influential functionaries within the Office of the President to push friends and others into various positions, irrespective of whether or not such individuals had the qualification and integrity for public service. Once in the corridors of power behind the scenes, one could pick up on whispers and rumors of how some of the "fat cats" took kickbacks to push individuals into various positions in the government.

The problem of influential officials in government soliciting bribes in exchange for giving others a job or promotion is an age-old one in Liberia. Over the years, many presidential confidants have been known to have exploited their access to the highest office in the land to perpetrate criminal activities to enrich themselves and undermine public interest.

As the new Liberian leader began naming her cabinet team, as well as officials of various ministries and parastatals, she was nevertheless keen to demonstrate to Liberians and the donor community that anyone selected to serve in her cabinet would have to pass three basic tests: integrity, competence, and a good human rights record.

President Sirleaf made it a point that individuals with known records of human rights abuses would not be considered for appointment in her government, which generated public debates in Liberia at the time. One of the major casualties of that pronouncement was a prominent individual, Mr. Paul Mulbah, a longtime supporter of Madam Sirleaf who was nominated for a post in the new government. Notwithstanding his support for Madam Sirleaf, she promptly withdrew his appointment following public outcry regarding Mulbah's role as director of police during the brutal regime of Charles Taylor.

Even though he denied involvement in abuse of human rights, Mr. Mulbah, who was famous for his role in the development and promotion of soccer in Liberia, never recovered from that stigma until his death in January 2019.

Eventually, the composition of the new administration was a reflection of some of the brightest minds and respectable leaders of diverse backgrounds of our country. Many Liberians of different professional backgrounds, including myself, were recruited from abroad and deployed in positions of leadership in various ministries and agencies of government.

Among the appointments, that of George Wallace Jr. as minister of foreign affairs eloquently delivered the message Liberians were waiting to hear. Wallace—a career diplomat, lawyer, and administrator—is one of Liberia's most celebrated diplomats, having joined the then Department of State (now Ministry of Foreign Affairs) in 1954 as a cadet and rising through the ranks. His diplomatic route had seen all the important ports of call in Africa and elsewhere in the world, including the Court of St. James's in the United Kingdom and the United States. Before his appointment, he was a senior diplomat at large at the Foreign Ministry ("A New Cabinet Outlook," *UNMIL Focus*, December 2005–February 2006).

Another highly acclaimed appointment was that of Dr. Antoinette Monsio Sayeh, a brilliant Liberian economist, as minister of finance. Dr. Sayeh came to the job with extensive experience working for the World Bank in the financial, capacity building, and economic development areas. She had also served as the World Bank's country director in Togo, Niger, and Benin, as well as senior country economist for Pakistan and Afghanistan, among others. She earned a bachelor's degree with honors in economics from Swarthmore College and a PhD in international economic relations from the Fletcher School at Tufts University.

As minister of finance, Dr. Sayeh led post-conflict Liberia through the clearance of its long-standing multilateral debt arrears, the Heavily Indebted Poor Countries (HIPC) decision point, the Paris Club, and its first Poverty Reduction Strategy (PRS). She instituted policies and programs to significantly strengthen Liberia's public finances, championing public financial management reform.

Dr. Sayeh, who previously worked in Liberia's Ministry of Finance and Ministry Planning and Economic Affairs, termed corruption as "an economic crime." But she reminded Liberians that it would take more than the government alone to fight the vice. "The problem of corruption should be tackled by all Liberians. Giving better remuneration to civil servants is one of the ways of fighting corruption," she said ("A New Cabinet Outlook," *UNMIL Focus*, December 2005–February 2006).

Dr. Sayeh became Liberia's second female finance minister, after Madam Ellen Johnson Sirleaf, who was the first female to occupy the post during the administration of President William R. Tolbert.

At the time Dr. Sayeh introduced the original draft of the PRS during a cabinet meeting, I attended as acting minister of MICAT. After presenting the draft PRS document to the president and the cabinet, the president requested for comments from each member of the cabinet in attendance. In my comments, I recommended that a media component be developed to form part of the PRS. Through the PRS media component, I noted, communication programs can be developed in order to create public awareness about the PRS. It was through the PRS communication component that the slogan "Lift Liberia" was developed as part of the initiatives for Liberians to gain ownership of the PRS, a general framework for national development.

After she left government, Dr. Sayeh served as director of the African Department of the International Monetary Fund (IMF) from 2008 to 2016.

Dr. Antoinette Sayeh, former finance minister of Liberia (L), with the author, Gabriel Williams, at a ceremony at Georgetown University, Washington DC, in 2017 (courtesy of the Liberian Embassy Public Affairs)

Among the many highly respected personalities also appointed in the Sirleaf government were notable human rights activists Tiawan S. Gongloe and Samuel Kofi Woods, both lawyers. Mr. Woods, who worked tirelessly to expose child labor and other work-related injustices in Liberia, was appointed minister of labor; and he instituted commendable reforms in the country's labor sector. Mr. Gongloe, who was appointed solicitor general of Liberia at the Ministry of Justice, also worked toward reform of the judicial system.

Despite the president's laudable move to highlight the importance of human rights, the irony was that many of those elected at the time to serve in the national legislature, one of three branches of Liberia's US-modeled government that includes the executive and judicial branches, were warlords and prominent supporters of armed factions during the civil wars.

Take, for example, former rebel leader Prince Johnson, whose armed group captured and mutilated then military ruler Samuel Doe to death in September 1990, nine months after the civil conflict ignited to force Doe from power. During the 2005 presidential and general elections from which Madam Sirleaf became president, Mr. Johnson won the highest number of votes among senatorial contestants, becoming senior senator of his native Nimba County. Johnson would also shock most people when he came third among sixteen presidential candidates who contested in the 2011 elections, during which President Sirleaf was reelected to a second six-year term. He later won landslide reelection as senior senator of Nimba County, and he was also a major player in the 2017 presidential elections in which retired global soccer icon George M. Weah succeeded Madam Sirleaf as president of Liberia.

How individuals with such backgrounds as Mr. Johnson have managed to win freely contested elections in Liberia is another issue that will be explored further in this book, focusing on reality in life that somebody's villain may be another person's hero, liberator, or savior—roles that Mr. Johnson was known to have played. On the other hand, Mr. Johnson has been a peaceful and law-abiding citizen who has not been engaged in any activities to undermine the peace in Liberia.

Another prominent ex-warlord serving in the National Legislature of Liberia is Dr. George E. S. Boley, who was leader of the misnamed Liberia Peace Council (LPC), a notorious rebel movement during the civil war in the 1990s. The LPC was blamed for widespread atrocities and destruction in territories that the armed faction occupied. Dr. Boley was elected as a member of the House of Representatives for his home county, Grand Gedeh, during the 2017 general and presidential elections in Liberia.

A former government minister and close associate of then military ruler Samuel Doe, Dr. Boley was elected to the national legislature after he was deported from the United States in March 2012. While he was resident in the United States, the ex-warlord was accused by the US government of commissioning killings and recruiting child soldiers during Liberia's bloody civil war. This led to Boley's deportation to Liberia after being held in custody for two years.

As an example of the LPC's campaign of death and destruction, my beautiful home village, Neegbah, in Rivercess County (which is mentioned in chapter 1) was invaded, plundered, and laid to waste by LPC fighters. My most beloved aunt who played the role of mother and family matriarch following the death of my mother from childbirth was killed along with others during attacks on the village by Boley's LPC thugs. She was one of several close family members killed during the civil war. According to accounts from Liberia's Truth and Reconciliation Commission (TRC) hearings, marauding LPC thugs were involved in widespread atrocities and human rights abuses in southeastern Liberia, which includes Rivercess, as well as Sinoe County, where defenseless villagers, according to eyewitness accounts, were also massacred.

In the fullness of time, Boley and his likes will answer in the court of law for their murderous activities during the senseless Liberian civil war. Being members of the legislature will not shield Boley, Johnson, and other ex-warlords from being accountable for war crimes and crimes against humanity in Liberia and for the reign of terror they unleashed that cost the lives of our loved ones.

This absolute madness where individuals seeking political power and wealth would brazenly resort to violence and bloodshed to gain political relevance and power in Liberia will not end until the perpetrators of such acts are brought to account under Liberian and international laws. The rule of law must be affirmed in Liberia, where anyone who would contemplate violence for power grab would quickly realize that they are on the wrong side of history. The time is now to stop elevating murderous criminals and misfits with reward of position in government and public resources, as has been the case in Liberia and other parts of Africa.

The Path to Service in Government

Notwithstanding all of the issues that were brought to bear regarding my appointment at MICAT, I accepted the charge to return home and serve in government. I hopped on board the government train despite some level of skepticism and trepidation, still not fully convinced that this was the right decision that was being made, given that Liberia had been reduced to a failed state due to a dysfunctional system of governance.

My wife, Neiko Irene Williams, played a very critical role in helping me to decide on accepting to return home for public service. We both thoroughly discussed the implications of being away from the family for an extended period of time, as well as the financial challenges that came with it. The issue of my personal safety to live again in an environment that had recently experienced so much violence, death, and destruction also came through our thoughts and discussions. We both agreed that despite the challenges that may come along, there was a greater benefit to be derived from the opportunity to contribute to the recovery process of our war-torn country. We prayed for God's guidance. And all things considered, the Lord has been very good to us, and we remain grateful for His mercy and grace.

During the early years of the civil war, I was almost killed by armed men for my role as a journalist. At the time I started my journalism career in my early twenties close to around the mid-1980s, Liberia was under the rule of the military junta led by Master Sergeant Samuel K. Doe. In 1980, Master Sergeant Doe and a group of enlisted men of the Armed Forces of Liberia, all of them of indigenous backgrounds, staged a bloody military coup in which the president and many senior officials of his government were killed. Liberia's constitution was suspended as the military regime ruled by decree. Freedom of speech and of the press was criminalized and brutally suppressed. The era of the military regime was a very dangerous period to be a journalist in Liberia. Independent media outlets that were perceived to be critical of the regime were banned or vandalized. Journalists and political and rights activists who were seen to be critical of the government were harassed, intimidated, jailed, or murdered.

Despite the danger of being a journalist in Liberia during that period, I was nurtured in the orientation that journalists report out of a sense of responsibility to inform and educate the public and also to serve the common good of society. As a result of performing my reportorial duties, I also suffered from harassment to brutality, arrest, and death threats in Liberia from the period of the military regime through the early years of the Liberian civil war.

On one near-fatal occasion, several months following the outbreak of the civil war, I was apprehended on an otherwise-beautiful sunny afternoon in downtown Monrovia. A gun was placed to my head by a group of armed fighters from one of the factions that had occupied that area of the Liberian capital. The gunman who recognized me and blew my cover as a journalist accused me of biased reporting. I survived by the grace of God. I believe it was Divine Providence that made my then fiancée and now wife, Neiko Irene—who was with me when I was identified—fearless enough to confront those armed men, screaming and wailing to draw attention. I was eventually set free. She did so at considerable risk to her own life even as the armed fighters threatened to also shoot her or forcefully take her away to become their domestic servant and sex slave, as was a common practice during the civil war.

Seizing women and girls and then forcing them into domestic servanthood or sex slavery is a common practice that has also been reported in places around the world plagued by instability and war. An example of this evil practice is evident by reports related to Islamic jihadist movements like the Islamic State (IS) in the Middle East and Boko Haram in Nigeria, which openly make the enslavement of females as part of their way of life.

I eventually fled the country in 1993 due to death threats from some armed factions that were involved in the brutal civil war to control political power and loot the country's resources. I settled in Sacramento, California, where I pursued advanced education, worked with the media, and published my first book titled *Liberia:*

The Heart of Darkness—Accounts of Liberia's Civil War and Its Destabilizing Effects in West Africa. I also got married and raised my family in the beautiful California state capital, which has remained my home away from home. During my years in exile in the United States, I was actively involved in the process to restore peace and institute democratic governance in Liberia.

This is why, following the inauguration of Madam Ellen Johnson Sirleaf in January 2016 as the first democratically elected female president in Liberia and Africa, it did not come as a total surprise when I was among several Liberians of diverse professional backgrounds that Madam President recruited from abroad to join our compatriots at home to serve in various governmental departments. We were charged with the mandate to institute the government's aggressive reform agenda to rebuild our country, which was then regarded as a failed state.

Eventually, I was among many Liberian professionals, most of us young men and women, President Sirleaf recruited from abroad to join our compatriots at home to serve in various governmental departments, charged with the mandate to push through the government's aggressive reform agenda, which was intended to make the government more responsive in providing basic services to the general public.

After more than ten years in exile, I first returned to Liberia on a short visit on April 21, 2004, less than a week after the disarmament and demobilization of the armed factions under the auspices of the United Nations Mission in Liberia (UNMIL), which deployed what was then the world's largest peacekeeping force that also provided basic humanitarian services, including food and medicine, to the general public.

Ambassador Jacques Paul Klein, a retired American diplomat, was appointed by UN Secretary-General Kofi Annan to serve as special representative of the secretary-general and coames ordinator of UN operations in Liberia. Ambassador Klein proved to be very forceful and effective in getting the warlords to comply with UN demands relative to moving the peace process forward.

With the national economy collapsed and unemployment projected to be more than 80 percent in the country where the overwhelming majority of the population endured abject poverty, agencies of the United Nations and international nongovernmental organizations (NGOs) operating in Liberia were the most gainful employers during that period.

Activities of my 2004 visit to Liberia included meetings with then information minister Allen, as well as the leadership of the Press Union of Liberia and the independent media. Those meetings, which included visits to the offices of some media entities, were intended to enable me to acquire firsthand information regarding the state of the media in Liberia.

I was particularly honored to have been received in audience by the head of the Liberia National Transitional Government, Charles Gyude Bryant, and some of the representatives of the international community in the country. During my meeting with Chairman Bryant, the interim head of state reaffirmed his government's strong commitment to press freedom and the rule of law in the country. He said that the transitional government was working in concert with the international community to ensure that peace and the rule of law prevailed in Liberia after more than a decade of anarchy.

Following my return to the United States, I published an article in the fall 2004 edition of the *Nieman Reports*, published by Harvard University's Nieman Foundation for Journalism, under the title "Journalism at a Crossroads in Liberia." The article recalls significant progress made in the area of press freedom in Liberia following the signing of the 2003 Accra Peace Agreement, leading to an increasing number of print and broadcast media outlets.

Then information minister Allen, who had served as editor in chief of the independent daily newspaper *Footprints Today* and president of the Press Union before the war, demonstrated commitment to press freedom during his tenure at MICAT. Under his leadership, efforts began to transform the Information Ministry from an instrument of state repression that enforced antimedia laws to an agency that promoted press freedom, such as relaxation of media registration regulations and other draconian measures.

The article in the *Nieman Reports* also highlighted problems that affected the Liberian media at the beginning of the postwar reconstruction, including the chronic lack of financial, material, and human resources. From my meetings with various stakeholders, it was also clear that there were widespread concerns regarding what was seen as a serious decline in professional standards in the media, which, obviously, was largely due to the massive brain drain the country suffered in the wake of the war.

In 2005, I returned to Liberia and did a five-month consultancy as program officer for International Observation Mission with the US-based National Democratic Institute (NDI) for International Affairs. NDI, headquartered in Washington DC, partnered with the Carter Center (TCC) in Atlanta, Georgia, in fielding a joint team of international observers for the 2005 general and presidential elections in Liberia, which was won by Madam Sirleaf as Africa's first democratically elected female president. NDI, TCC, and the International Republican Institute, which is also based in the United States, operated respective offices in Monrovia.

My roles at the NDI Monrovia office included liaison with Liberian political parties, governmental agencies, and the National Elections Commission in order to facilitate the implementation of the International Observation Mission's activities; public relations advisor and liaison officer for the local media; and analyst of political developments relative to the elections.

The NDI Liberia office was headed by a fellow West African, Mr. Sidi Diawara from Mali, while the senior program manager for the NDI International Observation Mission was Ms. Joyce Titi Pitso, a very competent and progressive South African with years of experience in international election observation missions in various parts of the world. Serving with these two capable and wonderful fellow Africans was just as fulfilling as the knowledge and experience acquired dealing with Liberia's political parties and leaders during this historic electoral period.

That the 2005 NDI-TCC International Observation Mission was recorded as one of the most successful in the history of joint international observation missions indicates that Africans have the capabilities like those of other races in providing successful leadership at any level of human endeavors.

Upon my return to the United States following the end of my NDI assignment, I began exploring avenues for new international engagements, especially media development-related programs for Liberia, when Dr. Allen called to inform me about President Sirleaf's desire to have me serve at the Information Ministry.

It may be considered a coincidence when I stated in my *Nieman Reports* article the need to sustain the progress that was made in the media upon Allen's departure from the Information Ministry. In that article, I had expressed fear that those who would take over from the Allen administration could choose to reinforce antimedia laws that were on the books. Little did it occur to me that I would be requested to serve at the Information Ministry to help consolidate the gains made toward press freedom under Dr. Allen's leadership.

I went to Liberia particularly mindful of the history of many well-respected prodemocracy journalists and rights activists who had their credibility ruined and became subject of public ridicule when they accepted positions in regimes of the recent past. As a former government official told me, "Once you're in the government, you will not be able to criticize again, and you will also share the blame for anything that goes wrong with the government." This was what happened during the bloody 1980 military coup and the 1989–2003 civil wars, when many individuals—some of them otherwise-well-meaning people who served with honesty and dedication—were killed, imprisoned, or terrorized due to guilt by association.

In Liberian society, perceptions matter more than facts because of the long history of widespread corruption, abuse of power, and outright criminal acts perpetrated by many leaders in public service because of little or no confidence in public leaders. For example, the Sirleaf administration took over from a power-sharing transitional government dominated by warlords and their supporters who were responsible for the deaths of more than 250,000 people and the plunder of the country's resources during the civil wars.

The presence of known criminals and murderers in government reinforced long-held public perception that government jobs provided opportunities to acquire ill-gotten wealth. This was why anyone who took a prominent government position was easily perceived to have also ridden the gravy train.

The Liberian government was seen as a big "elephant meat," as the saying goes, from which anyone could slice as much a piece of the meat at any given time. Having survived trying to cope under predatory regimes and leaders, many Liberians had little or no confidence in whatever was called the government because of the confidence crisis related to anything government.

During my years in exile, I remained very actively involved in the campaign to advocate for an end to the civil wars and for the ushering in of democratic governance in Liberia. In addition to the book, I also published articles regularly to help create international awareness about the state of death and destruction in Liberia.

I also played a leadership role, along with my senior colleague and dear friend Isaac Bantu, in establishing the Association of Liberian Journalists in the Americas (ALJA), becoming the organization's first secretary-general. ALJA was established in 1998 by Liberian journalists living in exile to enable them in their collective to continue to advocate for press freedom and democracy in Liberia. ALJA members were mostly members of the Press Union of Liberia who were forced to flee their country during the years of civil upheavals and suppression of press freedom.

Even though ALJA became inactive immediately following the end of the Liberian civil war, the organization was reactivated by a group of members led by Mr. Moses Sandy, a broadcast journalist who worked at the state-owned Liberia Broadcasting System (LBS) in Monrovia before resettling in the United States. Since its revitalization, ALJA has continued to be proactive in advocating for freedom of the press and good governance in Liberia.

Other media colleagues who played commendable roles in the reorganization of ALJA included Volcano Shelton, Joe Mason, Jackson Seton, Gardea Woodson, senior colleague Patrick Kugmeh, Kadiatu Konteh, Melissa Chea-Annan, Sam Abu, Menekeh Pshorr, Pewu Baysah, and Akai Awuletey Glidden. These and other journalists not named are commended for continuing to support the cause of press freedom and democratic governance in Liberia.

During my period of exile in the United States, I also had the opportunity to work for some of the local media in Sacramento, including the *Sacramento Observer* and the *West Sacramento Press*. I also served as editor of the *Capital Gains*, then monthly publication of the Sacramento Black Chamber of Commerce. Writing for these media outlets, I reported stories that were more sedate than the experiences of my turbulent Liberian world.

However, the knowledge and experiences I acquired in the United States were very useful and would help prepare me for my responsibilities in managing the media when I entered government service in Liberia, especially regarding the critical importance of the media in a democratic society. In the discharge of my duties as one of the most prominent spokesmen of the Liberian government, I did so with an unwavering conviction that we as a country cannot build a fully unctioning democratic society without the media being a part of the main pillars or part of the foundation.

My conviction is grounded in the fact that the history of Liberia's foundation is intricately linked to the United States, which has been the greatest power in the world simply because Americans have the freedom to express themselves and to aspire in every human endeavor to the best of their abilities. To the contrary, Liberia has been a country that has suppressed and denied a vast mass of its population the opportunity to develop their potentials through destructive state-sanctioned policies.

Although Liberia is well endowed with abundant human and natural resources, the country that was once regarded as a beacon of hope for Africans and a land of liberty and freedom for people of color from around the world has been one of the poorest and most backward on the face of the earth. And this has been because of the corrupt and evil practices of those who have been in charge of the affairs of the country since its existence for nearly two hundred years.

CHAPTER THREE
Confronting the Taylor Fear Factor

As if the enormous challenges of maintaining the peace and beginning the process of rebuilding a failed state broken by years of devastating civil wars were not enough, President Sirleaf was suddenly confronted with a crisis that had the potential to plunge the country back into another round of civil upheaval less than three months into her presidency. To the shock of Liberians and the entire world, the media reported that President Sirleaf had taken the unprecedented, and what I consider to be a very courageous, step on March 17, 2006, when she requested regional power Nigeria to extradite former Liberian president Charles Taylor to face trial for his alleged role in the brutal eleven-year civil war in neighboring Sierra Leone.

As rebel forces seeking to oust Taylor invaded Monrovia, the Liberian dictator was forced out of power in August 2003 and exiled to Nigeria as part of a peace deal brokered by the international community under the auspices of the regional bloc Economic Community of West African States (ECOWAS). Under the peace accord, Mr. Taylor accepted to go into exile in Nigeria in exchange that he would not be prosecuted in the wake of indictment by the UN-backed Special Court for Sierra Leone.

In 2003, while Mr. Taylor was the sitting president of Liberia, the prosecutor for the Special Court for Sierra Leone filed an eleven-count indictment against him. He was accused of war crimes, crimes against humanity, and other serious violations of international humanitarian law, including pillage, murder, rape, and the use of child soldiers. Mr. Taylor stood accused of arming Sierra Leone's Revolutionary United Front (RUF) rebels, which unleashed a bloody civil war that led to more than fifty thousand deaths in that country. The RUF, which was notorious for hacking off the hands and legs of civilians, supplied Taylor with diamonds looted from Sierra Leone—dubbed "blood diamonds"—in exchange for arms and ammunition.

Indicted along with other Sierra Leonean warlords, Taylor became the first sitting African leader to be indicted by an internationally backed court for the crimes alleged against him. Under a deal brokered by African leaders and the international community, Taylor accepted to go into exile in Nigeria in exchange for immunity from prosecution for the crimes for which he was indicted.

One of the conditions for Taylor's exile was that he would not interfere in the affairs of Liberia. However, the African strongman, who had ruled the country as his fiefdom, would do just the opposite. From his exile in southern Nigeria, where he reportedly lived lavishly with hundreds of aides and hangers-on who accompanied him into exile, the flamboyant ex-dictator was reported to have played an active role in the selection of the chairman of the power-sharing Liberia National Transitional Government. Mr. Charles Gyude Bryant was picked as the chairman of the transitional government by Taylor and other warlords after Bryant declared that he would support neither the creation of a war crimes court for Liberia nor the prosecution of warlords and others culpable of war crimes and crimes against humanity in Liberia.

Regarded then as a political neophyte who was not well known outside his affiliations, Bryant was picked over a more seasoned politician like Madam Sirleaf, who had strongly advocated in favor of the establishment of a war crimes court for Liberia. To establish a hybrid international court like that of Sierra Leone, a country has to request the support of the UN.

At the time he was plucked out of near obscurity into the national and international limelight as head of Liberia's transitional government, Bryant was a prominent lay officer of the Episcopal Church of Liberia and an executive of the Liberia Action Party (LAP), of which Madam Sirleaf was a founding member in the 1980s to oppose military ruler Samuel Doe.

To sustain his extravagant lifestyle in exile, Mr. Taylor also had a stranglehold on Liberia's economy, which was criminalized during his regime, when he appropriated the country's natural resources as his personal property, turning Liberia into what one would call a "vampire state." The Strategic Commodities Act, passed secretly in 2000 by the rubber stamp legislature packed with his acolytes and criminal collaborators, gave Taylor "the sole power to execute, negotiate and conclude all commercial contracts or agreements with any foreign or domestic investor" for designated commodities, including timber, gold, oil, and diamonds.

When the UN Security Council imposed sanctions on the exportation of diamonds from Liberia and Sierra Leone as a means to stop the use of the precious gem to fuel conflict in West Africa, Taylor turned to the plunder of timber from Liberia, which has the largest remaining rain forest in the subregion with unique plant and animal species. The council then imposed sanction on the export of timber and a travel ban on Taylor, his family, and close associates. It also authorized the freezing of their assets. An existing arms embargo on Liberia was also reimposed. As noted earlier, Liberia under Taylor was reduced to nothing more than a massive criminal enterprise.

So it was that while he was in exile, Mr. Taylor continued to live extravagantly from his criminal enterprise as millions of dollars were reportedly funneled to him through various back channels from Liberia. With many of his supporters occupying strategic positions in the public and private sectors of the country and thousands of ex-militia members still loyal to the deposed despot at the time, there were justifiable fears that Taylor had the potential to continue to destabilize not only Liberia and Sierra Leone, but also the entire West African subregion, which also had to deal with the challenges of Taylor-sponsored armed insurgencies in neighboring Guinea and the Ivory Coast.

There were persistent reports that Mr. Taylor was violating the terms of his exile, including meddling in Liberia's affairs and making secret travels to other African countries, according to a UN Panel of Experts report.

Leading international environmental advocacy group Global Witness published a report on June 15, 2005, stating that despite the terms of his exile arrangements with Nigeria that forbade Taylor from engaging in active communication with anyone engaged in political, illegal, and governmental activities in Liberia, he continued to do so. The report added that Taylor had been accused by the Special Court for Sierra Leone as having been behind a coup attempt against then Guinean president Lansana Conte in January 2005; and he was able to bribe Nigerian state security forces to continue meeting in person and having telephone contact with various individuals related to his political, military, and economic interests.

The Global Witness report also noted that Taylor had maintained significant influence over West Africa and that he remained as much a threat to regional peace and security as he always was.

A confidential document that was among several reports completed in 2004 and 2005 by a UN investigative task force into misconduct within the UN system revealed that a senior UN official had an improper relationship with a local woman in Liberia who was suspected of passing secrets to Taylor.

The uncle of the woman accused of spying for Taylor was a prominent Lebanese businessman, Abbas Fawaz, who headed a major timber company during the Taylor regime. During hearings of Liberia's Truth and Reconciliation Commission, businessman Fawaz was linked to the massacre of more than three hundred civilians in River Gee County during the civil war, although he denied the allegation.

Fawaz—who partnered with Taylor in several logging companies, diamond trade, and the importation of arms and ammunition, among other businesses—was suspected of supplying arms and ammunition to the Taylor regime to attack neighboring Ivory Coast.

Taylor's Arrest and Extradition from Nigeria

It was in view of those developments, among others, that US president George W. Bush requested Nigeria to turn over the indicted war criminal to face trial, a request the Nigerian government of President Olusegun Obasanjo resisted vigorously. Nigeria maintained that turning Taylor over would violate the internationally brokered Liberian peace agreement granting him safe asylum. As pressure mounted during the tenure of Liberia's transitional government, President Obasanjo said Nigeria would oblige to turn over Mr. Taylor only if requested to do so by a democratically elected government in Liberia.

Accordingly, immediately following Sirleaf's inauguration, President Bush reportedly prevailed on President Sirleaf, as Liberia's democratically elected leader, to request Nigeria to extradite Mr. Taylor. President Bush reportedly told the Liberian leader that in order to ensure a strong US commitment in support of her government's efforts for Liberia's reconstruction and attainment of sustainable peace, it was imperative that Taylor be extradited for prosecution.

In this light, while on a visit to Nigeria, President Sirleaf requested President Obasanjo to hand Taylor over on March 17, 2006. This unprecedented development was to set off a drama that was nerve-racking for most war-weary Liberians at home and abroad as it also created fear of instability within the West African subregion. Upon her return to Liberia, information was reportedly leaked to the media from the Nigerian presidency that the new Liberian leader had requested Nigeria to turn over Mr. Taylor and that Nigeria had agreed that Liberia was free to have him detained and extradited.

Former Nigerian president Olusegun Obasanjo (in white) was the keynote speaker at the annual Armed Forces Day celebration in 2017 in Monrovia. On the left is President Sirleaf (courtesy of the Liberian Embassy Public Affairs).

The Liberian government was caught completely off guard by the sudden leak. Information Minister McClain, who was not aware because he had not been briefed by President Sirleaf about the said development following her return from Nigeria, strongly denied to the media that Liberia had requested for Taylor's extradition from Nigeria. The handling of Taylor's extradition information turned out to be a major public relations debacle for the government, which damaged the credibility of Mr. McClain as the government's chief spokesman. The Taylor extradition miscommunication, along with other problems that hampered the operations of the Information Ministry, which were not necessarily his fault, would lead to McClain's resignation nine months into his tenure.

The stakes regarding Taylor's extradition could not have gotten higher when on March 27, 2006, there were media reports that the exiled former warlord turned president had disappeared from his villa in Calabar, southern Nigeria; and his whereabouts were unknown.

Rumors were widespread that the Nigerians, who felt betrayed and humiliated by the pressure to turn over Taylor, had simply allowed him to flee and that the ex-warlord was headed to the jungle in Liberia, from where he would start another round of warfare. For fourteen years, Taylor had supported a series of conflicts throughout the West African subregion. Many of his loyalist soldiers were roaming freely in Liberia, Sierra Leone, and then civil war–divided Ivory Coast, from where Taylor launched his rebel incursion into Liberia on December 24, 1989. He had also been involved in military aggression against neighboring Guinea at the time he was in power.

So it was that the news that the man who terrorized Liberia and the subregion for more than a decade was on the loose inspired panic, dread, and anger. On the streets of Monrovia, there were rampant rumors of a coup or attack by Taylor supporters, many of whom held seats in the national legislature.

Mr. Taylor disappeared on the eve of a visit to Washington by President Obasanjo to meet with President Bush, who faced calls to cancel the meeting in protest at Nigeria's failure to place Taylor in custody after approving his surrender to Liberia. According to BBC reports, Desmond de Silva, chief prosecutor of the war crimes court in Sierra Leone, had warned that Mr. Taylor could use his vast wealth and contacts to organize his escape. He described Mr. Taylor as one of the three most important wanted war crimes suspects in the world.

Nevertheless, an hour before President Obasanjo's departure for the United States on March 29, 2006, BBC reported that Nigerian security forces had arrested Mr. Taylor at Nigeria's border with Cameroon in the northeastern Nigerian state of Borno. According to the report, Mr. Taylor, dressed in a flowing white robe, had arrived at the frontier in a Range Rover jeep with a diplomatic license plate. He passed through immigration, but when he reached customs, there were suspicions. The security officers insisted on searching the jeep, where they found him and two large bags containing various currencies, including US dollars.

Nigeria's information minister, Frank Nweke, told reporters that President Obasanjo had ordered Mr. Taylor to be sent back to Liberia immediately to be placed in custody there. As soon as the jet conveying Taylor landed at the Roberts International Airport near Monrovia, he was arrested, handcuffed, and turned over to the custody of UN peacekeepers, who quickly flew him to Freetown, the Sierra Leonean capital, where he was incarcerated. BBC quoted Mr. Nweke that President Obasanjo had been "very shocked" by Mr. Taylor's disappearance from his villa in Calabar.

The dramatic turn of events, especially the media images of Taylor in handcuffs and visibly dejected, were just unbelievable, especially for most Liberians who had been conditioned to seeing the ex-warlord as a "mighty lion" who could not be contained. It is an understatement to say that it was a complete shock to his supporters, particularly his thousands of ex-militias, who often boasted that they believed "the Pa-paye"—name used in local Liberian parlance for a senior male figure viewed with respect and reverence—would return to resume his rule over the country.

In order to deal with any possible security threat from Taylor's ex-fighters, UNMIL forces were placed on full alert.

In what seems like an interesting twist of fate, when the Nigerian government plane conveying the former Liberian leader landed at the Roberts International Airports about fifty miles from Monrovia, Mr. Taylor was received on behalf of the government by the solicitor general of Liberia, Mr. Tiawan Gongloe, who almost got killed and was forced to live in exile after criticizing Taylor's regime.

In April 2002, Mr. Gongloe, one of Liberia's most prominent human rights lawyers, was arrested, stripped nude, and brutalized in police custody after delivering a speech at a conference in neighboring Guinea. In that speech, the human rights lawyer condemned the use of violence as a means to state power, a reference to the situation that prevailed in Liberia. Upon arrest following his return to Liberia, he was severely beaten and tortured. Following a night of torture, Mr. Gongloe lost some hearing in his left ear, his left eye was swollen and bloodied, and his head and body were badly bruised ("Leading Liberian Human Rights Lawyer Tortured by Police," Human Rights Watch, April 26, 2002).

Following strong international pressure on the Taylor regime, the noted human rights lawyer was taken out of the detention cell and hospitalized in Monrovia while police guards were posted near his hospital bed. Mr. Taylor eventually yielded to international pressure to allow Mr. Gongloe to leave the country to seek medical treatment abroad for his injuries. There were reports that he suffered some internal bleeding. He sought refuge in the United States and never returned to Liberia until Taylor was forced out of power and exiled.

This brings me to a popular Liberian expression, which goes "No one knows tomorrow." So it was that Gongloe became the solicitor general of Liberia just a few months before Taylor's arrest. After receiving the former warlord from the Nigerian government, Gongloe had Taylor read his Miranda rights, handcuffed, and turned over to the UN to be flown aboard a UN helicopter to Freetown, Sierra Leone, for detention. Solicitor General Gongloe told the media that Taylor's arrest was the beginning of the end of impunity in Liberia. Gongloe would recall how surreal it was the moment the fugitive former president was brought before him and turned over by the Nigerians to be placed in custody.

The local and international media were saturated with images of a visibly broken and pathetic-looking Charles Taylor being led away in handcuffs. It was a very sad spectacle for a showman who had projected himself as a lion in full control of his domain and had abused that power by terrorizing the people of Liberia, Sierra Leone, and the other neighboring countries.

Here is an interesting example of the global media coverage and impact of Taylor's arrest: A copy of the March 30, 2006, edition of the *New York Times* containing the photos and story of Taylor's arrest and transfer to Sierra Leone, placed in a large beautiful frame, was mounted on the center of the wall in the Capitol Hill office of Congressman Ed Royce, member of the US House of Representatives from California from 1993 to 2019. A Republican, Congressman Royce served as chairman of the US House Committee on Foreign Affairs from 2013 to 2019. He regarded the strong US-backed international interventions to bring an end to the civil upheavals in West Africa and the prosecution and conviction of Mr. Taylor for war crimes and crimes against humanity as parts of the foreign policy accomplishments during his congressional tenure.

A strong advocate for human rights and democratic governance around the world, Congressman Royce played an important role in getting the Liberian crises on the front burner of US policy, which resulted in ending Taylor's reign of terror and prosecution of the ex-warlord. He also deserves commendation as one of the friends of Liberia on Capitol Hill who ensured the provision of generous US support for postwar Liberia's reconstruction and UNMIL operations, among others. In 2018, Congressman Royce announced at a Capitol Hill event in Washington that he was pushing for more women military and paramilitary forces to be involved in UN Peacekeeping operations around the world, given the success of the Indian female contingent of the UN police in Liberia during UNMIL's operation in that country.

President Sirleaf, at an event on Capitol Hill, is seated on platform with (R–L) US Senator Chris Coons, Congressman Ed Royce, and moderator Tami Hultman of AllAfrica news service (courtesy of the Liberian Embassy Public Affairs).

Back to the drama surrounding Mr. Taylor's arrest, even though the Nigerian leader was reported to have been "very shocked" by Taylor's disappearance, Mr. Taylor would testify during his trial in The Hague in 2009 that he was betrayed by President Obasanjo. He said he was deceived by Nigeria into being arrested there. Taylor noted that Obasanjo had reneged on a promise to let him leave the country freely. "He lied to the world when he said I was escaping, and he knew nothing about it." He would also accuse the British and the American governments of masterminding his indictment, removal from power, and arrest.

Taylor's accusation of Obasanjo during his trial was earlier confirmed by other sources. As pressure heightened for Nigeria to turn Mr. Taylor over to Liberia, President Obasanjo reportedly ordered that he be dropped at some border post and allowed to go wherever he wanted rather than for Nigeria to formally hand him over to Liberia. It was while going on an official visit to the United States and President Bush refused to meet him until Taylor was located and turned over that President Obasanjo had a change of mind and ordered that Mr. Taylor be apprehended and returned to Liberia, according to sources close to the Nigerian presidency at the time.

African Leaders Alarmed by Taylor's Arrest

While Taylor's indictment and arrest were generally welcomed in Liberia and among ordinary Africans, many African leaders were reportedly alarmed by this unprecedented development. On a continent where the leaders and political elite squander or loot their countries' resources and engage in widespread abuse of power with impunity, bringing one of their kind to book was a frightening prospect. Indeed, the arrest of the former warlord turned president sent chills down the spines of those African leaders who were not accountable to their people, mindful that they too could face a similar fate.

President Sirleaf was reportedly seen by many African leaders as a traitor and an American puppet for violating an agreement brokered under the auspices of ECOWAS and the African Union, which was the basis for Taylor's exile. More importantly, she was seen to have thrown Nigeria under the bus, so to speak, in her effort to ingratiate herself with the US administration and European powers. The Nigerians would argue that after their country made so much sacrifice, with the blood of Nigerian soldiers and others, as well as spending hundreds of millions of dollars, to bring peace to Liberia and the subregion, President Sirleaf decided to abandon them and closely align herself with the Americans after her election.

Some within Nigeria's ruling circle may have reasons to have rightfully felt the way they did regarding the handling of Taylor's extradition, which they felt negatively impacted their national pride and African pride in general. For those who regarded the matter from the perspective of national or racial pride, the argument has been against white people or former colonial masters always telling Africans what to do, as was the case of Africans yielding to American and European demands for Taylor's extradition. It has been a common refrain among African leaders that Africans should be left alone to solve their own problems.

The argument that Africans should be left alone to solve their own problems is well noted if it is intended to empower collective African decision-making and actions for the common good. Unfortunately, we have seen how the argument of noninterference in the internal affairs of member countries have rendered even the AU as nothing more than a toothless bulldog, unable to control the gross abuse of power by African leaders who are emboldened by the culture of misrule and impunity.

A general perception has prevailed that many African leaders, with a few exceptions, tend to be birds of the same feathers, as the saying goes. The perception holds that such leaders have demonstrated that they are nothing more than incompetent and corrupt individuals who are not accountable to their people. Therefore, it would become a matter of necessity for them to shield one another, as has been the case with those who have been thrown out of power. It is common knowledge that deposed African leaders would easily be given asylum in another African country, where their friend and former "brother president" in power there would enable them to live peacefully and enjoy their ill-gotten wealth.

Such deposed despots include former Chadian president Hissène Habré, indicted for crimes against humanity, who was being harbored in Senegal. Another of the leaders is Colonel Mengistu Haile Mariam, who ruled Ethiopia from 1977 to 1991. In a campaign aimed at repressing political dissent that would be called the Red Terror, Mengistu's administration was alleged to have killed an estimated half a million people, including the last emperor of Ethiopia, Haile Selassie, according to the German-based news organ, DW ("Quest to Extradite Ethiopia's Dictator Mengistu as Mugabe Departs," Deutsche Welle, November 12, 2017). Following his overthrow, the former Ethiopian despot fled to Zimbabwe, where he has lived quietly under the protection of Zimbabwe's mercurial leader, Robert Mugabe.

Entrenched in power for thirty-seven years since 1980, Mugabe was himself forced out of power in 2017. Until his forced resignation, Mugabe was the world's oldest leader at ninety-three. A liberation hero, Mugabe took over the leadership of his country upon independence at a time the country was regarded to be one of the economically prosperous in Africa. At the end of his rule, Zimbabwe was reduced to one of the poorest countries in Africa and the world. Nevertheless, the nonagenarian president tried to make his fifty-two-year-old wife, seen to be a polarizing figure who also lacked the experience in governmental leadership, succeed him as president of Zimbabwe.

Habré, who came to power in a coup in 1982, fled to Senegal after he was deposed in 1990. He was accused of killing and torturing thousands of his opponents. However, Senegal had rejected several extradition requests to have Mr. Habré tried in Belgium, according to BBC News Africa online ("Hissène Habré: ICJ Rules Senegal Must Try Ex-Chad Leader Immediately," July 20, 2012).

Given the manner in which African leaders were seen to have handled matters regarding the Habré prosecution or the Mengistu asylum, for example, it is easy to see why many of them may have preferred that Taylor should have been left alone to roam about freely.

Sirleaf Caught between a Rock and a Hard Place

Even though the African leaders' disapproval of the Taylor situation was generally reduced to nothing more than stage whispers, their collective misgivings and anger found expression in Libya's mercurial leader, Colonel Muammar Gaddafi. The Libyan strongman did not hesitate to openly condemn the United States and other Western countries for conspiracy in the removal of Taylor from power and disgracing him by having him arrested because he was an African leader hated by Western leaders for his refusal to do their biddings. The Libyan strongman was also known to have expressed his vehement opposition regarding Taylor's arrest and detention to Madam President during meetings between them in Libya, where Madam President paid frequent visits to confer with her "brother leader."

As the unpredictable and erratic Libyan leader ranted, President Sirleaf always listened with patience. She succeeded in getting Gaddafi to basically focus on providing assistance for Liberia's recovery process through donations and reactivation of once-successful Libyan-funded economic joint ventures that existed between both countries before the civil crises in Liberia, among others.

I once traveled with President Sirleaf to Libya, using one of Gaddafi's small presidential jets for the round trip. I would say it is to her credit for treading very carefully with Colonel Gaddafi and ensuring that he remained in Liberia's corner as a friend. Despite the very close relationship that was known to have existed between Gaddafi and Taylor, the Libyan leader basically wanted to be assured that political and economic ties between Liberia and Libya would continue to row, under the new political dispensation in Liberia. Gaddafi badly needed Liberia's support as he pursued his grand dream regarding the creation of the United States of Africa, of which he badly wanted to become the first leader.

Still on the fallout from Madam President's request for Taylor's extradition, Liberian supporters of the ex-warlord also vehemently expressed their outrage at what they felt was an act of betrayal by President Sirleaf for turning over the former warlord turned president for trial.

Embittered by what they regarded to be a grave betrayal of Taylor and their cause, a group of wealthy Liberians, who were of Americo-Liberian descent, reportedly conspired that upon the conclusion of Madam Sirleaf's presidential tenure, they would support and fund any effort to have her imprisoned and prosecuted as a payback for having Taylor turned over to the international war crimes court. They were also angry for the imprisonment and prosecution of Charles Gyude Bryant for corruption. Bryant, who was also of Americo-Liberian descent, headed Liberia's interim government after Taylor was forced out of power and exiled.

The group of wealthy Americo-Liberians was among those known to have provided strong financial and moral backing to Taylor's armed insurgency to remove Samuel Doe from power. Under the guise of supporting democratic activities, these "old guards" from the deposed era also secretly plotted revenge against Doe for the killing of their loved ones during the military coup. They were also bitter and unforgiving for the loss of the exclusive political, economic, and other privileges the tiny Americo-Liberian ruling class enjoyed for over 130 years before the coup staged by Doe, a member of Liberia's indigenous population that was discriminated against by the then minority ruling class.

Mr. Taylor, born 1948 of Americo-Liberian descent, was a part of the anti-Doe movement who was daring enough to step forward and lead an armed insurgency that resulted in the collapse of the regime and Doe's assassination, a cause Madam Sirleaf and other anti-Doe individuals were reported to have supported or funded. Madam Sirleaf is on record for admitting that she was one of those who provided financial support to Taylor during the early stage of the armed insurgency and that she stopped supporting him after she realized that he was nothing more than a misfit who had taken the country on a course of unimaginable death and destruction.

Nevertheless, it was the position of the shady group of "old guards" that although the armed rebellion did not go as planned and Mr. Taylor made some mistakes, the ultimate objective to remove dictator Doe from power was realized. This was why they considered it a tragic mistake and betrayal for Madam President to have turned Mr. Taylor over for war crimes prosecution, using him as a sacrificial lamb to enjoy the favors of the United States and other Western powers that wanted to get rid of Mr. Taylor.

This was why the shadowy group decided that as they were able to employ every means possible to eliminate Doe and his regime, they would also explore every avenue that would lead to the arrest, imprisonment, and prosecution of Madam Sirleaf for war and economic crimes, simply to disgrace her as she did to Messrs. Taylor and Bryant.

So the group went to work and began to plot their strategies, through which they hoped to eventually have Madam Sirleaf disgraced as she did Taylor. During the 2011 election season, information surfaced that some key financial backers of one of the presidential candidates, who is of Americo-Liberian background and was also once a Taylor ally, had considered that Madam Sirleaf be prosecuted if their candidate came to power. This was to serve as payback to Madam Sirleaf for the betrayal of Mr. Taylor, the now-convicted war criminal, who has been incarcerated in a prison in the United Kingdom after he was tried and convicted in The Hague and sentenced to fifty years in prison.

This is why the group of wealthy Americo-Liberians decided that once the presidential candidate they supported successfully won the election, his government's immediate actions would have included the opening of investigations to identify corruption and other failures of the Sirleaf administration that were to result in charges being filed against Madam Sirleaf for her arrest and prosecution.

According to a source familiar with the group who gave a tip-off on the group's activities, the aim was to humiliate and disgrace Madam Sirleaf for what they regarded to be her betrayal of Taylor and Bryant. According to the source, the group wanted Madam Sirleaf to experience the humiliation and disgrace that Messrs. Taylor and Bryant suffered because of her betrayal.

After Taylor was forced from power in 2003, Mr. Bryant served as chairman of the National Transitional Government of Liberia (NTGL), a power-sharing interim government that included representatives of armed factions, political parties, and interest groups. The NTGL presided over the affairs of Liberia for two years, including the 2005 elections, which Madam Sirleaf won as Liberia's and Africa's first democratically elected female president.

As a manifestation of the Sirleaf government's determination to combat corruption during the beginning of the new government, former interim president Bryant was charged with embezzlement of public funds in February 2007 and was arrested and imprisoned in March, a couple of weeks after he was charged.

Many Liberians were surprised that a former president could be arrested on charges of corruption, which was another strong message to a public used to reckless and criminal behavior on the part of their leaders that the days of impunity were over. The government decided to prosecute Bryant and some of his officials on an ECOWAS audit report linking them to massive corruption during the tenure of the NTGL, which relinquished power to Madam Sirleaf on January 16, 2006. Mr. Bryant was acquitted by the court, and the Liberian government subsequently dropped all other charges of economic sabotage and theft of property against him in 2010.

It may be recalled that during Liberia's 2005 runoff election, in which Madam Sirleaf contested against popular international soccer star George M. Weah, she openly expressed that she would not seek the extradition of Taylor and the establishment of a war crimes court. Her remarks were apparently intended to seek the support of Taylor's supporters and other warlords, going into the runoff. With that declaration, many key Taylor supporters—including Taylor's current wife, Jewel Howard Taylor—publicly announced their support for Madam Sirleaf, who eventually won 59.4 percent of the votes cast during the presidential runoff. Mr. Weah had won first place, and Madam Sirleaf came second during the first round of the presidential race in which twenty-two candidates contested. A runoff was held because no candidate won 50 percent plus one of the overall votes as required by the Liberian Constitution.

Then a leading opponent of military leader Samuel Doe, Madam Sirleaf associated with Taylor, also then a strong anti-Doe element who lived in exile first in the United States and then in various parts of mostly West Africa. Doe had Taylor arrested in the United States and imprisoned while awaiting extradition to Liberia to face trial for alleged financial embezzlement to the tune of about US$1 million. However, Taylor reportedly escaped from an American maximum security prison and fled to other parts of Africa, from where he masterminded the destruction of his homeland, Liberia, and the destabilization of the subregion.

How Taylor escaped from the Plymouth Correctional Center in the state of Massachusetts and fled to Africa without being rearrested has remained a mystery, even though Mr. Taylor himself provided an account of how he left prison and departed from the United States during his trial in The Hague.

In a dramatic testimony in July 2009, Taylor told the court of his 1985 escape from the maximum security jail with alleged US government help. He said his prison cell was unlocked by US prison guards one night in November 1985; and they escorted him to a minimum security area, from where, using a sheet, he climbed out the window and over the fence to a waiting vehicle containing two men who whisked him to New York.

Bonded by a common cause grounded in the shared desire to uproot Doe's entrenched dictatorial regime, Madam Sirleaf was seen to be one of Taylor's key supporters when the warlord launched his rebel invasion of Liberia from neighboring Ivory Coast, with the backing of Libya, which provided training bases and other critical support for the rebels. Other countries that strongly supported Taylor included Burkina Faso and neighboring Ivory Coast, from where Taylor's rebels invaded Liberia on December 24, 1989, to begin Liberia's and the subregion's nightmare.

However, the relationship between Madam Sirleaf and Mr. Taylor soured when the armed rebellion turned into indiscriminate slaughter of defenseless people and looting of Liberia's resources in areas under the control of Taylor. In early 1990, several months into the rebellion, Taylor declared himself president when more than 90 percent of Liberia had been occupied by his notorious armed faction, the so-called National Patriotic Front of Liberia (NPFL). From then on, Madam Sirleaf became one of his leading critics, a situation for which Taylor threatened to have her arrested and tried for treason if she set foot on Liberian soil.

Madam Sirleaf's association with Mr. Taylor would come back to haunt her. Testifying before Liberia's Truth and Reconciliation Commission (TRC) in 2009, Madam Sirleaf publicly apologized to the Liberian people for her association with Taylor during the early stage of the armed rebellion and noted that Taylor fooled her. Despite the apology, TRC, established with the mandate to investigate causes for the country's civil crises, recommended that Madam Sirleaf and others, mostly former warlords and key supporters of the armed factions, be banned from holding public office for thirty years and be prosecuted for their roles in the civil upheavals. The TRC report was yet to be implemented because it has been very seriously mired in legal, constitutional, and political controversies. An overview of the TRC process and report is provided in chapter 7.

As if to confirm fear of Africa's brutal and barbaric leaders that their era of impunity had ended, Taylor's indictment by Sierra Leone's internationally backed hybrid war crimes court was followed by the indictment of the International Criminal Court (ICC) of several African leaders and members of the political elite for war crimes and crimes against humanity.

In 2009, Sudanese president Omar al-Bashir became the first sitting head of state to be indicted by the ICC. The second sitting head of state was Libya's erratic leader Colonel Muammar Gaddafi, indicted in 2011 along with his son Saif al-Islam and his military intelligence chief, Abdullah Senussi. Former Ivorian president Laurent Gbagbo, who was detained in The Hague, was also indicted in 2011 along with his wife, former First Lady Simone Gbagbo. The ICC has also issued indictments for several prominent Kenyan politicians and warlords from the Democratic Republic of the Congo, among others.

However, in January 2019, Mr. Gbagbo's conviction for war crimes and crimes against humanity was overturned by the ICC. Although she was also indicted by the ICC, Mrs. Simone Gbagbo was not turned over to the ICC by the Ivorian government. Instead, she was tried and convicted in the Ivory Coast and sentenced to twenty years in 2015 for her role in the violence that followed the 2010 elections in which more than three thousand people died. In August 2018, she was granted amnesty by Ivorian president Alassane

Ouattara, who then president Gbagbo and his wife, along with their supporters, tried to prevent from taking power after Ouattara won the presidential election to replace Gbagbo.

In April 2019, Sudan's military overthrew President Al-Bashir following weeks of mass protests by ordinary Sudanese, bringing an end to his thirty years of brutal dictatorship.

The overthrow of the brutal Sudanese despot and indicted war criminal came just over a week after a similar protest in Algeria forced the resignation of the military-backed regime of President Abdelaziz Bouteflika, who had held on to power in Algeria for twenty years. Although he had been wheelchair-ridden for a few years after suffering a stroke and was rarely seen in public, in 2019, Bouteflika had the nerve to still present himself as a candidate to continue his reign over Algeria for another five years. That was when the Algerian people decided that they have had enough of their disabled eighty-two-year-old leader, and they launched their protests, which led to his downfall.

Even though Taylor's destructive influence in West African continued for over a decade, the United States never seriously paid attention to the outcry from the West African subregion to contain this man who was starting to be seen as a mass murderer until after the September 11, 2001, Al-Qaeda terrorist attacks in the United States. According to reports, the United States then found out that Taylor sold diamonds to Al-Qaeda and that some members of the terrorist network were also harbored in Liberia before the attacks on the US mainland.

Caging Taylor for Peace in West Africa

Immediately following her election, there was a groundswell of international goodwill toward the government of Africa's first democratically elected female president, with the United States leading the charge. Madam Sirleaf became something like a superstar on the global stage. She soon developed a close bond with President and Mrs. Bush, as well as other senior officials within the Bush administration, including Secretary of State Condoleezza Rice. That special relationship paved the way for the Liberian leader to address the joint session of the US Congress, joining the ranks of very few African leaders to have been accorded such great honor, such as South African president Nelson Mandela. President Bush also awarded her the Presidential Medal of Freedom, the United States' highest civilian honor. A contingent of US Secret Service officers were deployed in Liberia to provide security for the president during the early period of her administration.

After years of neglecting Liberia, then regarded as America's stepchild because of the special historical bonds subsisting between both countries, the United States went all out to provide the necessary diplomatic, financial, and technical support to the recovery of the war-torn country. The United States played a pivotal told in the negotiations ending Taylor's misrule and the deployment of what was then the world's largest UN peacekeeping force in Liberia, of which the United States was the largest single contributor.

Then British prime minister Tony Blair deserves credit for reportedly getting President Bush to see the need for the United States to play a leadership role in the process to end Taylor's destructive influence in West Africa. In 2000, Prime Minister Blair ordered the deployment of British troops in Sierra Leone, a former British colony, after RUF rebels held five hundred UN peacekeepers hostage. The British military intervention was the beginning of the end of the destructive influence of Taylor's RUF in Sierra Leone. Before the UN peacekeepers were deployed to Sierra Leone, a Nigerian-led ECOWAS peacekeeping force sacrificed and paid the ultimate price in the struggle to stop the murderous RUF gang from gaining full control of the mineral-rich West African country.

During her inauguration on January 16, 2006, President Sirleaf had proclaimed the dawn of a new day in Liberia, a break with the past, and declared corruption "public enemy number one." However, my first strong conviction that the government would be different from previous regimes in recent Liberian history, in terms of reforms and moving the country forward, came when the president took the unprecedented and very courageous step to extradite Taylor to face trial.

As someone who had strongly advocated for Mr. Taylor to be brought to book for his crimes, the former warlord's arrest and extradition convinced me that, indeed, Liberia was on a new trajectory. I became convinced that the administration of President Sirleaf would definitely bring about the transformation of my war-torn country, Liberia. I had no doubt that there were numerous challenges ahead, but the arrest of Mr. Taylor was a significant step toward bringing about sustainable peace and progress not just in Liberia, but also in the West African subregion, which had faced a period of death and destruction over the past fourteen years.

Although Liberia had made significant progress in the consolidation of peace and progress, having Mr. Taylor to freely roam about in the subregion had cast a dark shadow on the long-term peace and stability not just in Liberia, but also in West Africa as a whole. It, therefore, became imperative that having this brutal warmonger apprehended and canned presented the best option to ensure sustainable peace and progress in Liberia, as well as for the stability of the West African subregion.

More than anything, it sent a very strong message to those jackbooted thugs who have long thrived on anarchy by resorting to the slaughtering of defenseless people and the plunder of resources to seize political power and enrich themselves that they are now on the wrong side of history.

Amid the increasingly loud drumbeats for the prosecution of alleged perpetrators of war and economic crimes in Liberia, could there be a hidden agenda of revenge being pursued by some of those who are advocating for Madam Sirleaf to be included among those to be prosecuted? Such elements must be made to understand that Liberians are sick and tired of their sinister deeds that have caused Liberia to be one of the poorest and least developed countries in the world.

Meanwhile, it may also be interesting to note that Mr. Taylor was flown from Freetown to The Hague on June 20, 2006, as the annual World Refugee Day, which falls on June 20, was being commemorated worldwide. On the day he was being taken for prosecution, a ceremony took place at the Liberian border with Sierra Leone to formally receive a group of Liberian refugees returning home to their war-ravaged country. His transfer was covered live on CNN International, which also featured refugee-related stories.

In commemoration of World Refugee Day, CNN had scheduled to also interview President Sirleaf live that morning from Monrovia. During that period, hundreds of thousands of Liberian refugees from various countries within the subregion and the internally displaced people (IDP) were being repatriated and resettled in various parts of Liberia through the auspices of the United Nations High Commissioner for Refugees (UNHCR) and the support of other international partners.

Visiting Liberia to commemorate World Refugee Day was UNHCR High Commissioner for Refugees, Mr. António Guterres, who was making his first visit to West Africa after taking over as head of UNHCR in 2005. Seen to be very warm, down-to-earth, and engaging, Mr. Guterres, who became the ninth secretary-general of the UN in 2017, decided to commemorate the day with returning families who had just been repatriated from neighboring Sierra Leone. The World Refugee Day celebration was held at a transit center in Bomi County, western Liberia, near the border with Sierra Leone, where the UNHCR boss was joined by President Sirleaf to commemorate the day.

Before departing Monrovia to join Mr. Guterres at the refugee transit center, the president's convoy headed to the American embassy, where she was scheduled to sit for the live CNN interview to commemorate World Refugee Day. Presidential Press Secretary Cyrus Wleh Badio, a dear colleague and friend, and I accompanied the president.

While the president was being prepared for the interview following our arrival at the embassy, the CNN anchor suddenly announced that there was breaking news that former Liberian president Charles Taylor, who was indicted for war crimes in Sierra Leone, was now being put on a flight in Freetown bound for The Hague. President Sirleaf sat there, and we all watched while Mr. Taylor was being led in handcuffs and put on an aircraft. After the segment ended, the anchor turned to the president, and much of the interview was now focused on Charles Taylor.

As she was entering her vehicle after we left the building, the president turned to me and asked, "Why nobody told me this was coming?" This was in reference to the timing of Mr. Taylor's transfer.

"Madam President, we didn't know either," I responded.

As we drove away, I kept wondering as to how our intelligence community could have also missed this. I could tell that Madam President was not happy. She did not like to publicly comment on anything regarding Mr. Charles Taylor even though she faced allegations that she was an ally and supporter of Mr. Taylor during the early period of his armed insurgency in Liberia.

While Mr. Taylor's supporters and ex-fighters were still fuming over his arrest, it was bad timing for the president to be seen on CNN live commenting on his detention as the former warlord was being flown to The Hague.

CHAPTER FOUR

The Struggle to Change a Dysfunctional
System of Governance

After a three-month delay following my appointment in the government, I finally returned to Liberia and basically hit the ground running. The government was drowning in a noise of miscommunication, where various functionaries of government agencies were making pronouncements contradicting one another. There was grand confusion, as the saying goes, to reflect the low level to which the government had sunk in terms of its inability to disseminate concise information to the public that made sense.

One very notable example of the government's struggle to effectively communicate with the public was in regard to the disastrous manner in which President Sirleaf's request for Charles Taylor to be turned over for prosecution was handled. Feeling betrayed and humiliated by the pressure to surrender Taylor, the Nigerians leaked information to the media immediately upon President Sirleaf's arrival from Nigeria that, during that visit, she had requested Nigeria to turn Taylor over for prosecution. The president had not even been able to meet and brief her officials when BBC broke the news to the shock of the world. The Liberian government was completely caught off guard and did not have the opportunity to devise a strategy on how to manage such delicate information for public consumption.

When President Sirleaf returned from her visit to Nigeria, during which she requested President Obasanjo to extradite Taylor to Liberia to face trial, she reportedly did not acquaint Information Minister Johnny McClain with this development in her briefing to him at the airport, where McClain, who presided over the affairs of the country in the absence of the president, led the official government delegation to welcome the president back home. In keeping with Liberian presidential protocol and practice, ceremonies are usually held at the airport to bid farewell or welcome the president to or from foreign travels. During such a welcome ceremony, the cabinet minister designated to coordinate the affairs of state in consultation with the vice president would usually give the president a brief overview of what transpired during their absence from the country. The president would then respond with a brief overview of the foreign trip.

Mr. McClain shared with me in conversation on a number of occasions that during the welcome ceremony, the president only provided information on certain aspects relating to her visit to Nigeria, but she did not disclose to him anything regarding her request for Taylor's extradition. It was against this background that he went on to brief the media about the outcome of the president's visit to Nigeria without mentioning anything about Taylor's extradition.

Therefore, when information leaked in Nigeria and the media contacted McClain to confirm that Liberia had requested Taylor's extradition, he categorically denied such a report as nonsense. He was confident that he had been briefed by the president from her Nigeria trip, and she never mentioned said situation. With thousands of Taylor's loyalist ex-soldiers roaming freely about in Liberia, Mr. McClain felt the need to vigorously deny the Taylor report, mindful of its potential destabilizing effects. The fact was that he was not in the know about what had actually transpired during the president's trip to Nigeria. Accordingly, when it became clear that President Sirleaf had indeed requested Taylor's extradition, McClain was subjected to public ridicule as an ineffective minister. However, why the president chose to not disclose such very sensitive information regarding her request for Taylor's extradition to her government's chief spokesman has remained unclear.

Nevertheless, the media fallout damaged McClain's credibility, and he never recovered until his resignation as minister of MICAT in October 2006, less than a year on the job. It should be noted that a very important reason for McClain's resignation was the government's inability to provide the needed financial and logistical support to help make MICAT more functional and effective. Also, he was often kept out of the loop of the day-to-day operations of the government, owing to a lack of effective coordination between the Office of the President and MICAT during his tenure as minister.

The following accounts regarding some of the challenges at MICAT during the inception of the Sirleaf administration are intended to give the reader a picture of what it took in the overall process of rebuilding a broken country with a dysfunctional system of governance. The Ministry of Information is herein being used simply as an example of the myriad of challenges in rebuilding and reforming all of the institutions and structures of a failed state decimated by years of war.

Mr. McClain's deep frustration and disappointment about the state of affairs at the Ministry of Information were shared by all of us who were his principal lieutenants, not to talk about the hundreds of employees, many of whom did not have a sitting office space for some time due to the dilapidated condition of the building housing the ministry.

Endowed with a wealth of national and international experience, Mr. McClain later served for a few years as Liberia's ambassador to Senegal before finally retiring from public service. According to the *Historical Dictionary of Liberia*, as part of his background, Mr. McClain was engaged in French study and journalism in Côte d'Ivoire, Senegal, and the University of Paris in France at the beginning of his career.

Minister McClain was a leader with so much to offer from his wisdom and experience at the national and international levels. Nevertheless, he met a country very broken and different in terms of how people conducted themselves and treated one another.

Struggle to Revive a Broken, Poorly Funded Agency

By the time I arrived in Monrovia at the end of May 2006, the rest of the other senior officials at the ministry were already at post, as I was the only MICAT official recruited from abroad. They included Richmond

Anderson, deputy minister for administration, and Elizabeth Hoff, deputy minister for technical services (who was appointed at the same time as I was). Anderson also had a long tenure of service at MICAT, having started there as a reporter with the Liberia News Agency (LINA). He rose through the ranks to become deputy minister for research during the tenure of the Liberia National Transitional Government before his latest appoint as deputy minister for administration. As reported earlier, Hoff served as a reporter of the *New Liberian* newspaper published by the MICAT before moving on to serve as news editor of the independent newspaper the *News*. She was the first female president of the Press Union, a position from which she resigned to assume her new responsibility in government.

Following my arrival in Monrovia from the United States the previous night, I reported to work at MICAT early the next morning. However, it took several days before I was given an office space, which was a dilapidated room with broken windows, walls and floors stained with dirt, and electrical wires and sockets ripped from the walls. Part of the building's roof was ruined due to years of lack of maintenance, looting, and vandalizing as a result of the war. I had to work with the janitors, using soap water, to scrub the walls and floor. There was no money to purchase paint for the walls and floor-cleaning materials. I also used plastic sheets with duct tape to seal off the windows, which, along with the walls, were not repaired or painted for more than a year due to lack of budgetary allocation.

The Information Ministry, housed in what was once an impressive office building with radio and television studios, as well as other media facilities, is located on Capitol Hill, which houses the headquarters of the three branches of the Liberian government: the Executive Mansion, official residence of the president of the Republic of Liberia who heads the executive branch; the Capitol Building, housing the national legislature; and the Temple of Justice building, housing the judiciary. From my second-story office windows, our country's once-majestic statehouse, the Executive Mansion, is closely within view as is the breathtaking view of the Atlantic Ocean, and part of the beachfront area of the Barclay Training Center, a military facility that was turned into the headquarters of the Ministry of National Defense.

Because there was no electricity, I used candles in my office while I worked late many nights for more than six months, as the minister's office was one of a couple of offices in the entire building with electricity that was initially powered by a small portable generator before a larger generator that provided electricity for the entire building was acquired. Worst still, I was assigned an old jeep with a driver after nearly two months on the job, and that jeep broke down numerous times due to inadequate maintenance because there was almost always lack of funds to pay for repairs.

This was at a time when the lack of transportation was one of the most difficult problems in the entire country. And despite my own transportation challenges, I was often heartbroken, while in traffic, seeing the mass of people along the way under the scorching tropical sun or heavy downpour of rain, trying to catch a ride to or from work and school or whatever their destinations were. Some of these people often had to trek long distances to get to their respective destinations. I recall that Sundays were among those days when the chronic transportation problem was highlighted. As you moved along intersections and roadways on Sundays, it was common to see beautifully dressed people, including women and children, struggle to board a taxi or bus or hop on "pen-pen," or motorcycles that were used as commercial transportation, in the absence of adequate commercial taxis and buses.

Mostly lacking formal training to operate a motorcycle and unfamiliar with established driver's road-safety rules and regulations, pen-pen operators posed a serious risk to the commuting public due to numerous accidents resulting in serious injury and death. The pen-pen drivers and owners were mostly teenage boys and young adults, many of them ex-combatants, who operated their own little businesses.

Liberians, who are predominantly Christians, would wear some of their best attires to church on Sundays, like African Americans across the United States do. This was to the extent that one would think that there was a fashion show while attending some Liberian churches, especially seeing gorgeous women moving about with grace and dignity in their elegant attires. Those beautifully dressed women often reminded me of my lovely wife, Neiko, in Sacramento, California, who would hardly miss a Sunday from church without serious compelling reasons; and she always appeared elegant mostly in her African attires. Despite their state of deprivation and destitution during the early postwar period, most Liberians carried themselves with grace and dignity, happy to be alive. There can be no question that Liberians are among the most resilient people in the world.

This was also a time when an overwhelming majority of the people, estimated to be some 85 percent of the entire Liberian population, was unemployed. A majority of the unemployed were young adults who had little or no formal education or employable skills due to the years of civil upheaval. The UN Mission in Liberia and various international NGOs provided more employment opportunities with better pay, which was a huge benefit to those Liberians with the requisite education and skill sets. Dispossessed as a result of years of carnage and devastation, most Liberians had to survive on handouts donated by friendly countries, international agencies, charitable organizations, and religious entities.

Majority of Liberians at the time lived in abject poverty, as it was very difficult for many families to even provide the bare minimum of one meal a day for their children on a daily basis. Not to talk about the very chronic housing shortage, caused by the massive destruction of the infrastructure, including residential homes, schools, and medical facilities. Electricity and pipe-borne water supply to the general public had stopped since 1990, when the power hydro and water treatment facilities were destroyed and left in disrepair during the years of war.

It is gratifying to also recall that despite those challenges, the Liberian people, always a resilient people, have managed to forge ahead in rebuilding their lives.

Because of the financial challenges, I lived for two years with my first cousin Mark Brumkanjay Saulwah. His family of six occupied a three-bedroom apartment in a partially dilapidated building, beautifully located on the bank of a lagoon that runs near the James Spriggs Payne Airport in the Sinkor suburb of Monrovia. The area is within a ten- to twenty-minute stroll from the Atlantic beach. I used to jog and swim in the ocean regularly in the morning before going to work. Nothing was more refreshing than plunging into the warm seawater in the morning, especially during the cold winter season.

As one of the challenges at the Ministry of Information, we inherited an agency with not just one of the lowest budgetary allocations in the entire government, but there also appeared to have been a lack of interest at the highest level of government to garner the necessary support that would have enabled the ministry to effectively carry out its function in disseminating information on the government's policies and programs to the general public. In a society where perceptions matter more than facts, the government's inability to effectively articulate its policies and programs to the general public only contributed more to the spread of misinformation and rumormongering.

Liberia has been a society where the government's failure to create a credible, proactive means of disseminating information to the populace had led to a culture of widespread rumormongering and misinformation, which were contributing factors to the country's upheavals. For example, it is reported that part of the reasons the bloody military coup took place on April 12, 1980, was because rumors had spread that the settler-dominated government of President William Tolbert was planning to secretly execute certain political prisoners, who were mostly of indigenous backgrounds. The seventeen noncommissioned officers who overthrew the government by assassinating President Tolbert were indigenous Liberians who reportedly acted to prevent the government from executing their kinsmen. It has been common knowledge that misinformation and rumors helped to fuel the civil wars and the destruction of many lives.

Therefore, it was unfortunate that the Sirleaf administration treated the dissemination of information to the general public as an afterthought and not as a priority. The government's inability to effectively articulate or adequately keep the public informed about the state of affairs in the country was to have serious negative consequences, as was the case with how the Taylor extradition was handled. This is why although President Sirleaf accomplished a lot during her first term and was viewed like a rock star on the international stage, public sentiments against her government intensified to the point that she was embroiled in a bitter struggle to win reelection.

I would surmise that the Sirleaf administration's negligible support for an effective state-owned public information establishment from the beginning was partly based on the widespread publicity the president and her government enjoyed from the international media, which, rightly so, were fascinated by the dawn of a new day in Africa with the democratic election of Africa's first female president. A very charming and charismatic woman with strong international credentials based on her experience and accomplishments, President Sirleaf was one of the most attractive leaders in the world on the international media stage.

While the president was sailing on the wave of favorable international press, the local media felt marginalized and treated in a somewhat unfriendly manner by the new government, a situation that caused considerable friction between both sides from the inception of the Sirleaf administration. The poisonous state of affairs with the local media came on the heels of a contentious presidential election that brought Madam President to power and left a significant segment of the population disgruntled, as well as the arrest of Charles Taylor, among other national problems, which made the atmosphere in the country really tense.

Ending the Culture of State Security Attacks on Journalists

Compounding the problem with the local media was the fact that a number of journalists were, at various occasions, harassed, beaten, and detained by state security personnel while covering the news in 2006. However, it is important to note that the attacks on the journalists by state security personnel were not sanctioned by the government, as was the case of Liberia's recent past, particularly during the civil war and the respective reigns of military ruler Samuel Doe and warlord president Charles Taylor. During the respective dictatorial regimes of Doe and Taylor, freedom of speech and of the press was criminalized. As a result, journalists and political and human rights activists were routinely harassed, imprisoned, terrorized, or even killed while media houses and facilities were vandalized.

The Sirleaf administration inherited state security agencies and personnel that were accustomed to seeing journalists as antigovernment or enemies of the state who needed to be contained by perpetrating acts of violence against them. As independent journalists reported on issues that were critical of the government of the day, they were perceived to be against the government. In an attempt to silence their critics, the respective Doe and Taylor regimes resorted to draconian measures, including harassment, torture, imprisonment, and sometimes death. Therefore, it was not a complete surprise that the security "leftovers" from those regimes that were in active service still operated with the mind-set from the old order even though Liberia was now in a new political dispensation.

For example, after a few weeks on the job, I was requested to accompany the president on the tour of a Monrovia district where there was a concentration of Liberian-owned small businesses. While waiting for the president's arrival in the vicinity of her office, a presidential aide introduced me to one of the assistant directors of the Special Security Service (SSS), the security agency responsible for the protection of the president, which was renamed the Executive Protection Service. The aide informed him that I would be part of the president's entourage on the tour. Immediately after I was introduced to him, the assistant director, while instructing officers who were being deployed for the president's tour, charged the officers that they should not hesitate to manhandle any journalists that would be covering the president's tour if the journalists failed to adhere to security rules and directives.

I immediately called the assistant director aside and quietly told him that the instruction given to the officers to be hostile toward journalists was not acceptable. In reaction, the director, in a loud and angry tone, said it was not in my place to tell him how to do his work—that the journalists were antigovernment elements who always reported activities of the government negatively. And then he reechoed his instruction to the officers to manhandle any journalists within the proximity of the president who would not follow security instructions.

In that light, I told him that I was left with no alternative but to inform the president regarding the instructions he gave the officers. A few minutes after the exchange, the president entered the room, and he was right there when I told her what had transpired. Upon inquiring from the director, the president simply told him that Minister Williams's job was to handle all media issues to ensure a better working relationship between journalists and security personnel, which was why he would be a part of the presidential party at various functions. She directed that any problems with journalists should be brought to the attention of Minister Williams or Mr. Cyrus Badio, then press secretary to the president. She noted that continued problems between the security officers and journalists were a distraction that was hurting the government's image.

Author, Gabriel Williams (center), with then presidential press secretary Cyrus W. Badio in 2007 (courtesy of the author)

Within weeks of working together, the assistant director and I soon became closely bonded, especially when we both found out that we shared a common birthplace in Rivercess County; and he knew some of my immediate family members. From that time on, whenever he was giving predeployment briefings to the officers at various presidential events, he did not hesitate to instruct officers to work in harmony with journalists—that they should report problems to senior government press officers immediately available, such as Minister Williams or Press Secretary Badio, and also that officers should desist from confrontational acts with journalists.

It is also important to note that on a number of occasions, some officials of the new government accused the media of acting unprofessionally. These officials, who were aggrieved by what they regarded to be negative reporting against them and their agencies, at times advocated that the Ministry of Information must exercise its statutory responsibility to impose sanctions against media entities, which included arbitrarily banning them. However, the MICAT was vested with the statutory power to regulate media activities and impose sanctions that included arbitrary ban and fines against news outlets that the government considered to have committed acts of transgression.

My response always was that anyone who was aggrieved by acts of the media should seek legal redress through the courts instead of having MICAT impose sanctions that were contrary to the constitution of Liberia. It was my considered opinion that arbitrary measures against the media for acts of professional impropriety would not induce professionalism. Rather, proper education and training and a conducive working environment would enhance professionalism at a time the media, like the rest of the country, faced massive brain drain as a result of the civil war.

At a meeting where a number of officials vented their frustrations with the media, my expressed disapproval of arbitrary actions as a recourse caused an angry official, with finger pointed at me, to inquire, "Who're you working for? The government or the journalists?" The official said that my actions amounted to encouraging the media to destroy the hard-earned reputation of people through unprofessional reporting.

The attacks and threats against the media by security personnel created a huge challenge and very serious embarrassment for the new president, who had taken over to change what I would call an "evil system," in which she was also victimized as a leading advocate for the rule of law and democratic governance in Liberia. Madam Sirleaf was harassed and jailed, faced death threats, and exiled under previous autocratic regimes for advocating for basic human rights and democracy.

In the wake of the series of attacks against journalists by state security officers, the Press Union of Liberia, the umbrella organization for journalists and media entities, along with independent media establishments, threatened to boycott coverage of government-related activities until there were assurances that the lives of journalists would not be threatened.

One of my first official acts immediately upon arriving in Liberia was to visit the office of the Press Union of Liberia and open dialogue with the union's leadership as to how we, together, could begin to work together to collectively find a solution to the security problems affecting journalists in the performance of their reportorial duties. During my meeting with the PUL leadership, I assured them that the maltreatment of journalists by state security officers, as well as threats against journalists by some government functionaries, was not sanctioned by the new government and that the government was prepared to work with them to put an end to such unfortunate developments.

I recalled that before going to the PUL office, I had attended my first presidential function at the Executive Mansion, where the president was presiding over a ceremony. As the president got up to leave the hall at the end of the ceremony, she walked over to me, shook my hand, and said, "Welcome, Minister Williams. I'm glad that you've decided to return home to serve." She said she looked forward to seeing that I use my media background to help build a healthy working relationship between the government and the local media and to improve the government's information dissemination to the public.

Since my first handshake and interaction with Madam President, those few words from her calling me to service became my charge and marching order over the years of my service in the Sirleaf government.

As a former leader of the Press Union who headed the organization during part of the brutal and barbaric period of our country, I was cognizant of the threats posed to press freedom by state security apparatus or renegade officers and was fully prepared to help put an end to such abuses during my tenure at the Ministry of Information.

My unwavering determination to do what I could to protect and promote press freedom at all costs would draw the ire of some officials who questioned my loyalty to the government or whether I was simply around to seek the interest of those "irresponsible journalists." I recall many heated meetings when some officials vented their anger at me for cautioning against arbitrary actions when the media reported negative stories against them or when journalists were thought to have committed acts of professional impropriety. Whatever the situation was, I always recommended that due process of law was the most acceptable means of recourse for those who may have been aggrieved by media reports.

Over the next several months, the Information Ministry worked with the Press Union and the independent media, through a series of meetings, in putting together what could be considered as the "rules of engagement" on how state security personnel and journalists would interact when assigned at presidential and other state functions. With the full backing of the president, the Information Ministry announced constantly that state security agencies or personnel must refer all complaints against journalists and media entities to the ministry and desist from taking actions that could be tantamount to harassment or maltreatment of journalists.

The Information Ministry publicly announced repeatedly that harassment or manhandling of journalists was totally unacceptable and that the government would not condone such acts under the new political dispensation. With the approval of Minister McClain, with whom I had regular briefings on how to articulate the issues, I was in the media constantly, especially programs on radio, to emphasize that the government of Liberia will in no uncertain terms tolerate any acts of abuse against journalists. Radio was the most popular medium of information dissemination to the public at the time.

How Indiscipline within the Security Sector Threatened National Security

The hostilities between state security and the media are highlighted because my responsibility was to manage the media and disseminate information on the policies, programs, and activities of the government.

Nevertheless, the new government was faced with a major challenge of indiscipline and criminal activities within the respective ranks of the then newly reorganized Armed Forces of Liberia, the Liberia National Police, and the Special Security Service (presidential security), now renamed Executive Protection Service (EPS), among others. Frequent reports of soldiers and law enforcement officers perpetrating abuses against the general public were as disturbing as having some of the officers caught being involved in criminal activities, including armed robbery.

There was a strong recognition from the president that the government needed to work very closely with UNMIL and our international partners to accelerate the pace of reform within the security sector. The president understood that besides the general public who were being victimized, her own life could be endangered if the government failed to institute the necessary measures to consolidate the peace and security.

During a high-level meeting I attended in the president's office, where the security situation in the country was being discussed, I was struck and have never forgotten when she said something along the lines of "Sometimes when I'm alone with these security officers, I wonder whether one of them will not turn on me and shoot me when I turn my back."

As the president expressed concern about her own safety, my mind drifted to the incident in the Democratic Republic of the Congo, where, in 2001, rebel leader turned president Laurent Kabila was shot dead by one of his bodyguards while Kabila was seated in his office having a meeting with an economic advisor. According to the *Guardian*, when the teenage assassin, who was one of the child soldiers in Kabila's army, entered the president's office, Mr. Kabila leaned over, assuming the teenager wanted to talk to him. The boy soldier then pulled out a revolver, shot Kabila four times, and then escaped with other conspirators ("Revealed: How Africa's Dictator Died at the Hands of His Boy Soldiers," *Guardian*, February 10, 2001).

Kabila came to power after ousting brutal dictator Mobutu Sese Seko in 1997, ending Mobutu's thirty-two-year rule. Following his assassination in 2001, Kabila's son Joseph Kabila replaced his father at the age of twenty-nine, and he remained in power through 2018.

Following a controversial election in January 2019, opposition candidate Felix Tshisekedi was declared the winner of the presidential election to succeed Kabila. Another leading opposition candidate, Martin Fayulu, alleged that the vote was rigged against him in a deal made by Tshisekedi and the outgoing president, Kabila, whose party won a majority in legislative elections. According to Reuters News Agency quoting diplomatic sources, vote tallies by Congo's highly influential Catholic Church showed second-place opposition candidate Fayulu as victor. Felix Tshisekedi is the son of the late veteran opposition leader Etienne Tshisekedi, who died in 2017.

Because of serious concerns for the safety of Madam President in such a fragile security environment, the US government deployed Secret Service officers to provide security for the president with the backing of UNMIL peacekeepers from the onset of her administration until Liberian officers were retrained to perform in keeping with international best practices. Some opposition elements often went on radio and threw verbal gibes that the president did not trust and was afraid of her own people so much that her security was in the hands of foreigners.

Among the immediate postwar security challenges was armed robbery—a terrifying crime that often left defenseless people terrorized, women and girls raped, property stolen, and, in more tragic circumstances, people killed. There was no electricity; and Monrovia, like the rest of Liberia, was in complete darkness, except for those that operated electric generators. Ex-combatants, who were mostly without skills and unemployed, were the main perpetrators of armed robberies. Regrettably, though, some soldiers and law enforcement officers of the newly reorganized military and paramilitary forces during that time were also caught red-handed perpetrating such heinous crimes against the very public they were under oath to protect. Some of the culprits were caught in military or police uniforms. There were also the fearful instances of carjacking, where giving a stranger a lift, in a society where people easily assist others they do not know, could prove tragic for the driver.

As I reminisce on the period when carjacking had become alarming, I had an experience that is an indication that we should be careful not to allow fear to get in the way of what God can do to use us, during unusual circumstances, to make a difference in the lives of others. In the wake of growing media reports of an increase in carjacking, my elder cousin Mark Saulwah became very concerned about my safety because I was someone who did not hesitate to pick up folks from along the wayside once there was space in my vehicle. Mark, who helped to ensure my security those days, strongly advised me to be extremely careful in giving lifts to strangers, especially at night.

Standing at the height of about six feet and well-built, Mark, who died suddenly in 2019 of an apparent heart attack in Monrovia, joined the Armed Forces of Liberia (AFL) in the 1970s; and he retired after the AFL was disbanded to establish a brand-new military force. With the rank of colonel, he was employed with the Bureau of Immigration and Naturalization, where he has played a critical role in the effort to reestablish central government security control in Liberia's border areas.

One day, while driving from a function past midnight, as I turned from the main road and began to drive down this dark muddy road filled with potholes leading to my residence, there were two women standing on the side of the road, waving me down. They stood in a remote part of the road with no houses or people around at a time of the night during the rainy season when anyone could not just venture out because of the criminal activities.

As I drove past them, I stopped ahead and woke Mark from sleep when I called to tell him that I just drove past two women in this remote part of the road, but they looked like they were in need of help. Mark advised that I proceed driving and not stop because the criminals would use women and children to lure potential victims. While we were talking, I saw the two women walking toward my vehicle. With Mark still on the line monitoring the development, I ensured my doors were locked and partially brought down one of the windows to talk to them while my engine was running. The lady who was ahead of the two told me that her sister was in child labor, but they could not find a vehicle to get them to the hospital that time of the night, so they were walking there when they saw my vehicle. She said they could not even find a wheelbarrow, which could be used to convey the woman in labor to the hospital, as was the case in some instances those days to transport the sick to the hospital due to a lack of ambulance or absence vehicle.

Having listened to them, Mark said I could take the chance to open the car and allow them in but expressed that it was a very dangerous move. With my eyes scouring the nearby bushes to spot any movement, I opened the door for them to enter, and I sped off to the John F. Kennedy Medical Center, where I had the lady admitted at the maternity ward before returning home. Following her release from the hospital, the lady came looking and found my residence to express thanks and to inform me that they had decided to name their bouncing baby boy Gabriel, after me.

Because of the precarious security situation, various communities organized themselves into what was called "neighborhood watch." Members of the neighborhood watch teams were mostly able-bodied young men who stayed up at night and kept watch over the neighborhood to discourage individuals from outside the neighborhood from coming in to engage in criminal activities. They also helped to apprehend criminals, but sometimes the criminals were brutalized or killed by mob violence perpetrated by community members frustrated by the lack of adequate security protection and legal redress. The neighborhood watch operated under the auspices of community leaderships, which collected contributions from residents to purchase food and other materials such as flashlights, batteries, and raincoats for the community watch teams.

Some of the leading radio stations, such as UNMIL Radio, operated by the UN Mission in Liberia, and the privately owned Truth FM radio, broadcast live programs throughout the night, where residents from various parts of Monrovia and beyond called in to report suspicious activities or incidents in their neighborhoods or to simply say, "Everything in my area here is cool and calm." Many early mornings, between 1:00 a.m. and 4:00 a.m., I used to enjoy monitoring the live neighborhood watch radio programs. There were times when calls came in reporting armed robberies and other criminal activities in real time due to the growing availability of cell phones. There were also police hotlines to report armed robbery, but you would be lucky if the police responded to your call for help.

Even in instances where the police engaged armed robbers, there was not much they could do because the newly reorganized police force at the time was not armed. In view of the immediate past history of the country where the police and soldiers terrorized the people, Liberians were hesitant to accept the immediate rearming of the police under the new dispensation. There was a real fear among the population that an armed police force would turn the guns on the people, as was the case during the war, in the absence of good professional training and reforms.

It may be recalled that Liberia's military and paramilitary forces were factionalized during the civil war. Instead of protecting the defenseless population, soldiers and paramilitary officers turned their guns on their own people, and they were involved in committing atrocities and other unspeakable crimes against defenseless civilians.

Because they were not paid by the various factions they represented, the marauding armed thugs were accustomed to a way of life that was to prey on the defenseless population to sustain themselves.

This is why, in the August 2003 Comprehensive Peace Agreement (CPA), signed in the Ghanaian capital of Accra, which ended Liberia's civil war, parties involved in the negotiations agreed that the country's armed forces and paramilitary be demobilized and reorganized with a focus on adherence to respect for human rights and ensuring that the people enjoy safety and security. The need to establish new military and paramilitary forces that the public would run to and not run from at all times could not be overemphasized.

There was a strong recognition that reorganizing the military and paramilitary forces with which the general populace would feel safe and secure was very critical to ensuring durable peace and progress. For example, while most Liberians yearned for a robust law enforcement outfit to curb the alarming crime rate at the time, they did not hesitate to express apprehension about arming the police and other law enforcement officers. The public sentiments were necessitated by fear that if the police or law enforcement officers were to be armed, those officers could use the guns to terrorize the general population. Public fear was against the background that a significant number of those that made up the newly organized military and paramilitary outfits were ex-combatants.

According to reports from the UN and other sources, more than thirteen thousand soldiers of the old Armed Forces of Liberia were demobilized. Overall, more than one hundred thousand ex-combatants from the various warring factions were disarmed under the auspices of the National Commission on Disarmament, Demobilization, Rehabilitation, and Reintegration (NCDDRR), which was funded by the UN and other international partners.

The ex-soldiers and former rebel fighters often acted with violence and rioting when they had not received their benefits promised them under the agreement to lay down their arms and demobilize. The ex-soldiers, in particular, posed a very serious threat to national security as they regularly unleashed waves of violence and rioting to demand salary arrears and other benefits from the government. The ex-soldiers were always engaged in their acts of destabilization during the period around July 26, Liberia's Independence Day, which is a major holiday season, as well as around the Christmas season in December. The ex-soldiers carefully chose these seasons to force the government to yield to their demands in order to keep the country calm for the general public to enjoy peaceful celebrations.

It is interesting to note that the violent actions of the ex-soldiers were not necessarily intended to destabilize the country as much as they were motivated by the desire to squeeze some money out of the government to cater to themselves and their families. It may also be recalled that Mr. Taylor launched his armed rebellion to unseat military ruler Samuel Doe on December 24, 1989, (Christmas Eve) when the entire country was in a state of celebration during the Christmas holidays.

The irony of the ex-soldiers' behavior was that the overwhelming majority of defenseless Liberians they terrorized during the war were not demanding compensation from the government. There were some Liberians who openly raised concerns as to why the ex-soldiers should keep threatening the peace by acts of violence to demand compensation when what they did during the war was mostly to terrorize the people instead of protecting them.

While the government often yielded to the demands of the ex-soldiers simply to maintain a peaceful atmosphere in the country, I always did not hesitate to use my "bully pulpit" as a government spokesman to tongue-lash them for threatening to undermine the fragile peace by extorting money from the people, whom they had victimized during the civil war.

With majority of the ex-soldiers and former rebels unemployed at the time, many of them were also involved in criminal activities in the country, including armed robbery.

These accounts provided are intended to give the reader a gist of how the new government of President Sirleaf had to deal with a myriad of challenges, all of which were a priority, as it struggled to reestablish governmental control over the entire territorial jurisdiction of the country, with the full backing of UNMIL and Liberia's international partners.

There were also instances where some national security leaders would employ some of the tactics of the evil past by deliberately misleading the president and general public regarding matters of national security for pecuniary gains and other sinister motives. Liberia's history, especially from the 1950s through 2000s, is replete with accounts of how leaders within the national security sector concocted plots to overthrow the government and assassinate the president; and they would use such allegations to implicate or eliminate others they might deem to be a threat to them for whatever narrow interest they served.

Here is an example of how an individual in a senior security position violated the public trust during the early period of the Sirleaf administration. The director of national police called a press conference to announce that the security forces had uncovered a cache of arms and ammunition in central Liberia. Such an announcement coming from the director of national police at a time when the UNMIL was dealing with ensuring a successful disarmament of the various armed factions certainly created reasons for public concern.

However, the fact of the matter was that the information released to the press by the police director was completely false and may have been intended to show that she was hard at work at a time she was coming under scrutiny for gross financial impropriety, among other problems, which eventually led to her dismissal and prosecution.

What happened was that the police had seized several bags of spent shells or empty casings from bullets that were fired during the years of civil bloodbath. The empty bullet casings were collected and sold by petit traders while the shells were melted and turned into aluminum pots and other products.

Following the police director's press conference to make such a false claim, UNMIL informed Madam President that the report was untrue and that there was a need to correct such misinformation, which had the propensity to affect the image of the country as being unstable.

Immediately after the BBC reported about the ammunition seizure in Liberia, I received a call directly from the president, who instructed that I should immediately proceed to contact the police director and have the false information corrected, which was done.

A few days after working with the police to handle the media clarifications, the director of the Criminal Investigation Division (CID) of the Liberia National Police visited my office and gave me a tip-off that his boss, the director of national police, had hidden the original copy of the security report given to her by investigators involved with the case and that she had forwarded a falsified copy of the report to the president. He wanted to know if I could ensure that the president would get a copy of the original report and for him to remain anonymous to avoid possible negative backlash.

Having perused a copy of the falsified report sent to the president and the original copy, which was being suppressed, it was clear that the facts were distorted to support the police director's position in the matter. It was a sad reflection of the length to which many people would go to abuse the public trust.

With the facts confirmed, I went to the Executive Mansion, briefed the president on my discovery, and presented her a copy of the original report. After some time, the police director in question was fired and sent to court for economic crimes. She and a gentleman with whom she was romantically involved allegedly set up a bogus company through which tens of thousands of dollars were funneled supposedly to purchase new uniforms and other accessories for officers of the police force. This was at a time when the police officers appeared really poorly with their faded and worn-out uniforms and shoes. Many of the officers did not even have uniforms. Yet some of the resources that were made available to help improve their conditions were squandered with such brazen audacity by those entrusted to provide leadership for the force. This has often been the case without regard for national security implications.

Lessons from the Gray Allison Experience

A vivid example of the dog-eat-dog viciousness of Liberian politics played out in 1989 with Major General Gray D. Allison, the minister of national defense during the regime of military leader Samuel Doe. He fell from grace to grass, as the saying goes, in a plot allegedly concocted by his enemies within the regime who felt threatened by his power. General Allison—regarded as a soldier's soldier, trained in the United States and the United Kingdom—was widely seen to be the most powerful individual in Liberia second only to Head of State Doe himself. Allison, who earned a master's degree in mass communications from a university in the United States, was a former minister of information. He had earlier served as liaison officer of the Liberian contingent to the UN forces in the Congo during that country's civil war in the 1960s.

Always very smartly attired in his military outfit and a man with a strong commanding presence, General Allison gained infamy for being a ruthless leader during his tenure as minister of national defense. For example, in 1984, with the endorsement of Commander in Chief Doe, General Allison ordered heavily armed soldiers to invade the main campus of the University of Liberia in Monrovia, where students were peacefully protesting the arrest and detention of several of their professors, along with political activists and others. The detainees, who were mostly outspoken critics of the Doe regime, were accused of plotting to overthrow the regime.

The army attack on the student protesters left several dead, many women raped, and over one hundred injured (introduction, *Historical Dictionary of Liberia*, second edition, page 8).

The lives of many promising young people were extinguished and shattered as a result of the barbaric attack on the university campus, which I covered as a young reporter with the *Daily Observer* newspaper. In desperation to conceal evidence of the killings and other human rights abuses perpetrated on the university campus, government security forces reportedly visited medical facilities and collected the bodies of those killed during the attack. Some of the wounded, who were found undergoing treatment at various medical facilities, were also reportedly taken away by state security.

When the *Daily Observer* and other news organs published reports regarding families who claimed that their loved ones at the university were missing following the attack, the government announced that those who said their loved ones were missing should make a formal report to the government for such matters to be investigated. Liberians were consumed by so much fear that families of victims were afraid to go public. Imagine families who lost their loved ones but did not dare to grieve openly for fear of retribution from the Doe regime.

As reported in chapter 1, General Allison was seen to have become too powerful to the extent that some of those within Doe's inner circle reportedly conspired to have him eliminated. Doe was reportedly made to believe that Allison was plotting to overthrow him. In 1989, Allison and his wife, Mrs. Angeline Watta Allison, were arrested and accused of the ritualistic killing of a man identified as J. Melvin Pyne, a police officer, whose decapitated body was found lying across a railroad track near the Allisons' residence in the township of Caldwell outside Monrovia. Government prosecutors alleged that Allison was made to believe that he needed a portion of human blood and body to perform juju, a fetish or ritual intended to derive supernatural powers. According to the prosecutors, the portion was then to be used to kill Doe and overthrow his government.

Following his arrest, General Allison was publicly paraded and humiliated, barefoot and in rags. He was dismissed as minister of defense and charged and convicted of murder and unspecified political offenses by a military tribunal, in what was widely seen as a kangaroo trial. General Allison vigorously denied the charges as a plot concocted by his enemies to eliminate him.

After he was declared guilty by the kangaroo military tribunal, Allison was then banished to the notorious Belle Yella, a maximum security prison in the interior Liberian jungle. In 1990, he was discovered there and killed by rebel forces loyal to Charles Taylor. The rebels reportedly tortured him to death in retribution for the gross human rights abuses he allegedly perpetrated during his days in power.

Mrs. Angeline Watta Allison and nine others who were also indicted as co-conspirators were tried separately by a civilian court. In May 1990, she and two other accused were found guilty and sentenced to life imprisonment for complicity to murder. In a submission to the TRC in September 2006, Amnesty International noted that Mrs. Allison and the two other people sentenced to life imprisonment appeared to be prisoners of conscience.

As Monrovia descended into total bloodshed and destruction in the wake of the invasion of rebel forces, the prison where Madam Allison was being detained was reportedly overtaken by Prince Johnson's forces, who took the prisoners to their base in the township of Caldwell outside Monrovia. It was while in detention at the base that Mrs. Allison was allegedly interrogated and killed by Johnson.

Johnson was the leader of the rebel faction Independent National Patriotic Front of Liberia (INPFL), which broke away from the main National Patriotic Front of Liberia rebel movement headed by Charles Taylor.

As reported in chapter 1, a female friend who was displaced in the Caldwell community during the early period of the civil war provided some refreshing accounts regarding Mrs. Allison's death. According to her, during that period, she visited Johnson's INPFL base frequently for food; and she was acquainted with the then warlord, as well as the accounts related to the death of Mrs. Allison. She said Mrs. Allison was killed by some female INPFL rebels, who were close associates of Johnson, upon orders of the then INPFL leader.

According to her, she was personally acquainted with a senior female INPFL fighter who was a member of Johnson's Gio ethnic group and inner circle. Following news of the killing of Mrs. Allison, she added, the female fighter visited where she resided and narrated that Mrs. Allison begged them to spare her life. The female fighter said Mrs. Allison offered them (female fighters) her jewelries and other valuables in a futile attempt to secure her release. Mrs. Allison was regarded to be a wealthy woman as she served as commissioner of the township of Caldwell. She, like her husband, was widely perceived to be evil.

My friend stated that she saw her female INPFL acquaintance wearing rings and other jewelries said to belong to Mrs. Allison. The rebel fighter said that after taking her jewelries, Mrs. Allison was beaten to death while she was pleading for her life, and her body was thrown in a nearby river. The female fighter also said that she and her comrades did not have any sympathy for Mrs. Allison because she and her husband were involved in acts of wickedness against their fellow Liberians.

There is a video that has been played on social media in which, following her arrest, the INPFL strongman, who was also responsible for the capture and assassination of President Samuel Doe, is seen interrogating Mrs. Allison. The INPFL leader is seen questioning Mrs. Allison about some acts of human rights abuse committed by her husband, including the invasion of the main campus of the University of Liberia in Monrovia, where many students were reportedly shot, killed, or wounded by soldiers under General Allison's command. At one point in the video, while Mrs. Allison is attempting to answer a question Johnson asked, she is slapped in the face by the INPFL leader.

Testifying before Liberia's Truth and Reconciliation Commission (TRC) in 2008, General Armah Youlo, former assistant director of the National Security Agency, who was a leader of one of the armed factions during the civil war, said everyone in the Doe government was afraid of General Allison, including President Doe himself. He noted that General Allison had enemies in high places, which led to a conspiracy for his downfall. According to Youlo, Allison was a man who could intimidate anybody, so everyone was really afraid of him. However, Youlo, who hailed from President Doe's ethnic group and was a key government security leader, said he did not believe that General Allison was plotting to overthrow the government when he was purged. Youlo said, "Gray D. Allison did not look like someone planning a coup. If he was planning a coup, I did not see any soldier that will refuse his order" ("Even President Doe Feared Gray D. Allison . . . Youlo at TRC," *Liberian Journal* online, October 6, 2008).

I have decided to highlight this account because in 1987, about two years before his fall from grace to grass, the all-powerful General Allison had ordered soldiers to have me arrested, publicly stripped naked, manhandled, and detained for what he considered as a disrespect because I refused to disclose the sources of an article I wrote as a reporter of the *Daily Observer.*

The article in reference relates to the kidnapping of one Reverend Gabriel Swope, a clergyman of the Methodist Church of Liberia, allegedly by state intelligence officers. Seen to be a regular critic of the Doe regime, Reverend Swope was the assistant pastor of the First United Methodist Church in Monrovia at the time he was reported kidnapped on a late Friday night in Monrovia. While on his way home from a church library, he was reportedly standing on the sidewalk waiting for taxi when a vehicle pulled up. He was reportedly forced into the vehicle by some men, who sped away from the scene. Reverend Swope was known to be one of those members of the Liberian clergy who did not hesitate to use the pulpit to draw attention to the transgressions of the Doe regime.

As a reporter, having been tipped off about the kidnap of Reverend Swope, allegedly by government security officers, I did the necessary investigation and filed a report, which was a front-page lead of the *Observer.* On the day the article was published, I was summoned to the Defense Ministry to provide information I had to the state security agencies, supposedly to aid in the investigation of the clergyman's kidnap.

I was brought in for questioning during a meeting of the Joint Security Commission, Liberia's supreme policy-making body on defense and security matters, chaired by then defense minister Allison. The meeting was attended by other top brass of the commission, including then justice minister Jenkins K. Z. B. Scott, the directors of the national police and the National Security Agency, and the chief of staff of the Armed Forces of Liberia, among others.

After I was questioned and I explained as to how I got the report that was published by the *Daily Observer*, General Allison demanded that I disclose the names of the sources I mentioned in the article. The unnamed sources that I cited in the report were prominent members of Liberian society and the Methodist Church who were quietly involved in a negotiation with the government for Swope's release or were knowledgeable of what transpired.

When they secured the release of Reverend Swope during that Sunday morning, the eminent persons who negotiated his release drove him in a white van straight to the First United Methodist Church on Ashmun Street, Monrovia, where the congregation had gathered for the Sunday morning worship service. As reflected in the church's program for the service that Sunday, Reverend Swope was scheduled to preach on the theme "How Long?"

The atmosphere at the church was tense because of the reported kidnapping of the reverend. As he was brought into the church shivering and barely able to walk, the congregation was literally in tears. Dressed in a T-shirt with his hair shaved in a style akin to prisoners in Liberia, prayers were offered over Reverend Swope, after which he was rushed to the hospital and admitted.

As part of my investigation as a reporter, I was at the church when the visibly distressed Reverend Swope was brought there, and the accounts cited were reflected in my report.

During the Defense Ministry meeting, General Allison maintained that those individuals whom I referred to in the report as sources must be identified for them to be apprehended and questioned regarding the alleged kidnapping of the Methodist Church clergyman. He argued that the kidnapping might have been staged by antigovernment elements to smear the image of the government and that I was being used as a pawn by those who were exploring every opportunity to overthrow the government.

Even though I cooperated with the investigation in every way possible, I refused to disclose the names of my sources for the professional reason that I did not get their permission to publicly disclose their names. General Allison took my refusal as an act of defiance, and he decided to have me punished.

Angered by what he called a "gross disrespect" toward him by my refusal to disclose the names of the sources, General Allison ordered his guards to place me in custody until I could make the disclosures he demanded. With that instruction, the soldiers knocked me down and dragged me away from the conference room. One of the soldiers pressed my neck down to the floor with the boot he had on. I was stripped naked, manhandled, and detained for about two hours.

Given the level of cruelty to which I was being subjected when I did nothing wrong in the first place, I simply concluded that Allison could do as he was pleased, but I was not going to disclose the names of those people to him. From the way he spoke during the meeting, I became afraid that the lives of my sources would be in peril if I were to disclose their names. Since Doe's regime came to power, many Liberians, including those who had no military or security background, were arrested or killed for alleged complicity in plotting to depose the regime. Those who dared to openly criticize the regime were often among those arrested for involvement in subversive activities against the government.

General Allison said the regime was aware that there were remnants of the "old guards" from the deposed government who were determined to destroy Doe because of the 1980 coup. He said the government was closely monitoring the activities of certain individuals associated with the deposed regime, who gathered regularly under the guise of social interactions at a residence called the Porch, which was located in downtown Carey Street in Monrovia.

General Allison said I was basically an innocent young man who was being used by those antigovernment elements to smear the image of the government by staging the kidnap and getting me to report a story implicating the government. He said that no one was going to know that I gave to the government the names of the sources quoted in my story and that it was only intended for the government to identify these with knowledge related to the kidnapping. He said that I was not the target for the investigation, but that my cooperation was only needed. However, he warned sternly that if I did not cooperate, I would suffer the consequences for my noncooperation.

During the course of the interrogation, as I realized the gravity of what was unfolding and how it would be more dangerous to name my sources, I decided not to say anything more. I did not panic and maintained my composure even while I was publicly stripped naked, detained, humiliated, and traumatized simply for doing my job as a news reporter. I had appeared at the Defense Ministry for the kidnap investigation dressed in a suit and tie, a quality for which my boss at the *Observer*, Kenneth Y. Best, often commended me. Mr. Best lauded me for usually coming to work appropriately attired because you did not know where you would go as a reporter to cover an assignment.

In view of what was unfolding at the investigation, I could only imagine the worst for my sources if I were to name them. And this is why, no matter how much he growled, General Allison failed in his attempts to pressure me to reveal the names of my sources even when he earlier assured me that whatever information I provided would be treated confidentially.

Apparently, after realizing that they could not force me to confess the names of my sources, Justice Minister Jenkins Scott, who sat through the period of interrogation without saying a word, eventually spoke and made an appeal to his colleague Minister Allison to have me released. I sat between General Allison and Minister Scott in the conference room during the investigation. At the head of the conference table, General Allison sat in a large rocking chair with a soldier standing right behind him. Minister Scott sat quietly and closely observed me as I engaged the generals in the room, especially General Allison, who previously served as minister of information before being appointed as minister of defense. I never gave in to fear, as I articulated my responsibilities as a journalist and that I was under no obligation to disclose the names of my sources to government authorities.

Following an appeal from Justice Minister Jenkins K. Z. B. Scott for me to be pardoned, General Allison ordered my release. In his parting words before Minister Scott personally ensured that I got dressed and escorted out of the Defense Ministry building onto the main street, General Allison told me to thank God for Minister Scott for appealing on my behalf. With his eyes peering above the rim of his small-framed glasses that basically hung on the tip of his nose in the style of an intimidating professor, Allison said he would have taught me a lesson I would never forgot for the rest of my life. He said he did not tolerate anyone to disrespect him without serious repercussions, such as the disrespectful conduct that I exhibited by refusing to disclose the names of the sources in my story.

When the Press Union of Liberia and the *Daily Observer* newspaper protested my detention, General Allison went on national television and referred to me as a "gbarpleh," a tiny bony fish eaten by mostly the poor who cannot afford the cost of the more nutritious and delicious-tasting fishes. In Liberia, the bony fish called "gbarpleh" is regarded to be of little taste and nutritious value. By this expression, General Allison was telling the Liberian people on national television that I amounted to nothing, as far as he was concerned, and that he could have taken any action against me without any consequence as a result of.

After the Press Union of Liberia and the *Daily Observer* protested what was regarded to be my illegal arrest and detention, a gentleman I later found out to be an officer of the National Security Agency (NSA), the state intelligence outfit, paid one of his regular visits to the offices of the *Daily Observer* newspaper to meet with his fellow soccer enthusiast and drinking buddy, T. Maxson Teah, then news editor of the *Observer*. T-Max, as Mr. Teah was affectionately known, and the gentleman (name withheld since I am not sure whether his background as an intelligence officer was publicly known) were each ardent supporters of the two top rival national soccer clubs: Invincible Eleven (IE), called the Yellow Boys, and the Mighty Barrolle, known as the Rollers. While T-Max was simply a staunch Barrolle supporter, the gentleman rose through the ranks of the IE leadership to become president of the then-famous national club, whose past players include Liberia's current president, George Weah, who became Africa's and the world's best player during his remarkable playing time in Europe.

While they were engaged in their usual sports arguments, the gentleman tipped off the news editor that there were plans afoot to have me secretly apprehended. He told T-Max that someone I was familiar with would drop by that night to ask me to walk with him down the road to a nearby bar for a drink. He said I should decline the offer and also that I should not spend the night and the next few nights at my residence until the tension cooled. As journalists during those days, when we went to work in the morning, we did not leave until nighttime because of the tedious process of producing a daily newspaper in an era of limited technology. Those were the days when we used typewriters to write our stories before the current computer and Internet age, which has made the process of reporting and production much easier.

Not long after the gentleman departed and T-Max alerted me, a guy he and I would occasionally hang out with for drinks came by and offered for us to go and check out one of our regular spots nearby. I pretended to be very busy trying to finish writing a report; therefore, I could not leave the office. Immediately after he left, it became clear to us that there was danger, and I became terrified. T-Max ordered that I leave the office immediately and go anywhere but home to spend the night. Having sneaked out of the building, I ran out of the compound through the back, and I never the spent the night at my residence for a few days until the tension regarding this matter eased.

When Reverend Swope was admitted at the hospital in the wake of his kidnapping, state security personnel were stationed at the door of his room. For a few days following his release from the hospital, he moved about with security guards. This, according to the government, was intended for his protection.

It may be interesting to note that because of the courtesy and honor extended him by the government following his kidnapping, Reverend Swope went on state television and said he did not believe that the government was involved in his kidnapping. He said he was being so well treated by the government since the incident that he could not see how the government could have been the culprit.

Reverend Swope was at the Defense Ministry when I was manhandled and emotionally abused for reporting his kidnapping. As he left the Defense Ministry while I was in custody, I was hopeful that he would have alerted my office about my plight. However, he did no such thing, and he publicly appeared to be more on the side of the government.

Encouraged to do an interview on state television, Reverend Swope proclaimed that the government was not involved in his kidnapping. Words from Swope's own mouth exonerating the government was the opportunity General Allison needed for his next move. Allison followed the next day with his own press conference, at which he described Swope as a "double agent." He said although Swope appeared to be critical of the government, he was being used by the government to spy on the bishop of the United Methodist Church of Liberia, the Reverend Arthur F. Kulah, who was known to be a staunch critic of the regime.

According to General Allison, although fingers were being pointed at the government for complicity in the kidnapping, Reverend Swope himself had openly absolved the government of responsibility. This, he added, was an indication that Swope was playing games to conceal his activities as a double agent. And that was the end of Swope's special treatment by the government.

Swope was literally crushed by General Allison's allegations. His credibility severely damaged and disgraced by the revelation that he was a "double agent" who was spying on his own boss, Swope was forced to leave Liberia with his family and settle in the United States. Nothing has been publicly heard of him since then.

The 1987 encounter with General Allison occurred a few months following my return to Liberia from the United States, where I had benefitted from a prestigious journalism program, the Dag Hammarskjold Memorial Fellowship, at the United Nations headquarters in New York. Allison was aware from the news that I had recently returned from further studies abroad, but he cautioned that I should not be fooled by what I had learned in America, to challenge authorities.

Because of the increasingly dangerous security situation in Liberia during that period, especially regarding how journalists, opposition politicians, and rights activists were targeted by the regime, I was advised by many not to return to Liberia. I was encouraged by many well-meaning people who cared for my safety and well-being to take advantage of the opportunity to stay in the United States and pursue my career.

Back in Liberia during that period, the *Sun Times* newspaper, where I was a senior reporter before taking up my fellowship in the United States, was banned by the government for alleged antigovernment reporting. The *Sun Times* managing editor, legendary journalist Rufus M. Darpoh, and the editor in chief, Westmore Dahn, were under constant security harassment for the paper's reportage. Before the establishment of the *Sun Times*, Mr. Darpoh was arrested and imprisoned for six months at Belleh Yallah, a notorious prison located in the jungle, for allegedly publishing antigovernment articles in foreign news organs.

The *Daily Observer*, where I began my journalism career, was shut down by the Doe regime in 1984, principally to prevent the paper from covering the 1985 presidential election. Having ruthlessly suppressed the media and the political opposition, Doe rigged the election and was declared president. This was how I went to work for the *Sun Times*, from where I traveled to the United States in 1986. While I was in the United States, however, the ban on the *Observer* was lifted; but the regime also banned the *Sun Times* for antigovernment reporting. This was how, upon my return home in 1987, I was working with the *Observer* at the time Allison ordered my detention.

Notwithstanding the encouragement to stay put in the United States during those very challenging days, I was determined to return home to contribute to the development of Liberia with my newly acquired knowledge to help make a difference for the common good. I am grateful to God that, irrespective of the challenges along the way, nothing has prevented me from fulfilling the desire to help make a difference in the life of my beloved country and people.

My foster mother, the beautiful and elegant Mrs. Martha Gene Mason-Williams, who was born in Lexington, Sinoe County, and was married to my foster father, the Honorable A. A. Williams in Grand Bassa County, had a favorite church hymn that she usually sang at home, where we were imbued with a strong sense of trust in God. This old song, which was played occasionally on the Christian station Eternal Love Winning Africa

(ELWA) Radio, has a line that goes: "Hold your peace, and the Lord will fight your battle." It is that blessed assurance that has taken me through every challenge in life, including my encounter with General Allison.

So it was that, in 1989, the all-powerful General Allison was disgracefully brought down from power due to what was mostly seen to be trumped-up charges to get rid of him. This reminds me of a Liberian parable: "Town trap is not for rat alone." A literal meaning of this wise expression is that any trap that is set in a town to catch rat could also catch other animals, such as a goat, sheep, dog, and chicken, among others.

The reality of the parable relates to General Allison, who was widely seen to have been destroyed in the similar manner he had participated in destroying the lives of many others by concocting charges against them.

There were speculations that as part of the process to weaken Doe's grip on power, his enemies had conspired to eliminate Allison, whose leadership of the military apparently made it difficult to contain the military and prevail over Doe. A few months after Allison's fall from power and his imprisonment at the notorious Belleh Yallah prison, the civil war began. As reflected earlier in this chapter, the TRC testimony by former National Security Agency assistant director Armah Youlo regarding General Allison is a testament to Allison's power over the military and within the Doe regime.

How sad that Allison became a victim of the vicious process he and his likes used over the years to rise to power and maintain a grip on power by eliminating others, including otherwise-well-meaning citizens who were falsely implicated in one plot or the other.

When I returned to Monrovia to work in the government following the end of the civil war, I encountered the NSA gentleman who was associated with T-Max and once offered him a lift. During the ride, I used the opportunity to thank him for what he did in 1987 to save my life. In response, he said even though he was part of the government, his primary goal was service to country. He said it was that guiding principle that informed his public service and that was why he did what he could to protect journalists like me and others as well as newspapers like the *Daily Observer*, which were striving to advocate for the common good of society.

As a biblical saying goes, "He who lives by the sword shall die by the sword." This proverb comes from Matthew 26:52, in which one of the disciples of our Lord and Savior Jesus Christ is described as having struck the servant of the high priest and cut off his ear. "Then Jesus said unto him, put up again thy sword into his place; for all they that take the sword shall perish with the sword." According to the Bible, this incident occurred at the time of Jesus's arrest, which led to his crucifixion on the cross to save mankind from the bondage of sin.

Whatever were the transgressions of Mr. and Mrs. Allison, however, the manner in which their lives ended is totally unacceptable. The manner in which they were tortured and killed was against the rule of law and the Christian principle to care for one another and protect the sanctity of life.

Following General Allison's downfall, I was interviewed by the media to give my impression about the fate that had befallen the once-powerful defense minister. I made it clear that it was unacceptable for General Allison to be denied the right to due process of law. I indicated that even though General Allison violated my civil rights and denied many others due process, there was no justification to deny him his legal rights. And I suppose the same goes for his wife.

CHAPTER FIVE
Confronting the Reality of a Broken Country

I n an interview published in *Newsweek* magazine on October 2, 2011, President Ellen Johnson Sirleaf said she did not realize just how broken Liberia was before she was sworn in office in 2006. She said it had taken longer than she expected to begin building a functioning state. "We found a totally collapsed economy, dysfunctional institutions, lack of proper laws and policies, low capacity, and a value system upside down," she said.

My responsibilities in the government were nowhere near the burden of the entire country, which was rested on the shoulders of the president. However, the challenges I encountered were so daunting that many nights I would lie awake looking toward the ceiling in the darkness and tropical heat, wondering, "Lord, what have I gotten myself into?" In the absence of electricity, everywhere around was pitch-dark, which added to the heat and mosquitoes that made the night rest uncomfortable.

Equally important was that everywhere, from one end of Liberia to the other, was devastated by the war. The general population, those who survived the carnage, was destitute and in a state of desperation for relief. There was no time for procrastination. People were very desperate for answers and solutions to those daunting problems, such as the restoration of basic services, including medical, education, job availability, and food to feed millions of people rendered dispossessed by the war.

McClain's Resignation

For anyone abroad who went to Liberia to work to have succeeded at the time, you had to be physically, emotionally, and psychologically prepared for the challenges that you were to encounter in such a broken country with its dysfunctional institutions. And it became clear early on that Minister McClain did not seem fully prepared for the daunting task that confronted him as the government's chief spokesman in an immediate postwar country that had limited skilled and disciplined manpower as well as financial and material resources.

McClain's acceptance of the president's request to serve as the minister of information was like stepping back into a minefield or wading into unchartered waters. As reported in chapter 2, he was the minister of information at the time of the bloody April 12, 1980, military coup d'état in which President William R. Tolbert was murdered and thirteen senior government officials were publicly executed. I would learn from him that he very narrowly escaped death when he was pulled from the bus that was conveying those officials to be executed on the beach. He said it was a miracle when someone among the heavy security taking the prisoners to the beach recognized him. Amid the frenzy of the moment, McClain recalled how he was pulled off the bus by a man who recognized him and said, "This man is a country man. He is not a Congo man"—a reference to the ruling class that had been overthrown from power.

The military junta detained McClain for several months, and following his release, he left the country and never lived in Liberia again until the end of the civil upheaval. While in exile, he served as an Africa executive of the United Nations Educational, Scientific and Cultural Organization (UNESCO). It was following his retirement from UNESCO that he returned home to just quietly live in retirement.

From interacting with Mr. McClain, it was clear that he was still affected or haunted, to some extent, by the trauma from the 1980 bloody military takeover, during which he was almost executed.

Having lived out of the country for two decades, Mr. McClain appeared to have been caught completely off guard in relation to what it would have taken to again lead the Ministry of Information and manage the new Liberian media, which had been hardened by years of abuse under the previous regimes of Samuel Doe and Charles Taylor, as well as the brutal civil war.

After surviving those brutal regimes and the war, the Liberian media, despite limitations caused by brain drain and inadequate resources, had become aggressive and probing in their reportage under the new political dispensation. The postwar media landscape in Liberia was far different from those days when the state-owned media dominated the news in the 1970s. In those days, the state-run national broadcaster, ELBC radio and television, dominated the airways. Back then, there was only one major nongovernmental radio station, the Christian evangelizing ELWA Radio. Also in those days, there were only a few official and semiofficial newspapers.

Within the first year of the Sirleaf government, there were nearly forty radio stations, fifteen of which broadcast regularly in Monrovia and about twenty-four local stations in other parts of the country. UNMIL also operated one radio station that transmitted to most parts of the country, as well as one government-operated station, the Liberia Broadcasting System (LBS), which was rehabilitated with support from the Chinese. Added to the media list were over a dozen newspapers and three television stations. The number of media outlets has continued to increase.

A notable aspect of this new era was that the media operated mostly without government restrictions and were free to openly criticize public officials, including the president, without retribution. And the media's criticism of the government of the day and its officials were often scathing, a complete difference from those days of mostly government promotional or patronizing journalism.

There were also no government restrictions on the growing access to the Internet, nor did the government monitor e-mail or Internet chat rooms. Widespread public access to cell phones—where individuals could call in to radio and television studios and participate live in discussions, pose questions to studio guests, or text their comments or questions—was also a new phenomenon that was gaining popularity. Many newspapers and radio stations also subsequently established online editions, some with blogs for public comments.

Nevertheless, the most difficult challenge that forced McClain's departure less than a year on the job was the very limited financial and technical support to undertake the very critical task of articulating the government's policies and programs to the general public. The Liberian people were now beginning to openly question their government and demand answers. The Ministry of Information, which is supposed to provide information to the public regarding the activities of their government, was clearly unprepared to cope, considering that the government's first national budget was just a puny US$80 million, from which humanitarian and other programs were funded to help bring relief to the war-weary populace. Mostly confined to his office and kept out of the loop of the day-to-day affairs of the government, Minister McClain decided to resign less than a year on the job.

After McClain's resignation was made public, there was a media report that certain other officials of the ministry were also planning to resign due to the lack of adequate financial and logistical support from the government, which had seriously hampered the ministry's ability to ineffectively manage the dissemination of government information to the general public. I was one of those who had contemplated departing out of frustration due to the challenges at the ministry, which made one appear inefficient and like an idiot.

Upon hearing the report, Mr. McClain invited me to dinner at his residence and encouraged me to remain at the ministry. He said that he did not want it to appear like he was encouraging the departure of competent individuals like myself to also leave as he was leaving. "My young friend," as he always referred to me, "I have no doubt that you will continue to play a critical role at the ministry because of your experience and performance."

A confidant of the president also called me and appealed to me to reconsider my decision to resign. She said that I would have a critical role to play in administering the affairs of the ministry because the new minister being appointed did not have a trained media background. She also assured me that the president was now keen on providing the necessary financial support to enable the ministry become more effective.

Mr. McClain was later appointed Liberia's ambassador to Senegal, where he served for several years before his retirement.

Bropleh's Appointment

Mr. McClain was succeeded by the Reverend Dr. Laurence Konmla Bropleh, a gifted eloquent speaker and minister of the gospel. Also a young person like most of us within the leadership of the ministry, Bropleh's appointment brought some needed boost in the function of the ministry as we complemented each other very well.

With a strategy focused on frequent press conferences and interviews broadcast mostly on radio, which has been the most popular medium of information dissemination throughout the country, the Information Ministry became proactive in articulating the government's policies and programs to the general Liberian public. Minister Bropleh and I coordinated very well in keeping the Liberian people abreast of issues regarding the government and the state of the country that the government itself and the general populace soon began to appreciate the relevance of the Information Ministry in the dissemination of public information.

Part of our information-dissemination strategy also included arranging regular press conferences and interviews, which also involved officials from various ministries and agencies, among others, to address the public on issues related to their respective agencies and functions. The Ministry of Information's weekly press conference, which was launched during our tenure, has continued as the ministry's primary media forum, carried live on radio. Even on a regular basis, the president herself conducted live interviews from studios of radio stations, which enabled members of the general public to ask her questions on issues of importance to them.

Minister Bropleh fondly referred to me as his "secret weapon" because of the appreciable level of professionalism and effectiveness in the performance of my responsibilities as the chief technician in the collecting, processing, and dissemination of public information. Long before he got on board, I had coined an expression—"the government inherited a dysfunctional system of governance," which became really popular. Many people often made joke of the "dysfunctional system of governance" phrase because I used it very frequently in interviews.

At a time when most Liberians, in a state of desperation due to deprivation, wanted quick fixes to the myriad of problems, I always used this phrase to remind them that it would take enormous effort and resources over a considerable period to rebuild our broken country. Over time, the expression resonated as the public began to understand that the rebuilding process was not going to be overnight.

Upon taking office, the eloquent and well-engaging Minister Bropleh also coined his own slogan—"changing minds, changing attitudes," entreating Liberians that national progress would be snail-paced as long as people are stuck in the old mind-set, which proved to be counterproductive in the past. He often opined that the government could build skyscrapers and other modern infrastructure, but all that would amount to nothing if people remained in their old mind-set, which was responsible for the destruction of our country and kept the general population impoverished.

During the first two years of Bropleh's tenure, MICAT became more effective in executing its functions to keep the Liberian public informed about the government's policies, programs, and functions.

Despite these groundbreaking developments in public information dissemination that positioned the Information Ministry in the center of government operations, not much was done in terms of institutional building. There was a lack of serious effort to revitalize the Liberia News Agency (LINA), the Department of Press and Public Affairs, the *New Liberian* newspaper, the broadcast division, MICAT television division, and the Central Printing Press—all critical components to fully enhance the capacity of the ministry and position it back to its prewar status.

The Sex Scandal

Even though Minister Bropleh and I had a very close working relationship, there were moments of serious policy differences, which would rock the boat and eventually make working together difficult. Our first major difference of opinion occurred in February 2007, following the outbreak of a sex scandal involving a prominent government official in the Office of the President, which led to the resignation of that official.

The sex scandal became public when a local newspaper, the *Independent*, published on its front page a photograph of the minister engaged in a sexual act with two women. The publication of the photo was clearly a violation of Liberian laws regarding public obscenity.

When the photograph was first published, the Justice Ministry wanted to immediately have the paper's editor, Sam Dean, arrested for publishing pornography, which is illegal under Liberian laws. At the Information Ministry, I took the lead in engagements with the Justice Ministry regarding how to resolve what turned out to be a major crisis for the government, which resulted in the resignation of the minister of state for presidential affairs—a position equivalent to that of the White House chief of staff. During those meetings, which involved Deputy Minister Elizabeth Hoff and myself, we were able to prevail upon Justice Ministry officials to allow the Press Union of Liberia, the professional body responsible for media entities and journalists, to look into the matter and institute whatever sanctions that were necessary against the media entity instead of the government immediately taking actions. I strongly subscribe to the view that whatever is legal may not necessarily be politically expedient.

Our recommendation, which was accepted by the Justice Ministry, was against the background that having the editor arrested would be wrongly interpreted in the public domain that the new government was beginning to clamp down on the local media by instituting actions against the newspaper for exposing an official caught in a very embarrassing sex scandal.

Considering the history of the Liberian media and journalists when they were terrorized under regimes of the recent past, most Liberians would have simply regarded the arrest of the editor as similar to the manner in which previous regimes operated to clamp down on press freedom. We wanted to ensure that this would no longer be the case under the new political dispensation.

Both Liz and I strongly supported the proposal to have the PUL take the lead in dealing with this ethical and legal breach on the part of the *Independent* because of our backgrounds as journalists who had led the Press Union. We also understood the need for the government to help empower the PUL to police its membership. It was our considered opinion that giving the Press Union the opportunity to handle matters of professional and ethical transgressions on the part of its members would help empower the PUL and prevent the government from getting easily involved in media-related matters. This would prevent the government from instituting actions that could be tantamount to abuse of press freedom.

Having conducted their own investigation without any involvement of the government, the Press Union found the *Independent* newspaper culpable of serious ethical misconducts and imposed some penalties against the newspaper. However, the *Independent* flatly refused to accept the PUL's decision on grounds that the organization was not clothed with the legal authority to sanction it. The paper asserted its constitutional right to freedom of speech and of the press and then went ahead to defiantly publish the pornographic photos for the second time on its front page. This development caused consternation within certain circles, especially among religious leaders, who brought the government to task for allowing individuals to flagrantly violate the law, as was the case of the newspaper, in the name of freedom of the press.

While the *Independent*'s edition containing the pornographic photos was on the newsstands on the morning of February 27, 2007, I did a live interview in the studio of a radio station. By the time I walked out of the studio and turned my cell phone on, there were already several missed calls from Minister Hoff. "What's up,

Liz? I noticed that you've been trying to get to me, but I was in studio," I indicated when I quickly returned her call.

"Where are you, Gabriel? We have a very serious problem here this morning, and you need to come to the office as quickly as possible for us to figure out how to deal with it," she stated. "The *Independent* has published the sex photos again. Larry came to my office pissed, and he's gone to the mansion to see the president because he said he will shut down the paper for defiantly breaking the law."

Larry is the nickname for Dr. Laurence Bropleh. As children of the 1960s and 1970s, we usually address one another informally by first name. In light of the *Independent*'s defiance by reproducing the pornographic photos, Minister Bropleh had gone to the Executive Mansion to consult with the president and seek her approval for him to arbitrarily shut down the newspaper, an action that was deemed to be in keeping with the Information Ministry's statutory responsibility.

Immediately after I got off the phone with Deputy Minister Hoff, I called Minister Bropleh's cell phone. "What's up, Larry? What's going on?" I inquired.

"I just arrived at the mansion to see the president," he responded. "We have to shut down that paper today for breaking the law and continuing to be defiant. We cannot allow that."

Although I expressed the need for us to meet as a cabinet and agree on a course of action before the matter was taken to the president, it was already late. The minister reminded me that I was the very one who led the charge in advocating for the Press Union to handle this matter. However, given the newspaper's refusal to abide by the PUL's decision and defiantly decided to publish the pornographic photos the second time, the government was left with no alternative but to step in and act in the public interest.

As I entered my vehicle, I told the driver to do whatever it took to get me to the office as soon as possible. Upon my arrival at the ministry, I rushed to Minister Hoff's office. We both began to brainstorm on how the government could take appropriate actions against the newspaper without imposing an arbitrary ban, which could be tantamount to a violation of press freedom. We both understood that shutting down the newspaper outside the due process of law would be contrary to the Liberian Constitution even though the Information Ministry had the statutory authority to arbitrarily ban news organs.

The statutory power of the Information Ministry to proscribe news organs emanated from a decree of the People's Redemption Council, the Samuel Doe-led military junta that seized power in 1980. Upon the coming into effect of the new Liberian Constitution of the second republic on January 16, 1986, all decrees contravening the constitution should have been rendered ineffective in keeping with the provisions of the said constitution.

However, the problem with Liberia's return to civilian or constitutional rule in 1986 was that Doe brutally maintained power by rigging the 1985 presidential election. Although he took off the military uniform and adorned civilian attire to give his regime a civilian outlook, he still operated like a military ruler. And following the end of Doe's rule, the Taylor regime also relied on the decree empowering the Ministry of Information to criminalize freedom of speech and of the press. Under the respective regimes of Doe and Taylor, news organs were often closed without due process of law while journalists and political and human rights activists were harassed, terrorized, jailed, or even murdered in cold blood.

This was the authority, and I may add, problem we inherited when we assumed leadership at the Ministry of Information. We, therefore, had to use our discretion when to enforce and not to enforce the ministry's statutory responsibilities regarding arbitrary closure of news organs. The laws regarding arbitrary closure of news organ were unjust, and there was no need for their enforcement in a democratic environment. Rather, there was a need to scrap all laws that criminalized freedom of speech and of the press off the books.

So it was while I was still in Minister Hoff's office as we discussed what to do in order to prevent the banning of the *Independent* that Dr. Bropleh walked in from the mansion and told us that the president had endorsed his recommendation to close the newspaper in light of the prevailing circumstances. He then instructed me to immediately organize a press conference for him to announce the government's action against the newspaper.

While the three of us were in Minister Hoff's office, Liz and I pleaded in vain with the minister to reconsider the decision to arbitrarily shut down the newspaper. Having realized that we had failed to persuade him, I simply told him that the decision to ban the newspaper would backfire with condemnation from the Press Union, international rights organizations, and others. However, the minister expressed confidence that he had been assured by leaders of the Press Union that they would support his decision as the newspaper had defied the PUL regarding the matter related to the pornographic photos.

At the press conference during which then Press Union president George Barpeen, who had been invited, sat together with the minister and myself, Minister Bropleh announced the revocation of the *Independent* newspaper's license for one year and ordered the closure of its offices with immediate effect. Following the press conference, riot police were sent to the paper's offices, the staff violently thrown out, and the doors sealed with padlocks.

This development set off a wave of condemnation, as I had predicted, from the Press Union, international human rights advocacy groups, and opposition politicians, among others. Although Barpeen had attended the press conference supposedly as a show of support for the ministry's action, he declined to comment, only saying that the PUL would study the situation and respond accordingly. The following day, the PUL issued a strongly worded press statement in which it condemned the government for the arbitrary closure of the *Independent* newspaper without due process of law.

Following the PUL's lead, several international organizations that promote press freedom and human rights around the world (including the New York–based Committee to Protect Journalists) issued statements condemning the government for the arbitrary closure of the newspaper.

The Press Union also condemned the seizure of the newspaper's offices without a court order and called on the government to unlock the newspaper's door and "submit to the rule of law." The PUL said while "it acknowledges the reckless ethical misconduct" of the newspaper, it would resist any attempt by the government to "institute mob justice" against the paper.

As professional journalists and former leaders of the PUL, Liz and I had a better understanding of the media landscape unlike Minister Bropleh, and we could foresee what the national and international impacts of the government's arbitrary action against the newspaper would be. The government had dug itself into a hole.

Concerned by what they considered to be a very serious development, the US ambassador to Liberia, H. E. Donald E. Booth, visited MICAT and met with Minister Hoff and myself to hear the government's reasons for the newspaper's closure. After igniting the firestorm, Minister Bropleh traveled abroad, and Deputy Minister Hoff was left to act in his stead.

During the meeting, the ambassador noted that freedom of the press was a critical requirement for US foreign assistance and that they did not want the new Liberian government, despite the abundance of American goodwill, to be affected because of the action related to the *Independent* newspaper. Plans were to soon begin for the historic visit of President George W. Bush to Liberia, although information about the visit was still a closely held secret.

The meeting appeared to have gone well. We provided Ambassador Booth with the necessary information without having to defend such an unconstitutional act. We reaffirmed the government's commitment to creating the enabling environment to promote freedom of speech and of the press. We briefed him about laws on the books and some of the statutory functions of MICAT that inhibited free speech, as well as the need to repeal them. We did caution that while efforts were being made to ensure that MICAT was generally restrained in executing some of its statutory responsibilities, such as the arbitrary closure of news organs, there was a possibility for such laws to be enforced until they were scrapped off the books.

The American ambassador and his information officer, Ms. Meg Riggs, left the meeting after expressing that they were well pleased with the efforts that were being made to reform an agency that had long been an instrument of state terror by the enforcement of laws to stifle freedom of speech and of the press.

Having come to serve at MICAT with the conviction that I would not support the arbitrary closure of any news organ without due process of law, I became deeply disturbed about the developments regarding the *Independent*. During that time, my dear friend Mr. James E. Cooper Jr. and I decided to have lunch one afternoon. When we met at a restaurant, Jimmy, which is his nickname, noticed that I was withdrawn and not upbeat as usual; and he inquired as to what was happening.

I explained to him the developments regarding the closure of the newspaper, how it would negatively affect the image of the country, and how it had the potential to ruin my credibility as a journalist and former leader of the PUL, who was expected to protect and promote press freedom. I recalled that in Liberia's recent history, many otherwise-well-meaning journalists who became officials at MICAT have had their credibility destroyed by being made to enforce antimedia laws—the very laws that negatively affected them when they were also practicing as journalists.

Just a few years older than I am, Jimmy stood at the height of about five feet plus. At the time, he weighed between two hundred and three hundred pounds, and he was an avid weight lifter with a muscular physique. He and I have been very good friends since we got acquainted during my days in exile in Sacramento, the capital of the great state of California, which is ranked as one of the largest economies in the world.

A retired police officer from California, Jimmy served as chief of office staff for then senator Leroy F. Greene of the California State Assembly. He also served as deputy director general of the Library of Congress in Washington DC during the administration of President Bill Clinton, among other responsibilities, before he returned to Liberia at the end of the war to reclaim and manage his family properties, including a rubber farm. His father, James E. Cooper Sr., was one of the earliest Liberians sent to the United States for study to return home and establish the Civil Service Agency (CSA), which was aimed at professionalizing the government workforce. It was while in the United States that the senior Cooper met and married an African American woman, who was Jimmy's mother.

Jimmy was like a mentor, given his vast experience in security and governmental matters. I told him that I wished I was in a position to have gotten to the president to make a case against the paper's closure before the government decided to do so. I was also acutely aware that appearing to oppose a decision the government had made could get me fired. So I poured my heart out to Jimmy, giving him a sense of how I found myself between a rock and a hard place, so to speak.

Jimmy's response to me was direct and specific, and I was emboldened to move forward to request a meeting with Madam President with immediacy. Using a biblical context to make his point, Jimmy reminded me that this might be the time that God might have placed me in the position I held to help move Liberia in the right direction. He said failure to take a principled position now would be the beginning of compromises that might help undermine Liberia's progress and, eventually, my credibility. He noted that if I felt very strongly that the government's action was unconstitutional and that the president needed to be given a broader picture regarding the implications surrounding the arbitrary closure of the newspaper, then I should make an effort to meet her and give her the benefit of the doubt.

Regarding the possibility of dismissal for raising such a matter with the president, Jimmy simply said, "Well, I don't think that's something that you should worry about. Just focus on doing what is right, and God will take care of the rest." As we conversed, I took notes on salient points that could be raised in the meeting with the president, including some recommendations for a possible resolution of the matter.

Speeding from the restaurant to my office to establish contact with the president's office, my thoughts wandered back to the 1980s when I was a cub reporter interning at the *Daily Observer* newspaper. I recalled that the first front-page lead story of the paper that carried my byline was titled "Be Prepared to Say No." The article quoted the Reverend Father Christopher Kandakai, a priest of the Episcopal Church of Liberia who served as the keynote speaker at the 1983 baccalaureate service for the graduating class of the University of Liberia. In his charge to the graduates, Father Kandakai noted that as they go into the world, they should be prepared to stand up for what is right and say no to any situation they may encounter that might be inimical to the public good.

Upon my arrival at the office, I immediately contacted my dear friend and colleague Cyrus W. Badio, then press secretary to the president. Cyrus and I go many years back to the 1980s, when we were both out in the field as news reporters. Cyrus was a rising star as a broadcaster with the state-run Liberia Broadcasting System (LBS) when the civil war began. He was among a large group of Liberian journalists, including myself, who voted with our feet to seek refuge in the United States due to the civil upheavals. During our days in exile, Badio also served as president of the Association of Liberian Journalists in the Americas (ALJA), the organization established in exile by Liberian journalists to continue to advocate for free speech and democratic governance in Liberia. After the war ended, we both returned to work in the new government in senior leadership positions related to public affairs.

Mr. Badio then put me in contact with Mr. Amara Konneh, the young and enterprising then deputy chief of staff in the Office of the President, who scheduled me to meet with the president that very evening. Both Messrs. Badio and Konneh also disagreed with the decision to arbitrarily shut down the newspaper.

Madam President was magnanimous enough to grant me audience in her office around 7:00 p.m. to 8:00 p.m. that night. She began the meeting by saying that she endorsed the minister's decision to close down the newspaper in light of the paper's defiance and blatant disregard for the law by publishing the pornographic photographs the second time after they were made to understand that doing so was in breach of the law. She also indicated that the minister assured her that the action to shut down the newspaper was in line with the statutory authority of MICAT.

"Minister Williams," the president noted, "I heard that you have reservations regarding the decision to close down the newspaper. Let me hear the reasons for your objection."

In my response, I told the president that I was not opposed to the government taking action against the newspaper for its violation of the law. However, I was strongly opposed to the arbitrary manner in which the paper was shut down, which I felt was unconstitutional and, therefore, illegal.

The president leaned back in her chair behind her desk and just nodded her head as I briefly took her down memory lane by reminding her that when media houses were arbitrarily shut down and journalists were brutalized and imprisoned during the respective Doe and Taylor regimes, they were enforcing the very laws that we were also now invoking. I told her that the statutory authority that was being enforced by MICAT was derived from Decree 88A, which was promulgated by the People's Redemption Council regime led by Master Sergeant Samuel Doe. Decree 88A criminalized freedom of speech and of the press. Following the 1980 coup d'état, the military regime suspended the constitution of Liberia and ruled by imposing decrees.

I also told the president that article 15 of the Liberian Constitution, which came into effect in 1986, guarantees freedom of the press and that according to my limited knowledge of the constitution, all decrees and laws that contravene the said constitution have no legal effect. This meant that Decree 88A had been nullified since the new constitution came into effect at the end of military rule in 1986. Therefore, I continued, it was my considered opinion that if the newspaper were to go to court to seek legal redress against the government for wrongful closure on constitutional grounds, the court was very likely to rule in favor of the newspaper.

I reminded the president that those of us who were strong advocates for press freedom, including herself, did not hesitate to condemn those regimes for failure to adhere to the rule of law. "If we're doing the same things today that were done in the past, as reflected by this arbitrary action, how different are we from those regimes?" I inquired, looking the president straight in the eye.

As I concluded to get her feedback to my submission, it was clear that the president was moved by the merits of my argument, and she ordered a reversal of the decision to close the newspaper with immediate effect. The president acknowledged that as a result of my submission, it was now clear to her that mistakes were made in the decision to close the newspaper. She had been advised by the minister that the closure of the newspaper would be within the statutory authority of MICAT as a consequence of the newspaper's legal and professional transgressions. Then she asked me, "So what do we do to correct the mistakes?"

I told her that the government should acknowledge publicly that there was a mistake in how the newspaper was closed because of its failure to pursue due process of law and promise the Liberian people that such a mistake would not be repeated. I also recommended that the arbitrary ban imposed on the newspaper should be lifted. I indicated that the acknowledgment of mistake should be publicized in the local media and communicated to relevant international entities. I assured the president that such public admission, which was unprecedented in the history of any government in Liberia or unusual of governments in Africa, would calm the wave of local and international condemnation that was already against the government for the action.

I had no doubt that this unprecedented decision to publicly admit error would be an added boost to the reform and democratic credentials of the government, for it has been a rare occurrence in Africa or many parts of the world for a government to publicly admit mistakes or apologize to its citizens for wrong policies or actions.

The president accepted the recommendations as noted, and she added her wisdom with a directive regarding how MICAT should proceed in quickly bringing an end to the problem.

Those in the president's office during the meeting were then presidential press secretary Badio and presidential deputy chief of staff Konneh, a confidant of the president, whose formal title was deputy minister of state for public affairs. Mr. Konneh would later become minister of planning for economic affairs and minister of finance (the ministry was later renamed the Ministry of Finance and Development Planning). However, the two gentlemen only listened and did not participate while the president and I discussed. Nevertheless, both of them disagreed with the closure of the newspaper. My buddy Cyrus told me that had the president sought his input before endorsing the minister's decision, he would have advised against it.

Indeed, following dissemination of the government's position in the media beginning with a front-page report in the *Inquirer* newspaper, the strategy worked so well that it undercut almost all of the activities of those who advocated for boycott of the government and had begun a smear campaign to liken the new administration to brutal regimes of the recent past. Many of those who had condemned the government soon began to praise it for the unprecedented admission of error, and they urged against any further antigovernment protest actions.

Meanwhile, the *Independent* newspaper went to the Supreme Court of Liberia seeking redress for wrongful closure. The supreme court ordered the contending parties to return to status quo ante, interpreted by lawyers to mean that the paper should return to its normal function while the matter was under determination. In May 2007, Minister Bropleh announced the reinstatement of the *Independent*'s license.

The Struggle and Sacrifice to Make a Difference

Amid the developments regarding the *Independent* newspaper, a former senior official, who had served in previous Liberian governments, came to my office to thank me because he said he had closely followed the effort I had made to amicably resolve the media crisis. Nevertheless, he warned me to be extremely careful because what I had done in resolving the media problem, however laudable, could create some enemies for me in the government. It was his thought that there were those within the government who could now see me as a threat to their interests. He spoke of how there have been individuals, otherwise found to be promising and well-meaning, who have been lied upon and made to suffer retributions—including job dismissal, prosecution, imprisonment, or even death because their activities were seen as a threat to the interest of others in government or the political realm.

He indicated that even though the president endorsed the recommendations that I made in order to resolve the problem, certain powerful individuals within the government who might oppose the move or begin to feel threatened by my action could retaliate by going to the very president and pressure her to have me removed from the ministry based on allegations they could dredge up as a justification. "My young man, you have to remember that this is Liberia, and things are not always done the way rational people would normally expect," he added. "I just want you to watch your back from now on."

Several days after the discussion with the former official, I got a call from a senior official at the Executive Mansion, a confidant of the president, who blasted me for undermining the minister of information for having the president reverse the minister's decision against the *Independent*. She indicated that it was about time that the government set an example to show that irresponsible reporting within the media would be seriously dealt with. She reminded me that certain journalists were Charles Taylor loyalists, such as the *Independent*'s editor, who were using a section of the media to wage a destructive war against the government and its officials in order to undermine the government.

I was very much aware that certain journalists and media entities at the time were supporters of Charles Taylor, and as a result, they were hostile toward the new government. Those journalists and media entities were mostly negative in their coverage or reportage related to the government because most Taylor supporters felt that President Sirleaf had betrayed the former warlord turned president by having him arrested and turned over for prosecution for his role in Sierra Leone's civil war.

Here is an example of how some of Taylor's supporters reacted to the manner in which they felt he was betrayed by Madam Sirleaf: Fellow journalist Gus Jaeploe and I have been good friends since the 1980s, when he was a reporter with the government-owned *New Liberian* newspaper published by MICAT while I was a reporter with the independent *Daily Observer* newspaper and later the *Sun Times*. He was a leading figure in the government media establishment during Taylor's regime.

At the start of the Sirleaf administration, Mr. Jaeploe was unemployed. Seeing the need to help my old friend, I once invited him to lunch and offered him a job for him to return to work at MICAT. He said he could not see himself working for the government to promote Madam Sirleaf because of her betrayal of Taylor. Even while he was broke and I had to give him money for commercial transportation after our lunch, Jaeploe's parting words were that he would rather die in poverty than betray his conscience for financial gains. Well known for his rhetorical jabs and parables, I was deeply touched by the conviction of Jaeploe—a man who was prepared to say no to what did not seem right to him irrespective of the consequences.

Whatever were the issues between Taylor's supporters and the government of President Sirleaf, there was no justification to arbitrarily shut down any news organ even though such draconian measures were very common during the Taylor regime, with which the pro-Taylor journalists were associated. This is why I was not prepared to support any extrajudicial action to make the editor of the *Independent* the poster child for press freedom in Liberia, especially when the government was seen to be making progress in the promotion of freedom of speech and of the press.

As noted in chapter 2, I accepted to serve at MICAT with a determination to help change the ministry from an entity of state repression to an agency of the government focused on promoting free speech. We, as a people, could not continue to repeat the mistakes of the past and expect different results. The failure to learn from past mistakes and change course for the better has been the main reason why Liberia has experienced mindless death and destruction, progress has been snail-paced, and a vast mass of the people have endured abject poverty.

Needless to say, I was taken aback by the manner in which I was addressed by the official, whom I respected a lot because we were all together in the vanguard advocating for press freedom during the days of the Doe and Taylor regimes. To avoid a confrontation on the phone, I simply told her that everything that was done to resolve the problems regarding the *Independent* newspaper was approved by the president and that if she had any reservation in this regard, she needed to take that up with the president herself.

Immediately after I got off the phone with the lady from the president's office, I called my special assistant in my office and instructed that I did not want to see anyone or take any phone call at that time except when it was extremely important. I was upset by the manner in which I was berated by the lady for doing nothing wrong, and I simply needed time alone to regain my composure in light of the unprovoked verbal attack.

As for the minister, the only reaction I got from him regarding my intervention in the *Independent* matter was when he returned from a trip to the United States and conveyed greetings to me from some mutual friends. Also recruited from the United States to serve in the government, like myself, the minister and I shared many mutual friends and acquaintances in America. As we casually discussed in his office about friends abroad and the prevailing situation on the ground in Liberia, the conversation quickly drifted briefly to the *Independent* situation. As we exchanged views regarding developments surrounding the newspaper, the minister said, "Gabriel, your friends are not happy with you for what you did."

I then quickly inquired, "Which of the friends, and why?"

He then responded, "Never mind, they just wanted me to let you know that they're not happy with the way you handled this newspaper thing."

We both briefly went back and forth as I tried to explain to him that my intervention was meant to save the government and us from the unnecessary embarrassment and backlash generated as a result of such an unconstitutional decision. Meanwhile, he was of the opinion that once the decision was made, we should have just left it alone because the ministry acted in keeping with its statutory authority.

Bropleh's Campaign to Eliminate Opponents

Following the *Independent* newspaper's brouhaha, there were growing policy differences between the minister and virtually all of the deputy and assistant ministers who comprised MICAT's cabinet, especially those of us with a journalism background. Besides Deputy Minister for Administration Cletus Sieh, my fellow media colleagues were Deputy Minister Hoff and Abu Kamara, the assistant minister for information services. The growing policy divide between the minister and key members of the MICAT cabinet had led to normal functions of the ministry being partially stalled.

Meanwhile, there were stage whispers within the corridors of the presidency that the president was becoming very concerned about developments at MICAT, which could lead to possible dismissals. However, instead of instituting changes at MICAT, which the president could have simply done without question, the president decided to visit the ministry and meet with the cabinet and relevant senior staff in order to better understand matters and shake up things to get MICAT back on course in its public information dissemination.

The meeting was held in the office of Minister Bropleh even though he was not inside to participate. He had first met the president in person and given his side of the story, so to speak. During that meeting, the president indicated that there were certain media programs that MICAT had not undertaken, such as the public awareness programs on the Poverty Reduction Strategy (PRS), the general framework for national development. Therefore, she came to inquire from leaders of the ministry what was wrong. Each of my colleague officials in the office gave their views on what they thought were responsible, major among which was the seriousness of inadequate financial and material resources to make the ministry more functional.

Among MICAT officials at the meeting were Deputy Ministers Sieh and Hoff, as well as the Reverend J. Emmanuel Z. Bowier, who was a consultant assigned at MICAT. Reverend Bowier was assigned at MICAT under a government program to build institutional capacity by recruiting retired government officials and other professionals and have them deployed in various government ministries and agencies. Reverend Bowier, who started his journalism career as a cadet at MICAT in the 1970s, rose through the ranks to become minister. He also served in a diplomatic capacity as minister counselor for press and public affairs at the Embassy of Liberia in the United States. He is widely respected as a walking encyclopedia on all things Liberia. It was a blessing to have him at the ministry to help provide guidance for us, who were mostly young officials born in the 1960s and 1970s. More on Reverend Bowier can be read in chapter 15.

After the president spoke during the meeting, she requested the input of everyone in attendance regarding what the challenges were and what needed to be done to remedy the situation. Accordingly, all my colleagues gave their perspectives regarding the state of affairs at MICAT. I was the last in the group to speak.

As I began to speak when it was my turn, giving an overview of what could be accomplished at MICAT with the requisite support, the president immediately interrupted me. She said, "You have these great ideas, and you have demonstrated the capabilities in the performance of your duties. But in recent times, you have not been performing. When I inquired what was going on with you, I was told that you said that you no longer wanted to work in the government, that you wanted to return to your family in the States. Why do you want to leave?"

In response, I told Madam President that it was completely false that I had decided to leave the government and return to the United States. I indicated that if I had reached such a decision, I would have done the honorable thing of talking to her or writing her about it. Regarding the matter of slacking on the job lately, I presented to the president a folder containing media program proposals with budget inclusive, which had not been funded for months because I was told that there was a lack of funds. As I handed her the folder, I said, "Madam President, you know there is no way anyone can implement these programs without the requisite funding."

I was aware that a few months before the meeting, the president had authorized a certain amount of funding that was released to MICAT to begin the Poverty Reduction Strategy (PRS) media programs and other activities. However, the funds were not disbursed for the intended purposes. While visiting the Office of the President one day, I stopped by to pay a courtesy call on one of the principal advisors to the president. As we chatted in his office, the advisor then wanted to know as to why MICAT had not begun to execute certain media programs for which the president had provided some funds. I told him that the programs had not been executed because of lack of funding and that I was not aware that funds had been provided to the ministry in that regard.

The presidential advisor then showed me a photocopy of a check issued to the Ministry of Information, along with a photocopy of a letter addressed to the minister indicating the purpose for the check, which, he said, he personally hand-delivered to the minister. Nevertheless, other than the minister, almost everyone on the ministry's cabinet was not aware about the transfer of the funds to MICAT. During the meeting with the president, however, I simply said that I had not received any funding to implement the programs and left it at that. This was because I had not been officially informed that the funds in question had been authorized for MICAT.

As I attempted to delve further into the matter, the president interrupted me again and said, "Minister Williams, having heard what you've said, I will invite you and the minister to a meeting for us to talk when I have some time to do so. What I want all of you to do right now is to work together to get the ministry more functional."

I never heard anything about that money again. After the meeting, I learned from an aide close to the president that whenever she inquired about the media projects, the minister had repeatedly informed her that I was the obstacle to the projects' implementation. And that was how he told her that I wanted to leave the job and return to my family in the United States.

During the meeting at MICAT, having gotten a sense of the prevailing state of affairs at the ministry, the president decided to make available some funds directly to my office so as to enable me to undertake a quick media project. Liberia was less than a week from hosting the International Colloquium for Women's Empowerment, Leadership Development, International Peace and Security, which brought together hundreds of women from various parts of the world, on March 7–8, 2009. The conference was co-convened under President Sirleaf and then President Tarja Halonen of Finland, in concert with the Pan-African parliamentarians.

The media project, which had been stalled because of a lack of funds, was the production of a special edition of the government-owned *New Liberian* newspaper, published under the auspices of MICAT. The special edition profiled a number of Liberian women who have made or were making outstanding contributions to Liberian society and the world at large. Copies of the paper were distributed as a souvenir for the colloquium, also attended by thousands of women from across Liberia who jam-packed the stadium where the event was held in Monrovia.

Because of the puny budget of MICAT those days, the government had to consider other discretionary funding to support various media programs undertaken by the ministry.

The president then departed the MICAT building and headed straight to tour the Providence Island, the place the settlers who founded the modern state of Liberia first landed. The island, which is located on the Mesurado River near the Atlantic Ocean, is managed as a historic site under the auspices of MICAT. Minister Bropleh, who had a very close relationship with the president, rode with her to the Providence Island. On their way, the president advised him to nurture a good working relationship with the ministry's cabinet. As she closed the meeting with us, the president said the Minister was riding with her to the Providence Island, and that she was going to use that time to caution him on the need for a cordial working relationship at MICAT, something the Minister later confirmed.

However, there was no longer any good working relationship to be nurtured. Things got more conflicted from there on between the minister and myself. A deliberate campaign was already afoot to have me removed from the ministry, including such an unbelievable lie to the president, as narrated, that I wanted to leave the government. This was a deliberate campaign similar to those of our recent evil past in which innocent people were killed on trumped-up allegations.

The scheme was to suppress my work and make me appear ineffective and then inform the president that I was not performing. That would have been the basis for the president to fire me without question. The scheme backfired because the president was already well impressed with my performance as she had expressed on a number of occasions, including during that meeting. She recognized that something was not right with the accusations against me.

In June 2009, I received a call from the Office of the President indicating a date and time the president wanted to meet with me at the Executive Mansion. I had no idea what the meeting was about, but I reported for the meeting, which was held around 7:00 p.m. After I greeted her and she offered me a seat upon entering her office, the president quickly started off by asking, "What is going on between you and the minister? I have received numerous complaints from him against you lately."

I sat calmly and attentively, looking straight in the president's eye as she spoke, both of us alone in her office. Within a couple of minutes of speaking, the president began to say things that just blessed my heart at a time when I was beginning to battle many demons, as the expression goes, for a job that I did not even want to take in the first place.

"I want you to know that I have thoroughly checked into the allegations brought against you, and there has not been a single evidence of wrongdoing on your part," she said. She stated that I had been one of the most effective officials since the government's inception, at one time shouldering the leadership of MICAT even while I did not receive salaries for months.

The president understood very well that I was not one of those in the government driven by greed and the desire to squander public resources. As she acknowledged in her comment above, during my first year at MICAT, I worked for almost that entire year without a salary due to some bureaucratic mix-up. Having been informed about my salary situation, the president intervened herself and made some funds available to help sustain me while that challenge was addressed. She did so when I did not go to her to complain, nor did I even ask her for financial assistance.

After thanking me for a job well done at MICAT, the president then informed me that she had, nevertheless, decided to reassign me from MICAT to another post. This was to avoid an open conflict between the minister and myself, something that was a common occurrence at many government entities, especially during and since the war. Infighting hinders progress of any entity or body. In Liberia, it has sometimes resulted in physical altercation.

During the Taylor regime, the minister of information and his principal deputy were locked in a fistfight in the minister's office due to differences. A notable example of the danger of infighting in government was during the civil war when leaders of warring factions served together in a power-sharing government. Occasionally, differences among factional leaders resulted in violence and unnecessary destruction of life and property.

It was from that meeting with the president that I eventually ended up in a diplomatic post in the United States. As I was planning to depart the country, MICAT was engulfed in a major financial scandal that resulted in Minister Bropleh's removal from office, and he was sent to court for prosecution.

The accounts narrated reflect part of the challenges that are encountered in the process of transforming a broken country with a dysfunctional system of governance, such as Liberia. The country's progress has been snail-paced due to limited vision and greed, as has been the case in many other African countries. I am grateful to President Sirleaf for the confidence she reposed in me, without which I would have simply been dismissed when those lies and complaints against me reached her.

An ordained clergy of the United Methodist Church, the Reverend Dr. Laurence Bropleh was known to have exploited his relationship with the president, also a staunch Methodist, to influence the dismissal of certain officials within the government who incurred his ire. He had no compunction in going after individuals in the government who he regarded to have crossed him the wrong way.

For example, Minister Bropleh openly spoke of how he engineered the dismissal of Richmond Anderson, then deputy minister for administration at MICAT, by regularly complaining to the president that Anderson was not performing well and that there was a need for his replacement in order to enhance the operation of MICAT. Before the press statement from the Executive Mansion announcing Anderson's removal was released publicly, Bropleh told me that an official press statement to that effect was expected to be issued on that day by the Executive Mansion.

After I left Minister Bropleh's office, I went straight to Anderson's office to see if he had any inkling of what was unfolding regarding his dismissal. When I bolted into his office, everything seemed normal as he was in his usual jolly mood. After interacting with him, I retired to my office pondering what was unfolding. I returned to his office a couple of times before the call came from the president to thank him for his service, with a promise that he would be considered for a new appointment in due course, which did not happen.

As news of the dismissal sunk in, Anderson would joke about how I had gone to his office a few times behaving quite strangely by showing an unusual level of affection, and he was beginning to wonder what the heck was going on with me. Irrespective of the circumstances at the time, I regarded him as a friend and colleague I worked together with as part of a team of wonderful people at MICAT.

Anderson got out of favor with Minister Bropleh after he tipped off economic crimes investigators that he had given a check intended for MICAT to the minister, but the minister had failed to account for the check. Unfortunately, the investigators who were involved with the case were allegedly bribed by the minister, and that was the end of the investigation. An audit conducted by the General Auditing Commission a few years following his removal from MICAT revealed that Deputy Minister Anderson had alerted the government's economic crimes investigators to cover himself from liability after he failed to get the minister to account for the check concerned despite several inquiries.

After quashing the investigation, the minister apparently then set out to have Anderson removed from MICAT, apparently in retaliation for Anderson reporting him to be investigated for the funds in question. Anderson had spent many years at MICAT, rising from the level of a civil service employee to a presidential appointee. He first became a deputy minister at MICAT during the power-sharing Liberia National Transitional Government (LNTG), which came to power following the end of Taylor's reign and the civil war.

I had known Anderson since our days as news reporters, when he was a reporter with the Liberia News Agency (LINA) under the auspices of MICAT while I reporter for the independent newspaper *Daily Observer*. After he left MICAT, Anderson contested for and won a seat in the national legislature as a member of the House of Representatives.

Minister Bropleh also devised another scheme to have Cyrus Badio, then press secretary to the president, removed from his post. In what appeared to be a classic tale of divide and rule, the reverend prevailed upon the president to have me transferred to the Executive Mansion to succeed Mr. Badio as press secretary to the president. This move would have undoubtedly damaged the very good relationship that existed between my dear friend Badio and me, as he would have felt that I was part of a conspiracy to undermine him to take his job.

The move to have me succeed Badio was also part of the Methodist clergyman's plan to remove me from MICAT after I had begun to raise questions on matters of administrative malpractices at the ministry. Following an embarrassing encounter with the president on the day of the student riot at the Kendeja Cultural Center, which you will read about in the following pages, I was deeply pained by the thought of how I looked stupid and inefficient when the president asked me what caused the riot and I did not have the foggiest idea. From then on, I decided to become more proactive in terms of inquiring and speaking openly on matters of concern at MICAT.

Accordingly, I was invited to a meeting at the Executive Mansion, during which I was informed about the pending changes to have me succeed Badio as press secretary to the president. The meeting also covered an interview as to what programs and activities I would undertake during my tenure to enhance the efficiency of the office.

In response, I expressed thanks and appreciation for the confidence reposed in me for my preferment to serve as press secretary to the president. However, I noted that I could not accept the position considering the circumstances under which Badio was being relieved. I indicated that Badio and I had been good friends for nearly two decades.

I emphasized that given the circumstances under which Badio was being removed from the position, he could have reasons to believe that I was involved in a conspiracy to remove him from his post for me to take over. I said that I wanted to continue to enjoy a good relationship with my friend Cyrus when the government job was no more. In this light, I respectfully declined to accept the job. And that was how the meeting ended.

When I returned to my office, I called Badio and told him I wanted to see him in person as soon as possible for us to discuss a very urgent matter related to him. I told him not to come with his driver or anyone else and that he should pick me up from the gate at the back of the ministry.

As we drove alone, I informed Badio that I had been interviewed for his job to replace him but that I declined because of our friendship and also because I disagreed with the orchestrations that were at play to get rid of him. I told him that even though I declined the offer, someone else might be selected for the job if he did not move swiftly enough to counteract what was unfolding.

And sure enough, upon hearing that I had declined to succeed Badio, Minister Bropleh went back to the president with the fancy idea of appointing Elizabeth Hoff, who would make history as the first Liberian female to serve as press secretary to the president. The president thought that was a great idea, and Hoff was offered the post. She was also not interested, but it seemed like there was no alternative but for her to accept the job, especially after I had declined.

As Badio maneuvered to stall any appointment, tension increased between him and Bropleh. The reverend had openly expressed how he would frustrate Badio to the extent that Badio would leave Liberia and return to the United States. He also openly boasted that he would "clip my wings."

In the wake of growing tensions, the president decided to convene a meeting with Minister Bropleh, Press Secretary Badio, and Deputy Minister Hoff. According to information from the meeting, both men had a shouting match in the office of the president, who reportedly seemed to lean more toward Reverend Bropleh's point of view.

Sensing what was unfolding and realizing that he had nothing else to lose, Badio said he told the president something like "I'm glad you have so much trust in Reverend Bropleh. I hope that by the time he reveals his true character and you get to know who he is, it will not be too late."

Reverend Bropleh reportedly responded angrily to Badio's comment, and both men were engaged in intense verbal exchanges. The president then intervened to calm both men down, noting that she first did not realize that the problems between them appeared to be deep-rooted. She called an end to the meeting and instructed that the parties concerned should remain at their respective positions until she had time to sort things out.

Reverend Bropleh's Downfall due to Another Financial Scandal

Badio remained as press secretary to the president until 2012. Meanwhile, President Sirleaf was forced to let go of Bropleh in 2010 in the wake of a major financial scandal at MICAT, for which he was forwarded to court for prosecution. The scandal that resulted in his dismissal followed reports of a series of financial malpractices or scandals.

These included the scandal related to the Kendeja relocation program in 2008, for which the Reverend Dr. Laurence Bropleh could not account for more than $200,000. No actions were taken against him for the Kendeja scandal, which was the first major scandal for which Reverend Dr. Bropleh was investigated.

Before touching on the financial scandal that led to his dismissal in 2010, it is important to reflect on the first major scandal, which related to the Kendeja relocation program.

According to an audit of MICAT conducted by Liberia's General Auditing Commission (GAC), under then auditor general John S. Morlu II, $360,000 was allotted to MICAT for the relocation of residents and inhabitants of Kendeja, the national cultural center located near Monrovia, as well as to acquire a large piece of land to rebuild a new cultural center. The GAC audit of MICAT, which covered the period from 2006 to 2009, found that a total of $200,659.90 could not be accounted for, as the funds were paid off to certain individuals who were not residents of Kendeja without documentation to justify the disbursement.

In its founding, the GAC states, "We observed however, that payments were made in these individuals' names from the Kendeja relocation account number . . . with a total deposit of USD$213,000. The amount of USD$200,659.90 was withdrawn as per the bank statement without stating the purpose for the disbursement as there were no documents provided" (GAC Audit of the Ministry of Information, Culture Affairs, and Tourism, FYs 2006/07, 2007/08, and 2008/09).

The GAC audit also found that Dr. Bropleh was the custodian of the checkbooks and that he and now late deputy finance minister Tarnue Mawolo were signatories to the Kendeja account. The audit report recommended that Reverend Dr. Bropleh and then deputy minister Mawolo be held liable to provide justification for disbursing the Kendeja relocation funds.

The need to relocate the national cultural center became apparent after most of the land originally allocated by the government for the Kendeja Cultural Center was encroached upon during the civil war while the infrastructure at the center was in a dilapidated state due to years of disrepair.

This was why when business mogul Robert L. Johnson, the first African American billionaire, expressed interest in acquiring the beautiful beachfront property to build a resort during a visit to Liberia, the government jumped at the opportunity to lease the land to him. Kendeja is located near the highway leading to the Roberts International Airport, about a thirty-minute drive. It was under the agreement with the Liberian government that portion of the funds provided by Mr. Johnson was to be used to relocate the residents for the infrastructure that existed to be demolished to make way for the construction of what is now known as the RLJ Kendeja Resort and Villas.

The funds were intended to assist with the relocation of performers and other artists who were residents at Kendeja National Cultural Center to find new accommodation while the government was to acquire a new property to build a modern cultural center.

Because of the misuse of the relocation funds and poor coordination of the relocation process, aggrieved young people, who were Kendeja residents and students at the Kendeja School, staged a violent protest during which they set vehicles ablaze and blocked the main highway leading to the Roberts International Airport with burning tires.

Upon hearing about the riot, President Sirleaf rushed to Kendeja to calm things down. Before the president's arrival, I was already on the scene helping to bring the riot under control. When she was informed about the riot, Deputy Minister Hoff, who was then acting minister due to the travel of Minister Bropleh, requested me to immediately go to Kendeja to work with the police and relevant authorities to bring the situation under control.

Before the president's arrival, the police had managed to bring the riot under control, but the aggrieved young people were still chanting their demand for redress to their grievances. For example, they complained that the government did not complete the renovation of the building that was to be temporarily used as a school until the end of the semester. The students complained that the building was not safe for children and not conducive for learning.

After hearing some of the grievances of the protesters, President Sirleaf went on a tour of the building in question, accompanied by officials of the Ministry of Education, the Kendeja School principal, myself, and other relevant authorities at the scene. As the tour progressed, the president was visibly angry that people's children were being housed in such dilapidated condition as a school.

While the tour was concluding, the president turned to me and asked, "Minister Williams, what happened here?" I was caught completely off guard by the question. However, I responded candidly that I was not aware of what led to the riot except that acting minister Hoff had asked me to come and assist in bringing things under control after we heard about the riot. The president then responded with a threat that "heads will roll" for those officials who bore the responsibility for the Kendeja problem. And that became a major media headline as journalists reported what was called the "Kendeja financial scandal."

When I said that acting minister Hoff had sent me to help calm things down, to my surprise again, the president also asked for the whereabouts of Minister Bropleh; and I told her that he had traveled. There were instances where the minister traveled abroad using taxpayers' money without official communication to the Office of the President, as was required.

Immediately upon her return to the Executive Mansion, the president summoned acting minister Hoff to better understand the problems surrounding the Kendeja relocation process. As was in my case, Minister Hoff told the president that she also was not kept abreast of the Kendeja relocation process until she received information regarding the riot.

Undoubtedly, the president expressed that she was baffled that we, who were members of the MICAT cabinet, were saying that we were not aware of what was going on at MICAT related to the Kendeja relocation exercise. And indeed, we were not involved. Minister Bropleh and Assistant Minister for Culture Jailee Quiee were the only two officials from MICAT who dealt with the transactions related to the Kendeja relocation exercise without keeping the rest of the MICAT team in the know.

This was why, as noted earlier, I decided to be more proactive in the affairs of the ministry in order to never again appear stupid in front of the president, such as what happened during the Kendeja riot.

Meanwhile, believing that Bropleh would be fired, there was a celebration at MICAT involving some members of the cabinet and staff when news spread that the president publicly threatened that "heads will roll" as a result of the scandal. I kept away from those who were celebrating. It turned out that certain staff loyal to Minister Bropleh called and informed him regarding what had transpired at the ministry and that they did not see me with those who celebrated.

Upon my return home from work late that evening, I received a call from Minister Bropleh, who was in Accra, Ghana, waiting for a connecting flight to Monrovia the following day from an overseas trip. He said he had been briefed by his staff regarding what was transpiring, including the celebration at the ministry, of which I was not a part. He expressed appreciation that I was not among those at the ministry who wanted him out as they had demonstrated. He also sought my input as to how he should proceed upon his return to Liberia.

I told him that since he was scheduled to arrive in Monrovia from Accra in the afternoon, he should first visit Kendeja, especially the school, to have a sense of things before his meeting with the president later that day. I gave him a heads-up on the situation on the ground and some of the things he needed to do before and during his meeting with the president.

Minister Bropleh arrived and had an evening meeting with the president. After he returned from his meeting with Madam President during that night, he called to give me an update from the meeting. He said that the president had decided to fire Assistant Minister for Culture Jailee Quiee and to set up a special committee to inquire into what went wrong with the Kendeja relocation exercise. He added that the president decided to include one official from MICAT to form part of the investigation committee and that he had prevailed upon her to select me to represent the ministry because he was confident that I would not stab him in the back.

He said that the president's office would contact me the following day, during which the official statement regarding the assistant minister's dismissal and the setting up of the investigation committee would be issued by the Executive Mansion.

And that was how developments unfolded the following day. I got a call from the Office of the President, followed by the press statement from the Executive Mansion announcing Assistant Culture Minister Qiuee's dismissal and the setting up of the committee of inquiry. The committee was headed by human rights advocacy lawyer Augustine Toe, who was head of the Catholic Justice and Peace Commission (JPC), a respected nongovernmental human rights advocacy organization in Liberia. Another member of the committee was Mr. Willard Russell, then director general of the General Services Agency (GSA), the principal government procurement agency.

Attached to the president's letter appointing me as a member of the committee to inquire into what went wrong with the Kendeja relocation exercise were bank statements from the Kendeja relocation account and other relevant documents. I noticed from the bank statements that a certain amount of the money had been disbursed for a media project under the Department of Public Affairs, of which I was the head. How could it be that such an amount was disbursed for a media program in a department that I headed without my knowledge?

With that question, I went to Minister Bropleh's office with the bank statements to inquire about the funds that were disbursed in the name of the department that I headed, as reflected by the bank statements, and knew nothing about it. He apologized for what he called an "oversight" and noted that since the president had authorized an investigation, I should wait until the investigation is completed, and then he would explain what happened. That was the last time such a conversation was held.

Other members of the MICAT cabinet who saw the bank statements were infuriated. Some of my colleagues suggested that the Kendeja scandal presented an opportunity to have Bropleh removed from the ministry. In order to mount public pressure on the president and force her to fire Bropleh, some of my colleagues suggested that I should acquiesce for the financial records to be leaked to the media.

However, I told my colleagues that Larry would fall on his own sword, and therefore, I did not want to be involved in anything that would get me to be blamed for undermining him to lose his job.

Although the committee concluded its report and submitted the same to the president, no further actions were taken besides the dismissal of Assistant Minister Quiee, who had direct supervision over Kendeja. Reverend Dr. Bropleh, who was the custodian of the checkbook and one of the two signatories to the relocation fund account, was left untouched. I am not aware that the funds in question were ever accounted for.

Reverend Dr. Bropleh remained in his post as minister until another financial scandal. This time, he was disgracefully removed from MICAT in 2010 after a GAC audit report also found that he had again swindled the government to the tune of about $260,000 through fraudulent processing and payments of salaries and allowances to several ghost employees.

According to the audit report, among the ghost names on the MICAT payroll was that of the late Sarbatoe Weah, then minister counselor for press and public affairs posted at the Liberian embassy in Nigeria. Reverend Dr. Bropleh was accused of keeping the name of the late Weah on the payroll and collecting his funds until the outbreak of the financial scandal that led to his suspension as minister in October 2009.

Amid mounting public pressure due to intense media coverage, President Sirleaf was forced to request that Reverend Dr. Bropleh resign or be fired in January 2010, after he was indicted by the GAC audit for defrauding the Liberian government. He denied the charges, and the case was forwarded to court for prosecution.

President Sirleaf was left with no alternative but to let Reverend Dr. Bropleh go because of intense publicity from documents leaked to the media related to the financial scandal. Then Finance Minister Augustine K. Ngafuan, who had a meeting with the president and informed her about the financial scandal, told her that there was no way that the government could keep a lid on the financial scandal that was to become public because the media were already in possession of information relation to the economic crimes allegedly involving Reverend Dr. Bropleh.

Mindful that it would be a serious public embarrassment for the media to first publish information regarding the scandal before the government took action, the president rushed out of her office, got in her vehicle, and the presidential convoy sped to the Justice Ministry. Following a meeting with then justice minister Christiana Tah, orders were given for the immediate arrest and detention of the comptroller and the chief accountant at MICAT. Normal activities at MICAT were interrupted that sunny October afternoon when police descended on the ministry and conducted a swoop, leading both men away from their offices in handcuffs as other MICAT staff looked on, bewildered.

How amazing that the media were in possession of documents related to the financial scandal before the president even got wind of it! It is notable that the media reports were critical in bringing an end to a criminal streak at MICAT. The press deserves commendation for playing its role, which is to shed light in darkness and hold public leaders accountable for their actions.

On the afternoon the scandal became public, I was on my way from town to the Sinkor suburb of Monrovia when my old government-assigned vehicle broke down. While having it repaired at a roadside garage, my phone rang. When I answered my phone, the caller said, "They got him!"

I responded, "Got who?"

And he said, "Bropleh is finally being exposed."

The caller was a prominent journalist who said the president was on her way to the Justice Ministry after Finance Minister Ngafuan briefed her about the financial scandal at MICAT.

The journalist who called me had been involved for weeks with the media investigation that led to public exposure of the scandal. Through my media connections and contacts at the Finance Ministry, I had earlier been tipped off regarding what was unfolding at MICAT. However, under the circumstances, all I could do was watch from the sidelines. During my tenure at MICAT, managing the media to ensure that the government's public image was not undermined by unnecessary negative headlines and reports was critical in my engagement with the media. Being accessible to the journalists and respecting them for what they do can keep a lot of misinformation out of the news. I have always told my principals that no one, no matter how powerful, can ever win in a war against the media. When it is all said and done, journalists will write the last story about you.

Meanwhile, Minister Bropleh was on an official visit to China at the time the scandal broke. The president ordered him to return home immediately. Even though the two MICAT financial officers implicated with the minister in the scandal were immediately arrested and placed in custody, the president directed that Bropleh should not be detained upon his return to Liberia. However, after he returned and met with the president, he was suspended from office pending the outcome of the corruption investigation and audit.

A press statement issued by the Executive Mansion on October 16, 2009, states as follows: "The Minister of Information, Cultural Affairs and Tourism, Dr. Laurence Bropleh, has been suspended by President Ellen Johnson Sirleaf, pending results of an ongoing investigation by the Ministry of Justice, into an alleged scandal at the Ministry."

An Executive Mansion release says the action by the President follows the return of Minister Bropleh to the country. The President met with the Minister on the evening of October 16 and informed him of his suspension.

Meanwhile, the Deputy Minister of Information, Elizabeth Hoff, has been designated Acting Minister by the Liberian leader. ("Information Minister Laurence Bropleh Suspended," Executive Mansion press release, October 16, 2009)

Hoff was designated instead of then deputy information minister for administration Cletus Sieh, who was the acting minister in Bropleh's absence at the time the scandal broke. Bropleh had told the president and also publicly said that Sieh was involved in the conspiracy to undermine and remove him from MICAT.

Sieh, who was also investigated by the police and GAC and cleared of any wrongdoing, reacted to Bropleh's allegation against him as nonsense as he was never involved in any of the economic crimes for which Bropleh was accused. Bropleh recommended Sieh for the position of deputy minister for administration after Richmond Anderson was removed.

At the time the scandal broke, I was preparing to leave the country to take up my new diplomatic assignment as minister counselor for press and public affairs at the Liberian embassy in Washington. Abu Kamara, who succeeded me as assistant minister for information services at MICAT, was also appointed along with me as minister counselor for press and public affairs, posted at the Liberia Permanent Mission in New York.

Our departure from the country was delayed for months because funds allocated in the budget as salaries and benefits for those positions for that fiscal year had been squandered. I had been informed by officials at the Finance Ministry with knowledge of the financial situation that it would take the president's intervention to authorize funds from different budgetary appropriations for Mr. Kamara and me to travel and take up our respective assignments. It was while the president was involved in the effort to find money for our departure that the scandal broke at MICAT.

The president's mandate to the Justice Ministry directed that all deputy ministers at MICAT who served from 2006 to the date of the financial scandal should also submit to the investigation and audit. As a result of the foregoing, my bank account was frozen, and all salary transactions were blocked pending the outcome of the investigations and audit. I felt humiliated by media reports that we, as past and present deputy ministers during that period, were also under investigation, in addition to the financial hardship that I incurred due to the inability to access my bank account or take delivery of my salary checks.

While resting at home on a Saturday afternoon a few days after the scandal broke, I received a call from the police to report to the police headquarters immediately for an investigation related to the financial scandal. I immediately contacted my first cousin Mark Saulwah, the now late veteran security officer who had worked in the Office of the Solicitor General at the Justice Ministry, to accompany me to the investigation.

Upon arrival at the police headquarters, I was asked to present a written statement, followed by questions from the investigators, to which I dutifully complied. However, the investigative process turned into a shouting match between one of the investigators and myself. The investigator said that he could not understand how Minister Bropleh alone could be held liable for the financial scandal that was being investigated when other deputy ministers, like myself, were also involved in financial transactions on behalf of MICAT. He argued that it was unlikely that Minister Bropleh and the two financial officers were the only ones involved in acts of financial impropriety while other officials of MICAT operated with clean hands.

I responded that I rejected what I thought was his twisted logic and insinuation as there was no record that would establish from the investigation and audit that I was involved in financial malpractices simply because I served as a deputy minister. As we argued, he said that the investigation would uncover my culpability and that they were set to get me. I also responded that he was a damned liar and that Liberia had continued to linger in a state of dysfunction because of poorly trained and unprofessional people the likes of him serving in critical positions, such as the security service. As I walked from the conference room following the end of the investigation session, the investigator shouted that they would get me, and I shouted back that he should go to hell.

In Liberian society, perception matters more than fact while guilt by association can lead to innocent lives being put in danger and also result in tragic consequences. For example, during the civil upheavals, many innocent people were terrorized and killed because they were perceived to be enemies by one group or the other. Along similar lines, many people who did nothing wrong were killed for no reason other than their ethnic, political, religious, and other differences.

Needless to say, I was never invited back for the police investigation. I also appeared before GAC auditors and investigators once. Even though I was informed that I would be summoned again if the need arose during the course of the inquiry, I was never invited back until the police investigation and audit reports were completed and presented to the president. Like I told the police investigator, I was never a party to the financial scandal, which was what the audit reflected.

From the day the financial scandal broke, the manner in which the police conducted the investigation left much to be desired in terms of their professionalism and impartiality. The police were seen to be compromised in the handling of the investigation and their report to the president. The police, who sealed off the finance office at MICAT for several days as part of their investigation, reportedly took away critical financial records and other evidence that were not shared with the GAC.

At the conclusion of their investigation, the report from the police, which was sent to the president before the audit report was completed, basically exonerated Minister Bropleh from any wrongdoing. The police report, which was leaked to the media, found that there was no serious financial malpractice involving Minister Bropleh. The police report concluded that the discrepancies at MICAT were of poor financial record keeping and not necessarily due to financial mismanagement. The report blamed Minister Bropleh, along with the other deputy ministers at MICAT, for the poor financial record keeping at the ministry.

The Justice Ministry or the minister of justice has oversight responsibility of the police and other state security agencies. Then justice minister Christiana Tah was seen to be a close associate of Minister Bropleh, who once told me that he had a family connection with Madam Tah. The justice minister, who is the attorney general of the Liberian government, was known to have tried unsuccessfully to prevail on the GAC to conduct their audit to conform to the conclusion of the police investigation.

Despite the pressure from high places that was brought to bear, the GAC, under the leadership of Auditor General John S. Morlu II, remained resolute and uncompromising in exposing the gross financial malpractices that occurred at MICAT, as was the case with other government agencies and officials that were investigated for economic crimes.

More on then auditor general Morlu and his positive impact in the struggle against corruption in Liberia in chapter 7.

It was after the GAC audit found Bropleh responsible for embezzlement and other financial crimes and recommended his prosecution that the president was forced to terminate him as minister in January 2010.

Deputy Minister Cletus Sieh was appointed as minister to replace Bropleh. A savvy politician who was a former executive of the Liberia Unification Party (LUP), Minister Sieh served honorably until his dismissal in December 2011. According to an Executive Mansion release, Minister Sieh was dismissed for his indiscretion in the manner he handled security information relating to disturbances by vacation job students, which occurred a couple of days before his termination on December 24, 2011.

The decisive campaign to leak information regarding the financial scandal involving Reverend Dr. Bropleh to the media was coordinated at high levels between MICAT and the Finance Ministry. That was the only way to force the president's hand to get rid of Bropleh, who usually boasted that there was nothing those who opposed him could do to remove him as long as he continued to enjoy the confidence of the president. Some of the colleagues at MICAT, who wanted me to leak information regarding the Kendeja relocation exercise, were now better positioned with access to all relevant information.

From the Finance Ministry's end, there were reports that Reverend Dr. Bropleh had also started to put in the president's ear the need to transfer Minister Ngafuan, another young rising star in the government, from the Finance Ministry. This was apparently because the Finance Ministry had begun to inquire into matters of financial malpractices at MICAT, including the presence of ghost names on the payroll. In the wake of the Finance Ministry's inquiry, Reverend Bropleh reportedly started complaining to the president that Ngafuan, who later served as minister of foreign affairs, was not doing a good job as minister of finance.

And that was how Reverend Dr. Bropleh got forced out of office as minister of information and forwarded to court for prosecution during the Sirleaf administration.

Unfortunately, the Justice Ministry, which is the prosecuting arm of the government, bungled the case, thus providing an opportunity for the judge to dismiss the case against the accused. The judge dismissed the case when prosecuting lawyers went to court late. By the time the prosecutors entered the court that morning, the judge had dismissed the case, for which they (prosecutors) took an appeal to the supreme court. However, no further legal action was pursued as of this publication.

Prior to the dismissal, the judge was seen to have been favorably disposed to the defendant. For example, the judge had previously denied prosecutors' request to have the accused sit in the seat reserved for defendants when court was in session. It was the next court session following that development that the judge dismissed the case because prosecutors came to court late.

With a Ministry of Justice known to be tainted by conflict of interest and a corrupt judicial system, there were public sentiments that the Bropleh case was compromised, similar to many others in which those accused of squandering hundreds of thousands or millions of dollars of public funds were simply let go to enjoy their loot. Even though some progress has been made in Liberia's judicial reforms, corruption has continued to undermine public confidence in the integrity of the courts.

It may be interesting to note that in 2019, Reverend Dr. Bropleh returned to government service with his appointment in dual capacity as special envoy and communications advisor to President George M. Weah, who succeeded President Sirleaf in 2018. According to media reports, his responsibilities include working with MICAT and the other government media-related entities to devise and disseminate government-related information.

It may also be interesting to note that in March 2018, US-based international watchdog organization Global Witness issued an investigative report in which former justice minister Christiana Tah was named among several senior Liberian government officials who allegedly received large payments for authorizing the sale of Liberia's oil block 13 to ExxonMobil in 2013. The Global Witness investigation showed that ExxonMobil's purchase of the license for Liberia's oil block 13 also likely enriched former government officials who might have illegally owned the block.

"In 2013, oil giant Exxon signed a $120 million deal with the Liberian government for an oil block it knew was tainted by corruption. As our expose reveals, Exxon negotiated the deal despite its concern over 'issues regarding U.S. anti-corruption laws'" ("Catch Me If You Can: Exxon Complicit in Corrupt Liberian Oil Sector," Global Witness report, March 29, 2018).

According to the Global Witness investigation, Exxon's purchase of the oil block was accompanied by over $200,000 in unusually large payments made by the corruption-tinted Liberian agency to six officials who approved the deal. The agency that made the payment was the National Oil Company of Liberia (NOCAL), at the time one of Liberia's most financially solvent agencies, which reportedly went virtually bankrupt under the leadership of Robert Sirleaf, son of President Sirleaf who served as chairman of the board of NOCAL, and Mr. Randolph McClain, chief executive officer of NOCAL.

The Global Witness investigation found that shortly after the authorization of the Exxon deal, the officials involved were paid "bonuses" of $35,000 each by NOCAL—more than doubling their annual salaries.

Officials who received the large payments and the posts they held were Justice Minister Christiana Tah; Finance Minister Amara Konneh; Lands, Mines, and Energy Minister Patrick Sendolo; National Investment Commission (NIC) Chairman Natty B. Davis; NOCAL CEO Randolph McClain; and NOCAL Board Chairman Robert Sirleaf.

Global Witness reported that oil block 13 was originally awarded by NOCAL in 2005 to Broadway Consolidated/Peppercoast (BCP) and that the block was ratified in 2007 by the Liberian legislature through bribery.

The international watchdog's investigation found that BCP was likely part-owned by former Liberian politicians who had illegally granted themselves the block. Those officials were former minister of lands, mines, and energy Jonathan Mason and former deputy minister Mulbah Willie. Former ministers Mason and Willie were suspected of granting the oil block to a company in which they held interests while they were government ministers in 2005, which was illegal under Liberian laws.

In its report, Global Witness recommended that Exxon, BCP, and those who received the unusual large payments should be investigated to determine if they broke laws in the United States and Liberia. No such investigations have been undertaken in both the United States and Liberia.

Meanwhile, some of the officials named in the Global Witness report for receiving large payments have responded to the report. Former justice minister Christiana Tah, former NIC Chairman Natty B. Davis, and former NOCAL board chair Robert Sirleaf noted in separate reactions in the media that the payments they received were bonuses authorized by NOCAL's Board of Directors for their roles in negotiating the Exxon deal.

In their respective reactions published in the media, Madam Tah and Mr. Sirleaf said all other staff of NOCAL also received bonuses following the conclusion of the Exxon deal.

In her reaction published in the *Daily Observer* newspaper, former minister Tah said President Sirleaf instructed NOCAL to pay bonuses to all those who participated in the negotiation of the Exxon contract because the president said she was very pleased with the performance of the team.

Madam Tah said that the president then communicated "her instructions to the Board of Directors chaired by her son, Robert A. Sirleaf. Therefore, when the NOCAL Board passed a resolution to pay bonuses, it specifically referred to the 'approval of the President of Liberia,'" ("Former Justice Minister Tah Speaks Out on Global Witness Report on the Exxon-Liberia Contract," *Liberian Observer*, June 12, 2018).

It may be equally interesting to note that during her tenure at the Justice Ministry, Minister Tah made a very courageous decision to hedge in the enforcement of what was regarded to be an unjust law, for which she was sanctioned by the Supreme Court of Liberia.

In 2013, the court had imposed a five-thousand-year prison sentence on the publisher of the newspaper *FrontPage Africa*, Mr. Rodney D. Sieh, for failing to pay a $1.5 million libel fine to a former minister of agriculture, Dr. J. Chris Toe.

While he was in jail, Sieh got critically ill and fell unconscious, prompting public concern and outrage for his condition. This led Minister Tah to release him on "compassionate" grounds to enable him to seek medical treatment.

In October 2013, the supreme court ordered the justice minister, who is the attorney general of the Liberian government, to explain why she should not be held in contempt for releasing Mr. Sieh from prison. In January 2014, the supreme court suspended Minister Tah from practicing law in Liberia for six months after finding her in contempt.

The suspension of the attorney general, who is also the chief prosecutor of Liberia and legal advisor to the president, amounted to essentially getting her out of the job. Her case was not helped with what was seen to be the lukewarm approach of the president regarding her problem with the supreme court. Sieh and *FrontPage Africa* had become a thorn in the flesh of the government and many officials close to the president because of the unrelenting reports of corruption within the government. Many government officials openly expressed their support for the legal action against Sieh for his aggressive anti-corruption reporting.

Even though she remained in office until the end of her six-month suspension, in October 2014, Madam Tah tendered her resignation as minister of justice, saying President Sirleaf had blocked her investigation into fraud allegations against the country's National Security Agency (NSA), which was headed by the president's stepson, Fumba Sirleaf.

In her letter of resignation, Minister Tah said she could not remain in office. "I cannot be the Minister of Justice and not supervise the operations of the security agencies under the Ministry of Justice. What is the 'rule of law' if the President asserts that she does not trust the Ministry of Justice to independently investigate allegations of fraud against the National Security Agency?" ("Liberia Justice Minister Quits, Says President Blocked Investigation," Reuters, October 7, 2014).

The government did not officially react to the allegations of former minister Tah, a seasoned lawyer who holds a graduate degree in law from Yale University and a master of arts degree in sociology and criminal justice from Kent State University in the United States. According to her biographical information, Madam Tah, who has previously worked at the Justice Ministry and other Liberian government agencies from the late 1970s, has served as a professor of sociology and criminal justice for more than fifteen years in the United States, where she has also practiced law.

Madam Tah was one of the many professional Liberians who returned home from the United States and other parts of the world to serve in the government during the administration of President Sirleaf. Nevertheless, it is unfortunate that many Liberians who returned home from abroad with high levels of education and professional expertise have proved to be very disappointing in their conduct and a deterrence to Liberia's progress. They play by the rule of law when in America; but when in Liberia, they resort to the rule of the jungle, as these accounts narrated reflect.

In her resignation letter, Minister Tah's pronouncement that the president did not trust the Ministry of Justice to independently investigate allegations of fraud against the National Security Agency was right on the mark. I would never have trusted her or the Ministry of Justice to preside over any credible investigation, given my terrible experience regarding her role in the Bropleh scandal and how the Justice Ministry was comprised with respect to how investigations are conducted and cases are prosecuted. The president, very certainly, knew better.

With these kinds of developments as reflected, is there any wonder why Liberia and other countries that function like it have been stuck at the bottom of the Human Development Index (HDI) as the poorest in the world? More information regarding Liberia's ranking on the HDI is found in chapter 15.

Beyond Liberia, many of those within the leadership of various African countries have obtained education and resided or worked in the United States, Europe, and other developed parts of the world where everyone adheres to the rule of law and enjoys the benefits of good governance. Once they return to their respective countries and assume leadership, they usually forget about good governance and resort to the rule of the jungle.

Like my professional father, legendary journalist Kenneth Y. Best, once said, "if you want to see the true nature of an African, give him power." The use of power not for the common good but to prey on or subjugate others for self-aggrandizement is a fact of life in many parts of Africa. The bottom line for most of them is to abuse the public trust or squander public resources without accountability.

Sierra Leone's president, Julius Maada Bio, who launched a vigorous anti-corruption campaign in Sierra Leone immediately upon his ascendency to the presidency in 2018, was right to the point when he said that those who indulge in corruption see it as a source of wealth, a source of privilege, and a route to or a demonstration of power that they often abuse.

In a nationwide address to commemorate International Anti-Corruption Day in December 2018, President Bio said the following:

Corruption in all its forms has a cost and it has real human victims when critical infrastructure like hospitals and schools are not built and when citizens are denied their rights and equitable access to service delivery . . . Corruption also stalls economic development, compromises ethical conduct and national values, and, violates the fundamental rights of all citizens. Above all, corruption undermines democratic institutions of governance and the stability of a country. For the foregoing reasons, corruption is a national security threat.

If we are to develop as a nation, we must draw a line under the perverse, arrogant, and reckless looting of the state. (Statement by His Excellency, President Julius Maada Bio in Commemoration of International Anti-Corruption Day 2018, December 9, 2018)

Since the 1970s, a healthy exchange of ideas and competition to show competence in Liberian society have degenerated to nothing more than blood sport, where well-meaning people get wounded or eliminated for daring to make a difference. Amid the clamor for power and wealth, competence has been relegated to mediocrity. Liberia can be likened to the pit associated with what is called "crab mentality," regarding how people consume their time and energy trying to climb over one another by pulling one another down.

I am often left to wonder, where is our humanity? Have we lost our sense of humanity amid the clamor for transient material gains?

Because of the foregoing, many successful African professionals and entrepreneurs in the diaspora are usually afraid or hesitant to return to their respective countries. They fear returning home to be victimized by those "vultures."

Liberia's president, George M. Weah (L), shakes hands with his Sierra Leonean counterpart, Julius Maada Bio, during Bio's first visit to Liberia as Sierra Leonean president in 2018 (courtesy of the Liberian Embassy Public Affairs)

All things considered, it has been nothing but the grace of God that has shepherded me through the many challenges in order to help make a difference in my country. I bless the Lord, fully aware that there have been many well-meaning Liberian patriots who have suffered and perished along the way because they were targeted by powerful hands who felt threatened by new ideas and those who are results-oriented. It is all about them—that they do not want anyone else to outshine them. This is the true character of individuals with small minds who are insecure in their own skin despite the facade of confidence with which they carry themselves.

That is indicative of the mind-set of some Liberians and, for that matter, many Africans who find themselves in leadership. The former senior official of government who visited my office following the *Independent* newspaper brouhaha was very mindful of this destructive tendency that is pervasive in Liberia and Africa when he warned me to be extremely careful, as there were those in government who now saw me as an enemy and a threat to their interests.

It is pleasing to note that following the experience with the *Independent*, the government was very restrained in shutting down any news organ outside of the due process of law. A notable exception was in August 2014, when police were sent to shut down the offices of the *Chronicles* for publishing articles that were deemed to be subversive at a time the country was under a state of emergency imposed by the government to deal with the alarming spread of the Ebolepidemic, which had killed hundreds of people; and the entire country was being brought to its knees.

The Need to Repeal Unconstitutional and Unjust Laws

When I was requested to serve at the Information Ministry, my first concern for which I was hesitant to take the job regarded the ministry's power to arbitrarily shut down news organs without due process. I had expressed that I was not prepared to take a job that would make me to enforce unjust laws under which I had been victimized and which I had challenged in the past as a journalist. It is therefore gratifying to note that our refusal to support the enforcement of what was regarded as an unjust law to proscribe the *Independent* newspaper became a significant turning point in the promotion of press freedom in Liberia.

During the twelve-year leadership of President Sirleaf, the government had its share of challenges and fights with the local media. Nevertheless, one of the major accomplishments of the Sirleaf administration was the tolerance of dissent, which has birthed an unprecedented level of freedom in Liberia. This is manifested by the fact that in 2010, Liberia became the first country in West Africa to pass into law a Freedom of Information (FOI) Act, a law that grants public access to documents or other data in the possession of a government agency or public authority unless the information falls into a certain category that is specifically excluded from the terms of the legislation.

The passage of the FOI Act was followed by Liberia becoming a signatory to the Declaration of Table Mountain, which calls for the repeal of criminal defamation and "insult" laws across the African continent and was adopted at the World Newspaper Congress held in Cape Town, South Africa, in 2007. Despite these accomplishments, freedom of speech and of the press remained under threat in Liberia while the laws on libel, defamation, and sedition, which are inimical to free speech, were on the books.

This is why it is pleasing to note that in May 2018, four months after taking office, President George M. Weah resubmitted to the national legislature a bill to repeal some sections of the Penal Law of Liberia in an effort to decriminalize free speech and create the unfettered flow of news in the media environment. The bill was first submitted to the legislature during the Sirleaf administration, but it failed to gain passage.

The bill, which was passed by the House of Representatives in July 2018 and approved by the Senate in February 2019, repealed the Penal Law of 1978, which impedes freedom of speech with criminal libel against the president, sedition, and criminal malevolence.

President Weah and the national legislature must be highly commended for the passage of the landmark legislation, which is known as the Kamara Abdullai Kamara Act of Press Freedom, in memory of deceased journalist Kamara Abdullai Kamara, former president of the PUL who died in 2018. During his leadership, Kamara was actively engaged with the Sirleaf administration for the passage of the bill even though the efforts were not successful.

I met Mr. Kamara, who headed a PUL delegation from Liberia, at the 2016 annual convention of the Association of Liberian Journalists in the Americas (ALJA) in Philadelphia, Pennsylvania. During that event, after which he was replaced as PUL president, I inquired from Mr. Kamara as to what the PUL was doing to repeal antimedia laws that were on the books in Liberia. He briefly explained efforts that were being made and challenges that were faced, including the bill submitted by President Sirleaf that stalled.

The PUL is applauded for staying the course to ensure freedom of speech and of the press in Liberia. The minister of Information, Cultural Affairs and Tourism, Hon. Lenn Eugene Nagbe, is also applauded because the passage of the landmark legislation occurred during his tenure at MICAT.

Having served during the first four years of the Sirleaf administration as assistant minister and deputy minister for public affairs, respectively, at MICAT, and tasked with the critical responsibility to manage the expectations of the media and the public, I am grateful to God for the opportunity to help institute necessary reforms that created the enabling environment that has brought about the gains made toward freedom of speech and of the press in Liberia. However, I am on record for stating that the gains made toward freedom of speech and of the press in Liberia were under threat as long as there were laws on the books that criminalized these fundamental rights.

One of the very few examples of how the laws on defamation and libel were used to undermine press freedom in Liberia during the Sirleaf administration regarded the detention and prosecution of Rodney D. Sieh, editor of Liberia's leading independent daily, *FrontPage Africa*, in 2013.

A court in Monrovia sentenced Mr. Sieh to five thousand years in prison for failing to pay libel damages of $1.5 million won by a former minister of agriculture in the Sirleaf administration who sued *FrontPage Africa* after the newspaper published the findings of a government audit. The audit report revealed that funds worth $6 million intended to combat an armyworm epidemic that destroyed crops in some parts of rural Liberia were unaccounted for.

What an outrageous imposition of a prison sentence simply to enforce an unjust law!

Imprisoned for four months, the government was forced to release Sieh from further detention following strong international outcry and public protests in Monrovia with supporters and sympathizers carrying placards demanding his release, among others.

Ever since launching *FrontPage Africa* in 2005, Sieh has had run-ins with the judicial system in connection with his paper's investigative reporting on corruption within the Liberian elite and government mismanagement.

Mr. Sieh hails from a family with a background in advocacy for the common good of society. His late grand-uncle Albert Porte was a pioneering pamphleteer, crusader, and journalist who is famously remembered in Liberia for standing up to the corrupt political system during his days. Mr. Porte, who started his sociopolitical activities in the 1920s, endured constant harassment as well as imprisonments for his advocacy, a cause to which he was consistent till his death in 1986.

It may be interesting to note that Mr. Porte was also sued for libel for drawing public attention to the excesses of a government official with presidential connections. The suit, *Stephen Allen Tolbert v. Albert Porte, "Damages for Libel,"* was in connection with Porte's publication in 1975 of *Liberianization or Gobbling Business*. Mr. Stephen Tolbert, then minister of Finance, was the younger brother of then president William R. Tolbert Jr. What started as a lawsuit between Stephen Tolbert and Mr. Porte led to an outpouring of public support for Porte and outcry against the abuse of public office (*Historical Dictionary of Liberia*, second edition, page 269).

Sieh's uncle Kenneth Y. Best, who introduced him to journalism and mentored him, was the founder of the *Daily Observer*, Liberia's first independent daily newspaper, where I also began my career as a journalist. From its establishment in 1981 to the civil crises in 1989, the *Observer* suffered five closures, including one that lasted nearly two years, for alleged antigovernment reporting. There were several government imprisonments of the *Observer* staff, including Mr. Best and his wife, as well as several arson attacks, the last of which completely destroyed the building housing the newspaper's offices and facilities during the early stage of civil upheavals.

In the wake of the civil war, Mr. Best fled with his family to the Gambia, where he established yet another *Daily Observer*, that country's first independent daily newspaper. He was expelled from the Gambia in 1994 by the military regime of Yahya Jammeh after the *Observer* ran a series of articles critical of the military regime on human rights violations.

Mr. Rodney D. Sieh is the author of the book *Journalist on Trial: Fighting Corruption, Media Muzzling and a 5,000-Year Prison Sentence in Liberia*, published in 2018.

As a former leader of the PUL, I recall the many journalists and others who have suffered and sacrificed over the decades, some losing their livelihoods and their lives in the process, due to the imposition of decrees and draconian laws such as provisions of the laws on defamation, libel, and sedition, among others.

A few historical examples among the many tales of repression include Liberia's 1925 False Publication Act, which stipulated heavy penalties for "harmful and false" statements against the president and other government officials. In the 1950s, C. Frederick Taylor, editor of the *African Nationalist* newspaper, languished in prison for nearly fifteen years for publishing what the establishment did not like. Meanwhile, editors Bertha Corbin and Tuan Wreh of the *Independent Weekly*, like Mr. Taylor, also served prison sentences for criminal libel of the political elite, including the president.

An American-born, but naturalized Liberian, Ms. Corbin was denaturalized and deported to the United States while Mr. Wreh was severely tortured and reportedly forced to clean feces and toilets with his bare hands in prison. The PUL was founded in 1964 by a group of journalists to advocate for their collective interest, following the arbitrary detention of Stanton B. Peabody, then editor of the *Liberian Age*, for publishing an article that angered some establishment elites.

I have remained a strong advocate for the repeal of unjust laws relating defamation, libel, and sedition, which have been used over the years to criminalize freedom of speech and of the press and to penalize the media and those who dared to exercise their right to free speech.

CHAPTER SIX

Tackling Challenges in the Rebuilding Process

D espite being endowed with abundant natural resources and a considerable human capital base, years of conflict, corruption, and mismanagement left Liberia as one of the poorest countries in the world with massive brain drain.

By the time Liberian leader Charles Taylor was forced out of power and exiled to Nigeria in August 2003, the country had basically crumbled into a failed and criminal state, and the national economy had essentially collapsed. Extreme poverty was pervasive, and more than half the population was internally displaced and became refugees in neighboring countries. About 80 percent of Liberia's population was estimated to be illiterate.

With the deployment of peacekeepers under the auspices of the United Nations Mission in Liberia (UNMIL) as the civil war ended in 2003, Liberia began to benefit from tremendous goodwill from the international community. There was a massive deployment of financial, material, and human resources by the United Nations system, as well as very critical support from the US government, the Economic Community of West African States (ECOWAS), the African Union, and the European Union (EU), among others.

While providing massive humanitarian support in the form of food, medical, and other emergency services to sustain the war-afflicted Liberian population, the international community also put in place what was called the Governance Economic Management Assistance Program (GEMAP). Implemented during the period 2006–2010, GEMAP was a partnership between the Liberian government and the international community to promote accountability and transparency in the fiscal and financial management of Liberia's resources.

Driven by the United States, GEMAP was instituted during the period of Liberia's transitional government to assist the country in putting in place sound economic policies and programs to ensure accountability and transparency in managing the resources of Liberia in keeping with best international practices. Under GEMAP, expatriate financial experts were deployed in various government ministries and agencies responsible for the collection of revenues and management of the country's resources. The foreign financial experts worked with their Liberian counterparts.

Immediately following her inauguration in January 2006, President Sirleaf instituted short- and long-term national development plans aimed at stabilizing the country, providing emergency relief services for the disaffected and traumatized population, as well as putting the country on a path of sustainable peace and progress to alleviate poverty. The first of the national development program, called the 150-Day Action Plan, was followed by the launch of the Interim Poverty Reduction Strategy (IPRS), which was under the theme "Breaking with the Past: From Conflict to Development." The IPRS, a national strategy endorsed by the government with a focus specifically on poverty reduction, guided the development management process for the period spanning July 2006 through June 2008.

The president also labored tirelessly to restore Liberia's tainted international image as a criminal and failed state. She immediately instituted policies and programs to rebuild the country's ruined economy and infrastructure and also to put into place a system of good governance.

The Iron Lady, as President Sirleaf was popularly known, basically hit the ground running as her government launched an ambitious transitional development program that was focused on consolidating national peace and positioning the country on a path of poverty reduction through economic growth and human development.

The Sirleaf government inherited a dysfunctional system of governance, as well as a collapsed economy, which recorded a staggering 90 percent decline in gross domestic product (GDP)—the greatest decline by any nation since World War II. Her administration also inherited an unsustainable external debt level of US$4.9 billion—more than six times Liberia's GDP—brought about by debt unserved for more than two decades. A large verified domestic debt of over US$900 million lingered in the arrears. The national treasury was virtually broke—facing salary arrears, unmet obligations to international bodies, and continuing food and fuel crises. With only US$80 million in annual revenues, "Liberia was at the bottom of a very deep hole, desperately needing revival and emergency measures" (Annual Message of President Ellen Johnson Sirleaf to the Joint Session of the National Legislature, January 23, 2017).

The country had been blacklisted by international lenders for default in loan repayment, and it was also placed under United Nations sanctions and treated as a pariah nation for involvement in destabilizing activities in the subregion during the regime of Mr. Taylor.

With only a budget of US$80 million, the new government was faced with many challenges, including the reintegration of war-affected populations, restructuring of security services, extension of state authority throughout the country, creation of jobs, and restoration of basic services, such as rebuilding health and educational systems.

The government began with the launch of the 150-Day Action Plan, which was successfully concluded in collaboration with the Liberian people and the country's development partners. The action plan focused on the restoration of limited basic services, initiating democratic governance, beginning restoration of the economy, and maintaining peace and security.

Under the Interim Poverty Reduction Strategy (IPRS), which is the temporary general framework for national development, the government prioritized key development issues into four pillars: (1) enhancing national security, (2) revitalizing economic growth, (3) strengthening governance and the rule of law, and (4) rehabilitating infrastructure and delivering basic Services.

After the IPRS phased out, the government then launched a three-year Poverty Reduction Strategy (PRS). The PRS, popularly known as Lift Liberia, was also based on four pillars: (1) consolidating peace and security, (2) revitalizing the economy, (3) governance and the rule of law, and (4) infrastructure and basic services.

The PRS articulated the government's overall vision and major strategies for moving toward rapid, inclusive, and sustainable growth and development during the period 2008–2011. This was a period of critical importance as Liberia shifted from post-conflict stabilization to laying the foundation for inclusive and sustainable growth, poverty reduction, and progressing toward the Millennium Development Goals (MDGs).

The new terminal at the Roberts International Airport near Monrovia, partially completed during the Sirleaf administration (courtesy of the Liberian Embassy Press and Public Affairs)

An aerial view of the modern fuel unloading facilities at the Freeport of Monrovia, dedicated in 2017 (courtesy of the Liberian Embassy Public Affairs)

This newly paved road outlet is an example of the efforts made to improve road infrastructure around Liberia during Sirleaf's administration (courtesy of the Liberian Embassy Public Affairs).

Aligned with the government's broader PRS, what was regarded to be a comprehensive Civil Service Reform Strategy was put in place under the government's vision of "Smaller Government, Better Service." Under a policy called "rightsizing," a painful widespread layoff process of civil servants was undertaken. The bloated number of forty-five thousand civil servants the government inherited was reportedly brought down to about thirty-four thousand.

Under the rightsizing program, nearly seven thousand "ghost" names were reportedly removed from the government's wage bill. According to Dr. C. William Allen, then director general of the Civil Service Agency, the ghost names cost the Liberian government $2.6 million annually.

Dr. Allen was quoted in media reports that the civil service became bloated from more than twenty-five thousand to about forty-five thousand as successive interim governments and warring factions took power in Liberia. Those who came to power at the time employed their own people not necessarily based on qualifications or the merit system.

As the civil service became bloated during the years of crises, the successive interim governments became incapable of making monthly salary payments to employees. Throughout the Charles Taylor regime and during the different periods of interim governments, there were times that civil servants were not paid from six months up to a year and beyond. In the absence of their wages, most civil servants at the time had to create various corrupt means to make ends meet.

The following are a few examples of how government employees created the means of compensation for themselves: Customs and revenue officers or officials responsible for the collection of government revenues created their own mechanisms to pocket fees collected. Schoolteachers and administrators collected money from students, and some of them had sexual relationships with female students, many as young as their own children, in exchange for higher grades and promotion. Police, soldiers, and other security outfits in charge of traffic, at checkpoints, and border posts took bribes from motorists and travelers to let them move on freely. Judges and the jury in the courts rendered verdicts in favor of the highest bidders. Officials and personnel at various government entities demanded payment from businesspeople and others for document preparation and signature or awarding of contracts.

Even though the Sirleaf government endeavored to address these corrupt practices by the incremental and timely payment of salaries, employment of qualified personnel, more training, and major reform of the systems of government, these problems have continued to hinder Liberia's progress. Corruption is a systemic problem that has been ingrained in Liberian society due to decades of a dysfunctional system of governance.

Despite the reforms undertaken during the early years of the Sirleaf government to streamline and improve the civil service, it is unfortunate to note that patronage and a lack of or limited transparency in the recruitment of civil servants have again undermined the quality of staff replacement in the civil service. Because of the loopholes that allow for those in authority or people of influence to employ or recommend others for employment, the civil service has once again become bloated. So then what was the sense and benefit in throwing those many well-experienced people from their jobs, which created some void in terms of knowledge transfer? Regrettably, part of Liberia's reconstruction challenges has been that many young people occupying positions of importance have not benefited from the knowledge of experienced mentors who are well schooled in those specific areas of discipline or service. The transfer of knowledge is critical to any society that must grow and develop because it is the knowledge from the past and the present that shapes the future.

Of course, corruption at the level of the civil service has been nothing compared to the tens of thousands, hundreds of thousands, and millions of dollars allegedly squandered by individuals in public leadership as the several dozens of audit reports prepared by the government's auditing and anti-corruption agencies indicate. While the mechanism to identify graft in public service has been established, the weakest link has been the failure to adhere to the rule of law. I would underscore the critical importance of holding accountable, through prosecution and severe punishment, those culpable of economic crimes against the state. The sense that nothing will come out of squandering public resources is a major encouragement for continued rampant corruption.

A very critical part of the government's effort to restore basic services was the rehabilitation of the electricity grid of the capital, Monrovia, starting with a small part of the city, specifically focused on medical and educational facilities, such as the John F. Kennedy Medical Center and the St. Joseph's Catholic Hospital, among others. This also included streetlights being installed to illuminate a few main streets in the capital.

Before the civil crises, the JFK Medical Center, a university teaching public hospital, was a major medical center that not only catered to the general Liberian population but also attracted patients from other parts of Africa. It was one of the few medical facilities in Africa with a cancer treatment center, which was massively looted and destroyed during the war. The cancer treatment equipment, like many other facilities in Liberia, were reportedly looted and taken to certain African countries that had deployed peacekeeping troops during the early years of the war.

Similarly, the St. Joseph's Catholic Hospital, operated by the Catholic Church of Liberia, was also reputed to be one of the best medical facilities in that part of the world before the war. The hospital, like the JFK Medical Center, has been struggling to get back to the level of being able to provide high-quality medical service to the general population. Improvement in the quality of health care is of critical importance to winning the war on poverty. It is sad that since the end of the civil war, many people have died from preventable and treatable illnesses like malaria, typhoid, diarrhea, and hypertension, among others, due to the lack of or limited access to quality health care services.

On the economic front, the government negotiated the cancellation of an external debt burden of US$4.7 billion, out of the US$4.9 billion, in a record period of five years, and returned the country to the path of economic recovery by expanding the fiscal space to pursue the national agenda of inclusive growth and development. Relationships with the World Bank, the African Development Bank, and the International Monetary Fund (IMF) were restored, providing technical and financial support for the formulation of policies and laws aimed at achieving macroeconomic stability (Annual Message of President Ellen Johnson Sirleaf to the Joint Session of the National Legislature, January 23, 2017).

During the 2005 presidential campaign, Madam Sirleaf had promised the Liberian people that she would restore electricity to the entire city of Monrovia within six months if she was elected president. After an assessment was made following her inauguration, it became clear that, given the massive damage to the electrical facilities, it would take years and hundreds of millions of dollars to restore the electricity grid to its prewar status or better.

President Sirleaf would acknowledge that when she promised to restore electricity to Monrovia in the first six months of 2006, she did not realize the extent of damage to the country's electric grid or the extent of the massive destruction of the entire country as a whole.

After his rebels overran the St. Paul Hydro Plant outside Monrovia, the main hydro facility that supplied electricity to Monrovia and other parts of the country, Mr. Taylor reportedly ordered the looting of the main hydro equipment, which he gave to Burkina Faso.

It is well known and documented that the Burkinabe leader, Blaise Compaoré, who later masqueraded as a champion of peace in West Africa before he was also forced out of power in November 2014, was a very strong ally and partner in crime of Mr. Taylor. In the fullness of time, there would be a day of reckoning, through legal proceedings, for the now-deposed Compaoré, who has lived in exile in Côte d'Ivoire since he was swept from power by a violent popular uprising.

Compaoré, one of Africa's longest-serving despots for twenty-seven years, along with then Libyan leader Colonel Muammar Gaddafi, gave Mr. Taylor the military support that enabled him to ravage Liberia and extend his destructive influence to other parts of the West African subregion. After Liberia's brutal civil war, Colonel Gaddafi met his end at the hands of Libyan rebels during the armed rebellion that caused his regime's collapse. Gaddafi was captured and killed in October 2011 while hiding in a culvert during the battle of his hometown, Sirte.

Let There Be Light

Faced with the first major challenge of one of her most important campaign promises, which was to restore electricity to the entire city of Monrovia within six months if she was elected, President Sirleaf had no alternative but to turn to some friendly countries and development partners for support. An international donors group that included Ghana, the European Commission, the United States Agency for International Development (USAID), and the World Bank became something like a saving grace when they formulated a $7 million Emergency Power Program (EPP) to restore electricity to parts of Monrovia.

In four months, the donors group, with the active participation of the Liberian government, and the state-run Liberia Electricity Corporation, which was moribund with no infrastructure, imported generators, rebuilt distribution networks, and began commercial service.

Because the LEC lacked manpower and logistics at the time, the Ghanaian government had its state-run electricity agency, Volta River Authority (VRA), to bring utility crews to Liberia to reinstall poles and rerun wires.

Taylor's rebels looted the hydro equipment while some of the displaced people also looted electrical wires from the poles and sold them to merchants for little money or food in order to survive. Many of the light poles were taken down for firewood, and whatever was left standing of the poles were strewn with bullet holes.

Despite the fact that Liberia has 40 percent of the remaining rain forests in West Africa with some of the best timber species, light poles were exported from Ghana due to the lack of means in Liberia to harvest and process the poles within the few months that was required to get the lights back on in Monrovia.

As the Ghanaian crews went about reinstalling light poles within the designated areas, some Liberians complained about the small size of the poles from Ghana compared with the bigger size of Liberian poles before the war. However, the Ghanaian crews attracted large crowds wherever they worked as many people stood around and cheered them on. The Ghanaian crews, no doubt, were very encouraged by the appreciation and gratitude shown them by the general Liberian populace, as many of the Ghanaians publicly expressed.

Mindful that the government would only be able to provide electricity to very small parts of the city within the first six months, those of us who were in charge of the government's public information machinery began to brainstorm and strategize on how to manage the public's expectations in this regard.

With the support of our American media consultants who were assigned to assist government media officials in the planning and execution of public information dissemination, we were able to fashion a communication strategy that basically drowned out those that tried to portray the president as reneging on her campaign pledge to provide electricity to Monrovia within six months upon taking power.

Even though electricity was restored to a very small part of the city, we took to the airwaves to highlight this as a major achievement, when lights were switched on during the July 26, 2006, Independence Day celebrations of Liberia, as many teenagers who were born during the war saw streetlights for the first time in their lives.

Our media campaign was centered around the slogan "Small Light Today, Big Light Tomorrow" as a way of managing the expectations of our people and assuring them that bit by bit, the government would do everything possible to rebuild our broken country, including the provision of electricity throughout not just Monrovia, but the entire country.

On the morning beginning the celebrations of Liberia's 159th independence anniversary, then Ghanaian president John Agyekum Kufuor flew to Monrovia and joined President Sirleaf on the grounds of the JFK Medical Center to switch on the streetlights, restoring electricity and ending fifteen years of darkness in Liberia.

There was heavy downpour of rain during the early part of that morning, but the rain stopped around 8:00 a.m. to 9:00 a.m. It was cloudy during much of the morning, with the sun coming up around 11:00 a.m. Those areas where the new streetlights were installed turned bright and beautiful as the two presidents symbolically switched on the lights. And there were cheers and celebrations. A large crowd had gathered across the street from the JFK Medical Center, singing, dancing, chanting, and waving Liberian flags as President Sirleaf and her Ghanaian counterpart entered and left the compound. People across the country followed the festivities through live radio broadcasts while holding their own celebrations.

It was a moving event that rekindled the hope of many Liberians that the country had truly embarked upon a course of reconstruction and renewal. For the first time in more than fifteen years, the Independence Day celebrations had a feel of what things used to be before the war. Besides the president of Ghana, then Ivorian president Laurent Gbagbo and former Sierra Leonean president Alhaji Ahmad Tejan Kabbah were among the many high-profile guests from around the world for the event.

Fire Engulfs the Executive Mansion (Presidential Palace) during Independence Celebrations

However, the festivities were interrupted when fire broke out in the Executive Mansion, the official presidential residence, while the guests were assembled there for the state luncheon following the formal ceremonies at the Centennial Pavilion, which was also beautifully renovated.

On my way from the pavilion to the state luncheon at the Executive Mansion, I stopped over at my office, which was a block across from the mansion. While I was talking on the phone standing at the window looking toward the Executive Mansion, I saw smoke coming from the mansion grounds. I initially wondered with disgust as to why the gardeners would choose burning the leaves and dirt on the mansion grounds at a time the guests were already arriving for the state luncheon. Because there was hardly any organized garbage-collection program in the country, people usually burned leaves and dirt or buried them underground. Even though garbage collection has improved over the years, the practice of burning or burying dirt has continued despite the obvious harmful effects from the smoke and bad odor, not to mention possible underground contamination.

As the smoke intensified, I rushed downstairs from my office to the security desk on the ground floor and inquired from the security officer on duty about the smoke billowing from the Executive Mansion grounds. I realized within a second that he had no idea what I was talking about when he asked me if I wanted him to go and check out what was happening. I simply told him never mind and that I would go and find out myself. I then bolted out of the Information Ministry compound and ran toward the Executive Mansion to get a sense of why the smoke was getting thicker and spreading.

Plumes of smoke were billowing from the building as I arrived at the Executive Mansion gate. I then noticed that a stampede had begun as well-dressed local and international guests from various backgrounds and colors were rushing out of the building and compound in panic. The lights in the mansion had gone out, and the elevators were out of service, so people from as high as the eighth floor had to run down the dark stairs. Among those at the mansion were the visiting heads of state and government, who had to be rushed out to safety.

A view of the beautiful seaside Executive Mansion, the official presidential residence (Courtesy, Liberian Embassy Public Affairs)

A partial view of the Executive Mansion ablaze during the national independence celebrations on July 26, 2006 (courtesy of Liberian Observer)

The guards at the gates of the presidential palace recognized me as I joined them and sprang into action, helping them to direct guests out of the compound and stopping the growing crowds of onlookers from the surrounding residential communities from entering the presidential compound. There was mass confusion and panic. The entire country was quickly on edge when radio stations that were doing live broadcasts of the official event soon began to announce that the Executive Mansion had caught on fire and there was mass chaos.

Imagine dignitaries from around the world at such a historic national event, dressed in their very best, taking to their heels to get away as fast as possible. As a popular saying in Liberia goes, "Foot give me way," meaning taking to your heels and running away as fast as you can when you are in a danger zone and not knowing how things would play out. No one could tell what really caused the fire, and speculations were widespread that the fire was caused by sabotage or a terrorist act carefully timed to plunge the war-torn country back into chaos.

The fire started in the president's office on the fourth floor and spread to other parts of the building. During that time, the state-run fire service department did not own a single fire truck, as their equipment had been lost in the war. Because of the lack of government-owned fire equipment and manpower, it took about an hour waiting for fire trucks from the Firestone Rubber Plantation, nearly fifty miles from Monrovia. All we could do was watch helplessly in agony as the fire raged. Many people were openly wailing and weeping, watching our official presidential residence being consumed by the fire, and there was nothing anyone could do but wait until the fire trucks from Firestone arrived. This was at a time when the road to Firestone, which also connects the Roberts International Airport, was in a very deplorable condition, as was the case in most parts of Liberia.

Looking back on the situation at the time, I can only say that God once again came to the rescue of Liberia as the fire trucks were able to drive through those ditches and potholes in time to tackle the fire and contain some before the entire structure succumbed to the inferno.

Following an investigation, it was concluded that the fire was caused by an electric shock due to old wiring emanating from decades of lack of repairs.

I believe that no national security information is revealed by simply acknowledging that the Executive Mansion, constructed in the 1960s by the Israelis, is indeed a fortress specifically built to withstand massive attacks and other acts of destruction such as the fire under discussion.

During the civil war, the Executive Mansion endured extensive bombardment both from the ground and sea by forces seeking to capture and occupy it, but the structure did not crumble. It was because of the security of the structure that military ruler Samuel Doe and remnants of his loyalists were able to be holed up there, and they could not be conquered by opposing rebel forces attacking them from various sides during the early years of the civil war.

While the war raged, many Liberians would recall a BBC interview by Madam Sirleaf during which she called on rebel forces to destroy the Executive Mansion if that was what it would take to get Doe out of power, and it would be rebuilt. Doe was only captured and killed by one of the rebel groups after he left the Executive Mansion grounds to visit the headquarters of the West African peacekeeping force at the Freeport of Monrovia several miles away. That the statehouse again survived the fire that raged for several hours is a testament to how the building was specifically constructed.

A technical assessment following the fire indicated that it would cost some $6 million to repair the Executive Mansion, which is said to be located at the exact point where Brazil is closest to Africa.

In the wake of the fire, the Office of the President was relocated, with a skeletal staff, to the Ministry of Foreign Affairs—a beautiful five-story building next door to the Executive Mansion. The president had continued to reside at her private residence while the government sought for resources to repair the statehouse.

Six months following her inauguration, the president had not moved into the residential quarter of the Executive Mansion when the fire occurred. There were public speculations and rumors that the president was afraid to take residence at the Executive Mansion for fear of her life because the building was haunted as a result of numerous killings that occurred there, especially dating from the 1980 military coup through the nearly fifteen years of civil war. It may be recalled that President William R. Tolbert was murdered inside the presidential suite in the presence of his wife when Samuel Doe and his group of noncommissioned officers of the Armed Forces of Liberia staged their military coup deposing Tolbert in 1980. From the Doe through the Charles Taylor regimes, many perceived or real enemies were reportedly murdered at the mansion, including journalist Charles Gbenyon, who was butchered to death in 1985.

In the midst of a myriad of challenges to provide basic services to the Liberian population in a state of desperation, the government took the approach that renovation of the statehouse was not an immediate priority and that the country was better off allocating its scarce resources for the immediate improvement of the medical and educational facilities and road rehabilitation, among others, to better the lives of the poverty-stricken Liberian masses.

And so when critics lashed out at the president for neglecting to renovate the statehouse, which is a source of national pride, I was one of those, as a government spokesman, who did not hesitate to make it absolutely clear that the president and her government were focused on allocating most of our country's very scarce resources toward improving conditions in the war-ravaged country rather than concentrating on the renovation of the mansion for the president's comfort.

Since the fire, the government was known to have allocated a certain amount in the national budget every year for the gradual renovation of the Executive Mansion. From the annual allocations, the renovation of the statehouse has been ongoing, albeit at a disappointing slow pace.

Regarding the restoration of electricity, some of the major immediate positive effects were that criminal activities were curtailed in areas where there was electricity while students would gather under the lampposts at night to study their lesson and play. Areas with electricity also experienced a sudden revival of commercial and social activities.

While most Liberians were elated by the restoration of electricity to Monrovia, however limited, several critics, including some in the media, saw the president's Emergency Power Program as a halfhearted attempt to live up to her campaign promise to restore full electricity within six months following her inauguration. They argued that her attempts were no different from previous failed efforts of past Liberian governments, especially Charles Taylor, who was the prime agent for the country's destruction.

When he was trying to clinch power, Mr. Taylor had also promised to restore electricity upon becoming president. However, after taking power, he told the Liberian people that electricity was not a priority and that those who wanted electricity should purchase their private generators. This was when Mr. Taylor and his cronies enjoyed twenty-four-hour electricity at their private residences, some of them with swimming pools for the added comfort of the "lords" over the Liberian people. Those who dared to openly question such pronouncements of the dictator risked being arrested, tortured, or murdered.

Since the launch of the first phase of the Emergency Power Program in 2006, there has been an expansion of the electricity grid to various parts of the capital, also with the support of the kingdom of Norway and other donors.

In 2012, Liberia's finance minister, Amara Konneh, announced that the Mount Coffee Hydropower Plant would be rehabilitated and operational by 2016. He put the rehabilitation cost at US$350 million.

The Liberian government's effort to electrify the entire country got an added boost when, in August 2012, the government of Liberia and the World Bank signed a financing agreement for the West Africa Power Pool (WAPP) program at the World Bank headquarters in Washington DC. Liberia's ambassador to the United

States, Jeremiah C. Sulunteh, signed on behalf of Liberia while Shantayanan Devarajan, acting regional vice president of the International Development Association, signed on behalf of the World Bank.

The World Bank Board of Executive Directors approved US$144.5 million in zero interest financing and a US$31.5 million grant for two projects under the WAPP program to increase electricity supply and lower energy cost in the Ivory Coast, Liberia, Sierra Leone, and Guinea. The project was intended to integrate electricity systems, increase electricity supply, and improve system reliability. The project was intended to provide electricity to border towns between the Ivory Coast and Liberia's southeastern areas such as Maryland, Grand Gedeh, and Nimba counties.

Applauding Strong US Support for Liberia

In June 2013, US president Barack Obama announced Power Africa, a new initiative to double access to sub-Saharan Africa where more than two-thirds of the population was estimated to be without electricity and more than 85 percent of those living in rural areas lacked access. The initial group of countries selected to benefit from Power Africa included Liberia, Ethiopia, Ghana, Kenya, Nigeria, and Tanzania. Power Africa was intended to harness a wide range of US government tools to support investment in Africa's energy sector, from policy and regulatory best practices to prefeasibility support and capacity building and technical assistances, among others (Fact Sheet: Power Africa, Office of the Press Secretary, the White House, June 30, 2013).

In November 2015, US support for the rebuilding of Liberia gained an added boost with the signing of the Millennium Challenge Corporation (MCC) compact between both countries, under which Liberia was set to benefit from a $257 million grant to focus on the development of key critical sectors of the country. The compact combined infrastructure investments with policy and institutional reforms that are expected to modernize Liberia's power sector and strengthen its road maintenance systems.

The MCC compact included funding for the rehabilitation of the Mount Coffee Hydropower Plant, development of a training center for technicians in the electricity sector, support for the creation of an independent energy sector regulator, and building capacity and strengthening institutions for a cost-effective approach to nationwide road maintenance.

US Pres. George W. Bush with Liberian Pres. Ellen Johnson Sirleaf during Bush's visit to Liberia in 2008 (Courtesy of Liberian Embassy Public Affairs)

From a historical perspective, the United State is seen as a part of Liberia's unresolved past. However, there can be no question that the United States has been a very critical partner in Liberia's postwar recovery and progress—a lifeblood, so to speak, for a country that was terribly wounded and dying. The administration of President George W. Bush—who used the United States' "bully pulpit," as the saying goes—forced Mr. Taylor out of power and out of Liberia in August 2003 as government and rebel forces battled for control of Monrovia. In July 2003, CNN television reported that the United States had given the embattled Liberian leader forty-eight hours to give up power and leave the country. President Bush said he would "look at all of the options to determine how best to bring peace and stability to Liberia, including the possibility of sending troops as part of an international peacekeeping team" ("Liberia Reports US Ultimatum for Taylor," CNN.com, July 3, 2003).

During the early morning of August 15, 2003, about two hundred US Marines landed at the Roberts International Airport near Monrovia as part of an advanced team of international peacekeepers, led by Nigerian Brigadier General Festus Okonkwo. Many Liberians in Monrovia still recall the ships of the US Marine task force on the ocean coming within view minutes after Mr. Taylor resigned and went to Nigeria on August 11, 2003.

Since then, the United States became the single largest contributor to Liberia's postwar recovery. The country has also enjoyed strong bipartisan support in the US Congress, which has made it possible for the necessary support provided for Liberia's recovery through the foreign appropriations programs. The Liberian people are grateful to the US Congress, including the Congressional Black Caucus, for the strong support toward Liberia's postwar reconstruction.

The United States has been a leading partner in assisting Liberia institute aggressive forms in areas such as the security sector, economy, and the rule of law, among others, which enabled a country that had degenerated into a failed state to quickly reemerge as a postwar success story in the world. The United States led the way for the forgiveness of nearly $5 billion of Liberia's debt burden, for which the country had been blacklisted for years by international financial lenders. Due to very strong US engagement, the International Monetary Fund (IMF) and the World Bank's International Development Association (IDA) announced the US$4.6 billion of debt relief for Liberia on June 29, 2010. Liberia gained debt relief under the Enhanced Heavily Indebted Poor Countries (HIPC) Initiative. The boards of the IMF and the World Bank Group determined that Liberia had taken the necessary policy actions to reach HIPC completion point ("IMF and World Bank Announce US$4.6 Billion Debt Relief for Liberia," IMF press release, June 29, 2010).

The United States also provided financial and technical support to assist with capacity building in various areas of Liberian society and government, including education, which led to the rehabilitation of some teacher-training institutions in the country to provide quality training for public school teachers, as well as the return of the US Peace Corps volunteers, hundreds of whom have been deployed for educational and medical services in various parts of Liberia. For example, at MICAT, we also had US government–sponsored media consultants to assist in reforming the process of government information dissemination during the early days of the Sirleaf administration.

For reasons I would only attribute to the saving grace of God over Mama Liberia—as my beloved country is affectionately known—President Bush made Liberia a foreign policy priority of his administration.

During the historic inauguration of President Sirleaf as Liberia's and Africa's first female democratically elected president, First Lady Laura Bush led a high-powered official US delegation that included Secretary of State

Condoleezza Rice to the inauguration, which was attended by an array of world leaders, many of them from Africa. Mrs. Bush said the election of Madam Sirleaf as president was a significant event worldwide and was "particularly important" to Africa. She noted that women had been traditionally excluded in many African cultures. By becoming the first female president in Africa, said Mrs. Bush, Madam Sirleaf served as a very important role model for little girls on the continent as well as around the world.

Madam Sirleaf's election generated a wave of euphoria around the world, particularly among women in Africa. Besides the African and other world leaders, thousands of women from around Liberia and Africa converged in Monrovia for the inaugural celebrations. With US Navy warships anchored off the coast of Monrovia as a show of support for Liberia, the inauguration signified the dawn of a new day on the continent.

On February 21, 2008, President Bush and First Lady Laura Bush paid a one-day visit to Liberia on the fifth and last stop of the president's second African visit, which also took him to Benin, Tanzania, Rwanda, and Ghana.

The visit was a huge boost for our country's international image. Also importantly, the Bush visit created a major psychological and confidence boost among Liberians, including this writer, that, indeed, our country was back on a course of peace and progress.

Even when Liberia was faced with an existential threat following the outbreak of the Ebola virus epidemic, which killed over 11,300 people in the West African countries of Guinea, Sierra Leone, and Liberia, the administration of President Obama ordered the deployment of American troops and every medical means possible to Liberia to fight and contain the pandemic. The United States supported the other countries affected by the Ebola virus disease; but the focus was Liberia, which was the worst affected by the pandemic, with a death toll of more than 4,800 people.

On February 27, 2015, President Ellen Johnson Sirleaf was received at the White House by US president Barack Obama (courtesy of the Liberian Embassy Public Affairs)

President Sirleaf with former US president Bill Clinton at a lecture at the University of Arkansas at Little Rock in 2017. She was a guest of the Clinton School of Public Service and the Clinton Foundation.

Liberian president Ellen Johnson Sirleaf with now late US congressman Donald Payne Sr., former chair of the Congressional Black Caucus, who was a strong advocate for Liberia (courtesy of the Liberian Embassy Public Affairs)

Then assistant secretary of state for Africa Linda Thomas-Greenfield greets President Sirleaf during a US visit. Left is Ambassador Deborah R. Malac, who replaced Thomas-Greenfield as US ambassador to Liberia (courtesy of the Liberian Embassy).

Considering the long-standing historical ties subsisting between Liberia and the United States, one of the notable foreign policy accomplishments of Madam President was the establishment of the US-Liberia Partnership Dialogue in 2013. The first of its kind with the United States since Liberia's establishment, the US-Liberia Partnership Dialogue is the institutional framework for cooperation between both countries. The partnership dialogue is intended to promote diplomatic and economic cooperation between Liberia and the United States by providing a flexible, nonbinding mechanism to ensure sustained, high-level, bilateral engagement on issues of mutual interest.

In this light, irrespective of who is in the Executive Mansion in Monrovia or in the White House in Washington DC, there is an established institutional framework by which the relationship between both countries is governed.

Convened every two years on a rotational basis between Washington and Monrovia, the third round of the US-Liberia Partnership Dialogue took place on January 10, 2017, in Washington to build on the special historical and bilateral ties between the two countries and to convene four working groups focused on overcoming challenges to Liberia's economy, expanding agriculture production and trade, enhancing Liberia's investment and infrastructure climate, and supporting post-Ebola recovery and health system strengthening efforts.

US support for the rehabilitation of the Mount Coffee Hydropower Plant is an example of what has been achieved under the US-Liberia Partnership Dialogue, which also covers energy or electric power and road development, as well as human development.

In December 2016, the Mount Coffee Hydropower Plant successfully began generating power with the completion of the first of four generating units. Distinguished international guests who joined President Sirleaf at the dedication of the 22-megawatt turbine included the foreign affairs minister of Norway, the commissioner for Africa of the German Federal Ministry for Economic Cooperation and Development, and the assistant secretary of state for African affairs of the US government. The European Development Bank and the governments of Germany and Norway were also part of the partnership to support the rehabilitation of the hydroelectric dam.

Liberia was long regarded as United States' most reliable and closest strategic partner in Africa during the periods of the First and Second World Wars. The Roberts International Airport, which became a regional hub, and the Freeport of Monrovia, which was one of the largest deepwater ports in Africa, were constructed by the United States for military purposes during the World War II. The US military maintained rights to use the country's international airport, which was managed for decades by Pan American Airways. During the era of the Cold War, strategic facilities the US operated in Liberia included one of the largest Voice of America relay transmitters in the world and the Omega navigation tower, reputed to be one of the world's tallest structures, which was used to track the movement of ships and aircrafts in Africa and beyond. Other major private US companies included Chase Manhattan Bank, which, like Pan Am, pulled out of Liberia in the 1980s.

Having served in Washington DC as a Liberian diplomat, I can say without any doubt that there has been a groundswell of goodwill toward Liberia in the United States since the end of the country's civil war. The main challenge has remained as to how we, Liberians, would be able to adequately harness the abundance of goodwill for Liberia in the United States to help push the development of our country. Lack of proper organization and focus, as well as the systemic problem of corruption, has been a serious hindrance to how much Liberia could benefit from the myriad of opportunities and support from the United States to accelerate the pace of the country's development.

In Washington, my responsibilities focused on public diplomacy, a critical function, considering the special historical ties subsisting between Liberia and the United States, which is also Liberia's most important bilateral partner. Even though I accepted the diplomatic posting with reservations because I preferred to have worked on the ground where I felt my professional expertise was most needed, serving in Washington DC—the capital of the most powerful country on earth and leader of the free world—has been very insightful and exceptionally rewarding in terms of the experiences and exposure I have acquired.

Having the opportunity to sit in meetings at the highest levels between both countries, including meetings and other activities when the president of Liberia visited, has given me greater understanding regarding diplomatic intercourse among countries, especially the special historical ties subsisting between Liberia and the United States. I am amazed and deeply impressed by the strength of America's political and economic institutions and how such inclusive political and economic systems have made the United States to become the most powerful country the world has ever known. Indeed, America's greatness is in the strength of its democratic institutions and not due to strong authoritarian rulers.

Because of President Sirleaf's global appeal, including the honor and reverence she enjoyed in Washington, it was a period of great pride representing Liberia in what is, without question, the greatest country in the world. Navigating Washington is like being in the center of the universe because you encounter people from virtually every corner of the world. I have gained experience money can't buy, as the saying goes, and I am grateful to God.

Another source of great pride was serving in Washington during the administration of President Obama, the first black president in the history of the United States. I am most proud because his administration was virtually scandal-free. During his two terms in office, history shows that Obama upheld the dignity, honor, and sanctity of the American presidency. He inspired the world to strive collectively for the greater good of humanity and ensured that America continued to provide positive global leadership.

America did not retreat from its responsibilities as the leader of the free world during the administration of President Obama, who demonstrated that the United States must lead where necessary to ensure global peace and progress. An example of decisive US leadership was during the outbreak of the Ebola virus disease epidemic in West Africa from 2014 to 2016, which caused the death of over 11,300 people. As the deadly Ebola pandemic spread to the United States and other parts of the world due to human movement, President Obama came under strong pressure to ban people from the affected countries from entering the United States.

However, rather than yield to pressure to erect barriers against defenseless people who were perishing from the mysterious disease, President Obama took unprecedented measures to deploy US forces to West Africa to combat the pandemic under one of the most massive medical operations the world has ever known. It was because of strong American leadership under President Obama that the pandemic was contained, as detailed in chapters 9, 10, and 11 of this book.

According to the US Centers for Disease Control and Prevention (CDC), quoting 2014 projections from the World Bank, an estimated $2.2 billion was lost in 2015 in the gross domestic product (GDP) of the three West African countries worst affected by the Ebola epidemic—namely, Liberia, Guinea, and Sierra Leone.

The American media deserves special commendation for covering the Ebola crisis from a humanitarian standpoint. Many Liberians of diverse backgrounds in various states across the United States were featured in human interest reports on American television and radio and in the print media during the widespread campaign to raise support to contain Ebola. In Washington, then Liberian ambassador Jeremiah C. Sulunteh also made the media rounds from CNN to Fox to BBC to VOA, among others, to create awareness and support in the fight against the deadly pandemic.

American churches, charity organizations, and philanthropists also deserve high commendation for providing strong support to Liberia and the other countries affected by the Ebola epidemic.

Please see chapters 9, 10, and 11 for more on the Ebola pandemic, which posed an existential threat to Liberia and also plunged the global community in a state of fear and mass hysteria.

Also deserving high commendation is American billionaire Robert L. Johnson for his strong engagement with Liberia at the beginning of the Sirleaf administration as the war-ravaged country embarked upon the process of rebuilding.

Mr. Johnson, an African American who was the founder of the popular Black Entertainment Television (BET) Networks, now a unit of Viacom, was also owner of the Charlotte Bobcats basketball franchise.

In September 2006, Mr. Johnson was part of an audience at the Clinton Global Initiative in New York, where the lady who had become the new president of Liberia, Madam Sirleaf, spoke passionately about the challenges in Liberia, as well as the opportunities that abound that would be mutually beneficial to Liberia and its partners in progress.

The billionaire investor has said that President Sirleaf's courage and vision inspired him and other colleagues to commit to revitalizing the historic, but dormant relationship between African Americans and Liberia.

In an interview with Forbes.com, Johnson said that he was trying to rekindle the historic ties between African Americans and Liberians and would begin lobbying the US government and the US business community on Liberia's behalf. "What we want to do is build a permanent interest group in the US that will advocate (for) Liberia in the same way Jewish people lobby on behalf of Israel" ("Billionaire Robert Johnson Plugs Liberia," *Forbes*, September 27, 2006, https://www.forbes.com/2006/09/27/johnson-billionaire-liberia-face-cx_po_0926autofacescan01.html#2505382129ba).

During a meeting in Washington DC with President Sirleaf, Mr. Johnson shared his business ideas with the Liberian leader and told her that he would assemble a high-level delegation of African Americans from business, politics, and entertainment to visit Liberia as part of an initiative to invest at least $30 million there.

This led to the creation of the $30 million Liberia Enterprise Development Fund, which was designed to make credit available to Liberian entrepreneurs working to build viable job-creating businesses.

In 2007, the billionaire investor headed a twenty-five-member high-powered delegation to Liberia. He and his party were well received by a very delighted President Sirleaf, along with the government and people of Liberia.

The atmosphere surrounding the visit was like a homecoming for our African American brothers and sisters, who included the legendary actress Cicely Tyson. As an official at the Information Ministry involved with the delegation's visit, I remember Ms. Tyson breaking down in tears when she and some members of the delegation visited a market in Monrovia, which was in a dilapidated state. She said she was heartbroken seeing women, some with children on their backs, laboring under such deplorable conditions to provide for their families. Ms. Tyson is renowned for her career as an actress spanning more than fifty years and for her portrayal of strong African American women, for which she has won many awards, including the Presidential Medal of Freedom—the highest civilian honor in the United States.

A gentleman who was part of the delegation expressed how, despite his initial apprehension regarding the trip, he felt so much at home from the time they landed in the country. He said his interactions with many of the Liberians he encountered reminded him about some of his close family members back in America. Despite the challenges Liberians faced, he said, he found them so hopeful, warm, and loving.

During the visit, the delegation also toured some of the natural and historic sites in Liberia that were accessible by vehicle, as most parts of the country were impassible. One of the most important historic sites visited was the Providence Island in Monrovia, where the freed men and women of color from America first landed in

1822 to establish the Africa's first independent republic at a time almost the entire African continent was colonized by various European powers. How unfortunate that Providence Island, the historic point of return for a freed people whose forebears were taken away in slavery, has remained in a state of neglect. It is only with awareness that Providence Island will be celebrated as a point of return for freedom.

Among the places Mr. Johnson visited was the Kendeja National Cultural Center. Kendeja is beautifully located on the Atlantic coast near Monrovia, on the main highway leading to the Roberts International Airport.

Because of the war, the infrastructures at Kendeja were dilapidated, and a large portion of the land the government originally appropriated for the cultural center was encroached upon, and many structures had been erected. The government could not institute any action to reclaim the many acres of land encroached upon because some of those who built their beautiful homes on a portion of the beachfront property were influential political figures.

In view of the foregoing, when Mr. Johnson visited Kendeja and expressed interest in leasing whatever was left of the cultural center for him to build a world-class hotel, the government took kindly to the offer. The plan was that portion of the initial revenue from the RLJ Kendeja deal was to be used to relocate residents who were employed at the center and purchase a piece of land large enough to build a modern national cultural center, among others. However, the government was criticized by some citizens for leasing out what was left of the Kendeja Cultural Center.

This is how Mr. Johnson built the impressive beachfront RLJ Kendeja Resort and Villas, located within thirty minutes from the airport.

Mr. Johnson also advocated for an American carrier to make direct flights to Monrovia. This, he added, would aid the growth in commerce and make it easier for Liberian residents in the United States to travel home. Through the efforts of Madam President, Mr. Johnson and other friends of Liberia in the United States, Delta Airlines began direct flights from the United States to Liberia in 2009. Unfortunately, Delta announced the suspension of all its flights to Liberia in 2014, shortly before the outbreak of the Ebola epidemic.

Despite the enthusiasm with which he took on the Liberian cause, Mr. Johnson seemed increasingly less engaged regarding Liberia during the second term of the Sirleaf presidency.

Speaking at an event in Monrovia during the first term of the Sirleaf administration, the billionaire investor had called on the Liberian government to do more to curb corruption, which was a hindrance to the economic growth and progress of the country. He indicated that corruption will discourage foreign investors from investing in the country.

It may be interesting to note that the first amount the RLJ Companies paid to the Liberian government for the lease of the Kendeja land—more than $300,000—mostly went down the corruption drain at the Ministry of Information, as reported in chapter 5.

That is just one example of how we, as Liberians, have squandered opportunities and turned away those with their arms stretched out, willing to help us.

My only plea to Mr. Johnson is that he should never allow his desire to build a permanent interest group in the United States that will advocate for Liberia in much the same way Jewish people lobby on behalf of Israel to go unfulfilled. There is a need to continue to build the bridges he has already started through his notable and historic engagement with Liberia.

I have been deeply touched by Mr. Johnson's contributions to postwar Liberia because he invested millions of dollars in the country at a time it was common when most with the resources to also invest adopted an attitude of "wait and see." He helped to build international confidence in Liberia as an attractive destination for investment.

Irrespective of geographic differences, we are all one people. It is only with better understanding that African Americans and other people of African descent, as well as Africans on the continent of Africa would realize how much we are one people. That reality and understanding would lead to further empowerment of the people of Africa and African descent. This is why Mr. Johnson and other successful African Americans who are engaged in meaningful endeavors in various parts of Africa must be highly commended for helping to make a difference in the lives of our people.

While on a Delta Airlines flight in 2019, I was left with the memory of their statement welcoming passengers on board, which included something to the effect that "no matter where we're from, we're more alike than we're different."

Applauding Sustained International Engagement

Thanks to the international community as a whole for the sustained engagement with Liberia since the end of the civil crises and the beginning of postwar reconstruction. Besides the role of the United Nations, as already reflected, the Economic Community of West African States (ECOWAS), African Union (AU), European Union (EU), and also to mention major partners such as China and Japan, among others, must be highly applauded for staying the course with Liberia.

It is equally well to single out for mention some of the European countries like Germany, Sweden, Norway, and the United Kingdom, as well as African countries like Nigeria and Ghana for the strong support to Liberia's reconstruction. With continued, deepened engagement and support, as manifested by the involvement of the international community in bringing a peaceful end to the civil crises, there is reason to be hopeful that Liberia would remain on a steady course of peace, democracy, and economic progress.

Words are inadequate to express profound gratitude for the role of ECOWAS—the subregional body established on May 28, 1975, in Lagos, Nigeria—to promote cooperation and integration in order to create an economic and monetary union for the promotion of economic growth and development in West Africa. As you will read in chapter 11, Liberia was a founding leader of the fifteen-nation ECOWAS.

Following the outbreak of Liberia's civil war in December 1989, ECOWAS was confronted with the challenge of organizing a regional force, the ECOWAS Monitoring Group (ECOMOG), which intervened in the war in 1990 to end the bloodshed and restore peace to Liberia. The ECOWAS military intervention in Liberia, led by Nigeria, is said to have cost hundreds of millions of dollars and hundreds of lives of fellow West Africans. Before then, there was no precedence in how countries could work in their collective to successfully resolve regional conflicts. From the experiences and lessons learned in dealing with the Liberian crises, as well as strong encouragement that have resulted in peaceful resolution of conflicts in member states, ECOWAS has emerged as one of the more effective and proactive regional organizations.

It is also noteworthy to particularly mention the People's Republic of China for being a major partner in Liberia's reconstruction and economic recovery processes since the end of the civil war. It is hoped that the Liberia-China relationship, as well as Africa-China ties, would continue to grow to be mutually beneficial in terms of realizing Africa's economic growth and infrastructural development as Chinese investors, and other foreign businesses for that matter, generate profits from their investment. From the construction of roads and bridges to the erection of buildings and other infrastructure throughout Liberia, Chinese companies have been major players in the nationwide rebuilding process. Chinese companies like China Union, which is one of the leading iron ore mining concessions in Liberia, are contributing to Liberia's economic recovery.

Chinese support for Liberia in the educational sector is reflected by the rebuilding of the Fendell Campus of the University of Liberia outside Monrovia into a modern university campus. In the health sector, Chinese support for Liberia is also shown by the construction of a modern hospital in northern Liberia, the Jackson F. Doe Memorial Hospital in Tappita, Nimba County. Among other projects, the Chinese constructed a large annex to the Capitol Building in Monrovia, seat of the national legislature, while the construction of a ministerial complex that will house several government ministries and agencies under one roof is nearing completion in Monrovia. In the 1980s, the Chinese constructed the largest sports stadium in Liberia, named the Samuel K. Doe Sports Complex, in Monrovia.

As a manifestation of Liberia's reemergence as a respectable member of the comity of nations, several world leaders, including US president Bush, as reported earlier, visited the country. Other world and regional leaders who visited Liberia included then Chinese president Hu Jintao, German chancellor Angela Merkel, then British prime minister David Cameron, and Canadian prime minister Justin Trudeau, as well as then Nigerian president Olusegun Obasanjo and then Ghanaian president John Agyekum Kufuor. Both Presidents Obasanjo and Kufuor played critical roles in bringing about a peaceful end to Liberia's civil crises. Before the end of their respective presidential tenures, Presidents Obasanjo and Kufuor each visited Liberia and were honored by the state for their invaluable contributions toward the restoration of peace in Liberia.

Good Governance Yields Dividends of Peace and Prosperity

Because of the national development programs undertaken by the government despite the challenges, the economy expanded rapidly. By the end of President Sirleaf's first six-year term of office, the country had attracted several billions of dollars in direct private investment in the reactivation of the country's mining, agriculture, and forestry sectors. Oil exploration became a new potential in Liberia's private sector development in 2012.

The government also made significant progress in rebuilding Liberia's war-ravaged infrastructure, which includes roads, medical and educational facilities, as well as an increase in agriculture production.

Due to the aggressive reconstruction efforts undertaken especially during President Sirleaf's first term, a visit to Monrovia is now characterized by paved roads and street and traffic lights. In contrast, just a few years following the end of the civil war, the city was dark; and traffic on any major road was snarled due to potholes and puddles. During those days, most parts of the country were inaccessible or extremely difficult to reach because of the deplorable conditions of almost all existing roads while many other places lacked access to roads. Since then, the government has focused on the rehabilitation and construction of roads throughout the length and breadth of the country, making travel to many parts easier.

Before the war, it took a drive of about one and half hours from Monrovia to the commercial port city of Buchanan because the highway was paved. After conditions of the highway became very deplorable and at times impassable due to lack of repairs, it took between four and half hours to five hours from Monrovia to Buchanan. So terrible was the road condition, with the violent rocking and banging in the potholes and ditches, that while I was traveling with a group to attend a funeral in Buchanan, a young lady bled profusely, apparently due to the violent rocking of the vehicle. The Monrovia-Buchanan highway is now repaved.

It is equally noteworthy to point out that Liberia had successfully carried out reforms required under the Heavily Indebted Poor Country (HIPC) Initiative that more than US$4.7 billion of external debt, which had burdened Liberia and caused the country to be internationally blacklisted, was written off the books by bilateral and multilateral lenders. Thanks to the critical role played by the United States, along with other countries and international institutions, such as Germany, the International Monetary Fund (IMF), and the World Bank Group, in Liberia's debt-forgiveness process.

There were also considerable gains in the areas of governance and the rule of law, as manifested by the passage of key pieces of legislations, implementation of policies and programs, and enhancing the capacities of the judiciary and law enforcement agencies—all of which were aimed at improving public services.

Regarding reforms in Liberia's security sector, in July 2006, the first group of recruits for a new professional army began training in Monrovia. Even though the number of the first group of new recruits was small, just over one hundred, the significance of the exercise was huge. Liberia's former army, the bloated Armed Forces of Liberia (AFL), disintegrated during the years of the civil war, having become factionalized, and was an instrument of brutality and oppression. It was in consideration to prevent the evil of the past from reoccurring that necessitated the importance of creating a new well-trained armed forces.

In view of the above, the 2003 Comprehensive Peace Agreement, which was reached by parties to the Liberian conflict in Accra, Ghana, called for the restructuring of the AFL and other state security apparatus. UN Security Council Resolution 1509 mandated UNMIL to assist the creation of a professional army for Liberia as part of a broad security sector reform.

During the two-year transitional period following the peace accord, the former AFL was disbanded. Over nine thousand former soldiers recruited after the 1989 civil uprising were demobilized and served severance benefits while nearly 4,500 soldiers who joined the army before 1990 were retired. The latter group was decorated by President Sirleaf during the 159th independence anniversary of Liberia in July 2006, the month the first recruit for the new AFL began training ("Training Begins for New Army," *UNMIL Focus*, June–August 2006).

Since the end of UNMIL's mandate in Liberia at the end of March 2018, the security of the country has been fully under the control of the reformed military and paramilitary forces. Liberian troops have also been on peacekeeping duty under the auspices of the UN Peacekeeping mission in Mali while the country is playing an active leadership role in regional security matters.

An infantry platoon of the reorganized Armed Forces of Liberia preparing to depart for peacekeeping duties in Mali in 2013 as part of the UN Peacekeeping mission (courtesy of the Liberian Embassy Public Affairs)

Lieutenant Stephen V. Mulbah of the Liberia National Coast Guard with Honorable Gabriel I.H. Williams and US Coast Guard Vice Admiral Manson Brown after completion of training at the International Maritime Officers School in Virginia

It is interesting to note that the minister of national defense, Honorable Brownie J. Samukai Jr., was the only cabinet minister who served in the same position for the entire twelve years of the Sirleaf administration. A retired AFL soldier and veteran security expert of international repute who worked with the UN Department of Safety and Security, among others, Mr. Samukai is credited for providing effective leadership for the creation of the new Armed Forces of Liberia. Despite the challenges in organizing the new army, including a series of attempts by disbanded soldiers to engage in violent protest and disrupt the peace in demand of more financial benefits from the government, the country never relapsed into violence and war, as has been the case in certain countries of the subregion because of the leadership.

Following the inauguration of the Weah administration in 2018, Honorable Samukai was succeeded as minister of national defense by Brigadier General Daniel Dee Ziankahn, who was the first chief of staff of the newly organized Armed Forces of Liberia.

Another individual who played a notable role in Liberia's security sector reforms, however behind the scene, was Dr. H. Boima Fahnbulleh, national security advisor to President Sirleaf. A political science professor, veteran politician, activist, and Pan-Africanist, Dr. Fahnbulleh's understanding of the political and security dynamics within Liberia and the West African subregion helped the administration to ensure sustainable peace in Liberia. As noted in chapter 1, Dr. Fahnbulleh, a former minister of education and foreign affairs, respectively, has been a leading figure in Liberian political activities since the 1970s. He is well connected and respected within the West African subregion.

Those connections would serve well in the government's overall security strategy, which was focused on ensuring that there was no outbreak of subversive activity in Liberia and other countries within the subregion that could undermine Liberia's fragile peace. Thanks to the leadership of Dr. Fahnbulleh, Minister Samukai, and other security professionals who were involved with the security sector reforms, Liberia has enjoyed sustainable peace and is becoming a major player within the regional and multilateral security arrangements.

During my ministerial tenure at the MICAT, I interacted with Dr. Fahnbulleh on many national security-related matters, which gave me a better understanding of issues relating to national and international security. The fact that postwar Liberia did not experience any resurgence of armed insurrection is a testament to the notable success of the UN Peacekeeping mission, working along with local law enforcement leaders and professionals. This appreciation is in consideration that there are postwar countries within the subregion that have experienced renewed violence since the official end of their respective crises.

Another major accomplishment by the Sirleaf government was in the area of freedom of speech and of the press. After decades of suppression under past brutal regimes that criminalized freedom of speech and of the press, free expression was at an unprecedented level during the Sirleaf administration. One of the major accomplishments of the administration was the tolerance of dissent, which birthed an unprecedented level of freedom in Liberia. This is manifested by the fact that in 2010, Liberia became the first country in West Africa to pass into law a Freedom of Information (FOI) Act, a law that grants public access to documents or other data in the possession of a government agency or public authority unless the information falls into a certain category that is specifically excluded from the terms of the legislation.

This was followed by Liberia becoming a signatory to the Declaration of Table Mountain, which calls for the repeal of criminal defamation and "insult" laws across the African continent, and was adopted at the World Newspaper Congress held in Cape Town, South Africa, in 2007.

Despite these accomplishments, it should be noted that freedom of speech and of the press remains under threat in Liberia while the laws on libel, defamation, and sedition, which are inimical to free speech, are on the books.

According to President Sirleaf, on account of wide-ranging economic reforms, Liberia "attracted US$16 billion in foreign direct investment in concession agreements programmed to inject resources into the country over a period of up to twenty-five years. These were in iron ore mining activities, large-scale oil palm operations, resuscitation of coffee and cocoa production, and petroleum exploration. To date, largely on account of land and labor disputes, exacerbated by economic shocks, only US$4.2 billion of the amount mobilized has been operationalized to create jobs, improve infrastructure and generate national income" (Annual Message of President Ellen Johnson Sirleaf to the Joint Session of the National Legislature of Liberia, January 23, 2017).

Due to proper planning and execution in the national reform process, Liberia recorded an average growth of 7.53 percent between 2006 and 2013, thus placing it among sub-Saharan African countries recognized as fast-growing economies.

As part of the efforts to engender a countrywide economic viability, the Central Bank of Liberia and other commercial banks opened branches in various parts of the country, and some of them established the automated teller machine (ATM) system to enhance transactions. Government employees or civil servants now receive their monthly salaries through direct deposit rather than standing in long lines for hours, rain or shine, to cash their checks, as was the case in the past.

CHAPTER SEVEN
Growing Demand for Accountability to End Culture of Impunity

Despite the abundance of human, natural, and material resources, as well as the blessing of tremendous international goodwill, especially since the onset of the postwar reconstruction, there has been a struggle to get the country grounded and headed in the right direction because of many grave foundational problems. There are too many contradictions and fault lines created from the foundation of Liberia that have not been addressed or rectified. This is in regard to those acts of man's inhumanity to man, which culminated to years of bloodshed and destruction, and the culture of impunity as seen by the lack of accountability for the mismanagement of public resources.

In 2013, Liberia began to experience significant shocks that adversely impacted the economy, two of which include the following: the decline in global commodity prices, as well as the outbreak of the Ebola virus epidemic in Liberia and other West African countries, which led to an exodus from the country. The Ebola pandemic brought most production-related operations to a virtual halt, and Liberia's GDP plummeted to 0 percent.

As of this publication, the country has been going through another painful struggle to get back on the path of economic recovery and progress. Meanwhile, the accomplishments of the twelve years of the Sirleaf administration have been overshadowed by the general awareness of widespread corruption, which has generated grave negative perceptions among Liberians regarding their hopes and aspirations for their country. As a result, the goals of the Poverty Reduction Strategy have yet to be realized because the economic benefits have yet to trickle down fast enough to the impoverished population. The scourge of corruption has indeed hindered Liberia's progress.

As President Sirleaf acknowledged in her 2017 annual message to the Joint Session of the National Legislature, her government failed in tackling two major challenges facing the country: corruption and reconciliation. On the question of national reconciliation, she said, "Our country's long struggle for national reconciliation has its genesis in history. A coup d'état and years of civil conflict exacerbated long-standing divides that have left deep wounds" (Annual Message of President Ellen Johnson Sirleaf to the Joint Session of the National Legislature, January 23, 2017).

Addressing the UN General Assembly in September 2010, President Sirleaf informed the global community that tackling corruption and mismanagement represented the greatest challenge that Liberia faced as it continued to rebuild its economy and society after the UN helped the country end decades of either civil war or misrule.

While most Liberians have hailed the president for her accomplishments in developing the country since her presidency, corruption and impunity within the government were seen as serious matters that undermined public confidence in the government. For example, in an interview with the independent newspaper the *New Democrat*, published on December 5, 2012, the then chairperson of Liberia's Anti-Corruption Commission, Madam Francis Johnson-Allison, said, "Unless the Liberian nation takes a different approach in the fight against corruption, the legitimacy of this government may be undermined."

Madam Johnson-Allison, a former chief justice of Liberia's Supreme Court and the first minister of justice in the Sirleaf government, noted that despite the government's achievements in the fight against corruption, the "limited success scored could be weakened by the uncooperative tendencies on the part of government institutions that stand accused of acts of corruption. People are plundering and siphoning government's money out of the coffers." She emphasized, "I can only hope that we do something because a society that is corrupt cannot be stable for a very long time" (*New Democrat*, December 5, 2012).

President Sirleaf was often accused of weakness in seriously tackling corruption, especially due to her failure to take action against individuals with close ties to her. The president had expressed on several occasions that Liberia was well endowed with natural resources, but the country and its people were poor because of mismanagement. It is common knowledge that corruption and mismanagement of public resources were among the key reasons that led to the civil upheavals and collapse of Liberia as a nation-state.

For example, a report released on September 4, 2012, by the London-based watchdog organization Global Witness drew attention to corruption and criminalization of Liberia's rain forests involving Liberian government officials, which had the potential to destabilize the fragile country.

The Global Witness report stated, "A quarter of Liberia's total landmass has been granted to logging companies in just two years, following an explosion in the use of secretive and often illegal logging permits, an investigation by Global Witness, Save My Future Foundation (SAMFU) and Sustainable Development Institute (SDI) shows. Unless this crisis is tackled immediately, the country's forests could suffer widespread devastation, leaving the people who depend upon them stranded and undoing the country's fragile progress following the resource-fueled conflicts of 1989–2003."

The report also stated that the logging contracts, termed "private use permit (PUP)," covered 40 percent of Liberia's forests and almost half of the country's best intact forests. The forest scandal involved officials in several government agencies, including the state-run Forestry Development Authority, the Ministry of Agriculture, and the Ministry of Lands, Mines, and Energy, as well as a close presidential confidant.

Another report by the UN Panel of Experts in December 2012 also drew attention to the effect that the PUPs had grave implications for the fragile country, given the fact that the PUPs often pertain to areas that were vulnerable and outside the effective control of the government.

According to the UN Panel of Experts report, "Areas covered by the Private Use Permits overlap with locations that mercenaries and Ivorian militia members use as staging grounds and support bases for cross-border attacks into the Ivory Coast, particularly Grand Gedeh County. Moreover, these areas also contain many artisanal gold and diamond mining claims that the mercenary and militia groups use to sustain themselves."

It may be recalled that diamonds and timber were among the primary resources that fueled Liberia's and Sierra Leone's respective brutal civil wars and nearly destabilized the entire West African subregion.

In view of the foregoing, the government's apparent failure to institute appropriate policies and programs to effectively address the unresolved past, coupled with the scourge of corruption, has compelled Liberians to begin demanding for justice and accountability. Frustrated by the culture of impunity that has long emboldened perpetrators of war and economic crimes, Liberians are now making their voices louder in their demand for the establishment of a court for war crimes and crimes against humanity, as well as economic crimes.

Judging from the growing chorus in Liberia and abroad calling for the creation of a war and economic crimes court for Liberia, it can be said without fear of contradiction that a strong consensus has emerged affirming the need for the establishment of such a court. For example, on July 5, 2018, seventy-six Liberian, African, and international nongovernmental organizations made a submission to the UN Human Rights Committee in Geneva, Switzerland, calling on the Liberian government to undertake fair and credible prosecutions of international crimes committed during Liberia's civil wars. A release from Human Rights Watch, one of the international organizations involved with the initiative, stated that the submission was made ahead of Liberia's appearance before the committee, which monitors implementation of the International Covenant on Civil and Political Rights by its state parties, scheduled for July 9–10, 2018, in Geneva ("Liberia: 76 Groups Seek Justice for War Crimes," Human Rights Watch, July 5, 2018).

According to the consortium of organizations, Liberians suffered tremendously over the course of the armed conflicts spanning more than fourteen years. The abuses Liberians suffered included summary executions, large-scale massacres, rape and other forms of sexual violence, mutilation and torture, and widespread forced conscription and use of child combatants.

The submission presented by the seventy-six groups identified steps to be taken without delay by the Liberian government to help ensure accountability for serious crimes in Liberia, to be considered by the Human Rights Committee. It also made recommendations for additions and changes to the TRC's proposed court to enable fair and credible trials.

A *FrontPage Africa* report identified some of the leading international organizations in the coalition as follows: Civitas Maxima, a Swiss organization devoted to the independent legal representation of victims of war crimes; Center for Justice and Accountability, an international human rights organization based in San Francisco, California; Amnesty International, a leading global human rights organization; and Human Rights Watch, a leading international human rights body. Other organizations that have also been involved in leading the charge for the creation of a war crimes court in Liberia include the Global Justice and Research Project, Coalition for Justice, National Student Movement, Flomo Theater, Fubbi Foundation for Development and Sustainability, Citizens Actions, Liberia Trust Communications, and the International Justice Group.

Meanwhile, the UN Human Rights Committee issued strong concluding observations on Liberia's continued impunity for past crimes and human rights violations and called upon the Liberian government to establish, as a matter of priority, a process of accountability for war crimes, according to an Amnesty International press release.

On July 26, 2018, following the first-ever review of the human rights situation by the UN Human Rights Committee, which concluded a dialogue with the Liberian government, the committee concluded that it "regrets the very few steps taken to implement the bulk of the Truth and Reconciliation Commission (TRC) recommendations of 2009." It also expressed concern that "none of the alleged perpetrators of gross human rights violations and war crimes mentioned in the TRC report, has been brought to justice, and that some of those individuals are or have been holding official executive positions, including in the government" (Amnesty International, August 8, 2018).

As another indication of the growing international support for the establishment of a war crimes court, the US House of Representatives' Committee on Foreign Affairs passed a resolution on October 4, 2018, calling for the establishment of a war and economic crimes court for Liberia. The resolution was cosponsored by Congressman Daniel Donovan, a Republican, of New York's Eleventh Congressional District.

Congressman Donovan said his constituency, which includes Staten Island and part of southern Brooklyn, New York, is home to one of the largest Liberian communities in the United States, where many diaspora Liberians have been pushing for the establishment of a war crimes court in Liberia.

A growing number of Liberian individuals and groups have begun to hold regular street marches and protests in Liberia with placards displaying calls for justice and photos of their loved ones who were killed.

Liberians are of the growing opinion that an internationally backed war crimes court similar to that of the Special Court for Sierra Leone, which tried and convicted Mr. Charles Taylor and other Sierra Leone rebel leaders for their roles in Sierra Leone's civil war, is needed in Liberia for similar accountability. Liberians are becoming increasingly aware that holding public leaders accountable for their public stewardship is one way to remove the cover of impunity that has kept the country stagnant and to ensure steady progress.

Indications are that Liberians have begun to show their anger that the government has yet to satisfactorily implement the recommendations from the TRC, which evolved from the 2003 internationally backed Accra Comprehensive Peace Agreement, signed by warring factions and other parties to the Liberian peace process in Ghana. The TRC process was intended to help find ways to heal the deep wounds and breach the divides among the Liberian people outside a legal process. However, some of the warlords refused to testify, and those who did were mostly grandstanding and not remorseful.

Madam Sirleaf, then a sitting president, was the most high-profile individual summoned to testify at the TRC hearings regarding her role in the Liberian crises. Testifying before the TRC, President Sirleaf said she had endorsed Mr. Charles Taylor's rebellion against President Samuel Doe but had never been part of Taylor's National Patriotic Front of Liberia (NPFL) rebel group. She, however, admitted to being a part of a group of exiled Liberians who lent their support to Taylor without being aware of his true intentions. She also said even though she supported Taylor's war effort initially, she backed away as it became apparent he was a showman and not a true revolutionary.

President Sirleaf said her actions against the brutal dictatorial regime of Samuel Doe were done in consultation with other opposition political leaders and not unilateral. She apologized to the Liberian people for "being fooled by Taylor," noting that she did not realize Taylor's rebellion would be as bloody as it was.

Following the end of the public hearings, in June 2009, the TRC submitted its final report to the National Legislature of Liberia. The TRC report contains numerous recommendations, some of which have proven to be very controversial. Among others, the TRC report recommended that a number of politicians, including President Sirleaf, be banned from politics for a period of thirty years because of their past support for warring factions in Liberia's civil war.

The controversial TRC recommendation banning the sitting president from political activities had the potential to create a major constitutional crisis in the country, and there were legal challenges to the said recommendation by the president and other affected individuals. The politicization of the TRC report from then on undermined the full implementation of the report.

The TRC report also recommended that nearly a hundred individuals considered to be notorious perpetrators of gross human rights violations and war crimes be prosecuted in a court of competent jurisdiction.

Prince Y. Johnson, leader of the former Independent National Patriotic Front of Liberia (INPFL) armed faction, was named in the TRC report as a notorious perpetrator. Johnson, who was responsible for the capture and killing of President Doe during the civil war, has been the senior senator for Nimba County in the national legislature since 2006. Johnson and other former warlords have been vehemently opposed to the establishment of a war crimes court for Liberia. With former warlords and other former factional leaders and sympathizers in the national legislature and the upper echelon of government, there should be little wonder why much effort has not been put into implementation of the TRC report.

It is in view of such developments, as highlighted, that recommendations in the TRC report, submitted to the government for full implementation, were seen to have been partially implemented in a lackluster manner. Although the TRC recommended a war crimes court to investigate and try people responsible for grave violations of international law, Liberia had not moved ahead with this recommendation. Such developments have clearly caused more pain for the victims who suffered the unspeakable acts of human rights abuses and lost their loved ones during the crises.

While attending a gathering in the United States where issues related to the TRC and war crimes in Liberia were discussed, a young lady stood up and tearfully narrated accounts of how her father, a science teacher at the University of Liberia, was murdered by a rebel who was part of Charles Taylor's NPFL armed faction. She stated that the rebel who killed her father was once a student in her father's science class who failed the class. Blaming the teacher for failing him, the rebel went for the kill when he encountered the teacher, along with other displaced people, during the early period of the civil war.

With tears pouring down her face, the young lady said she was very broken by her father's tragic death that she once contemplated finding her way into Mr. Taylor's inner circle in the hope of going to bed with him so she could use that opportunity to kill him in revenge for her father. However, she devoted her energy to supporting quality education in Liberia, with a focus on science. This is in memory of her father, she said, in order for every child to have quality education, especially in science, that no child will fail in science and use their frustration to kill another innocent teacher out of ignorance.

Another young lady at the gathering also disclosed in tears how her mother told her that she was conceived after her mother was raped by an armed fighter. She disclosed that her mother had shown her the alleged perpetrator, who was still alive in Liberia, but she did not have any relationship with what she called the man who raped her mother.

As an example of how deep and widespread the wounds of the war are among Liberians, the fathers of four of the staff I have worked with at the Embassy of Liberia in the United States were violently killed during the civil crises. One of them was among the thirteen officials of the deposed government publicly executed following the 1980 military coup in Liberia while the three others were killed under different circumstances during the brutal and barbaric civil war. I have seen some of the affected staff at times in tears when recalling the memories of their killed loved ones.

As recorded in some of these pages, I was a journalist and the secretary-general of the Press Union of Liberia, the national journalists' movement, when the civil war started. I almost got killed for my role as a journalist before fleeing to the United States. In view of the foregoing, I was one of several journalists invited by the TRC commissioners to testify during the hearings, which focused on recording the testimonies of perpetrators and victims during the years of Liberia's civil crises from the late 1970s to the end of the civil war in 2003.

In October 2008, the TRC held what was called the special thematic hearings on "The Media and the Liberian Conflict." The special thematic hearings on the media sought to examine the role of the local and international media in the Liberian conflict.

It was a traumatic experience narrating the accounts of how I was arrested by rebels, with a gun placed to my head, and almost was executed because the rebels wrongly accused me of being a progovernment journalist. The fact was that I was on the run as one of those wanted by the government, dead or alive, because the Samuel Doe regime had accused the independent media and the Press Union, the student movement, and other progressive groups advocating for democratic governance of being supporters of rebels.

This was after Mr. Taylor had launched his armed rebellion to violently remove Doe's regime from power. The rebels had entered Monrovia, and there was fighting for control of the capital. There were checkpoints at street intersections and various parts of the city manned by armed men who interrogated those who passed by. Those they believed to be enemies based on ethnicity or perceived association with the government could be executed instantly. Similar atrocities were perpetrated at checkpoints manned by troops loyal to the government. It was through such a dangerous process at a street corner in downtown Monrovia that the rebels arrested me and almost killed me after wrongly identifying me as a progovernment journalist.

Reliving those experiences made me break down and weep openly. I remember now late legendary journalist Stanton B. Peabody, who sat next to me and was among the prominent national and international journalists who testified, rubbing his hand on my back to console me as I wept and tried to gain composure while narrating those traumatic accounts. I was one of the lucky few as many innocent people were slaughtered without justification.

The national and international journalists who testified at the TRC thematic hearings included *Liberian Observer* managing director Kenneth Y. Best, former BBC Liberia correspondent Isaac D. E. Bantu, former news director and anchor of the state-owned Liberia Broadcasting System (LBS) Kwame Clement, and managing editor of the Voice of Americas *Daybreak Africa* program Mr. James Butty.

The others included Robin White, former BBC Africa Service director; Stephen Ellis, author of the book *The Mask of Anarchy*, which deals with Liberia's civil crises; and Lamini A. Waritay, former president of the Press Union of Liberia and minister of information.

These journalists and others not named were involved in covering the Liberian crises. As journalists, we conveyed to the outside world the tragedy that Liberia had become, and most of us were victims of the circumstances that prevailed at the time.

Mr. Clement, a lawyer who was based in the United States, returned to Liberia to testify during the TRC hearings. He also broke down and wept openly when he was asked to narrate accounts of the killing of his very good friend and workmate Charles Gbenyon and his own imprisonment following the 1985 attempted overthrow of Doe's regime. As he cried, he said he never liked talking about Gbenyon's death and how he almost lost his own life during that incident.

On November 12, 1985, General Thomas Quiwonkpa, former commanding general of the Armed Forces of Liberia, staged an abortive coup to force Doe out of power after Doe rigged the presidential election held the previous month. Both Doe and Quiwonkpa were comrades in arms who staged the 1980 bloody coup. However, they became bitter rivals in the bloody contest for power. Quiwonkpa was forced to flee into exile, from where he plotted to seize power from Doe, who had been declared president by rigging the election, as noted.

During the early morning of November 12, 1985, forces loyal to General Quiwonkpa, who had infiltrated the country, seized LBS, the national broadcaster. Regular program on the station was interrupted with the playing of a recording of the national anthem, followed by the voice of General Quiwonkpa, who announced that he had overthrown Doe's regime. During the first few hours of that day, Quiwonkpa's coup appeared to have succeeded, sparking widespread jubilation in Monrovia and most parts of the country. Thousands paraded in the streets in a carnival affair in celebration of the fall of the brutal dictator.

General Quiwonkpa, regarded to be the most popular PRC member, drove around town and interacted with those who jubilated while the LBS radio and television crew, led by Gbenyon, was on hand to cover the activities of the general, as well as the mass jubilation around the city.

While Quiwonkpa was out and about, Doe was holed up inside the mansion with a few guards. He reportedly used a secured telephone line to reach the commander of the Schiefflin military barracks. The commander and many of the soldiers were members of Doe's Krahn ethnic group. Having told the commander that he was still at the mansion, troops from Schiefflin moved on the radio station and easily regained control from Quiwonkpa's loyalists, who were also celebrating instead of being alert.

Around 2:00 p.m. to 3:00 p.m., a recording from Doe was broadcast on LBS radio, stating that Quiwonkpa's coup had been foiled and that the government had regained control of the security of the country. As news of this latest development spread, everything went quiet, and people disappeared from the streets. As a reporter with the *Sun Times*, I was out covering the momentous event, which was to turn very brutal and bloody.

Just before Doe's announcement, I encountered my fellow journalist and friend John Vambo on the grounds of the Information Ministry, who told me that he had heard that Doe was still in the mansion. I had earlier visited the Post Stockade in Monrovia, where officials of Doe's regime who were being arrested by Quiwonkpa's forces were brought and detained. Among the officials who were brought at the Barclay Training Center (BTC) for detention while I was there were Doe's vice president, Dr. Harry F. Moniba, and Justice Minister Jenkins K. Z. B. Scott. Regarded to be one of the most hated members of Doe's regime for perpetrating widespread human abuses, Scott was brutalized with his eyes and head very swollen when he was brought to the Post Stockade prison, located at the BTC military barracks in Monrovia.

As officials of the deposed regime were being rounded up and placed in detention, General Quiwonkpa maintained in his radio broadcasts that this was a peaceful takeover and that no official of the deposed regime should be manhandled. He warned against looting and harassment of peaceful citizens. Quiwonkpa also announced the names of individuals appointed to various positions in the new regime. This caused many innocent people, who were named to positions without knowing anything about Quiwonkpa's plot, to be arrested, tortured, and killed after Doe regained control.

While at the BTC, I also saw Gbenyon sitting at the back of an LBS pickup wearing a white T-shirt while his crew filmed the officials who were being brought to the Post Stockade prison.

With the repeated broadcast of Doe's voice that Quiwonkpa's coup had failed and that government forces had been ordered to hunt down the rebels, everywhere went quiet as people went home and shut their doors. A great fear descended upon the country. A state of terror was unleashed across the country as the government rounded up its enemies, real or imagined. Political opponents, journalists, and rights activists were among those rounded up, imprisoned, tortured, or killed by the regime.

Worst targeted were members of the Gio and Mano ethnic groups, from which Quiwonkpa hailed. In reprisal for Quiwonkpa's attempted coup, Doe's Krahn-controlled security forces committed pogrom against the Gio and Mano people, especially in the Nimba County area, which is home to members of the two ethnic groups.

Charles Gbenyon and Kwame Clement were among numerous journalists arrested and detained by the Doe regime in the wake of Quiwonkpa's failed coup attempt. Unfortunately, while in detention at the Executive Mansion, Gbenyon was reportedly butchered to death at the mansion upon Doe's order.

Gbenyon was arrested in the front of the LBS building when Doe visited the national broadcaster after Quiwonkpa's dead body had been put on public display in Monrovia and openly butchered, which was something I saw with my own eyes. I was among the crowd of onlookers who gathered at the BTC when jubilant soldiers loyal to Doe began to dismember the body of Quiwonkpa with bayonets. It was such a traumatic sight that I ran home from the barracks consumed by fright from what I had just witnessed. I saw one of Quiwonkpa's smallest fingers being cut off and one of his eyes that had been plucked out in the hand of another individual.

In 1990, the global rights advocacy group Index on Censorship published a report from the London-based *West Africa* magazine detailing accounts of how Gbenyon was killed. Some of the accounts are as follows:

Gbenyon, the editor in chief of Liberian Television . . . walked up to the Head of State with microphone in hand and cameraman at his heels to ask a few questions. On seeing him, the smoldering bitterness which Doe had felt over the electronic media's betrayal of himself during the brief takeover boiled over and Doe screamed obscenities at the startled reporters. He asked in an excess of bitter fury, "Ain't you the one supporting Quiwonkpa? Take him away!"

With that peremptory order, his dutiful security aides immediately began clobbering Gbenyon. He was ordered to strip to his underpants if he wanted to be spared further suffering. He was then handcuffed and bundled into the back of a jeep . . .

Passersby saw Gbenyon sitting trussed-up in the jeep, his handcuffed hands resting on his knees. Later, the jeep drove off with its prisoner to the Executive Mansion.

Gbenyon was ushered into Doe's fourth-floor office still only wearing his briefs. Never imagining that he had committed any offense . . . [he] innocently continued to protest that all he had done was in line with his professional responsibilities . . . When it appeared that the newsman was only grudgingly repentant for both the personal as well as the collective "sin" of his Action Team (of TV reporters) the Liberian Leaders told the guards to go "fuck with him."

He was then taken to the second floor and beaten unconscious. They later bayoneted him to death. Gbenyon's distraught widow . . . and family members have asked for the corpse so that he could be given a decent burial, but the government has [refused]. ("Liberia," Index on Censorship report, June 1990)

The Executive Mansion issued a press statement "alleging that Gbenyon accidentally killed himself while struggling with a gun which had been found in his car" ("Liberia," Index on Censorship report, June 1990).

At the time he was murdered, the handsome and intellectually bright tall young Gbenyon was studying law at the once-prestigious Louis Arthur Grimes School of Law at the University of Liberia, which attracted students from across Africa and other parts of the world.

In the wake of this revealing report regarding Gbenyon's murder from an anonymous correspondent in Monrovia, the London-based *West Africa* magazine was banned from circulation in Liberia by the Doe regime.

Mr. Isaac D. E. Bantu was another journalist who almost got killed in the wake of Quiwonkpa's abortive coup. He was a local BBC correspondent who was seen as a thorn in the flesh of the Doe regime for his critical reporting. He had filed a number of stories about developments in Liberia in the aftermath of the coup, which irritated Doe and other officials of his regime.

Mr. Bantu is a 1992 Nieman Fellow under the Nieman Foundation for Journalism at Harvard University. Since fleeing Liberia in the early 1990s due to death threats, he has resided with his family in an area near Boston, Massachusetts, from where he has continued to advocate for issues concerning press freedom, civil rights, and democratic governance, among others. A mentor and very good friend, he narrated how he got arrested and imprisoned for more than six months following Quiwonkpa's abortive coup.

While the entire country was under a dusk-to-dawn curfew, Bantu said he was in bed at home when he heard the doorbell at his front door ring at around 10:00 p.m. What happened next could have also led to his death, similar to Gbenyon's fate.

Bantu said when he opened his front door, he was confronted by heavily armed men. The man who was in front of the group asked him, "Are you Isaac Bantu, the BBC reporter?" He said he answered in the affirmative, not knowing what was happening. Next, he said, the officer told him that he was under arrest for his reports on BBC. The officer said they were taking him to the Executive Mansion, where Gbenyon was also taken, for interrogation, as earlier reported.

According to Mr. Bantu, he was handcuffed and led away in his underwear. He said when he was brought outside, he noticed that the entire house had been surrounded by heavily armed troops. As he was driven away, the security forces set fire to his residence and burnt it down to ashes.

While he was being driven to the Executive Mansion, Bantu said the soldiers decided to detour and first go to the Defense Ministry before heading to the Executive Mansion. When they arrived at the Defense Ministry, the soldiers announced that they had apprehended Bantu the BBC reporter and that he was being taken to the mansion.

The chief of staff of the Armed Forces of Liberia, Lieutenant General Henry Dubar, was at the Defense Ministry when the soldiers arrived there with Bantu and said that they were taking him to the mansion. According to Bantu, General Dubar immediately intervened and ordered the soldiers to release Bantu into his (Dubar's) custody. General Dubar told the soldiers that he was not going to allow them to take Bantu to the mansion that time of the night. He said he was going to keep Bantu in protective custody overnight himself and send him to the prison the following morning. And this was apparently how Bantu did not suffer a fate similar to that of Gbenyon.

After more than six months in detention, Mr. Bantu was released by the Doe regime. However, he did not have a home to return to, considering that his residence was burnt down at the time of his arrest. Everything he had earned, including his university diplomas, was consumed by the fire that completely gutted his residence. He was also imprisoned on several other occasions for what was regarded to be his antigovernment reporting.

In addition to his popular status as a BBC correspondent, Mr. Bantu was one of the few brave journalists who took the risk to publish anonymous articles using ghost names in the *West Africa* magazine and other international media outlets to expose the excesses of the Doe regime.

For example, one of those who published anonymous articles in the international media to expose the evils of the Doe regime was legendary journalist Rufus Marmah Darpoh. Once suspected of publishing an article in an international media outlet critical of the regime, he was arrested, beaten with a water hose during interrogation, and imprisoned for six months at the notorious Belle Yella prison in 1984. Mr. Darpoh was a correspondent for several international media entities, including Deutsche Welle (German radio) and the Deutsche Presse-Agentur (DPA). He also published anonymous articles on Liberia in other international media outlets due to the danger associated with being known as the author of articles critical of the regime.

While serving as managing editor of the *Sun Times* following his release from Belle Yella, Mr. Darpoh was summoned to the Executive Mansion in June 1986 by an angry Doe. The military leader turned president was upset that the *Sun Times* had published a statement by a coalition of defeated political parties known as the Grand Coalition. In the statement, the opposition parties reaffirmed their refusal to recognize Doe, who was accused of rigging the 1985 presidential election.

During the Executive Mansion meeting, as Mr. Darpoh reported in the *Sun Times*, Commander in Chief Doe told him (Darpoh), "God give you long life but you are careless with it" ("Liberia," Index on Censorship, June 1990).

Following that development with Darpoh, the government announced a blanket ban on press coverage of the activities of the Grand Coalition. The coalition included the Liberia Action Party (LAP), whose candidate, Jackson F. Doe, was widely known to have won the 1985 presidential election rigged by Doe. The other coalition parties were the Unity Party (UP), led by Dr. Edward B. Kesselly as presidential candidate, and the Liberia Unification Party (LUP), led by then schoolteacher William Gabriel Kpoleh as its candidate.

For their refusal to recognize Doe as victor of the fraudulent presidential election, the three opposition leaders were arrested and banished to the notorious Belle Yella, which was intended to incarcerate the most hardened murderers and criminals in Liberia. Located in the deep tropical jungle, Belle Yella was accessible only by air, linked by a small airstrip connected to the prison compound. There were accounts that prisoners who dared to escape from Belle Yella were eaten by wild animals. Because of the conditions and circumstances, Belle Yella was known to be a place where those condemned to die were sent to perish.

Accordingly, it did not come as a surprise when rumors soon circulated that one of the opposition leaders who was sent to Belle Yella had died as a result of the vicious conditions at the prison. Anxious to dispel the rumors, the government dispatched a team of government and independent journalists to Belle Yella.

I was among the group of journalists who were flown in a small military plane to Belle Yella in an effort by the government to dispel rumors of the death of one of the political leaders. When we landed in Belle Yella, we met the opposition leaders alive, but they appeared to be distressed. They pleaded to be taken from Belle Yella, where we saw some of the prisoners chained to their waist, neck, or legs. It was a horrifying spectacle. In my book *Liberia: The Heart of Darkness*, which was published in 2002, I provided detailed accounts of my experience at Belle Yella, where I noticed that some of the prisoners appeared to be so disfigured that they looked like cavemen of the ancient past whose photos I have seen in printed materials and videos.

In the wake of the political leaders' desperate appeal to be rescued from Belle Yella, Bishop Augustus B. Marwieh and other religious leaders intervened to get the three men returned from the notorious prison. Bishop Marwieh, who was a veteran educator and founder of the popular Christian television evangelism program *Ministry of Hope*, often recounted his experience dealing with that crisis, as well as being one of the earliest African students at the world-renowned University of California at Berkeley (UC Berkeley) in Berkeley, California. I got to associate with Bishop Marwieh when we both resided in Sacramento, California, during the years of the Liberian civil war. The television evangelist, who was well known and admired for his constant smile and cheerful demeanor, died in 2007 in Liberia.

During his era, Mr. Darpoh put in more than three decades of service in various areas of journalism. He served the government of Liberia as director of press and publications in the Ministry of Information, edited the *New Liberian* newspaper, and pioneered the creation of the Press Union of Liberia (*Historical Dictionary of Liberia*, second edition, page 98).

Following his release from Belle Yella, I was blessed to benefit from the mentorship of the legendary journalist, a fearless warrior with the pen and a gentle giant, during my tenure as a reporter at the *Sun Times*. Mr. Darpoh, who also taught journalism at the University of Liberia, was the first editor in chief of the *Daily Observer* and the founding managing editor of the *Sun Times*. He died at the age of sixty-seven in Accra, Ghana, where he was taken for medical attention in 1994. He reportedly never recovered fully from the wounds he sustained as a result of being tortured during his arrest and imprisonment at Belle Yella.

Very mild-mannered and pleasant to be around, Mr. Darpoh did not to like to talk about his experience at Belle Yella. He always said, "Belle Yella is a Zoe Bush"—one doesn't publicly talk about what goes on there. In Liberia, the expression "Zoe Bush" refers to something like a secret society. What Mr. Darpoh meant was that what goes on in a secret society is not discussed in public.

Another warrior with the pen who literally pierced the heart of the Doe regime with his revealing anonymous articles in *West Africa* and other international media outlets was Mr. Lamini A. Waritay, a prolific writer and seasoned mass communications professional. He was regarded as a radical journalist by regime functionaries for fearlessly calling out the regime for its dictatorial practices.

Mr. Waritay served as secretary-general of the Press Union of Liberia (PUL) and subsequently became president of the PUL during the tumultuous rule of Samuel Doe. He later served as minister of information under the Interim Government of National Unity (IGNU) led by Dr. Amos C. Sawyer during the early years of the war.

A seasoned media scholar, Mr. Waritay received his bachelor's degree in general studies from Fourah Bay College in Sierra Leone, once acclaimed as the "Athens of West Africa," and a master of science degree in mass communication from Boston University in Boston, Massachusetts. He served as a lecturer and acting chair of the Department of Mass Communication at the University of Liberia.

The struggles and sacrifices of Messrs. Kenneth Best and Stanton Peabody to bring about press freedom and good governance in Liberia are also noted in chapter 15 of this book.

The tales of repression regarding how Liberia descended into absolute madness and bloodshed are recounted in various chapters of this publication.

Listening to the testimonies of victims during TRC hearings was very difficult and traumatic for me. For example, while listening once to the testimony of a lady who said that she was raped in front of her family before her husband and other male family members were killed by armed men, I bolted out of the hall, anguished and in tears.

I once asked Ms. Massa A. Washington, a professional journalist and good friend who served as a commissioner of the TRC, how the commissioners were able to listen to those many tales of horrors and keep their composure or sanity. She responded that listening to the testimonies of human tragedy was one of the most difficult tasks of the TRC process. She said the TRC commissioners and staff concerned with the investigations and hearings regarding the unspeakable crimes that were committed in Liberia simply managed to cope from one day to another.

Chaired by Jerome J. Verdier, Liberian human rights activist and environmental lawyer, other commissioners of the TRC were the following: vice chair Dede Dolopei, retired Methodist Bishop Arthur F. Kulah, Muslim leader and prominent peace activist Shiek Kafumba F. Konneh, registered nurse and social worker Oumu K. Syllah, veteran lawyer Pearl Brown Bull, Rev. Gerald B. Coleman, and journalist and rights activist John H.T. Stewart.

In view of the mindless brutality, death, and destruction that have consumed Liberia, there can be no question that an opportunity was lost during the past administration of President Sirleaf to allow for the TRC process to take its course. The opportunity was lost to establish a process of reconciliation, which would have helped to heal and reconcile some of the victims. Now that there is a growing public demand for the establishment of a court for war and economic crimes in Liberia, it is important for the government of the day to create the necessary conditions for Liberians to decide on this very critical matter.

Meanwhile, as Liberians tussle over whether or not to establish a war and economic crimes court, several Liberians have been arrested and prosecuted in the United States and Europe for their respective roles in Liberia's civil upheavals. Few of the high-profile cases include the following: Charles McArthur Emmanuel, a.k.a. Chuckie Taylor, son of Mr. Charles Taylor, who was commander of the notorious Anti-Terrorist Unit (ATU), commonly known as the Demon Forces. He was arrested in 2006 at Miami International Airport in Miami, Florida, and prosecuted. He has been serving a ninety-seven-year sentence in Florida for his role in human rights violations perpetrated by the ATU in Liberia.

Another high-profile individual prosecuted in the United States was Jucontee Thomas Woewiyu, former defense minister of Taylor's notorious NPFL. He was arrested in May 2014 and tried on sixteen counts related to immigration violations. In July 2018, he was convicted on eleven of the sixteen counts. Woewiyu was one of the ex-warlords who refused to testify during the TRC hearings even though he published a series of articles and conducted numerous radio and television interviews in some of which he, like Mr. Taylor, often bragged about the NPFL's heroic armed insurgency to liberate the Liberian people from Doe's brutal regime. I cannot recall where he ever expressed regret for the unspeakable acts of death and destruction brought about as a result of what has come to be known as the senseless civil war.

Former rebel commander Mohammed Jabbateh, who goes by the rebel nickname Jungle Jabbah, was also arrested in the United States in 2016. He was indicted on two counts related to gaining US asylum by lying about his role as a rebel commander of one of the armed factions during the Liberian civil war. He was accused of committing civil war atrocities, including murder and conscripting child soldiers. After being found guilty as charged, in April 2018, Jungle Jabbah was sentenced to thirty years in prison.

In Europe, the ex-wife of former president Charles Taylor, Mrs. Agnes Reeves Taylor, was arrested in the United Kingdom in June 2017 on war crimes–related charges. In September 2014, authorities in Belgium arrested one Ms. Martina Johnson, who was said to be one of Charles Taylor's few female personal bodyguards. Ms. Johnson has been implicated in direct participation in the mutilation and mass killing in 1992, when NPFL forces invaded Monrovia in an attempt to seize the Liberian capital. Both cases have been ongoing as of this publication.

Whether on corruption or on war crimes, Liberians are now demanding accountability and an end to the culture of impunity in order to ensure sustainable peace and progress in the country. As Liberians intensify their demand for accountability, an unease has overtaken the country since 2018, and there has been a sense that Liberia's postwar gains are being threatened to be reversed because of the entrenched culture of corruption and impunity.

On the question of how Liberia failed in the fight against corruption, it can be argued that the failure started when the government began to disregard adherence to the process of good governance and accountability. A turning point along that line was the government's decision to not renew the contract of Mr. John S. Morlu II as auditor general of Liberia following the end of his tenure. In 2006, following an extensive international search, the European Union recruited Morlu to become auditor general of Liberia.

A brilliant young certified public accountant who was in his thirties during his tenure, Morlu holds an MBA in finance from Johns Hopkins University, a master's in international commerce and policy from George Mason University, and double bachelors in economics and international relations from the University of Virginia—all in the United States, where he has been residing.

During his tenure as auditor general from 2007 to 2011, the General Auditing Commission (GAC) produced more reports, including financial, compliance, internal controls, operational, and also fraud investigative reports that indicted high-profile government officials. Short in stature, bespectacled, and always elegantly attired with a bow tie, Morlu produced reports that were widely covered by the local and international media, exposing the systemic culture of corruption and dysfunctional system of governance in Liberia. His reports named and shamed as well as recommended restitution or prosecution for high-profile officials. As a result, he was accused of unprofessional conduct for having audit reports published by the media.

Following the end of Morlu's tenure in 2011, the Liberian government decided not to renew his appointment as auditor general. He was literally a thorn in the flesh of many high-profile officials who could not wait to see him out the door. His aggressive, uncompromising stance against corruption drew the ire of many high-profile officials who had been publicly exposed for economic crimes.

Despite his unconventional approach regarding the auditing process, as some critics called it, Morlu's public awareness initiative helped to inform and educate many Liberians, including yours truly, about the process and preparation of the national budget and how the government was nothing more than a cash cow for corrupt individuals. Through public hearings and forums, he exposed fraudulent practices regarding the national budget and also educated the Liberian public about how such problems can be rectified.

For example, officials of some government ministries and agencies would insert one budgetary line item twice or multiple times in the entity's proposed budget. Once the budget is approved, the perpetrators would collect the money from the extra budgetary line items for themselves. This was because the national budget was never submitted to proper review and scrutiny before passage. During his tenure, Mr. Morlu demanded periodic budgetary performance reports from various government entities scrutinized and investigated, where necessary, to ensure compliance with the process of good governance and accountability. He demanded for the proposed national budget to be subject to public hearings and scrutinized before passage by the national legislature and that budget performance reports show evidence of how funds were expended.

Another notable act for which this brilliant Liberian and son of Africa is known was his very strong support to empower many young people through scholarship and other training opportunities abroad to advance their knowledge. He used a portion of the GAC's meager financial resources to send forty-five employees of the commission to attend universities in the United States and Kenya to pursue master of business administration (MBA) degrees in various disciplines ranging from finance, procurement and supply chain, human resources, and strategic management ("Comparing Africa's Greats: Is John Morlu Liberia's Tom Mboya?" *Liberian Observer* online, December 13, 2011).

During his tenure as auditor general at GAC, Mr. Morlu demonstrated, by his support for employees to benefit from advanced education abroad, his belief in the building of strong institutions through the empowerment of knowledge. This is why, in the *Liberian Observer* newspaper article referenced above, he was compared to Tom Mboya, one of the founding fathers of independent Kenya. Mboya was a trade unionist, educationist, Pan-Africanist, and cabinet minister in Kenya.

According to *Wikipedia*, Mboya worked with then US senator John F. Kennedy (later president of the United States) and Dr. Martin Luther King Jr. to create education opportunities for African students; this effort resulted in African airlifts of the 1950s to 1960s, which enabled African students to study at US colleges. Notable beneficiaries of this airlift were Wangari Maathai, who later won the Nobel Peace Prize, and Barack Hussein Obama Sr., father of the forty-fourth president and also the first African American president of the United States. In July 1969, Mboya—a promising thirty-eight-year-old African leader who won the admiration of people from all over the world for his intelligence, charm, and leadership and oratory skills—was assassinated under mysterious circumstances in the Kenyan capital of Nairobi.

On the Liberian scene, Morlu's departure from the GAC could be seen as the beginning of the end regarding serious effort to ensure adherence to the process of good governance and accountability in the government. And this was the beginning of the government's failure in the fight against corruption.

It is also equally noteworthy to state that one of the most effective public officials who made a profound impact in Liberia during the Sirleaf administration was Ms. Mary T. Broh, former mayor of Monrovia and deputy managing director at the National Port Authority (NPA). In an apparent recognition of her meritorious services, Ms. Broh was retained to continue to serve as director general of the General Services Agency when the administration of President George Weah succeeded the Sirleaf government in January 2018.

Through very aggressive cleanup campaigns, beautification programs, and enforcement of city ordinances, the ruined Liberian capital began to transform from the bullet-scarred eyesore it was at the end of the destructive civil upheavals. Ms. Broh demanded property owners or managers to clean their premises and paint their structures, and she was frequently embroiled in fights with squatters as she and her team went out to clean up one community after another, breaking down shacks built along main thoroughfares and other areas. The heaps of garbage amid the shacks created unsanitary conditions and hindered the normal flow of traffic and pedestrians. Her tenure at the NPA also saw improvement in the infrastructure and security of port facilities and the working conditions of employees.

Even though she generated a lot of controversy for her unconventional approach in the enforcement of city ordinances during her tenure as mayor, Ms. Broh deserves credit for cleaning up Monrovia and its surroundings after years of destruction and giving the city a face-lift, which began the process of rebuilding the Liberian capital. With many new skylines and other attractions being erected around the city, postwar Monrovia is becoming a bustling metropolis.

Then Monrovia City mayor Mary Broh being honored by the Philadelphia City Council during a visit in 2011. Right are Councilwoman Jannie Blackwell and Mr. Stanley Slaughter, and far left is Dr. Vera Tolbert.

The modern Central Bank of Liberia building, located in downtown Monrovia, was a testament that Liberia was back as a haven for international business (courtesy of Gregory Stemm of West African Journal).

The magnificent Boulevard Palace is one of several world-class hotels established in postwar Liberia, a testament to the country's huge business and tourism potentials (courtesy of Gregory Stemm of West African Journal).

This beautiful structure, which is the headquarters of the Liberia Revenue Authority, is an example of infrastructural development in postwar Liberia (courtesy of Gregory Stemm of West African Journal).

However, as of this publication, some parts of Monrovia have yet to benefit from the restoration of electricity and pipe-borne water while the city is overpopulated, and driving through the mostly narrow streets is becoming a nightmare jammed with traffic.

Outside the domain of government service, another Liberian who has generally impacted the course of postwar Liberia is veteran journalist and human rights activist Hassan Bility. Mr. Bility is the director of the Global Justice and Research Project (GJRP), a nongovernmental organization dedicated to the documentation of wartime atrocities in Liberia and to assisting victims in pursuit of justice for these crimes.

Bility's bio, published by the US-based nonprofit international human rights organization the Center for Justice and Accountability, captures the significance of his work. Under his leadership, the GJRP's documentation work has led to the investigation and arrest of alleged Liberian war criminals throughout Europe and the United States. These include the arrest of former Liberian rebel commanders Alieu Kosiah in Switzerland and Martina Johnson in Belgium, the arrest of Charles Taylor's ex-wife Agnes Reeves Taylor in the United Kingdom, and the arrest and eventual conviction of former ULIMO rebel commander Mohammed Jabbateh in the United States.

While serving as editor in chief of the *Analyst* independent newspaper in Liberia during the regime of Charles Taylor, Bility was arrested and brutally tortured in 2002 on Taylor's order because of his critical independent journalism. After a prolong campaign by international human rights organizations and widespread coverage of his arrest and detention by the media around the world, he was finally released following six months in detention on condition that he left the country. It was while in exile that he became fully devoted to the search for justice for Liberia's war victims.

He later testified in several war crimes trials, including the trials of Charles Taylor, and the Revolutionary United Front (RUF) Sierra Leone rebel movement at the Special Court for Sierra Leone. He also testified in the trial of the notorious Charles McArthur Emmanuel (Charles Taylor's son), commonly known as Chuckie Taylor, in the United States and the trial of businessman and gunrunner Guus Kouwenhoven in the Netherlands.

Mr. Bility, who is one of the leading advocates for the establishment of a war and economic crimes court for Liberia, must be applauded for his courage considering the potential risks and danger involved in this endeavor.

The need to prosecute war and economic criminals in Liberia cannot be overemphasized if the country is to realize sustainable peace and progress. Liberia's prevailing state of rampant corruption is an example that misfits and war criminals will continue to be entrenched in controlling the affairs of the country until they are made to account for the crimes that have been perpetrated against the people and the country.

CHAPTER EIGHT
The Urgency to Restore Liberia's Broken Educational and Health Systems

Despite the progress made in Liberia's postwar reconstruction, two very critical areas of the country that have continued to linger in a state of dysfunction are the educational and health systems.

Like the entire Liberia, the educational and health systems virtually collapsed during the brutal and devastating civil war. School campuses and facilities were looted, vandalized, and turned into displaced centers to accommodate hundreds of thousands of people driven from their homes by the war. In similar light, medical facilities around the country were abandoned by medical staff, looted, vandalized, or sometimes completely destroyed in the wake of the mindless bloodshed and destruction.

This chapter focuses on Liberia's educational and health systems, which have been mired in a state of neglect as of this publication due to failure to seriously prioritize these very critical areas to mold the minds of the people and improve the quality of their health conditions.

Recognizing that education was critical in reestablishing a sense of normalcy in the war-torn country, the Sirleaf government took immediate steps to get over a million children back in school. Many of the children, as well as many teenagers and young adults, never had the benefit of a formal education because of the years of war. It was very crucial to get the children, as well as the young people, many of whom were ex-combatants, off the streets and engaged in productive activities.

Due to the lack of infrastructure to accommodate the growing number of students, classes were conducted outdoors under trees in many areas around the country. Even on the main campus of the University of Liberia in Monrovia, many students took classes outdoors under trees because the university was overcrowded and there was lack of classroom space. The university campus was also devastated by the war.

Within a few years, hundreds of schools were constructed and renovated throughout the country while the government made primary public school education free and compulsory for all.

With support from the United States, the Liberian government reopened the Rural Teachers Training Institutes (RTTIs) to train teachers who are deployed mostly in rural parts so that students everywhere in the country would enjoy the benefits of quality education. The US Peace Corps have returned to Liberia, and most of them are deployed at the rural teacher-training institutes.

During his visit to Africa in 2008, which took him to five countries including Liberia, US president W. Bush announced that the US government was donating one million textbooks and desks for 10,000 children in Liberia. At the end of Liberia's civil war, the ratio of students to textbooks was estimated to be 36 to 1.

Meanwhile, as part of the effort to improve the Liberian educational system, the government raised teachers' wages from US$30 to a minimum of US$200 a month as measures were put in place for gradual increases. As a result, there are now over 50,000 teachers as of the time of this writing.

Even though majority of school-age children did not have the opportunity to go to school during the war, the number of students enrolled nationwide increased to 1.5 million. Emphasis on girls' education accelerated over the past few years, with competitive girls to boys ratio.

One of the major efforts to improve education was the passage of the Education Reform Act in 2011, aimed at decentralization of the education system.

The government also increased the level of support to state-owned institutions of higher education, provided subsidies to private ones, and expanded vocational and technical training for those not able to pursue a full academic program.

The University of Liberia, which has a student population estimated to be nearly 25,000, has moved to its Fendell Campus outside Monrovia, which was rehabilitated with modern facilities, thanks to support largely from the government of the People's Republic of China. Because the university was overcrowded and there was lack of classroom space, many students had to take classes outdoors under trees on the main campus of the university in Monrovia.

The government also endeavored to make higher education available to students in all parts of Liberia outside Monrovia. In Harper, Maryland County, the then William V. S. Tubman Technical College, which was ruined by the war, was rebuilt and elevated to university level. What is known as the Rubber Science and Technology Institute has been established as a component of the William V. S. Tubman University to train students to learn how to process rubber woods for technology and entrepreneurship.

It is also interesting to note that a few state-funded community colleges have opened or are opening in various parts of the country. Among them is the community college in Buchanan, Grand Bassa County, established under the leadership of veteran educator and former education minister, Dr. Levi Zangar, who is also former president of A. M. E. University in Monrovia, as well as the Bomi County Community College. One community college each have been under construction in Bong and Nimba Counties while President Sirleaf dedicated another community college in Voinjama, Lofa County, during the July 2011 Independence Day celebrations in Lofa.

The University of Liberia, established in 1862 as Liberia College, became the first degree-awarding institution in West Africa while Cuttington College, now Cuttington University, founded in 1889 by the Episcopal Church of Liberia, became the oldest private coeducational four-year degree-awarding institution in sub-Saharan Africa (Culture and Customs of Liberia; Education, p. 4).

The University of Liberia also produced Africa's first female university president, in the person of the eminent educator, now late Dr. Mary Antoinette Brown-Sherman.

Before the war, the University of Liberia and Cuttington University attracted students from across the continent and beyond due to the advanced quality of education.

Many Christian denominations, such as the Methodist Church, Episcopal Church, Catholic Church, Baptist Church, Lutheran Church, Seventh Day Adventist, Presbyterian Church, Assemblies of God, as well as numerous other religious institutions, have contributed enormously to the education of Liberians as they spread the word of God. There are also Islamic institutions around the country that have contributed to the advancement of knowledge in Liberia. Some of the major concessions doing business in the country have also operated some of the best schools and medical facilities in the region that once attracted patients far beyond Liberia's borders.

The churches and religious organizations also played a very critical role not just in spreading opportunity for education throughout the country but also quality education. Back in those days, most Liberians only traveled to the United States largely for further studies and vacation. And stories abound that many of them topped their classes or received double promotions due to the solid academic foundations they established in Liberia. As Liberians studied abroad in various endeavors, they could not wait to return to their homeland because there was an atmosphere of peace and high optimism. Our Sierra Leonean neighbors used to jokingly refer to Liberians as "born here, stay here, die here" because Liberians were regarded as a people who did not travel much outside their country.

I am a child of the 1960s, the era when Liberia was at the peak of peace and prosperity, kind of the "Golden Age." During my early childhood, my birthplace Neegbah, although a rural environment with no modern services such as electricity and pipe-borne water, was like a paradise in terms of the natural beautiful scenery and the cohesiveness of the family and community structures. Neegbah, which is not yet accessible by motor road, had only a public elementary school that held classes in a church edifice, and there was no clinic.

In Monrovia, I attended the Monrovia Consolidated School System (MCSS), a public school system established with USAID and modeled on the American public school system. Like American schools, Liberian schools hosted pageants, dances, sometimes with live bands similar to *Soul Train*, the popular American entertainment television show of the 1970s and 80s, which, along with other popular programs like Solid Gold, The Jeffersons, and Different Strokes, aired regularly on national television. Most schools had drill units, some with marching bands, dressed like American students.

Besides sports for extracurricular activities, Liberian schools had various organizations like drama and debate club, science and medical club, history club, mathematics club, music club, Bible club, among others. Through these organizations, many of us found our careers in life. I know of schoolmates that were once members of the science and medical club or Bible club who became medical professionals or clergypersons. My career as a journalist and writer began in the tenth grade when I joined the press club at D. Twe Memorial High School, which have produced several respected journalists at the national level in Liberia. D. Twe was then MCSS's second-largest high school that operated two school sessions conducted separately in the morning and evening.

Located on the beach of the Atlantic in the western suburb of Monrovia inhabited mostly by poor and low-income people, the school was originally named William R. Tolbert Jr. High School, in honor of President Tolbert who established the school to help bring enlightenment to people in that economically disadvantaged area. However, following Tolbert's assassination due to the 1980 military coup, the school was renamed D. Twe, in memory of a prominent Liberian of indigenous background, who was an advocate for equality in Liberia.

Like in various schools, both public and private, which operated two sessions, the evening classes provided opportunity for working people and adults to pursue their education at various grade levels. So it was that children and young people went to school in the morning while "night school," as we used to call it, was the domain of adults.

Some of the earliest Liberian educators to lead the MCSS were trained in the United States. For example, Mr. Timothy Nyan, the first principal of D. Twe High School, formerly the William R. Tolbert Jr. High School, received his master's degree in education from the San Francisco State University in San Francisco, California. About two hours from San Francisco is the California State University at Sacramento, where Liberians who played a pioneering role in the establishment of Liberia's Civil Service Agency, responsible to professionalize Liberia's civil service, were mostly educated.

Liberia has had an enviable history of strong partnership with various American universities and institutions. American churches and religious charities have also played a very critical role in the life of the country, providing education, medical care, and other services to the people.

For example, Liberia's relationship with Harvard University in Cambridge, Massachusetts, started from the founding of Liberia. According to historical accounts, Liberia's Independence Constitution of 1847 was drafted by Harvard College law professor Simon Greenleaf. The establishment of Liberia College (now the University of Liberia) in 1862, the second-oldest institution of higher learning in West Africa, was led and funded by the Trustees of Donations for Education in Liberia. Professor Greenleaf was the founder and president of the Trustees of Donations for Education in Liberia. America's oldest institution of higher learning, Harvard University, was established in 1636.

According to history, the first Liberian graduate of Harvard did so in 1920, and since then there has been a steady trail of Liberians to Harvard. President Ellen Johnson Sirleaf, a 1971 MPA (master of public administration) graduate from the Harvard Kennedy School of Government, was one of the Liberian graduates of the world-renowned university.

Other Liberian graduates include one of my first cousins, Moses Blonkanjay Jackson, who holds a master's degree in education leadership from the Harvard Graduate School of Education. Mr. Jackson served as assistant minister of education during the administration of President Sirleaf. He is founder and chief executive officer of the Diversified Educators Empowerment Project (DEEP), a nonprofit organization, focused on the following: social mobilization and community engagement, capacity development and teacher training, and economic empowerment.

Another Harvard product is veteran journalist, human rights activist, and mentor, Isaac D. E. Bantu, who was a 1992 Nieman Fellow under the Nieman Foundation for Journalism. The Nieman Foundation for Journalism is the primary journalism institution at Harvard University.

A BBC correspondent for Liberia in the 1980s, Mr. Bantu was arrested and imprisoned several times for his reporting during the regime of military ruler Samuel Doe. While Bantu was president of the Press Union of Liberia (PUL), the umbrella national journalists' organization, colleague Emmanuel Abalo, a notable broadcast journalist, served as vice president, and yours truly was the secretary-general.

Bantu was forced to leave the country and seek refuge in the United States due to death threats at the beginning of the civil war. Abalo and I respectively served as acting president of the PUL during the early years of the war, and we both fled the country separately and also sought refuge in the United States due to death threats from armed factions, which were embroiled in a brutal and bloody contest for state power. The PUL was opposed to the seizure of the country's leadership by force of arms.

Some of the institutions of higher learning in the United States with which Liberia has enjoyed close partnership are the following: Northwestern University based in Evanston, Illinois; Indiana University in the state of Indiana; Howard University and American University in Washington DC; Tuskegee University in Tuskegee, Alabama; Oberlin College in Oberlin, Ohio; and the Associated Colleges of the Midwest (ACM), a consortium of fourteen private colleges, primarily in the Midwestern United States, which maintained a close partnership with Cuttington University, Liberia's first private institution of higher learning, operated by the Episcopal Church of Liberia.

As an example of the partnerships between American and Liberian institutions, Tubman University in Maryland, Liberia, and Morgan State University in Baltimore, Maryland, USA, signed a landmark memorandum of understanding in June 2014. Under the memorandum, the two institutions of higher learning identified mutually beneficial objectives in cooperating in the delivery of instructional services.

The benefit of the MOU included but not limited to enhancing the preparation of a diverse and internationally competent workforce and developing undergraduate and graduate curricula that include theory and research on international topics relevant to Tubman University and Morgan State University. The MOU also included advancing new online and distance education instructional modalities appropriate for international students and cross-border studies.

According to the MOU, the mutual interest of both universities in collaborating on international and interinstitutional educational development initiatives, curricula development, academic programs, and workforce development projects was consistent with the objectives of the 2007 Sister State Program Agreement between the state of Maryland, USA, and Bong County and Maryland County of Liberia, as well as the US-Liberia Partnership Dialogue launched in 2013 by then President Sirleaf and then US secretary of state Hillary Rodham Clinton. The partnership dialogue is the institutional framework for cooperation between both countries.

The objectives of the Sister State Program Agreement is to enhance the many opportunities for cooperation in business and industry, arts and culture, education, and also to build long-term relationships, promote commercial cooperation, and develop joint programs of exchange in all the areas stipulated under the MOU.

Caring for the Less Fortunate through Donation of Textbooks

In 2006, I had a live interview with Capital Public Radio in Sacramento, California, an affiliate of National Public Radio, which resulted to the donation of about 14,000 textbooks from Sacramento to Liberia. As a journalist and activist who was active in the Sacramento area for a decade before returning to postwar Liberia to serve in government, some of the leading media entities in Sacramento, including the *Sacramento Bee* newspaper, provided favorable coverage regarding my return to Liberia, which created more awareness about the state of affairs in the country.

The live interview was conducted during the night while I was seated under some mango trees at my residence in Monrovia, under a bright moonshine because the city was in darkness as there was no electricity. Due to the seven- or eight-hour time difference between Liberia and California, it was during the afternoon in Sacramento.

During my interview, Casey Robbins, who was in the eighth grade at Mira Loma High School in Sacramento, was riding in a car with her parents listening to Capital Public Radio. I spoke of the urgent need to rebuild Liberia after years of devastation, especially the urgency to improve the educational system, in order to give the children an opportunity for a better future.

Inspired by the interview and with the strong encouragement from her parents, Casey decided to launch a project to donate textbooks to Liberia. One evening, while I was about to leave my office to attend a ceremony at the Executive Mansion in honor of former US president Bill Clinton, who was visiting as guest of the Liberian government, I received a call from the United States. The caller, Dr. David Seidenwurm, said he and his family had listened to and were deeply moved by my interview on NPR. As a result, he said, his daughter was interested in launching a project to donate textbooks free of charge to Liberia for the benefit of Liberian students. Dr. Seidenwurm, a neuroradiologist, said that he and his wife, Page Robbins, had endeavored to instill in their children a sense of responsibility to care for others, especially those who are less fortunate than they are.

This is why, he said, he had called for us to begin the process for the donation of textbooks from California to support Liberian schools. After sending them the curriculum from the education ministry, Casey began her textbooks for Liberia project. Hard work, coupled with support from others who were inspired by the humanitarian effort, as well as favorable media coverage in Sacramento, Casey's labor paid off with the transportation to the port and shipment to Liberia of about 14,000 textbooks for about five years. One of the major supporters was Firestone Company, which shipped the consignments to Liberia free of charge.

The first shipment of books were donated to the Monrovia Consolidated School System (MCSS), Liberia's largest public school system, of which I am a product. Subsequent consignments were delivered to the Ministry of Education for targeted distribution to public schools in various parts of Liberia.

While a high school senior, seventeen-year-old Casey and her parents visited Liberia in 2011, during which they were received by then president Sirleaf, Vice President Joseph Boakai, and the minister of education, Dr. Othello Gongar. The president lauded Ms. Robbins for her tremendous contributions to education in Liberia. President Sirleaf also thanked the parents for supporting their daughter in such a notable undertaking. Casey and her parents also visited several of the schools where the books were being used, and she interacted with students who were beneficiaries. Among the campus she visited was my alma mater, D. Twe Memorial High School, located in a poor area of Monrovia.

In appreciation for her contributions to education in Liberia, a school, Casey Robbins International School, was named in her honor. Following Casey's graduation from high school and her departure for further studies at Stanford University, the Textbook for Liberia project was continued by other students at Mira Loma High School for a few years before it became inactive. This was largely due to a breakdown in coordination from the Liberia end, following my departure from the country to take up diplomatic assignment in Washington.

During a 2013 visit to Sacramento, CA, Amb. Jeremiah Sulunteh (L) and Author Gabriel Williams with members of Textbook for Liberia. (L) Casey Robbins, (C) Anjanaa Sentil Kumar, and Orgilmaa Munkhbaatar (Robbins Famiy).

The Ministry of Education, by directive of the president, took charge to coordinate activities of the project in Liberia. However, following the involvement of the education ministry, there were attempts by unscrupulous individuals at the ministry to exploit the donors for financial gains. An example regarded an education ministry staff who called Casey's parents in Sacramento to request for $150 for something related to the project in Monrovia. I was quite upset and embarrassed when informed, and I urged that a brass penny should not be sent.

This was totally unacceptable. I reported the matter to the president, as I traveled to Monrovia just after being informed about the request from the education ministry staff. I could not understand as to how a government agency was not able to make available $150 after thousands of dollars were being expended by the donors to get the books collected, packaged, and shipped to Liberia. During my coordination of the project in Monrovia, whatever costs that were incurred in Monrovia to have the textbooks delivered to the intended receivers were personally covered by me. The donors were sacrificing their money and time to get the textbooks shipped to us, and therefore, it was unacceptable to make unreasonable financial requests that would be tantamount to exploiting their goodwill.

In a country consumed by personal greed and corruption, it was a serious challenge getting the books to the targeted schools without some of it being stolen to end up for sale on the market. In one incident regarding a consignment that arrived in Monrovia, after the books were removed from the container and packed in some classrooms on a school campus for a formal turnover to school authorities, the empty container disappeared overnight and was never retrieved despite police intervention. Even though the fellows who were in charge of the container and were suspected to have sold it were arrested and placed in police custody, the case went nowhere because the culprits bribed the police and absconded.

The San Juan Unified School District in Sacramento, of which Mira Loma High School is a part, as well as the other students and teachers who were involved in the project, deserve high commendation for supporting the textbook project for Liberia. Other individuals and entities involved in the project, including the community-based Liberian nonprofit organization Association of Citizens and Friends of Liberia (ACFLi) are also applauded for their contributions toward the success of the textbook project.

As with many promising projects or programs for Liberia, the Textbook for Liberia project faded largely due to the greed, narrow-mindedness, as well as lack of focus and priority on the part of some Liberians, such as the education ministry staff who attempted to exploit the goodwill of the donors. The mentality of such individual is all about what is in it for me, and not necessarily about seeking for the common good of general society. This mind-set of what is in it for me has permeated the Liberian society to the extent that many government officials and others in positions of authority in all walks of life would easily demand for kickbacks to approve or support the establishment of any entity for the common good.

It does not matter whether it is a company that would provide employment for local people and generate public revenues or a medical or educational facility to help enhance the quality of life of the people. Some Liberians in authority have the tendency to block the execution of a program or project because there is no personal incentive for them.

While chatting about the tendency on the part of some Liberians to demand kickbacks to approve or support services that are in the public interest, an American, who has been involved with humanitarian endeavors in Liberia for many years, said something to the effect like, "when you offer to give a million dollars to a Liberian, he will ask you how much you'll pay him to take it." The negative tendency of "what is in it for me" has become part of the Liberian mind-set, she said. That negative mind-set is what has continued to undermine the progress of the general Liberian society.

Applauding the Liberian Diaspora for Constructive Engagement

Before the signing of the MOU between Tubman University and Morgan State University as stated supra, nine architecture students from three Historically Black Colleges and Universities (HBCU) in the United States—Morgan State University; Howard University in Washington DC; and Tuskegee University in Tuskegee, Alabama—visited Tubman University in Harper, Maryland County, Liberia as guests of Tubman University. The students were involved in an architectural design competition for the Tubman University E-brary and Learning Center, a state-of-the-art futuristic project, designed as a regular library and learning center with electronic books intended to enable students, faculty, and researchers to have access to books and other academic materials globally through the Internet.

The design competition was named the Harriet Tubman Centennial Architectural Design Challenge, in homage to Tubman, an escaped American slave born in the state of Maryland, who became an abolitionist and political activist. She used the network of antislavery activists and safe houses known as the Underground Railroad for many enslaved to flee to freedom in the northern free states. The Harriet Tubman Centennial Architectural Design Challenge was aimed at bringing together the collective talents of African Americans from HBCUs to the growing marketplace of Africa's development.

The E-brary project was sponsored by the nonprofit W. V. S. Tubman University Foundation and the Marylanders for Progress (MFP), a philanthropic organization of Marylanders in the United States contributing to the progress of Maryland County and Liberia as a whole. Mr. Gerald F. B. Cooper, member of the board of Tubman University and the MFP, chaired the E-brary project. He and his wife, Mrs. Roberta Brown Cooper, along with other notable sons and daughters of Maryland County, have contributed significantly to the revitalization of Tubman University and other development initiatives in Maryland County.

These include Dr. and Mrs. James Elliott, as well as Mr. and Mrs. Victor and Leona Washington. Dr. Elliott is medical director, Division of Pathology and Laboratory Medicine at Doctor's Hospital in Lanham, Maryland, and clinical assistant professor of pathology at George Washington University in Washington DC. The E-brary project was estimated at more than US$19 million.

Dr. Elizabeth Davis Russell, who was appointed president of W. V. S. Tubman University following the end of the civil war, took a virtually nonfunctioning technical college suffering from the ruins of the war and neglect and turned it into what became one of the best institutions of higher learning in Liberia. Prior to assuming leadership of the devastated institution in 2008, Dr. Russell, who was born in Maryland, Liberia, served for more than thirty years in the field of higher education in the United States. Among other responsibilities in her professional career, Dr. Russell served as provost and vice president for Academic Affairs at the State University of New York College at Cortland and dean of Academic and Professional Affairs at the California School of Professional Psychology.

Tubman University, which was now under the leadership of veteran educator, Dr. Elliott Wreh-Wilson, has been strongly supported by the US-based Tubman University Foundation, whose leadership and membership included the following: Dr. Marsha Boveja Riggio, president, Maryland Association of Marriage and Family

Counselors (USA); Dr. Bernice Bass de Martinez of California State University, who has more than thirty years in various administrative roles in higher education; and Dr. Karen Webb, president, Antioch University Midwest, Yellow Spring, Ohio.

Activities of the Tubman University Board and the MFP are buttressed by the US state of Maryland and Liberia Sister States Committee (MLSSC), which has also been proactive in supporting development endeavors in Maryland County as a whole. Some of the leaders of the MLSSC include Ms. Sheila Durant, an American lawyer; Morris T. Koffa, a leading environmental activist; and Ms. Luana Kiandoli, a lifelong American advocate in the United States for the improvement of Liberia's health care. Ms. Kiandoli is a specialist in tropical disease and establishment of medical laboratories, and she has taught medical education in graduate school.

The MFP and MLSSC deserve commendation for being among a few Liberian-oriented organizations in the United States, which have been actively involved in promoting private sector ventures between Liberia and the United States. For example, both organizations have played a critical role in assisting in the development of a sister port relationship between the Port of Baltimore, Maryland, USA, and the National Port Authority of Liberia, which operates four commercial ports in the country, such as the Freeport of Monrovia; the Port of Buchanan, Grand Bassa County; the Port of Greenville, Sinoe County; and the Port of Harper, Maryland County. The Freeport of Monrovia, established during the Second World War by the United States, is a major deep water port in that part of the world.

In 2013, the presidents of Tubman University (TU) in Liberia and Morgan State University in the United States signed an MOU for academic engagement. Dr. Elizabeth Russell of TU and Morgan State's Dr. David Wilson signed.

At the 2013 MOU signing between Tubman University and Morgan State University were Morgan State lecturer Welma Mashinini Redd, Mr. Gerald Cooper, Author Gabriel Williams, Dr. Barbara Simmons, and Mrs. Roberta Cooper.

Immediately following the end of the Ebola virus epidemic in Liberia, Sierra Leone, and Guinea, MLSSC led several nongovernmental organizations in organizing a conference to review the state of national and international efforts to assist in rebuilding the health care systems, environment management, and to develop emergency preparedness in those three countries, which were affected by the Ebola epidemic. Other organizations that cosponsored the conference were Africa Environmental Watch (AEW), International Medical Corps (IMC), and Help Africa (HA).

Among the few Liberian-oriented organizations in the United States that are making meaningful contributions in Liberia, especially in the area of education, are the alumni associations of various public and private schools and institutions of higher learning. These include the B. W. Harris Episcopal High School Alumni Association, Booker Washington Institute (BWI) Alumni Association, University of Liberia Alumni Association, Cuttington University Alumni Association, and the Victor E. Ward Memorial Educational Fund, to name a few.

According to Ms. Vickie Ward, the very passionate and energetic founder and chairperson of the Victor E. Ward Memorial Educational Fund, the organization was established in memory of her father, Professor Victor E. Ward, former chairperson chemistry department at the T. J. Faulkner School of Science and Technology, University of Liberia. He was killed in 1990 during the civil war. There are accounts that Professor Ward was killed by a former-student-turned-rebel fighter, who had failed a science class under the professor before the war started. When the former-student-turned-rebel reportedly encountered the professor, he decided to revenge and went for the kill.

The Victor E. Ward Memorial Educational Foundation has been focused on supporting quality education in Liberia, with emphasis in science education. Ms. Ward has said that the effort was intended to continue to fulfill the desire of her father, who was regarded to be the first Liberian chemist, to promote science education in Liberia and also to ensure that good ultimately prevails over evil.

It is laudable to note that some of the alumni associations have provided or are providing budgetary and other support for the operations of their former alma maters to help keep the schools afloat since the civil war.

There are also ethnic, religious, and professional organizations in the Liberian diaspora that support various causes intended to help improve the livelihood of the people in the motherland. For example, the United Bassa Organizations in the Americas, commonly called UNIBOA, is an organization comprising mostly people of the Bassa ethnic group. According to UNIBOA, which has been actively involved in development programs in Grand Bassa County, its mission is to engage in social, humanitarian, and community development work in order to meet the needs of all Bassonians residing in the Americas and the homeland. The acronym UNIBOA can be interpreted in the Bassa language as "the child has grown."

While most Liberian-oriented organizations in the diaspora are focused on providing support that will directly impact the people back in Liberia, there are others that support educational and other professional endeavors to help and promote young immigrants and the Liberian Diaspora community.

The Liberian Awards (LA) is another US-based organization that is worthy of commendation for providing scholarships and mentoring for students from Liberia, as well as from other parts of Africa and the world. According to the LA website, its scholarship recipients represent ten countries on four continents. Other countries from which students have benefitted from LA scholarships and mentoring include Nigeria, Jamaica, United States, and Bangladesh. LA-sponsored students have attended colleges in several states in the United States while others have studied abroad in Turkey, Spain, and South Africa. The LA has provided scholarships and mentoring to many deserving but struggling students to pursue their bachelor's or master's degrees at various colleges and universities in the United States and abroad.

Having been in existence for almost a decade, the signature event for the LA, which is based in the state of Delaware, is an annual awards ceremony, which showcases the empowering stories of immigrant professionals and businesses that are excelling in the diaspora.

According to the LA, through the awards ceremony, which honors and celebrates the accomplishments of Liberian professionals in the Diaspora, "We introduce our youths to the brilliant pioneers before them and we pair them with these high-achieving Liberians as mentors. Liberian Awards brings our community together and displays our intellectual stars and future stars before the world."

The Liberian Awards is the brainchild of Ms. Samantha Divine Jallah, a young enterprising lawyer. She is an associate at a major law firm in Delaware, a member of the firm's health care practice group with responsibility in helping nursing homes, hospitals, and other health care providers, prevent, navigate, and resolve regulatory problems. She fled to the United States during the Liberian civil upheavals, and she said she almost missed out in pursuing her professional dreams because she did not know professional Liberians in the diaspora who could mentor her.

Attorney Jallah said she decided to lead the effort in organizing the Liberian Awards to help fill a void in the Liberian Diaspora community, which is to honor accomplished Liberians and pair them with young people for mentoring. "I believe that majority of our community lacks awareness of the successes of Liberians in the Diaspora partly because of the size of the Diaspora in comparison to home." As she rightly noted, the award is intended to educate the young people and build their confidence that they are standing on the shoulders of high-achieving people.

One of the honorees of the Liberian Awards is Dr. Dougbeh Chris Nyan, a Liberian medical doctor, biomedical research scientist, inventor, and social activist. He studied chemistry and zoology at the College of Science and Technology of the University of Liberia. Dr. Nyan holds a degree in human medicine (infectious diseases) from Humboldt University, Berlin, Germany. He did his postdoctoral fellowship as a biomedical scientist at the world-leading National Institute of Health (NIH) and the University of Pennsylvania, respectively, in the United States. He was also a scientist at the Laboratory of Emerging Pathogens of the Division of Emerging and Transfusion Transmitted Diseases at the US Food and Drug Administration.

The young Liberian scientist is the inventor of the Multiplex Infections Diagnostic Test, a rapid diagnostic test that detects Ebola, HIV, Zika, plasmodium (malaria), yellow fever, dengue virus, hepatitis B, C, and E, and West Nile virus.

Despite this groundbreaking invention, which could help address some of the critical health challenges especially in Liberia and Africa, the Liberian government has yet to make any serious effort to make the Multiplex Infections Diagnostic Test, which could be made available at various health centers to improve the quality of health care.

Thanks to President Paul Kagame, one of Africa's visionary leaders, whose government has announced support for Dr. Nyan's innovation. The Rwandan government announced support for Dr. Nyan's innovation during the June 2018 African Innovation Summit, held in the Rwandan capital of Kigali. Dr. Nyan's infections diagnostic test, for which he has received the patent from the US government, was exhibited as one of the top 50 innovations in Africa. Dr. Nyan's infections diagnostic test was among those selected from over 600 submissions.

Dr. Nyan's invention, a single test that rapidly detects at least three to seven infections simultaneously with results within an hour, could prove to be revolutionary and very useful in Liberia, Africa, and the world at large. His invention has been recognized worldwide, with Rwanda being the first African country to take practical steps in establishing a partnership through which resources would be offered in support of Dr. Nyan's innovation, according to the *Liberian Observer* newspaper ("Rwanda to Support Invention of Liberian Scientist, Dr. Dougbeh Chris Nyan," *Liberian Observer*, June 25, 2018).

I have known Dr. Nyan as a friend from our days as young people in the 1980s advocating for democratic governance in Liberia. An activist for democracy and social justice, we got acquainted when he was one of the emerging leaders of the Liberian student movement advocating for democratic change while I was also an up-and-coming reporter with the *Daily Observer*, Liberia's and one of West Africa's leading independent daily newspapers during the era of military rule.

The military era was a dangerous period especially for journalists, student activists, opposition politicians, right activists, and anyone who would dare criticize the regime, as freedom of speech and of the press was criminalized under decrees promulgated by the military regime. Like many others, Nyan suffered arrest and imprisonment for his activism before eventually being forced into exile.

During the outbreak of the Ebola epidemic in Liberia in 2014, Dr. Nyan headed the Diaspora Liberian Emergency Response Task Force on the Ebola crisis. As the Ebola crisis intensified, he gave a congressional testimony before the United States House Foreign Affairs Subcommittee on Africa, Global Health, Global Human Rights and International Organization, during which he recommended the establishment of an African Centers for Disease Control. The Diaspora Liberian Emergency Response Task Force, along with other teams of Liberian Diaspora professionals and organizations, contributed significantly in the fight to contain the Ebola pandemic in Liberia and the two other West African countries that were worst affected by the pandemic.

Among the medical practitioners who led the charge in harnessing support in the United States to battle the Ebola epidemic was Dr. Kondeh A. Greaves, an obstetrician gynecologist in Manassas, Virginia. She and many other US-based Liberian medical practitioners have been involved in supporting medical initiatives in Liberia.

As another example of the Liberian Awards' initiative to honor and celebrate accomplished Liberians in the Diaspora, the keynote speaker at the 2018 Liberian Awards Ceremony was Mr. Wilmot Collins, mayor of the city of Helena, Montana. The Liberian-born American politician defeated the four-term mayor in the 2017 mayoral election, making him the first black mayor of any city in the state of Montana, which is predominantly white. According to his biography, Mr. Collins, who retired from the US Navy Reserves after twenty-two years of service, fled Liberia as a refugee and came to the United States during that country's civil war.

The list of the 2018 honorees reflects the richness and diversity of Liberia's human resources, concentrated in the United States and scattered around the world. For example, the 2018 honorees were the following: Dr. Euphemia R. Brumskine, who operates her own family medicine practice in the state of Maryland; Judge M. Audrey Carr, who was appointed by the United States attorney general to act as an administrative judge within the Executive Office for Immigration Review in Bloomington, Minnesota; and Ms. Cori Thomas, an award-winning playwright.

Some of Liberian Awards' past honorees are Dr. D. Elwood Dunn, retired political science professor, eminent international scholar and author; Atty. Patricia B. Minikon, an immigration lawyer and a philanthropist who operates her own law offices in the Washington DC, Maryland, and Virginia (DMV) metropolitan area; and Dr. Anthony Barclay, a senior advisor at the World Bank, who has contributed to the promotion of strategic engagements of African countries with the World Bank Group in the areas of economic growth and poverty reduction.

Across the length and breadth of the United States, in both the public and private sectors, from the White House in Washington to the corporate boardrooms, as well as various professions, there are people of Liberian descent. For example, in January 2019, Mr. Mike Elliott, thirty-five, an immigrant who came from Liberia with his parents at age eleven during Liberia's civil war, was inaugurated as the ninth mayor of Brooklyn Center, Minnesota. Elliott defeated the twelve-year incumbent mayor to become the first person of color to lead Brooklyn Center, Minnesota's most diverse city.

In the neighboring city of Brooklyn Park, Minnesota, another young Liberian American, Wynfred Russell, also made history when he was inducted in January 2019 following his election as a councilmember of the city. A social activist and a prolific writer, Russell is the second person of color to serve on the Brooklyn Park City Council.

The state of Minnesota is reputed to be home to an estimated 40,000 Liberians and Liberian Americans, the largest concentration of Liberians in the United States. The Organization of Liberians in Minnesota, the umbrella community-based organization, as well as many other community-based civic, professional, and religious organizations, have contributed meaningfully to the reconstruction of postwar Liberia. Because of the growing importance of the Liberian Diaspora community in Minnesota, the state, city, and other local government jurisdictions have also been commendable partners in Liberia's reconstruction.

During the administration of President Sirleaf, then vice president Joseph Boakai beat a path to Minnesota as a regular visitor to the state, during which he emphasized the need for US expertise and workers to help rebuild Liberia's infrastructure and institutions. Those positive engagements brought some benefits to Liberia. For example, Brooklyn Park Fire Department, in partnership with the nonprofit group Fire Rescue Alliance, provided a couple of fire trucks, as well as other firefighting equipment and training to help build the capacity of the Liberia National Fire Service (LNFS).

In 2012, a fifteen-member delegation from Brooklyn Park Fire Department, headed by fire chief Ken Prillaman, visited Liberia under a partnership with the LNFS. Members of the team, all experts in firefighting, were on a return visit, during which they were engaged in various activities to enhance the capacity of the Liberia National Fire Service. These included carrying out repairs on the only fire engine owned by the LNFS, as well as the distribution of firefighting equipment and medical supplies.

When the Sirleaf administration took over the affairs of Liberia in 2006, the National Fire Service did not have a single fire truck, as narrated in the account in chapter 6 regarding the fire that destroyed the Executive Mansion.

As a manifestation of its growing importance, the Liberian government instituted measures to establish an honorary consulate in Minnesota to cater to the interest of Liberia and the Liberian Diaspora and also to promote economic and other ties between the Republic of Liberia and the state of Minnesota.

Mr. Jackson K. George, Jr., an enterprising Liberian professional, was appointed by President Sirleaf as honorary consul in 2017. In 2018, Ambassador Lois C. Brutus, then Liberia's ambassador to the United States, formally opened the offices of the Honorary Liberian Consulate, located in Brooklyn Park, Minnesota.

Mr. George, who is one of the founders and the executive director of the Liberian Business Association in the Diaspora (LIBA-Diaspora), has been focused on building strong ties between minority businesses in the Diaspora and Liberian-owned businesses in Liberia. LIBA-Diaspora has been engaged in advocacy, partnership, and projects that promote entrepreneurship, build minority business capacities, and foster dialogue on economic development and private sector issues affecting minority businesses.

It may be recalled that in an effort to enhance Liberia's representation in the United States and Canada, the Liberian government began a process in 2015 to establish four honorary consulates in both countries. In view of the foregoing, then Liberia's ambassador to the United States, H. E. Jeremiah C. Sulunteh, visited California and Minnesota in the United States, as well as Toronto and Edmonton in Canada, for the establishment of the consulates.

The establishment of the honorary consulate in Minnesota brings to two the number of honorary consulates of Liberia in the United States. The other is the honorary consulate of Liberia in Atlanta, Georgia, led by honorary consul Cynthia L. Blandford. Liberia also operates its Permanent Mission to the UN, headed by Ambassador D-Maxwell Saah Kemayah, and consulate general, headed by Consul General Rudolph E. Sherman Jr., both located in New York.

In January 2019, Ambassador Brutus was replaced as Liberia's ambassador to the United States by H. E. George S. W. Patten Sr., a long-serving energetic career foreign service officer. He previously served as Liberia's ambassador to Ethiopia and charge d'affaires AI at Liberia's Permanent Mission to the UN in New York, USA. The Liberian embassy near Washington also has jurisdiction over Canada and Mexico.

Liberian ambassador to US George Patten (2nd L), with Gov. Tim Walz (far-R), during a 2019 visit to Minnesota. (Far-L), Liberia's consul general to New York Rudolph Sherman and honorary consul to Minnesota Jackson George.)

Another community-based organization that has been a source of community togetherness is the Association of Citizens and Friends of Liberia (ACFLi), regarded as the oldest African community-based organization in Sacramento, California, whose membership is open to Liberians and non-Liberians alike. ACFLi was founded in 1990 by a group of Liberians fleeing the brutal civil war in that country.

ACFLi's a mission is to strengthen communities, provide humanitarian services, and to increase awareness of refugee and immigrant needs while sharing Liberia's rich cultural heritage. For example, the organization has awarded scholarships to deserving college students in the United States and Liberia and donated medical supplies to Liberia during the Ebola pandemic.

With favorable publicity from the local media and the outpouring of support from within the Sacramento area, the Liberian community succeeded in collecting and shipping a large quantity of medical supplies to Liberia during the global fight to contain the Ebola epidemic.

Sacramento's commendable response to the Ebola crisis was spearheaded by leaders of the Liberian community-based churches. The Reverend Timothy T. Wulah Jr., pastor of the Friends in Jesus International Ministries of the Church of the Nazarene, and Apostle MacDonald Jaa of the El-Shaddai World Evangelism, must be applauded for creating the conducive atmosphere for people of Liberian and African descent to congregate, worship, and engage in other activities together. They both have partnered well in bringing the community together in times of crisis, as was in the case of the Ebola or death within the community.

Liberians in the Diaspora have also begun to invest their professional expertise, resources, and time in the reconstruction process of the country. A growing number of Diaspora Liberians are returning to Liberia to be directly involved in the political and reconstruction processes. Such Diaspora Liberians should be applauded for their support and sacrifices to help keep the country on a course of sustainable peace and progress. An enhanced engagement of the Liberian Diaspora with the homeland is critical for Liberia's rapid transformation. Through continued and sustained engagement, Liberians in the Diaspora will help create the enabling environment that would engender the transfer of knowledge, skills, and resources to accelerate Liberia's development and progress.

Despite the tremendous challenges facing postwar Liberia, it is encouraging to note that there are many Liberian professionals in the Diaspora who are not only sitting back and just complaining about the problems in their native homeland but are also sacrificing their time and resources to be change agents.

One of the professional Diaspora Liberians who has endeavored to make a notable contribution in the health care system is Dr. Catherine Turkett-Kamara, founder and director of the SALT Rehabilitation Clinic, Liberia's first postwar trauma rehabilitation center with trained and certified experts in stroke and trauma rehabilitation. SALT services include physical, occupational, and speech therapies. In 2019, a new pediatric sensory room, the first of its kind in Liberia to provide children with developmental delay with cognitive and physical therapies, was added to the services being provided at the clinic, which is located in a suburb of Monrovia.

Having traveled to Liberia on a number of occasions, Dr. Turkett-Kamara saw the very pressing need for stroke and trauma rehabilitation services to assist the people, who did not have any access to such services. She said she was so moved by the plight of the people that she decided to personally do something to make a difference.

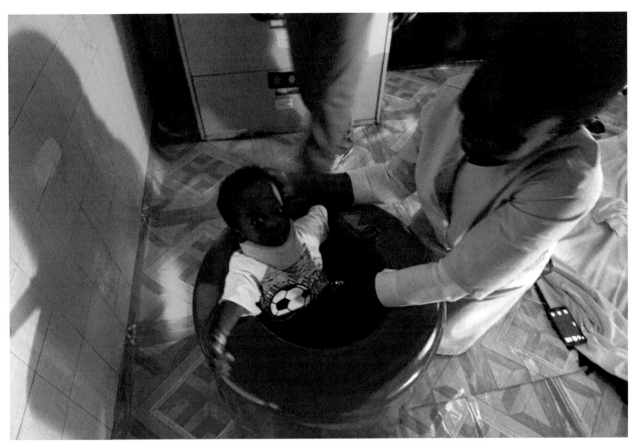

A child with developmental challenges being treated in the pediatric sensory room at SALT Rehabilitation Clinic in Monrovia. (Courtesy, SALT Rehabilitation Center)

The devastating civil war, the Ebola epidemic, and other factors have left many Liberians traumatized, physically deformed, and psychologically scarred. As a result, hypertension and stroke have left many Liberians dead or paralyzed. These health challenges have been at epidemic and alarming proportions since the civil upheavals. Many Liberians stricken with stroke who have the financial means have to travel to Ghana and other parts of the world for advanced medical treatment. This is why the opening of the SALT Rehabilitation Clinic has begun to make a difference in meeting the needs of Liberians who are being victimized by stroke.

Like thousands of other Liberians, Dr. Turkett-Kamara sought refuge in the United States as a young lady during the Liberian civil war, where she studied medicine and is a graduate of Rutgers University in New Jersey and New Jersey State University, respectively.

SALT Rehabilitation Clinic's immediate plans included the establishment of a pain management clinic and an autism center. In an interview with the *African Star* online news outlet, Dr. Turkett-Kamara said, "We see 11 to 13 children with developmental delays every day. Approximately five out of every 13 children assessed exhibit pervasive developmental delays (. . . symptoms of autism)" ("Liberia: Salt Rehab Clinic Seeks Merger With JFK Medical Center," *African Star.org*, February 19, 2018).

According to FrontPage Africa news, a 2008 study conducted by Harvard Humanitarian Initiative at Harvard University in Cambridge, Massachusetts, found that 40 percent of Liberians had symptoms of major depression, and 44 percent appeared to have posttraumatic stress disorder (PTSD), five years following the end of the brutal civil war.

Over the years especially since the end of the civil upheavals, Liberians in the Diaspora have invested their hearts and souls, resources, and time to be actively involved in the national rebuilding process. They have also been actively engaged in the electoral process supporting various political parties and candidates and causes. Many have traveled to Liberia to be directly involved in the political process. Thank you for your support and sacrifices to help keep Liberia on a course of progress. An enhanced engagement of the Liberian Diaspora with the homeland is critical for Liberia's rapid transformation. Through continued and sustained engagement, Liberians in the Diaspora will help create the enabling environment that would engender the transfer of knowledge, skills, and resources to accelerate Liberia's development and progress.

The Union of Liberian Associations in the Americas (ULAA) is the umbrella organization representing Liberians and their various organizations in the United States. Since the 1970s, Liberians in the United States have been actively engaged in the political life of Liberia, advocating for democratic governance, through ULAA. Some of the organization's past leaders such as Messrs. Charles Taylor and Thomas Woewiyu, who gained public relevance while they were residents in the United States portraying themselves as activists for change, returned home to unleash the civil upheavals that engulfed Liberia and the West African subregion.

Since the civil upheavals, ULAA has been positively engaged with the Liberian government and other stakeholders to ensure sustainable peace and progress. Recognizing the importance of the Liberian Diaspora, President Sirleaf established a department within the Office of the President to specifically deal with Diaspora affairs. In a similar vein, the Embassy of Liberia near Washington endeavored to cultivate a cordial and close working relationship with ULAA and the Liberian Diaspora during the Sirleaf administration.

President Sirleaf with leaders of ULAA during a 2010 US visit. (L-R) Samuel Slewion, Margaret Jones, Wilmot Kunney, Nee Allison, Isaac Zawolo, Anthony Kesselly, Ambassador Nathaniel Barnes, and Emmanuel Togba.

As an example of the cordial working relationship between the Liberian embassy and Diaspora community, the embassy usually cohosted an all-day cultural extravaganza with the Liberian Community Association (LCA) as part of festivities to commemorate Liberia's independence anniversary in July. The daylong summer extravaganza, which has attracted up to 10,000 people on the grounds of the embassy, showcases Liberia's rich and diverse cultural heritage. The LCA is the main Liberian community organization within the Washington DC, Metro Area, which incorporates parts of the states of Maryland and Virginia. The LCA is a chapter of ULAA, which has chapters in various states. The Association of Liberian Christian Ministers (ALCM), an organization comprising Liberian clergy based in the DC Metro area as an affiliate of the LCA, also usually partner with the embassy in cohosting an intercessory and thanksgiving service as part of annual festivities commemorating Liberia's independence.

Over the past decade, the Embassy of Liberia in the United States have worked closely with various Liberian organizations and friends of Liberia in advocating for the well-being of Liberians in the United States in dealing with various issues affecting members of the Diaspora community, including immigration support.

Even though the Liberian Diaspora is well positioned to help enhance Liberia's growth and development, the argument could be made that lack of strong collective approach in various undertakings, with too many splintered endeavors, have undermined the impact of the contributions of Diaspora Liberians. Diaspora Liberians need to be more organized and build mutual trust to work as a collective.

Cultural performers at a Liberian embassy event in the United States. Veteran performer Nimely Napla (R) is former director of the once-celebrated Liberian National Cultural Troupe. (Courtesy, Liberian Embassy Public Affairs)

Kandakai Duncan, popularly known as Ironside, now late Liberian musical star of the '70s, singing some of the oldies but goodies at a 2010 Liberian embassy cultural event in Washington. (Courtesy, Liberian Embassy)

Although not necessarily structured like many of the organizations mentioned supra, another US-based organization that has been a strong advocate for Liberia in the United States and has been actively involved in the country's reconstruction process is the Friends of Liberia (FOL). A nonprofit organization started in 1985 by former US Peace Corps volunteer from Liberia, FOL's membership now include Liberians, diplomats, missionaries, academics, development workers, and others committed to Liberia.

During the years of the civil war when the Liberian crises was on the backburner in Washington, Friends of Liberia was a loud voice screaming for help on behalf of Liberia. Since the end of the civil crises, FOL has been actively involved in Liberia's reconstruction process through various programs. The organization has been very actively involved in the effort to improve Liberia's educational and health systems, such as funding schools and children's libraries in various parts of Liberia, as well support for Liberian women organizations and other groups that promote sustainable peace, education, health, the environment, among others.

As of the release of this publication, the president of FOL is Ms. Sarah Morrison, who was a Peace Corps volunteer in Liberia from 1985–87, serving at the Ministry of Health in Monrovia as a national training and logistics coordinator for the Combating Childhood Communicable Diseases program. After that, she joined the US State Department and served as public affairs Officer at the US embassy in Liberia during the Taylor regime in the 1990s. She is well regarded within the Liberian media circle for her strong support of Liberian journalists in the struggle to defend freedom of speech and of the press during the brutal Taylor regime. Ms. Morrison went on to assume more senior diplomatic postings in other parts of the world before retiring in 2014. Nevertheless, there can be no question that her heart is in Liberia, as reflected by the regular visits she and other FOL officials undertake to the country to check on FOL projects and programs.

SOS for Liberia's Education System

Despite the prewar progress, Liberia's educational system has remained in a poor state since the war as of this publication. At the end of the civil upheavals, the country's illiteracy rate was estimated to be between 70–80 percent. An example of the weak education system was when nearly 25,000 students failed the test for admission to the state-run University of Liberia in 2013, a development that made news headlines around the world. Many schools around the country lacked basic education materials, and teachers were poorly qualified.

In a special Message to the Nation delivered March 14, 2013, President Sirleaf acknowledged the dire state of affairs when she said Liberia's "education system is a mess and in need of complete overhaul." Madam president had expressed on a number of occasions that the educational system was dysfunctional. She had pointed out that the country's universities and colleges were producing many graduates who could hardly read and write with comprehension, as their educational level was equivalent to that of a high school or secondary school. She also added that many secondary school graduates were only able to perform at primary school level.

And here is part of the main reasons for the decline in Liberia's educational standards. According to a report released in 2018 by the World Bank and quoted by the *Liberian Observer* newspaper, over 5,000 teachers, which made up 62 percent of all teachers that were assigned in government-owned primary schools across the country, did not hold a grade "C" certificate, which is the minimum teaching qualification ("62% of Public School Teachers Not Qualified, World Bank Reports," *Liberian Observer* online, November 13, 2018).

The World Bank report indicated that at the secondary level, teacher quality was low, with only a third of the secondary school teachers having the minimum qualification for their position, which requires a university degree or "A" certificate as described in the education policy.

It goes without saying that the national development goals of Liberia would not be fully achieved until the present and future generations of young Liberians are able to benefit from proper education and training in various areas of science and technology, as well as training in various employable skillsets.

Therefore, it is imperative for the Liberian government to work toward transforming the country's educational system with a focus on science, technology, engineering, and mathematics (STEM). This would better prepare the youth and future leaders to strongly compete at the global level. The educational system must be revamped to also focus on sound early childhood education that would enable children to learn how to read and write and develop the basic foundations to succeed.

Poor Health System Causes Human Tragedy

Since the end of the civil war, Liberia's health care system has also been struggling to adequately meet the needs of the war-affected population due to inadequate financial and material resources and manpower. A report on the state of the health system immediately at the end of the war indicated that there were only fifty medical doctors in the entire country.

In an effort to improve the health conditions of the people, the government rehabilitated or constructed numerous health facilities around the country, thanks to support from our international partners. Most notable of the new health facilities is the state-of-the-art Jackson F. Doe Memorial Hospital in Tappita, Nimba County, thanks to the government of the People's Republic of China.

The John F. Kennedy Medical Center, the largest public referral hospital in the country, which was looted and vandalized during the civil crisis, was being gradually restored. The JFK Medical Center, established by the United States government as a gift to the Liberian people, operated one of the very few cancer treatment centers on the continent and attracted patients from other countries. The JFK Medical Center has also been a teaching hospital for the A. M. Dogliotti College of Medicine at the University of Liberia, which attracted students from across the continent and beyond due to the advanced quality of education.

The government also prepared a national health policy, which was formulated as a result of extensive research and consultations, aimed at providing accessible and affordable quality health care to people throughout the length and breadth of the country.

Even though efforts were made to rebuild the broken health system, this was not taken as a critical priority. As a result, many resources and opportunities to transform the health system were lost.

An example regards how Liberia lost millions of dollars' worth of state-of-the-art medical equipment and other supplies in 2011 when the Walter Reed Army Medical Center (WRAMC) in Washington DC, was combined with the National Naval Medical Center to form the triservice Walter Reed National Medical Center. Following the merger, the Washington DC facility was shut down and its operations relocated to the newly constructed ultramodern center.

With the medical center relocated to its new facilities in Bethesda, which is equipped with the most advanced medical and scientific equipment, most of the medical equipment in the old medical center were left behind as there was no use for them in the new facilities.

Before the 2011 closure of WRAMC in Washington DC, a few good Samaritans who were part of the center's medical staff decided to organize a project to redirect the used but serviceable medical equipment and educational materials to West Africa. Two West African countries targeted for those generous donations were Liberia and Ghana. Liberia was given a priority for most of the medical equipment in order to help build the capacity of the postwar country's broken health system. The project also included an educational component to train Liberian medical professionals in the use and maintenance of the variety of medical equipment.

The project was spearheaded by Ms. Luana C. Kiandoli, chief medical technologist, nephrology laboratory, and consulting technologist, dialysis laboratory at WRAMC; and Dr. Byron K. Edmond, an anesthesiologist currently with Howard County General Hospital Pharmacy in Columbia, Maryland, and who is also on faculty at the Johns Hopkins University School of Medicine.

An American, Ms. Kiandoli was married to a Liberian, and she once lived in Liberia. Her husband died before the outbreak of the civil war, followed by the loss of her son during the war. In each situation, the individuals were sick and could not get the appropriate medical treatment. As a result of her family tragedy, she vowed to do all she could within her means to help improve Liberia's dysfunctional health system. Dr. Edmond was affiliated with a program between Johns Hopkins University School of Medicine and Korle-Bu Teaching Hospital in Accra, Ghana. Under the program, doctors abroad are able to participate in operating on patients in state-of-the-art closed-circuit operating rooms/theaters, known as telemedicine, at Korle-Bu Hospital. With the proper connectivity, surgeries can also be done using cell phones in remote areas.

Among the donations earmarked for Liberia under the project were breast cancer, prostate cancer, and neurological suites; closed-circuit operating theaters; operating room equipment; hospital laboratory; and office furniture.

About five hospitals, primarily the John F. Kennedy Medical Center, as well as three universities, including the University of Liberia, were targeted to benefit from the excess medical equipment and training programs that were earmarked to be executed under the project. This included the establishment of a biomedical equipment training program at the University of Liberia to train some students in medical equipment maintenance.

Other programs earmarked for Liberia under the project included the following:

> The **Walter Reed Health Sciences Collection** (medical library), which was intended to serve as an exemplary science library at the A. M. Dogliotti College of Medicine, in partnership with Howard University, University of Massachusetts, and George Washington University Health Sciences Libraries.

> The University of Liberia's Center for Excellence in Life and Health Sciences was to build toward having 1,000 students from the University of Liberia enrolled in an eighteen-month certified science training program. Under the guidance of the University of Indiana's agricultural geneticist Dr. Keithanne Mokatitis, the **Walter Reed Health Science Training Labs** at the University of Liberia was to begin producing sorely needed health care workers.

> The John F. Kennedy Hospital in Monrovia was to have a functioning **Walter Reed Pediatric Intensive Care Unit** that was intended to care for end-stage malaria children who were evaluated in an upgraded three-bed pediatric emergency bay (equipment reused from WRAMC Pediatric Clinic procedure room).

The project fostered collaboration between US academic institutions, nongovernmental organizations, and the governments of the United States, Liberia, and Ghana. The US government, through the US military, approved of the project, and the United States also offered to assist the project through a program where the government will assist in transporting humanitarian equipment into a foreign country.

Other partners that collaborated in the project were the Maryland Sister States Program health care initiative sponsored by the secretary of state of the state of Maryland; Partnership for the Advancement of Technical Training in Burke, Virginia; HEARTT Foundation, which has sponsored numerous medical missions to Liberia; Korle-Bu Neuroscience Foundation; and Mr. Billy Teninty, biomedical technician educator at Engineering World Health. Through Engineering World Health, volunteer engineers use their unique abilities to install and repair lifesaving equipment in resource-poor hospitals and to train local technicians in order to build sustainable capacity.

As the project gained momentum and approval, the University of Liberia and the J. F. Kennedy Medical Center, which were the main beneficiaries of the donations, were involved in the process. In order to ensure that the right types of equipment most suitable for Liberia were identified, some medical professionals of Liberian descent, such as Dr. James Elliott, were consulted. Dr. Elliott, director of the Division of Pathology and Laboratory Medicine at Doctor's Hospital in Lanham, Maryland, is also clinical assistant professor of pathology at George Washington University Medical School, Washington DC. He is a member of the board of the US-based William V.S. Tubman University Foundation, a nongovernmental organization aimed at providing support for Tubman University in Harper, Maryland County, Liberia.

A series of working meetings involving mostly professional experts from the various entities associated with the project were held at Howard University in Washington DC and elsewhere to plan regarding how the equipment and other materials would be transported to Liberia and reinstalled for operation, and they also formulated the training programs.

I accompanied the ambassador to several of the meetings, including at Howard University and at the WRAMC. One of the meetings at the WRAMC was presided over by a colonel in the US military, who was the WRAMC administrator. In remarks, the administrator said that when he was informed that the humanitarian project was intended for Liberia, he was motivated to do what he could to ensure its success. He said he grew up at home with a close family member who served a tour of duty in Liberia while enlisted in the US military. He added that until his loved one passed, he always talked about how his stay in Liberia was one of the best times in his life and that he had some beautiful traditional artifacts from Liberia in his home that he proudly talked about.

Among those at that meeting was the ambassador of Ghana and representatives from the Embassy of Sierra Leone, who came with a request for their country to be considered for whatever little that they could benefit therefrom.

As part of the meeting, we were taken on a tour of some areas of the medical center to see some of the equipment and operating suites that were earmarked for each country. We were very amazed and delighted by what was being given us free of charge to upgrade our health systems. In a concluding meeting following the tour, we were informed that the next phase of the project was for the equipment earmarked for each country to be disassembled, packaged, and moved to a warehouse by professionals with the expertise, pending shipment to Liberia and Ghana. A private firm with the expertise was to do an assessment and determine a reasonable cost to package and store the equipment for each country, which turned out to be not more than $25,000 for Liberia.

The Ghanaian ambassador, visibly excited, expressed thanks to the US government and all those who worked to make the donation possible. He said that even though the project was primarily focused on Liberia, his country was very grateful for those state-of-the-art equipment to help improve its health system. He said that as soon as he was informed how much it would cost to remove the equipment for Ghana, he will make the funds available.

For his part, the Liberian ambassador, who was intimately involved with the project through various engagements, expressed profound gratitude to the United States for yet another demonstration of its commitment to Liberia's reconstruction by such generous donations. He lauded Ms. Kiandoli, the WRAMC administration, and others involved in the project, which would contribute to the transformation of Liberia's health system. During the tour of the hospital, he said that what he saw went beyond his expectation, in terms of the variety and quality of the medical equipment earmarked for Liberia.

However, what the ambassador said next set the stage for Liberia to lose those state-of-the-art medical equipment and operating suites while the Ghanaians went away with basically everything. Regarding Liberia covering the cost to package and relocate the medical donations, the ambassador said he could not commit himself and that he will have to get directive from Monrovia to proceed with any payment.

After he was informed that the cost for Liberia was $25,000, he sent a communication to Monrovia seeking guidance, but there was no response for weeks. As the deadline approached for the equipment to be removed from the medical center, the company responsible for the package proposed that if Liberia made a $15,000 part payment, it will go ahead to move Liberia's donations to a warehouse, and the balance $10,000 can be paid subsequently.

As the deadline approached and the ambassador dug in his heels not to make any payment without authorization from Monrovia, tensions mounted between him and some of those involved with the project. Some of them could not contain their outrage at the ambassador for letting such a great medical opportunity for Liberia slip away and their time wasted in the process. In the wake of Liberia's failure to make the payment to remove the donations in keeping with the deadline, the Ghanaians, who made their payment and demonstrated a strong desire for the equipment, were given the opportunity to take all they could from what was set aside for Liberia and add those to what they were already given.

Even though the ambassador did not get the official authorization for the funds before the closure of the WRAMC, the embassy was financially positioned to make the payment. The Embassy of Liberia in Washington DC makes a significant contribution to the national budget with a regular remittance of hundreds of thousands of dollars in revenues generated from consular services. As a measure to control misuse of funds, there was a directive that all funds from consular services be remitted to Liberia and that no amount should be disbursed therefrom without authorization from Monrovia. However, it was not uncommon for consular funds to be used on government-related matters before formal authorizations were made. As a matter of fact, due to the tiny budgetary amount usually allocated for the embassy, consular funds have supplemented the budget for the operation of the embassy.

Therefore, it was a matter of discretion, given the urgency of a situation, such as the case of the deadline for the removal of the medical equipment. As one of the senior diplomats at the embassy involved with the project, I also unsuccessfully tried to prevail on the ambassador to go ahead with the payment, which I thought could be justified, given the deadline for the WRAMC closure. He once responded to me that if any questions arose from the payment, he was the one who would have to answer. Like I repeatedly indicated during that time, if I were in the position to authorize the payment from the embassy, I would have gone ahead without hesitation and wait to be questioned or fired for doing so.

Given the opportunities squandered as reflected supra, there is little wonder why, since the end of Liberia's devastating civil upheavals, numerous challenges have remained regarding access to quality health care. As a result of the limited access to quality health care, an unusually high death rate in the country has been attributed to preventable and curable diseases like malaria, typhoid, and diarrhea, as well as widespread conditions of hypertension and stroke since the civil war. As a result of the deplorable health conditions, life expectancy of Liberia as of 2018 was sixty-three years.

Nevertheless, nothing prepared Liberia and the world at large for the human tragedy that was to unfold in the country along with neighboring Sierra Leone and Guinea in the wake of the outbreak of the Ebola virus epidemic in 2014. Because of a broken health care system, Liberia suffered the worst effects of the Ebola epidemic in West Africa. The following couple of chapters reflect the devastating impacts of the Ebola disease, which posed an existential threat to Liberia.

CHAPTER NINE

Ebola Outbreak Exposed Health Care Crises in Liberia, Other Parts of Africa

Despite the encouraging progress made in the reconstruction of war-ravaged Liberia, enormous challenges have remained. Among the areas of challenges that have required urgent and robust intervention have been the health care delivery and education sectors. As a result of the civil war, the country witnessed a devastating loss of its human capital while the postwar country has been saddled with crises in its education and health care delivery systems. Many institutions in these sectors have performed poorly while others have been dysfunctional.

Regarding the state of the health delivery system, people have referred to health care facilities as "death trap" due to inadequate or lack of medical drugs and equipment, as well as inadequate and poorly trained medical staff. These problems are particularly acute in the rural or remote parts of Liberia, where the people are forced to trek for hours and sometimes for days to get from one destination to another because there is little or no access to passable roads for motor vehicles.

The outbreak and spread of the deadly Ebola virus in West Africa in February 2014, which the World Health Organization (WHO) declared the world's deadliest to date of this publication, brought to global focus the alarming rate of poverty in many parts of Africa. At the time Ebola struck, Liberia's impoverishment was characterized by very weak health care systems, inadequate safe drinking water and sanitation, and a high rate of malnutrition among children.

The health care systems of the three countries worst affected by the Ebola pandemic, Liberia, Sierra Leone, and Guinea, essentially collapsed, Liberia and Sierra Leone being most impacted.

Widespread television images of health workers dressed like astronauts in full body protective suits and gears, transporting body bags of Ebola victims, sent shock waves of fear and panic around the world regarding the deadly mysterious virus. There was little known about Ebola, and no cure existed. The WHO declared an international health emergency, as the virus spiraled out of control. From 2014 to 2016, more than 11,300 deaths were reported due to the Ebola disease while there were more than 28,600 cases of infection in Guinea, Liberia, Sierra Leone, and Nigeria.

Following the outbreak of the disease in Nzerekore, an area in southeastern Guinea, the virus spread to the country's capital, Conakry, and then to neighboring Sierra Leone and Liberia, wreaking havoc along the way.

A Liberian American who flew from Liberia to Lagos, Nigeria, was quarantined and later died of Ebola, which was the first case of the virus in Africa's most populous country with a population estimated at 178.5 million in 2014, according to the World Population Review. The effects of the Ebola epidemic were very minimum in Nigeria in comparison to the devastations experienced by the three worst-affected countries. This was attributed largely to Nigeria's advanced health system.

The West Africa outbreak, which is the thirty-fourth Ebola outbreak since the virus was discovered in 1976 in Zaire, renamed the Democratic Republic of Congo, manifested in a manner that posed a more serious existential threat to humans than previous outbreaks. According to the WHO, there were 318 cases of Ebola infection, 280 deaths, and only 38 serologically confirmed survivors from the first outbreak. Since the first outbreak, the number of deaths from each of the various known cases and outbreaks besides the West Africa outbreak were lower.

According to the US Centers for Disease Control and Prevention (CDC), "Ebola virus is the cause of a viral hemorrhagic fever disease. Symptoms include: fever, headache, joint and muscle aches, weakness, diarrhea, vomiting, stomach pain, lack of appetite, and abnormal bleeding. Symptoms may appear anywhere from 2 to 21 days after exposure to Ebolavirus though 8-10 days is most common."

It is stated that poverty and ignorance are the combustible fuel that fanned the flames, leading to the rapid spread and devastating impact of the Ebola epidemic in Guinea, Liberia, and Sierra Leone. These three countries are among the poorest in the world, with very weak health care delivery systems.

The rapid spread of the Ebola epidemic, leaving in its wake fear, panic, death, trauma, and anguish, exposed another aspect of how fragile most African countries are. They lack adequate services, such as affordable quality health care and education. In many areas, access to safe drinking water, sanitation, electricity, and good housing has remained a challenge. The transportation sector has also remained a challenge due to limited or lack of road networks.

In Africa, many people continue to die from curable and preventable diseases such as malaria and diarrhea, while malnutrition has been a factor in 45 percent of child deaths, according to the WHO, due to poor and dysfunctional health care systems. The basic health care and educational systems in many parts of Africa have suffered neglect because African leaders, including those of Liberia, along with the privileged few, usually travel abroad for advanced medical checkup, and they also send their children abroad for quality education. As a result, the health and educational systems, among other essential public services, have operated in a poor or dysfunctional state.

A glaring example of such neglect relates to Zimbabwe, where in December 2018, doctors and other medical practitioners went on strike to demand that the government address a very serious situation related to the unavailability of critical medicines, as well as medical and sanitary sundries.

The New Zimbabwe.com news outlet reported on December 17, 2018, that in their grievances, the medical doctors disclosed that they were being forced to resort to the use of condoms as protective gloves due to acute shortages. Can you imagine the level of frustration endured by those medical personnel who are supposed to serve people desperate for help under such horrible and unacceptable conditions?

It is common knowledge that many African countries have been in worst conditions economically and have declined in terms of infrastructural development under their own leaders who have been in charge since independence. It has also been argued that many African countries are worst off now than they were under colonial rule, considering the decline in the quality of health, education, and other basic services, as well as decline in the quality of life of majority of the people, who had so much hope and optimism at the time of independence.

Zimbabwe, which I mentioned supra, is a typical example of a country that has seen a reversal in its fortune since independence, due to what Zimbabweans have blamed on corruption and poor leadership. A country once regarded as the breadbasket of the southern Africa region, Zimbabwe has declined to a point where there had been reports of widespread food shortage. For example, in 2019, there was a shortage of bread, one of the main food consumed by Zimbabweans.

Because of widespread poverty and deprivation, many parts of Africa are like a powder keg waiting for a spark to ignite, as was the case of the Ebola epidemic, which overwhelmed the worst-affected countries shortly following its outbreak.

For example, it is common in some rural parts of Liberia to see a group of men toting a hammock on their heads, containing a pregnant woman experiencing labor complications or an individual in critical condition, who is being conveyed to a nearby medical facility that may be miles or hours away. Oftentimes the patients, who include those with all kinds of health complications requiring emergency treatment, would die before reaching the medical center.

Like many Liberians from poor and rural background, I lost my mother from childbirth because there was neither a clinic in my home village nor was there any health facility nearby that was equipped to handle the complications she suffered. As reported in chapter 1 of this book, Rivercess, my native homeland in southeastern Liberia, has been one of the least developed, as well as one of the most economically depressed parts of Liberia. This is notwithstanding the fact that the region is well endowed with natural resources, including minerals such as diamonds, rain forests, coconut and oil palm, and a beautiful coastline of white sandy beaches lined with palm trees stretching for miles.

In 2012, the Liberian government announced that a huge deposit of "oil block" offshore in Rivercess had been discovered. Rivercess also has an informal traditional fishing industry with enormous potential for commercialization.

It is, therefore, safe to conclude that the environment of ignorance, poverty, and deprivation, manifested by poor health care delivery system, were the perfect ingredients that accelerated the spread of the Ebola virus in Liberia, Sierra Leone, and Guinea.

Even though Liberia was the third country to be affected after the epidemic spread from Guinea to Sierra Leone, Liberia had the highest number of fatalities. For example, the WHO Ebola virus disease update of August 28, 2014, put the number of deaths in Liberia at 694 while there were 430 deaths in Guinea, 422 deaths in Sierra Leone, and 6 deaths in Nigeria.

The first case of the Ebola disease was recorded in Liberia on March 30, 2014, in Foya, Lofa County, Liberia's northern region bordering with Guinea, close to where the epidemic reportedly originated from in that country. People on each sides of the border share family, ethnic, and religious ties. Due to the level of cross-border movements, the virus spread quickly in Lofa and then to Margibi County with a crossover by a female marketer. On June 17, Ebola cases were reported in Montserrado County, where Monrovia is located. According to President Sirleaf, 2.1 million of the Liberian population of 4 million resided in various areas of Monrovia ("Congested Capital Alarms Pres. Sirleaf," *Liberia News Agency*, June 25, 2015).

After the Ministry of Health and Social Welfare, in partnership with the WHO office in Liberia, confirmed the first case of Ebola in the country, the report was greeted with widespread public disbelief and denial, even as the epidemic spread from Foya to other parts of the country with increasing infection and death rates. That a virus called Ebola was infesting and killing people, as was pronounced by the government, was taken to be a complete joke by many Liberians, who were deeply suspicious that the government was about to create a crisis in order to get more international financial support that benefitted mostly government officials and their families.

In an article published September 3, 2014, by the UN Integrated Regional Information Networks (IRIN), writer Kate Thomas reflects the history of mistrust in the following account: "Decades of corruption, deep-rooted mistrust of government and weak public services in Liberia have hastened the spread of the of the Ebola Virus" ("Liberia: Mistrust of Government Spurs Ebola Spread," AllAfrica.com, September 3, 2014)

During a press conference in late March of 2015 at the Ministry of Information, then minister of health and social welfare, Dr. Walter Gwenigale, announced measures to prevent the spread of the deadly virus. He urged people to avoid handshaking, touching, kissing, and coming into contact with persons infected or killed by the disease. He also called for abstention from sex for a certain period, noting that the virus can also be transmitted through sperm and vaginal fluids.

Dr. Gwenigale also announced a ban on the sale and consumption of bushmeat, amid reports that the virus was carried by bats.

The health minister indicated that the measures were intended to prevent people from coming into contact with bodily fluids or the blood of those infected, as this was a prime source through which the disease is transmitted from one individual to another.

Regarding whether or not Liberia should have closed its border with Guinea during the early stage of the outbreak, Dr. Gwenigale indicated during that press conference that the WHO had advised against the closure of the border, as doing so would have contravened WHO's health regulations. He added that the WHO had advised on the establishment of special centers to isolate infected people, so as to prevent the spread of disease.

The Ministry of Health also announced that US$1.2 million was urgently needed to combat the deadly Ebola plague. During that time, there were only 8 suspected and confirmed cases of Ebola and 6 deaths reported in Liberia. In neighboring Guinea, there were reports of 103 suspected and confirmed cases and 66 Ebola deaths while 6 suspected and confirmed cases and 5 deaths were also reported in Sierra Leone, according to the independent FrontPage Africa ("No Sex: Liberia's Ebola Epidemic and the Consequences," April 1, 2014, www.frontpageafricaonline.com).

Ironically, Dr. Gwenigale, became an object of popular Ebola-related jokes and a comic relief following that press conference in late March, during which he announced that one of the measures to control the spread of the Ebola virus was abstention from sex within a given period.

The Liberian media was abuzz with jokes and comical characterization of Dr. Gwenigale's pronouncement regarding abstention from sex. For example, the April 1, 2014, edition of FrontPage Africa was emblazoned with the headline: "No Sex for 45 Days." Social settings in Monrovia and the Liberian social media abounded with jokes, like "Ebola say we shouldn't eat something," a reference to sexual abstention. The FrontPage Africa publication carried a photograph of a gloomy-looking Dr. Gwenigale, seated at the press conference table with his head rested in the left palm of his hand on the table. Dr. Gwenigale's demeanor in that photo was a tiny depiction of the gloom that was to soon be cast upon Liberia by the Ebola epidemic ("No Sex: Liberia's Ebola Epidemic and the Consequences," April 1, 2014, www.frontpageafricaonline.com).

During the early stages of the Ebola epidemic, the Health Ministry made an urgent appeal to the government for US$1.2 million to fight the scourge. However, the ministry was given only US$250,000, according to Senator Peter Coleman, chair of the Senate Committee on Health. During a Senate session in early July 2014, he announced another appeal that the Health Ministry would urgently need US$1.5 million to combat the deadly virus, even though it had earlier requested for $1.2 million ("US$1.5 Million Needed to Fight Ebola," *Inquirer*, July 9, 2014, www.allafrica.com).

The government's effort to get Liberians to recognize the danger of the Ebola virus was not helped by some senior officials expressing doubt that Ebola was real. Senator Cletus Wotorson, a very influential member of the National Legislature, who once served as president pro tempore of the Liberian senate, exemplified the disbelief that existed even at high levels of Liberia's leadership about the existence of the Ebola disease. Mr. Wotorson's utterances during a regular senate session where he questioned the existence of the disease and asserted that the Health Ministry's pronouncements about Ebola were a ploy to attract international funding or extort money from donors were widely reported in the Liberian media.

The deep-seated mistrust that Liberians exhibited of their government during the Ebola outbreak was mind-boggling even though the government's credibility had been undermined by public outcry about widespread corruption and mismanagement of public resources. Widespread public misgivings about uncontrollable corruption and mismanagement in government had stigmatized Liberia as one of the most corrupt countries in the world.

Cultural and religious practices that are common in West Africa, such as shaking hands, hugging, washing of the dead, and other burial rites, contributed to the spread of the deadly Ebola pandemic. Many people did not believe that Ebola is real, and that was among the contributing factors for the spread of the deadly disease.

In neighboring Guinea and Sierra Leone, there were also strong public doubts that Ebola is real. Amid widespread rumors about the disease across the affected region, Ebola treatment centers were viewed by many as places set up to infect people or drain victims' blood to be carried away for sale. Health care workers, especially expatriates, were suspected of secretly carrying the virus around and infecting people. This level of ignorance would subsequently degenerate into violent attacks against health care workers and Ebola treatment centers, resulting in deaths, as you will read later in this chapter.

As the Liberian government struggled to ensure public adherence regarding the Ebola epidemic that had spiraled out of control, President Sirleaf delivered a nationwide address on the Ebola crisis on June 28, 2014, in which she said the following:

For those who do not believe that Ebola exists in Liberia, I want to inform all Liberians in this public manner that the disease is *real* and is in our country killing people. It is as I speak, taking the lives of our citizens in Lofa, Montserrado, and now Margibi County.

Ebola spreads through physical contact with a victim of the disease. The virus also spreads through: sweat, saliva, blood, by touching the vomit or urine of somebody who is sick with Ebola.

These deaths are mostly due to denial, touching dead bodies or participating in Burial Ceremonies. Avoid touching dead bodies or body fluids or materials of infected Ebola persons. Avoid direct physical contact, such as handshakes, kissing and direct contact with body fluids of infected or dead persons or animals.

Major issues confronting the response teams include but are not limited to keeping sick people in healing centers, prayer homes, and other nonmedical centers. These practices create public health hazards to families, neighborhoods, and other innocent people. It is illegal under our public health law to expose the people to health hazards such as Ebola. Let this warning go out, anyone found or reported to be holding suspected Ebola cases in homes or prayer house will be prosecuted under the laws of Liberia.

President Sirleaf dedicates the newly constructed ELWA Hospital in 2016 with US evangelist Franklin Graham, who has significantly contributed to Liberia's health care development. (Courtesy, Liberian Embassy)

In July 2014, the government declared a health emergency, ordered the closure of most of Liberia's borders with Guinea and Sierra Leone, and also ordered the indefinite closure of schools throughout the country. The government also set up a national task force chaired by the president, launched a National Action Plan prepared by the Ministry of Health and WHO, and also contributed an initial amount of US$5 million for immediate implementation of the action plan.

The reality that the Ebola disease was truly in existence began to sink in the minds of a growing number of Liberians as the death toll mounted from hundreds to thousands, among them health workers and doctors. The death of an Ugandan medical doctor on July 1 elevated public attention about the epidemic. Dr. Samuel Muhumuza Mutoro, who had worked for three years at the Redemption Hospital in the poor and congested Monrovia borough of New Kru Town, had become the latest of a growing number of health care workers to succumb to the disease, several of them from the Redemption Hospital.

On July 26, the day commemorating the 167th independence anniversary of Liberia, Dr. Samuel Brisbane, one of the country's high-profile doctors, became the first Liberian doctor to die from the Ebola disease. Dr. Brisbane was head of the emergency department and senior consultant at the John F. Kennedy Medical Center in Monrovia, Liberia's largest referral and teaching hospital.

Dr. Brisbane's death coincided with reports that a Liberian American, Patrick Sawyer, had died at a hospital in Lagos on July 25 from the Ebola disease. Mr. Sawyer, who traveled from Monrovia on July 20, reportedly collapsed upon arrival at the airport in Lagos, Nigeria's most populated city with an estimated 20 million residents. Sawyer's death heightened global fears and panic about how the disease can be easily transported to other parts of the world through movement of people from infected areas. Some of the medical personnel that came in contact with Sawyer were infected. And this was how the Ebola epidemic spread to Nigeria, Africa's most populous country.

The death of Sawyer, an American of Liberian descent, who was a consultant with the Liberian government, gained widespread media publicity around the world, especially the mainstream American media. The American media soon began to raise concerns of public interest regarding the possibility of the virus being easily transmitted to the United States through movement of people in a world that has become closely connected by airplanes. For example, there were media reports that Sawyer had planned to visit his family in the United States following the trip to Nigeria, where he died.

On the heels of the well-publicized death of Sawyer came reports in late July that two American humanitarian aid workers serving at ELWA Hospital, a Christian charity-run hospital in Monrovia, who were in the frontline to combat the Ebola epidemic, had also been infected by the disease.

Dr. Kent Brantly was helping to respond to the Ebola outbreak in Liberia, and Ms. Nancy Writebol, a hygienist, decontaminated those entering the hospital's Ebola care center. Dr. Brantly was the medical director for Samaritan Purse's Ebola Consolidated Case Management Center while Ms. Writebol, who was employed by the religious charity, Serving in Mission (SIM) in Liberia, was helping the joint SIM/Samaritan Purse team treating Ebola patients, according to a Samaritan Purse statement quoted by CNN television news ("Second American Affected with Ebola," *CNN*, August 22, 2014, www.cnn.com). *Both SIM and Samaritan Purse are US-based Christian humanitarian organizations that have operated in Liberia for decades.*

Dr. Brantly and Ms. Writebol were separately airlifted to the United States, where they were treated at Emory University Hospital in Atlanta, Georgia, and discharged after being cured from the Ebola disease. Bringing them to the United States significantly heightened public fear among Americans regarding the spread of the disease in the United States.

Confirmation of Sawyer's death in Lagos came after the Ministry of Health in neighboring Sierra Leone announced that a doctor who was playing a key role in fighting the Ebola outbreak in Sierra Leone had been infected with the virus.

Before falling ill, Dr. Shiek Humarr Khan had been overseeing Ebola treatment and isolation units at Kenema Government Hospital, about 185 miles east of the capital, Freetown. Dr. Khan, who died July 29, gained popular acclaim in Sierra Leone and international recognition for his inspiring leadership role in combating the disease. He was acclaimed as a national hero for helping to lead his country's charge in combating the pandemic.

Health workers were especially at high risk because they are in close contact with infected people and their bodily fluids. By October 2014, 443 health workers in the affected countries contracted Ebola of whom 244 died, according to the WHO.

In an address to the nation giving an update on the Ebola crisis on September 17, President Sirleaf said 172 Liberian health care workers had been infected and 82 of them had died. Giving an overall picture of the spread of the pandemic, she said there were 2,535 cumulative cases, which included confirmed, probable, and suspected cases of the Ebola disease. Of these, a total of 1,328 had died, she added.

As the death rate of health care workers and the general population increased, there were a series of strike actions by health workers to protest shortage or lack of basic medical supplies like protective gloves, low wages, among other problems in one of the world's poorest health care delivery systems. Many health care workers abandoned their posts and stayed away from work for fear of contracting the virus principally because of the very poor working conditions.

The infections exacerbated shortages of doctors and nurses in countries like Liberia, Sierra Leone, and Guinea that were already low on skilled health personnel and struggling with poor health care infrastructure that were being overwhelmed as the epidemic escalated.

On August 20, 2014, BBC News Africa published a report, quoting WHO statistics, which shed light on the health care challenges in the three worst-affected countries as follows:

In Sierra Leone, health spending stood at US $96 per person in 2002. This compares favorably to Liberia ($66) and Guinea ($32). By comparison, the UK (United Kingdom) spends $3,648 and US (United States) $8,895.

Sierra Leone has 2.2 doctors for every 100,000 people (2012 figures). Guinea has 10 (2005) and Liberia just 1.4 (2008), both far behind the UK (279) and Switzerland (395).

Resources in Sierra Leone and Liberia are drained by malaria treatment. Both had some1.5 million confirmed and probable cases in 2012, from overall populations of about 6 million and 4 million, respectively. ("Ebola Crisis: A Doctor's View from Sierra Leone," www.bbc.com/news/world-africa)

As the epidemic spiraled out of control with mounting death figures, on August 6, 2014, President Sirleaf declared a ninety-day state of emergency throughout Liberia to enable the government to step up its fight to restrain the spread of the lethal Ebola virus.

"The health care system in the country is now under immense strain, and the Ebola epidemic is having a chilling effect on the overall health care delivery," the president noted in an address to the nation. "Out of fear of being infected with the disease, health care practitioners are afraid to accept new patients, especially in community clinics across the country. Consequently, many common diseases which are especially prevalent during the rainy season, such as malaria, typhoid, and common cold, are being untreated and may lead to unnecessary and preventable deaths."

Tragically, by the time the president declared the state of emergency, the entire health care delivery system of Liberia had virtually shut down. Can you imagine that almost all the hospitals and clinics in the entire country basically shut down, and sick people, as well as pregnant women and children, had little or no opportunity to seek medical treatment?

According to the 2011 Liberia Malaria Indicator Survey quoted by AllAfrica.com online publication, on April 25, 2013, hospital records suggest that at least 33 percent of all in-patient deaths in Liberia and 41 percent of deaths among children under five were attributed to malaria ("Africa: Malaria in Liberia – 'The Struggle Continues,'" www.allafrica.com/stories).

In a country where a high death rate was also attributed to preventable and curable diseases like typhoid and diarrhea, as well as widespread conditions of hypertension since the civil war, it was also established that many people died from diseases not related to the Ebola virus, as medical tests conducted on many dead bodies proved to be Ebola negative. Lack of medical care equally affected pregnant women, as many of them died from childbirth because they could not get treatment at medical centers when they were in labor.

Following a period of temporary closures due to the devastating impact of the pandemic, health centers across Liberia, including major hospitals like the JFK Medical Center, St. Joseph's Catholic Hospital, and Redemption Hospital in Monrovia, as well as Phebe Hospital in Bong County, central Liberia, resumed operations. The health centers were reopened amid shortage of medical supplies, as well as the reduction of already limited number of health care workers due to deaths from the Ebola virus and many medical staff refusing to return to work under the circumstances.

Panic surrounding the Ebola disease affected health care workers and led to discrimination against patients suspected of being infected. The symptoms of illnesses like malaria, diarrhea, and typhoid, which include high fever, vomiting, diarrhea, sore throat, and mouth, are similar to the symptoms of the Ebola virus. As the sick were turned away from medical facilities, many died due to lack of treatment.

There are recorded images of sick people and dead bodies lying in the dust on the grounds of health care centers because they could not get admitted for treatment. Even pregnant women in labor or childbirth complications bleeding profusely were turned away at health centers out of fear that the bleeding was caused by the Ebola virus. A young pregnant woman related to an acquaintance of this author was taken from one hospital to another while she was bleeding profusely but refused admission. After she bled to death at home, medical test conducted on her body showed that she was Ebola negative and had simply suffered a miscarriage.

Another young lady, who was a college senior, died from asthma when she was denied treatment and turned away at a hospital, which demanded that she should bring clearance from an Ebola treatment center indicating that she was free of the disease before she would be treated. Unable to get treatment, she reportedly suffocated to death in the arms of her father, who was desperately seeking medical help for her.

Meanwhile, around late July to early August, residents of Monrovia began to experience the horror of seeing dead bodies lying about in various communities and streets of the city. Entire families and households were being infected and wiped out by the pandemic. It became clear that Ebola was out of control.

The Liberian media was now saturated with all kinds of reports of the soaring death toll. A report in Liberia's oldest independent newspaper, *Daily Observer*, on the death of nine members of a family reflected the state of desperation in the following paragraph: "As the fight against the deadly Ebola epidemic reaches uncharted territory, a maze of death continues to hit every sector of the Liberian population, both within the capital and its environs. There is a rising death toll in other parts of the country" ("Ebola Deaths Heighten in Monrovia, Hit Borbor Taylor's Family at Omega Station," *Daily Observer*, September 22, 2014, www.liberianobserver.com).

In an article published July 29, 2014, by FrontPage Africa online, the writer, Brenda Brewer Moore, captured the mood of growing desperation in Liberia during that time as follows: "I find myself being worked up each day almost into a frenzy panic, scouring the various online news and updates on the Ebola virus plaguing our country. Each day you wake up, you hear of more people infected, more deaths. These days it is no longer unnamed faceless victims in the most rural parts of the country but people we know, or we know people who know people who are victims. The disease has entered our social circles and is now staring us rudely, daringly in the face" ("Liberian Ebola and Sex," www.frontpageafricaonline.com).

With reports of mounting death toll at medical centers struggling to cope, the general public soon became distrustful of the health centers. There were fears that the health facilities were wrongly diagnosing patients with having the Ebola virus or contaminating them with the disease. Such fear resulted to sick people avoiding health care centers and seeking other means to cure their illnesses, such as self-medication, traditional herbalists, or spiritual healers.

For example, a young lady related to another associate of this author was afraid to seek medical treatment when she was experiencing severe headache and instead took some tablets to stop the headache. Shortly after taking the tablets, her blood pressure became very high. As a result, she suffered a stroke and was in coma for over a week. When she regained consciousness, she had lost her voice and an entire half of her body was paralyzed. She died several months thereafter.

Public panic, confusion, and anger regarding the growing state of desperation in the country degenerated into attacks against health works and medical facilities. The most daring and disgusting of the attacks that left the world stunned and in wonderment took place on late Saturday, August 16, 2014, when some residents of

West Point Monrovia's largest slum community inhabited by the mostly poor and unemployed raided an area quarantine center for suspected Ebola patients. Those who raided the quarantine center looted items such as bloody sheets and mattresses that were being used for the Ebola patients. An Associated Press (AP) report by veteran Liberian journalist Jonathan Paye Layleh quoted Liberia's assistant health minister Tolbert Nyenswah as saying that up to thirty patients were staying at the center, and many of them fled at the time of the raid.

Mr. Nyenswah said that the violence in West Point, a piece of land situated between the Atlantic Ocean and the Mesurado River with a population estimated to be between 50,000 to 75,000 was led by residents who were angry that patients were brought to the holding center in the area from other parts of Monrovia. "All between the houses you could see people fleeing with items looted from the patients," an official was quoted in the report. A resident of West Point was also quoted as saying that some of the looted items were visibly stained with blood, vomit, and excrement ("Liberia: Ebola Fears Rise as Clinic Is Looted," *AP*, August 17, 2014).

The looting of the quarantine center in a very congested slum that lacked basic services like pipe-borne water and sanitation, toilets, electricity, and health care facilities intensified fear regarding the spread of Ebola epidemic. Many residents of West Point used the beach, riverfront, and other open areas in the community to defecate and attend to other calls of nature due to lack of or limited basic services.

Following this very disturbing incidence of the quarantine center looting, the government instituted more stringent measures to combat the disease, including the quarantine of West Point and another area called Dolo Town in Margibi County as of August 19. The quarantined areas were placed under full security watch with personnel of the army, police, and other law enforcement agencies deployed to ensure that there be no movements in and out of those areas. West Point residents awoke to find themselves blocked in by checkpoints manned by armed security officers. The quarantine was to last for twenty-one days, which is the maximum time it takes for an infection to become apparent. The government also imposed a curfew from 9:00 PM to 6:00 AM.

Visibly shocked and angered by the action to restrict their movements, riot erupted as screaming West Point residents attacked security officers deployed to enforce the quarantine with rocks and other objects. Law enforcement officers responded by firing live rounds and tear gas and hitting protesters with their batons. In the process, a fifteen-year-old boy was shot in the leg and died later from bleeding. Several others were wounded. The security forces were able to maintain order and enforce the quarantine during the course of its duration.

The quarantine and imposition of the curfew coincided with rumors of an impending attempt to destabilize the country through unconstitutional change of government by some unscrupulous individuals who were about to exploit widespread public disenchantment with the government. There were speculations that a specific purpose for the curfew was to curb attempts to destabilize the country, even though such rumors were never confirmed.

Denials that Ebola is real, coupled with public suspicion and anger, also led to attacks on health care centers and medical workers in Sierra Leone and Guinea. The most fatal of all was an attack on a health team that included medical doctors and journalists who were trying to raise Ebola awareness in a village near the southern Guinea city of Nzerekore on August 17. Eight members of the team were killed by the villages using machetes and clubs, according to a Guinea official quoted by BBC News. Some of the bodies—health workers, local officials, and journalists—were found in a septic tank in the village, according to BBC ("Ebola Outbreak: Guinea Health Team Killed," BBC News Africa, September 19, 2014).

November, the Ebola crisis in Guinea would add another bizarre twist with a highway robbery during which armed bandits stopped a taxi and took off with blood samples that were believed to be infected with the deadly Ebola virus, according to the Associated Press. The samples, stored in tightly wrapped vials tucked into a cooler bag, were in the care of a Red Cross courier who was among nine passengers sharing a taxi when three bandits on a motorbike led the attack near the town of Kissidougou. The robbers, who reportedly fired in the air, also stole mobile phones, cash and jewelry. The blood samples were being transported to an Ebola testing center 165 miles away.

On August 29, Senegal's health ministry confirmed the first case of Ebola in that country after a young Guinea student infected with the disease turned up at a hospital in the Senegalese capital of Dakar.

CHAPTER TEN
Global Ebola Hysteria and Stigma

As the lethal Ebola scourge spread in the West African region, the international community was slow to respond, even though the French-based international medical organization Medecins Sans Frontieres (MSF), also known as Doctors Without Borders, and other aid organizations that were in the front line combating the deadly virus repeatedly sounded the alarm.

An Associated Press report on June 24, 2014, quoted Dr. Bart Janssens, MSF director of operations, as saying that the outbreak will require a "massive deployment of resources" by the governments and aid agencies to bring it under control. "We have reached our limits," Dr. Janssens noted. "Despite the human resources and equipment deployed by MSF in the three affected countries, we are no longer able to send teams to the new outbreak sites" ("Ebola Cases Rise in West Africa as Doctors Sound Alarm about Outbreak," *AP*, June 24, 2014).

MSF, which earlier reported that the outbreak was out of control, said it was stretched to the limit and having trouble responding to an epidemic that was breaking out in more than sixty locations across the three countries.

However, a WHO statement quoted by the AP report said the UN agency was working with local governments to provide the necessary expertise and was also planning a regional meeting in Ghana, which was scheduled to be held in a few days, to harness efforts in combating the pandemic.

It is interesting to note that the WHO statement reported by the AP indicated that there were only 567 Ebola cases with 350 deaths in Guinea, Sierra Leone, and Liberia during that time. Apparently because the world community had never experienced an Ebola outbreak of catastrophic proportions that the West Africa outbreak had become, it can be safely said that not much was done by the governments of the affected countries and the international community to contain the disease during its early stage. International response for assistance to combat the pandemic was slow and limited, even though MSF and other international aid agencies in the front line combating the scourge repeatedly raised the alarm that the Ebola virus was fast spreading and would have profound negative impact not just in Africa but also around the world.

The death of Patrick Sawyer, an American of Liberian descent, and the infection of the two American aid worker who were treating Ebola patients at a hospital in Monrovia generated enormous media coverage around the world, especially in the United States. Dr. Kent Brantly and Ms. Nancy Writebol were airlifted to the United States in early August, where they were treated at the Emory University Hospital in Atlanta, Georgia, and they both were among the earliest survivals of the disease. There was no cure for Ebola at the time, and being infected with the virus was like being given a death sentence.

It was, therefore, understandable that the United States government's decision to bring the two Ebola-infected American patients home generated tremendous media and public interest. There were fears that bringing the infected patients to the United States could lead to a spread of the disease in America. President Barack Obama and other appropriate US health authorities repeatedly assured the American public that there would be no Ebola outbreak in America because the country is well equipped to handle any Ebola problem.

The escalation of the Ebola scourge coincided with the historic US-Africa Leaders Summit, hosted by President Obama on August 4–6, 2014. The summit, attended by nearly fifty African leaders, was the first ever to showcase resource-rich Africa in the United States as the next frontier for economic progress and to further consolidate US-Africa relations.

At a time of heightened American interests in Africa's enormous economic potentials, the Ebola crisis in West Africa was an unwelcome distraction that became a part of the summit. A negative situation such as the Ebola crisis or civil unrest anywhere on the continent tends to reinforce age-old stereotypes of Africa as an unsafe and unstable place for foreign investment.

As the Ebola crisis intensified, President Sirleaf cancelled her visit to the United States to attend the US-Africa Leaders Summit in order to personally lead efforts on the ground to combat the deadly epidemic. She was represented at the summit by Vice President Joseph N. Boakai as head of the official Liberian delegation. Fond of poking fun, Vice President Boakai jokingly shared an observation during the summit, where, he said, he noticed that representatives from the three worst Ebola-affected countries were seated together at the various events.

Under the auspices of the Liberian embassy, Vice President Boakai attended a town hall meeting, which brought together hundreds of Liberians and friends of Liberia at the Trinity Episcopal Church in Washington DC amid growing anxiety about the Ebola pandemic.

The historic Trinity Episcopal Church, which was the venue of the jam-packed town hall meeting, also played a commendable role in raising humanitarian support to combat the Ebola pandemic. As earlier reported, Trinity, which is one of the most affluent predominantly black congregations within the Episcopal Church of the United States, is headed by the Reverend Canon John T. W. Harmon, a native of Maryland County, Liberia, as the rector and pastor.

Another Liberian native who is a prominent religious leader within the Washington DC Metropolitan Area, which includes parts of Maryland and Virginia (DMV) is Dr. Darlingston G. Johnson, founder and bishop of the Bethel World Outreach Church, a megachurch that has established branches in more than twenty countries in Africa and other parts of the world. Despite his responsibilities managing a multicultural church with global outreach, providing spiritual guidance for people of different races, ethnicity, and cultural background, Bishop Johnson has been a source of inspiration not just for Liberians in the Diaspora but for the African Diaspora as a whole. Located on a sixty-acre sprawling beautiful church campus called City of Hope in Olney, Maryland, Bethel World Outreach Church's Sunday worship services are aired on some national television channels in the United States.

Meanwhile, during the emotionally charged town hall meeting, many attendees expressed their fear and anxiety regarding the apparently increasing inability of the government to institute the requisite measures to contain the pandemic. Vice President Boakai did well in calming nerves when he briefed the anxious audience about the state of affairs in Liberia and appealed for increased support to combat the mysterious Ebola disease.

Even though they noted that they were fully committed to assisting the government in the fight to contain the Ebola epidemic, many Liberians in the Diaspora expressed disappointment by the government's handling of the Ebola crisis.

The spread of the Ebola virus and the government's handling of the crisis further heightened tensions in the country, which was already experiencing growing public disenchantment over widespread corruption and unemployment particularly among the youth who constitute more than 60 percent of the population.

There were rumors and fear of pending unrest in the fragile postwar country. It was being rumored that some ex-warlords and their supporters from the days of the country's civil upheaval were planning to take advantage of the state of disenchantment to launch an armed insurgency. Amid the increased tensions, there were other rumors that the president was spending the night in some secret hideouts and there was once an attempt on her life by individuals trying to forcefully change the status quo.

In a phone conversation between this author and a well-connected political figure in Monrovia, the person said, "Those of you who have access to the presidency should try to prevail on the president not to leave Liberia to attend the U.S. summit while the country is being consumed by Ebola. If she leaves the country under the circumstances, she may not be able to return because there might be an uprising against her government."

Another source with security connections in the United States also called me to give similar prediction of a popular uprising against the president if she were to leave the country for the US summit while Liberians were in a state of desperation.

In keeping with my responsibility as a diplomat, this author promptly informed a prominent member of the advanced presidential delegation to the summit with access to the president about these sentiments related to the possibility of unrest if the president were to leave the country. The government official indicated that the president was aware of those developments and was quietly contemplating whether it would be prudent for her to attend the summit in Washington. "She's studying the situation very closely and will make a decision within a couple of days," the official said.

On the second day following our discussion, the official informed me that the president will not be coming and that there will be an announcement in due course that Vice President Joseph Boakai will be heading the official Liberian delegation at the US-Africa Leaders Summit.

Liberia's vice president Joseph N. Boakai, (R), receiving a check from Ambassador Jeremiah Sulunteh at a 2014 town hall meeting in Washington DC during the Ebola epidemic. (Courtesy, Liberian Embassy Public Affairs)

A view of the large crowd that assembled during the 2014 town hall meeting with Vice President Joseph Boakai in Washington DC at the height of the Ebola epidemic. (Courtesy, Liberian Embassy Public Affairs)

Whether or not Liberia faced any real danger of civil unrest during this period under review has not been officially confirmed. However, some neighboring governments may have also received information about potential instability in Liberia. This is because an acquaintance associated with the Sierra Leonean embassy in Washington called and asked to meet with me in person to give me a heads-up on a very serious matter.

During that meeting, the acquaintance said there were intelligence reports of impending instability in Liberia, as some disgruntled individuals were planning to exploit the government's poor handling of the Ebola crisis to mount a popular uprising against the government. "Tell your government to be very careful and not to take this matter lightly," the source said. "We in Sierra Leone cannot afford to see another conflict in Liberia, especially at this time. As a diplomat, you know you are the eyes and ears of your government; this is why I decided to contact you."

Sierra Leonean president Ernest Bai Koroma also did not attend the US-Africa Leaders Summit and remained home to lead efforts in combating the epidemic in his country. Sierra Leone and Guinea, whose president, Alpha Conde, attended the summit, had also each declared a state of health emergency in their respective countries.

At the close of the US-Africa Leaders Summit, President Obama said the United States was deploying some medical first responders to West Africa to help control the Ebola outbreak while the United States was also working to strengthen public health systems. He added that the United States was joining the African Union to pursue the creation of an African Centers for Disease Control.

Days before the summit, there were concerns raised by the US media as to whether delegations from Ebola-affected countries should be allowed to attend the summit. President Obama and other relevant US authorities responded with assurances to the American public that there was no reason to prevent people from affected countries from traveling to the United States and that measures were being put in place to prevent those infected from traveling to the United States, including a special screening of passengers at airports to detect signs of the infection.

Realization that the Ebola virus can be easily transported from one country to another by a single individual in a world that has become a global village through air travel, as was the case of Sawyer's travel from Liberia to Nigeria, intensified worldwide fears and panic. Many countries reacted in something like a knee-jerk manner by closing their borders and imposing travel restrictions on the affected region. Ghana, Ivory Coast, Senegal, Kenya, Cameroon, South Africa, Chad, Zambia, Qatar, and Saudi Arabia were among countries that closed their borders or imposed travel restrictions on Ebola-affected countries, even though the UN warned that isolation of the affected region would undermine efforts to contain the spread of the pandemic.

Almost all the international airlines flying to the three worst-affected countries also cancelled services, as more African countries introduced measures to block visitors from the affected countries.

In Liberia, Brussels Airlines and the Royal Air Morocco were the two international airlines that stayed the course and continued to provide air services to the country during this very critical time. Liberians and people of the affected West African subregion are grateful to airlines that made the courageous decisions to continue to provide air services at such a very critical time when other countries, airlines, and ships were in a virtual stampede to isolate the affected countries. Brussels Airlines in particular holds a special place of deep appreciation in Liberia as the only major international carrier that had regular service to Liberia during the years of civil upheaval. Brussels Airlines, as well as Royal Air Morocco, are regarded as true partners of Liberia for staying the course when they were needed during this period of emergency. As a saying goes, "A friend in time of need is a friend indeed."

As the Ebola-affected countries became overwhelmed by the sheer magnitude of the epidemic, the international community increased support to combat the disease. However, as more support were provided those countries, it became increasingly apparent that the measures were too little too late. It seemed like the world was simply trying to play catch-up to a virus that was fast infecting and killing thousands.

Testifying at a US House Foreign Affairs subcommittee hearing August 7 on the margins of the US-Africa Leaders Summit, Mr. Ken Isaacs, vice president of Program and Government Relations of Samaritan's Purse, said the international response to the disease was a failure. Questioned by Members of Congress whether the American response to the Ebola outbreak had been effective, Mr. Isaacs said no country had done enough. His group employed Dr. Kent Brantly and nurse Nancy Writebol, who contracted the disease in Liberia and were brought back to the United States for treatment.

Also testifying at the congressional hearing, Dr. Thomas Frieden, then director of the Centers for Disease Control (CDC), said the Ebola outbreak in West Africa could be stopped but would take time and meticulous attention to detail. Dr. Frieden expressed confidence that there would be no large outbreak in the United States.

This author accompanied Liberia's foreign minister, Mr. Augustine Kpehe Ngafuan, who was in Washington for the summit, to the congressional hearing at which there was also testimony from Dr. Frank Glover, a medical missionary of the Christian charity, Serving in Mission (SIM), who had served in Liberia.

Dr. Glover's testimony basically summarized the magnitude of Liberia's health care challenges at the time of the Ebola outbreak, from poor infrastructure to limited resources and manpower. He urged immediate action in Liberia that included increasing efforts to isolate patients, developing an effective quarantine program and providing protective gear for health care workers and those charged with disposing the bodies of patients who have died.

"Given the episodic nature of Ebola, we must begin investing in health care systems, strengthening as we prepare to deal with future outbreaks," Dr. Glover said at the hearing.

Following a request to the US government, Liberia received three doses of the experimental Ebola drug called ZMapp on August 13. A few doses of ZMapp previously used to treat Ebola had shown positive early results. Dr. Brantly and Ms. Writebol were treated with ZMapp.

At a time of increasing despair, there was a glimmer of hope when the Embassy of Liberia in Washington took delivery of the carton containing the three doses of ZMapp for onward passage to Liberia. Liberia's ambassador the United States, H. E. Jeremiah C. Sulunteh, went to the airport to personally receive the cargo. Amid strict security at the airport and special flight arrangements, the carton containing the ZMapp was taken to Liberia by Foreign Minister Ngafuan, upon his return home from the US-Africa Leaders Summit.

Two of the three Ebola patients who were treated with the ZMapp experimental drug in Liberia survived.

Also in August, several foreign Catholic missionaries providing humanitarian services at St. Joseph's Catholic Hospital in Monrovia died upon contracting the virus. Miguel Pajares, seventy-five, a Roman Catholic priest, was flown back to Spain, where he died. Sister Chantal Pascaline, a Congolese nun who also worked with the Spanish priest, died in Liberia. The other Catholic missionaries who succumbed to the deadly disease in Liberia were Father George Combey from Ghana and Brother Patrick Nshamdze from Cameroon. Another nun, Sister Paciencia Melgar from Equatorial Guinea, also contracted the virus.

Amid the growing fear and panic around the world regarding the Ebola disease that was dragging Liberia to a brink of collapse, President Sirleaf sent a letter to President Obama on September 9, 2014. In the letter, Madam President implored President Obama for help in managing Liberia's rapidly expanding Ebola crisis and warned that without American assistance, the disease could send Liberia into the civil chaos that enveloped the country for two decades. She stated, "I am being honest with you when I say that at this rate, we will never break the transmission chain and the virus will overwhelm us" ("Liberian President Pleads with Obama for Assistance in Combating Ebola," *New York Times online*, Helene Cooper, September 12, 2014).

President Sirleaf also sent a "letter to the world" in which she said the whole world has a stake in the fight against Ebola. In her letter, broadcast on BBC on October 19, 2014, President Sirleaf said the disease "respects no borders" and that every country had to do all it could to help fight it. The Liberian leader added that a generation of Africans was at risk of "being lost to economic catastrophe" ("Liberia's Ellen Johnson Sirleaf Urges World Help on Ebola," BBC online, October 19, 2014).

Announcing his first major action to combat the pandemic on September 17, President Obama called the Ebola outbreak in West Africa "a threat to global security." He added that even though the world was looking up to the United States to take the lead in the fight, the outbreak required a global response. President Obama called on other countries to step up their response, as a worsening outbreak would lead to "profound political, economic and security implications for all of us," according to BBC News ("Obama says Ebola outbreak a 'global security threat,'" BBC News, September 17, 2014).

The previous day, the White House released the below information providing details of US plans to combat the pandemic:

The White House

Office of the Press Secretary

For Immediate Release
September 16, 2014
AibewhereFACT SHEET: U.S. Response to the Ebola Epidemic in West Africa

As the President has stated, the Ebola epidemic in West Africa and the humanitarian crisis there is a top national security priority for the United States. In order to contain and combat it, we are partnering with the United Nations and other international partners to help the Governments of Guinea, Liberia, Sierra Leone,

Nigeria, and Senegal respond just as we fortify our defenses at home. Every outbreak of Ebola over the past 40 years has been contained, and we are confident that this one can—and will be—as well.

Our strategy is predicated on four key goals:

- Controlling the epidemic at its source in West Africa;

- Mitigating second-order impacts, including blunting the economic, social, and political tolls in the region;

- Engaging and coordinating with a broader global audience; and,

- Fortifying global health security infrastructure in the region and beyond.

The United States has applied a whole-of-government response to the epidemic, which we launched shortly after the first cases were reported in March. As part of this, we have dedicated additional resources across the federal government to address the crisis, committing more than $175 million to date. We continue to work with Congress to provide additional resources through appropriations and reprogramming efforts in order to be responsive to evolving resource needs on the ground. Just as the outbreak has worsened, our response will be commensurate with the challenge.

New Resources to Confront a Growing Challenge

The United States will leverage the unique capabilities of the U.S. military and broader uniformed services to help bring the epidemic under control. These efforts will entail command and control, logistics expertise, training, and engineering support.

- U.S. Africa Command will set up a Joint Force Command headquartered in Monrovia, Liberia, to provide regional command and control support to U.S. military activities and facilitate coordination with U.S. government and international relief efforts. A general from U.S. Army Africa, the Army component of U.S. Africa Command, will lead this effort, which will involve an estimated 3,000 U.S. forces.

- U.S. Africa Command will establish a regional intermediate staging base (ISB) to facilitate and expedite the transportation of equipment, supplies and personnel. Of the U.S. forces taking part in this response, many will be stationed at the ISB.

- Command engineers will build additional Ebola Treatment Units in affected areas, and the U.S. Government will help recruit and organize medical personnel to staff them.

- Additionally, the Command will establish a site to train up to 500 health care providers per week, enabling health care workers to safely provide direct medical care to patients.

- The United States Public Health Service Commissioned Corps is preparing to deploy 65 Commissioned Corps officers to Liberia to manage and staff a previously announced Department of Defense (DoD) hospital to care for health care workers who become ill. The deployment roster will consist of administrators, clinicians, and support staff.

- Simple and scalable strategies that complement the use of Ebola Treatment Units are urgently required to disrupt the disease's transmission. A community- and home-based strategy that supports household and communities is a critical step to moving forward:

- USAID is supporting a Community Care Campaign, which will provide communities and households with protection kits, appropriate information and training on how to protect themselves and their loved ones. In partnership with the United Nations Children Fund, the Paul Allen Family Foundation, and other key partners, we will immediately target the 400,000 most vulnerable households in Liberia. The package will subsequently be scaled to cover the country and the broader region.

- As part of this effort, this week, USAID will airlift 50,000 home health care kits from Denmark to Liberia to be hand-delivered to distant communities by trained youth volunteers.

A Complement to Efforts To Date

Applying this whole-of-government approach, we have been engaged on this outbreak since March when the first cases were reported in West Africa. We currently have in the affected countries more than 100 specialists from multiple U.S. departments and agencies, including the Departments of State and Health and Human Services (HHS), the CDC, the U.S. Agency for International Development (USAID), and DoD. We also are working intensively on this effort with the United Nations, including the World Health Organization, the governments of the affected countries, and other partners, including the United Kingdom, France, Germany, Norway, the Africa Union, and European Union.

- To date we have spent more than $100 million to address this challenge, including the purchase of personal protective equipment, mobile labs, logistics and relief commodities, and support for community health workers. USAID also has announced plans to make available up to $75 million in additional funding to increase the number of Ebola treatment units, provide more personal protective equipment, airlift additional medical and emergency supplies, and support other Ebola response activities in collaboration with the UN, including the World Health Organization, and international partners.

- CDC has provided on the ground expertise in the largest international response in its history. More than 100 CDC personnel are on the ground in West Africa, and hundreds of personnel at their Emergency Operations Center in Atlanta have provided around the clock logistics, staffing, communication, analytics, management, and other support functions. The Administration has asked Congress for an additional $30 million to send additional response workers from the CDC as well as lab supplies and equipment.

- In August, USAID deployed a Disaster Assistance Response Team (DART) to West Africa to coordinate and prioritize the U.S. government's response to the outbreak. The DART assesses and identifies priority needs and coordinates key areas of the response, such as planning, operations, and logistics. The 28-member DART team is comprised of staff from USAID, CDC, DoD, and the U.S. Forest Service. The DART will be airlifting 130,000 sets of personal protective equipment to ensure that health care workers have the resources needed to safely do their jobs. The DART is also in the process of procuring generators that will provide electricity to Ebola treatment units and other response facilities.

- The National Institutes of Health (NIH) is developing an investigational Ebola vaccine, including recently starting phase 1 clinical trials, as well as supporting efforts to develop additional Ebola antivirals and therapeutics candidates. The Administration has asked Congress for an additional $58 million to support the development and manufacturing of Ebola therapeutic and vaccine candidates through Biomedical Advanced Research and Development Authority.

- In addition to the measures announced today, DoD plans to send a field-deployable hospital to Liberia and has provided more than 10,000 Ebola test kits to the Liberian Institute of Biological Research and to Sierra Leone's Kenema Government Hospital. DoD also has provided personal protective equipment and training to local medical professionals in affected regions.

- DoD also has requested to reprogram $500 million in Fiscal Year 2014 Overseas Contingency Operations funds for humanitarian assistance, a portion of which will be used to fulfill requirements identified by CDC, USAID, the Joint Staff, and U.S. Africa Command to provide military air transportation of DoD and non-DoD personnel and supplies; medical treatment facilities (e.g. isolation units), personnel protective equipment, and medical supplies; logistics and engineering support, and; subject matter experts in support of sanitation and mortuary affairs.

- DoD's Cooperative Threat Reduction program is redirecting $25 million to provide personal protective equipment and laboratory reagents, support for technical advisers, and other requests as validated by the DART. DoD has also requested to reprogram an additional $60 million to enable the CTR program to address urgent biosafety, biosecurity, and biosurveillance needs in the three countries most affected by the Ebola outbreak, as well as bolster the capabilities of neighboring countries and other partners in Africa.

- Last month, USAID airlifted more than 16 tons of medical supplies and emergency equipment to Liberia, including: 10,000 sets of personal protective equipment, two water treatment units and two portable water tanks capable of storing 10,000 liters each, and 100 rolls of plastic sheeting which can be used in the construction of Ebola treatment units. Additionally, in late August the DART airlifted 5,000 body bags to step up support for the safe removal and transport of the bodies of Ebola victims and 500 infrared thermometers to bolster Ebola screening efforts. These supplies will be distributed and used by the WHO and Liberian Ministry of Health and Social Welfare.

- USAID and the State Department are providing up to $10 million to support the deployment of an African Union mission sending more than 100 health care workers to the region. The State Department also has encouraged other governments to increase assistance; coordinate delivery of critical resources, including personnel, equipment, and medical supplies; and encourage airlines operating in the region to maintain or reinstate service while ensuring appropriate precautions.

- Additionally, the State Department has supported public education efforts in Liberia, Sierra Leone, and Guinea regarding prevention and treatment of the disease. The effort has included radio and television messages in local languages, the production of nearly 100 billboards and thousands of posters, program support to local nongovernmental organizations and a special song commissioned by a popular local musician.

- Earlier this month, President Obama released a message to the people of West Africa to reinforce the facts and dispel myths surrounding Ebola. The video was transcribed into French, Portuguese, and other local languages and was distributed to television and radio stations across the region. Tens of thousands of West Africans viewed or listened to the message.

Screening Efforts Overseas

In addition to our efforts to help the affected West African countries bring this outbreak under control, we have taken steps to fortify against the introduction of Ebola cases into the United States. It is important to note that Ebola is not highly contagious like the flu; to the contrary, the virus is spread through direct contact with the blood or body fluids of a symptomatic individual.

- CDC is working closely with Customs and Border Protection and other partners at ports of entry—primarily international airports—to use routine processes to identify travelers who show signs of infectious disease. In response to the outbreak, these processes have been enhanced through guidance and training. If a sick traveler is identified during or after a flight, the traveler will be immediately isolated, and CDC will conduct an investigation of exposed travelers and work with the airline, federal partners, and state and local health departments to notify them and take any necessary public health action.

- CDC is assisting with exit screening and communication efforts in West Africa to prevent sick travelers from boarding planes. It also has issued interim guidance about Ebola virus infection for airline flight crews, cleaning personnel, and cargo personnel.

- CDC also has issued advice for colleges, universities, and students about study abroad, foreign exchange, and other education-related travel, as well as advice for students who have recently traveled from a country in which an Ebola outbreak is occurring. Similarly, CDC has developed recommendations for humanitarian aid workers traveling to Guinea, Liberia, Nigeria, and Sierra Leone during the Ebola outbreaks in these countries. The recommendations include steps to take before departure, during travel, and upon return to the United States.

Preparedness at Home

Despite the tragic epidemic in West Africa, U.S. health professionals agree it is highly unlikely that we would experience an Ebola outbreak here in the United States, given our robust health care infrastructure and rapid response capabilities. Nevertheless, we have taken extra measures to prevent the unintentional importation of cases into the United States, and if a patient does make it here, our national health system has the capacity and expertise to quickly detect and contain this disease.

- CDC has worked to enhance surveillance and laboratory testing capacity in states to detect cases and improve case finding. CDC is developing guidance and tools for health departments to conduct public health investigations and improve health communication and continues to update recommendations for health care infection control and other measures to prevent the disease from spreading. Similarly, HHS' Office of the Assistant Secretary for Preparedness and Response and CDC are providing guidance documents to hospitals and other health care partners to support preparedness for a possible Ebola case.

- CDC also has prepared U.S. health care facilities and emergency medical service systems to safely manage a patient with suspected Ebola virus disease. CDC communicates with health care workers on an ongoing basis through the Health Alert Network, the Clinician Outreach and Communication Activity, and a variety of other existing tools and mechanisms. CDC developed <u>Interim Guidance for Monitoring and Movement of Persons with Ebola Virus Disease Exposure</u> to provide public health authorities and other partners with a framework for evaluating people's level of exposure to Ebola and initiating appropriate public health actions on the basis of exposure level and clinical assessment.

- The Food and Drug Administration is monitoring for fraudulent products and false product claims related to the Ebola virus and is prepared to take enforcement actions, as warranted, to protect the public health.

Securing the Future

The Ebola epidemic reminds us that our global efforts to build the capacity to prevent, detect, and rapidly respond to infectious disease threats like Ebola have never been more vital. In February, we came together with nations around the world to launch the Global Health Security Agenda (GHSA) as a five year effort to accelerate action.

- CDC is contributing to the GHSA by partnering with nations around the world to help them establish measurable global health security capacity. This includes core CDC partnership programs like the <u>Global Disease Detection Centers</u> and <u>Field Epidemiology Training Program, which enable the</u> laboratory systems, disease surveillance workforce, emergency operations center capacity, and biosafety and biosecurity best practices required to counter Ebola and other biological threats.

- Over the next five years the United States has committed to working with at least 30 partner countries to invest in model systems to advance the Global Health Security agenda. CDC and DoD will work with other U.S. agencies and partner countries to establish emergency operations centers, build information systems, and strengthen laboratory security to mitigate biological threats and build partner capacity.

The entire American society was swept into a virtual state of panic and hysteria following the breaking news that a Liberian national who traveled from Liberia to Dallas, Texas, had been diagnosed with Ebola at the Texas Health Presbyterian Hospital in Dallas on September 30. Thomas Eric Duncan arrived in the United States on September 20 without showing any signs of illness, as his temperature was normal when he went through airport screening put in place for early detection of symptoms. His was the first case of the deadly Ebola disease to be diagnosed on US soil.

Amid growing alarm of potential Ebola outbreak in the United States, fear took hold particularly at the apartment complex in Dallas where Duncan resided. While Duncan was in critical condition at the hospital, the four persons he was living with in Dallas, including Ms. Louise Troh, his fiancée with whom he was visiting, were quarantined and moved out of the apartment they shared with him. Some forty-eight individuals who interacted with him at some point were placed under what was called "close observation." Electronic scanners to check for fevers were set for use in the nursing stations at five Dallas schools after some of the students at the schools were exposed to the Ebola patient.

As fear and panic fueled by media hype on all things Ebola spread across the United States, parents pulled their children out of school and some residents reportedly moved out of the apartment complex in the Dallas neighborhood where the infected patient resided. There were calls from many circles of the American society for the United States to ban flights from the worst-affected Ebola countries. Some members of the US Congress joined calls for travel restrictions and stricter screening for travelers entering the United States from Ebola-affected countries.

The Obama administration rejected calls for mandatory travel restrictions to contain the Ebola virus in West Africa. Officials at the Centers for Disease Control and other public health experts stressed that the likelihood for an outbreak in the United States was minimal. President Obama, who had come under sharp criticism from some conservative members of Congress about his handling of the Ebola outbreak, underscored his confidence in America's doctors and national health infrastructure to handle this case effectively.

On October 8, the Obama administration announced that there will be enhanced screening for all travelers coming from Ebola-affected countries at five US international airports. They were the John F. Kennedy International Airport in New York, New York; Washington Dulles International Airport in Washington DC; Newark Liberty International Airport in Newark, New Jersey; Chicago O'Hare International Airport in Chicago, Illinois; and Hartsfield-Jackson International Airport in Atlanta, Georgia.

John F. Kennedy International Airport was the first to begin the process of enhanced screening on October 10. JFK, along with the other four airports, received more than 94 percent of travelers coming to the United States from the Ebola-affected countries, according to US authorities.

Europe's busiest airport, Heathrow International Airport in London, United Kingdom, also began screening for travelers from Ebola-affected countries on October 14. This coincided with reports of the first Ebola-related death in Germany. The fifty-six-year-old Sudanese UN employee, who caught Ebola while working in Liberia, died at a clinic in Leipzig, Germany. According to the London-based the *Guardian*, the Sudanese was the third Ebola patient to receive treatment in Germany.

It is interesting to note that it took the case of one patient like Duncan's to show the vulnerability of the US health care system, one of the best in the world. A series of missteps in the Duncan case showed the challenges involved in handling the Ebola outbreak, which is a complicated new threat to human existence.

For example, it is reported that after Duncan began to feel ill on September 24, he went to the hospital two days after, but the hospital sent him home with antibiotics. Duncan is said to have informed the nurse who treated him that he had recently traveled from Liberia, but this information did not raise any red flags and he was let go. As his condition deteriorated, he was admitted to the Texas Health Presbyterian Hospital and placed in isolation on September 28. On September 30, the CDC confirmed that Duncan's blood was positive for Ebola.

Over the following days, there were false alarms at some hospitals and airports across the United States. For example, a sick passenger on a flight from Brussels to Liberty International Airport in Newark, New Jersey, created panic after showing signs of fever and vomiting, but tests later proved that he was not infected with Ebola. At Orlando International Airport in Orlando, Florida, Ebola scare delayed a flight after a passenger showed signs of illness while there was also a state of fear and panic at O'Hare International Airport in

Chicago, Illinois, when a flight landed there amid reports that an ill passenger on board may have contracted the Ebola virus. From then onward, Ebola fear mongering intensified and took on a life of its own.

Following news about Duncan's infection, it was announced in Monrovia that the government might prosecute him upon his return to Liberia for lying on his airport questionnaire. Duncan reportedly answered "no" to questions about whether he had cared for an Ebola patient or touched the body of someone who had died in an area affected by Ebola, according to the Associated Press.

Days before he left Liberia, Duncan had helped carry to a taxi a pregnant woman who later died of Ebola, the Associated Press quoted neighbors. Her illness at the time was said to be pregnancy-related.

Duncan, forty-two, died October 8 after reportedly receiving experimental drugs for the treatment of the Ebola virus. He became the first person to die in the United States from the Ebola disease. His death raised questions regarding the quality of care he was given, considering the fact that three Americans who contracted the virus in Liberia and returned to the United States for treatment survived.

While Americans were digesting news about Duncan's Ebola infection on American soil, there were reports on October 2 that an American freelance cameraman working for NBC News in Liberia had also tested positive for Ebola and will be flown back to the United States for treatment. He arrived a few days later in the United States for treatment at the Nebraska Medical Center in Omaha, Nebraska.

The freelancer, Ashoka Mukpo, thirty-three, was a cameraman for NBC News chief medical editor and correspondent Dr. Nancy Snyderman, who was on assignment in Monrovia, reporting on the Ebola outbreak. Upon return to the United States, Dr. Snyderman and her crew were placed in isolation for twenty-one days.

Mukpo, who was the fourth American to contract Ebola in Liberia, became the second Ebola patient to be treated at the Nebraska Medical Center. The first to be treated there was Dr. Richard Sacra, who worked for the Christian charity SIM USA at ELWA Hospital in Monrovia.

Dr. Sacra, the third American missionary to contract Ebola, was working in the obstetrics unit of ELWA Hospital, where he was believed to have contracted the virus in early September. After being flown back to the United States, he was treated at the Nebraska Medical Center and discharged September 25.

As the global media and public attention was focused on developments in Dallas, there were reports on October 8 that a Spanish nurse had tested positive for Ebola in Madrid, Spain, becoming the first to contract the virus outside Africa. According to reports, Teresa Romero may have contracted Ebola while caring for two Spanish missionaries that contracted the virus in West Africa.

According to CNN News, after she began feeling sick, Romero sought help three times. Finally, one week after first seeing a doctor, Romero found out she had the deadly virus after her Ebola test came back positive at Madrid's Alcorcon hospital.

Even though Romero was diagnosed with Ebola, the CNN report quoted a health worker at Alcorcon hospital as saying Romero lay in the emergency room for eight hours before being transferred to a hospital in the

Spanish capital that specializes in infectious diseases. During her stay in the emergency room, she was exposed to other patients, as well as medical staff going back and forth, according to the CNN report.

Eight people who had direct contact with Romero, including her husband, were placed in isolation for monitoring. Ms. Romero's dog, Excalibur, was euthanized, provoking public protest of animal abuse. There was also protest in Madrid by some health workers, whose union called for the Spanish health minister to resign, indicating that training and protective suits provided to hospital staff had been inadequate.

Fear and panic intensified when there was breaking news yet again that a female caregiver at Texas Health Presbyterian Hospital, where the late Duncan was treated, also tested positive for Ebola in October 11. She was identified as Nina Pham, a twenty-six-year-old nurse. The director of the CDC, Dr. Thomas Frieden, said the woman had "extensive contact" with Duncan, according to Al Jazeera news.

While debates intensified across the United States on Ebola response and protocol on how to contain the virulent virus, Americans woke up in October 15 to news that a second nurse at Texas Health Presbyterian Hospital, identified as Amber Vinson, twenty-nine, was confirmed to have also contracted Ebola.

Ms. Pham was airlifted to the National Institute of Health (NIH) in Bethesda, Maryland, while Ms. Vinson was also airlifted to Emory University Hospital in Atlanta, Georgia, for treatment.

Amid the chorus of criticisms of the Obama administration for what was regarded to be its mishandling of the Ebola crisis, the administration came under more pressure to take further actions to combat the spread of the deadly disease. The Speaker of the US House of Representatives, John Boehner, added his voice to the growing chorus of calls for the United States to impose a travel ban on the worst-affected African countries. The CDC also came under increased criticism, with some calling for its director, Dr. Thomas Frieden, to resign.

Texas Health Presbyterian Hospital, where the two nurses contracted Ebola while caring for Duncan, was widely criticized for its demonstrated lack of preparedness as reflected by the Duncan case. Inadequate protective gears and instructions on protocol to care for Ebola patients heightened public concerns and fears regarding the level of preparedness at various medical facilities across the United States. On October 16, the hospital apologized for its handling of the Duncan case.

BBC's North American editor Jon Sopel captured the prevailing thoughts at the time in his article, titled "The Ebola Fumble in Dallas," as follows: "In the country with the most advanced health care of anywhere in the world, with the best trained health workers, with resources that any third world medical center would kill for, the question that—not surprisingly—is being asked is how in the name of God is this possible."

As public anxiety mounted in the United States, the Ebola situation degenerated into a case of political mudslinging between Democrats and Republicans, a few weeks leading to the American midterm elections. A political battle over Ebola eventually erupted, as American leaders clamored for the airwaves to pronounce what actions they were taking or would take to "protect the American people" from the deadly Ebola. On both sides of the political divide, the refrain was no longer just about protecting the American people against terrorism. It was also about protecting them against the newest global threat, Ebola.

Responding to pressure to impose a travel ban, President Obama said the imposition of a ban was "not the way to go," adding that it could further complicate efforts to combat the pandemic in West Africa.

President Obama instead issued an executive order on October 16, calling up the National Guard for deployment to West Africa to assist American troops being sent to the region to combat the pandemic, whose number had been increased from 3,000 to 4,000.

On October 17, President Obama appointed Mr. Ron Klain, an experienced Washington lawyer, to coordinate the federal government's response to the threat of widespread infection from the Ebola virus.

According to the *Washington Post*, the appointment of Klain, who also served as chief of staff to both Vice President Joe Biden and former vice president Al Gore of the Clinton administration, signaled the Obama "administration's recognition that an Ebola outbreak could overwhelm its management capacity. In Klain, 53, Obama had enlisted a legal expert and Democratic strategist with a reputation for handling complex projects such as the administration's economic stimulus package during Obama's first term, and the Democratic effort to challenge the 2000 presidential results" ("Obama Appoints Lawyer to Handle Ebola Response," *Washington Post*, October 17, 2014).

In a related development, then defense secretary Chuck Hagel ordered the military to train a thirty-member medical support team that could provide short-term help to civilian health professionals if there were more Ebola cases in the United States. The team, drawn from across the military services, included critical-care nurses, doctors trained in infectious disease, and trainers in infectious disease protocols.

Meanwhile, the first glimmer of global hope in the fight against the Ebola virus came October 18 when the WHO declared Senegal free from Ebola. This was followed by Nigeria, which the WHO also declared Ebola-free October 20. The WHO said Nigeria had gone forty-two days without a new case, which made it almost a statistical certainty that its outbreak, stemming from a single Liberian man who arrived in Lagos with the disease in July, had been solved. Senegal had also gone through a similar period without a new case since that of the one individual from Guinea.

In the United States, the late Duncan's girlfriend, Louise Troh, who and other individuals were quarantined for the duration of the deadly virus's twenty-one-day incubation period, were released October 20. A few days after, the two Dallas nurses who cared for the late Duncan, Nina Pham and Amber Vinson, were declared Ebola-free. Immediately upon her discharge from a special facility at the National Institute of Health in Bethesda, Maryland, Pham visited the White House, where she was given a hug by President Obama—a symbolic gesture that you do not contract Ebola from someone cured of the virus.

However, glimmers of hope in the fight against Ebola as reflected above were tempered by other negative reports regarding spread of the pandemic. The government of Mali, which neighbors Senegal and Guinea, confirmed the first case of Ebola in the country on October 23. BBC News quoted the Malian government as saying that a two-year-old girl, who was brought from neighboring Guinea by relatives following the death of her mother, tested positive for the deadly virus. The girl died a couple of days after the confirmation by the government of Mali, which became the sixth African country to be directly affected by the Ebola outbreak in West Africa.

During the same period, the WHO released a report, quoted by BBC News on October 25, 2014, that the number of Ebola cases had risen to 10,141, with 4,922 deaths. It was also stated in the WHO report that Liberia was the worst-affected country, with 2,705 deaths, while Sierra Leone had 1,281 fatalities and there were 926 deaths in Guinea. All but 27 of the cases had occurred in the three worst-affected countries.

In the United States, another Ebola case was reported with the diagnosis in New York of Dr. Craig Spencer, who had returned from treating Ebola patients in Guinea with the medical charity Doctors Without Borders a few days back. Amid increasingly heightened public fear and anxiety, the governors of the states of New York and New Jersey, quickly followed by the governor of the state of Illinois, ordered a mandatory twenty-one-day quarantine period for all doctors and other travelers who had contact with Ebola victims in West Africa. It was also ordered that travelers from affected West African countries who did not have confirmed contact with Ebola victims will be subject to monitoring by public health officials.

The first person to be quarantined under the new rules was Kaci Hickox, a nurse also with Doctors Without Borders, who arrived at Newark Liberty International Airport from treating patients in Sierra Leone. She only had a fever, but her Ebola test result was negative. Ms. Hickox said the experience was frightening and described seeing a "frenzy of disorganization, fear and most frightening, quarantine," according to BBC News. While in isolation, the lady alleged that her civil rights were violated and she was treated like a prisoner.

After threatening legal action, Ms. Hickox was released from the three-day isolation imposed by the state of New Jersey, and she traveled to the state of Maine, where Governor Paul LePage ordered her to be quarantined at home for twenty-one days. M.s Hickox vehemently objected to the quarantine order, leading to a legal collision with Governor LePage.

In what was seen as an act of defiance, with police and journalists looking on, television news images showed Ms. Hickox taking a morning bicycle ride outside with her boyfriend in the small town of Fort Kent near the Canadian border. The police did not intervene to stop her.

Following reported breakdown of negotiation to get Ms. Hickox to adhere to mandatory quarantine, the state of Maine instituted legal action to compel her to abide by the order. However, the court said Ms. Hickox could come and go as she desired, as long as she was monitored for symptoms and she let health officials know where she was going. Maine District Court chief judge Charles LaVerdiere said local health officials failed to prove the need for a stricter order enforcing an Ebola quarantine.

Meanwhile, Dr. Spencer was released from Bellevue Hospital in New York in November 11 after being cured and declared Ebola-free. With Dr. Spencer's release, America became free of anyone with the Ebola virus for the first time in months.

Ms. Hickox, who fought quarantine in New Jersey and Maine, also reached her twenty-one days without showing symptoms of the virus.

As fear and paranoia about the Ebola disease mounted globally, Africans also found themselves increasingly stigmatized in various parts of the world. Those who painfully bore the brunt of the Ebola stigma were citizens from the three worst-affected countries.

During most of the period of the Ebola crisis, the Embassy of Liberia in Washington DC played a very critical role in harnessing support in the United States to combat and contain the disease in Liberia. The embassy was inundated with calls from various individuals and groups who expressed their sympathy with the people of Liberia and the subregion and offered various kinds of support.

Liberia Becomes Ebola-Free

Efforts to combat Ebola paid off when, on Saturday, May 9, 2015, the WHO declared Liberia free of the virus disease, thus becoming the first of the three worst-affected countries to have brought an end to the epidemic. Liberia, which had the highest number of deaths of the three countries worst affected, was able to succeed in kicking Ebola out due to the collective effort of the Liberian people and government, with US-led international support.

Unfortunately, nearly two months after Liberia was declared Ebola-free, there was a new outbreak of the disease when the body of a seventeen-year-old boy, who died in June 28 in a village in Margibi County, was tested positive for Ebola. Fear that the disease could spread again intensified when a man in the village where the teenager died also tested positive for Ebola.

The WHO said that at the peak of transmission, during August and September 2014, the country was reporting between 300 and 400 new cases every week. The last official victim in the country was buried on March 28, 2015 ("Ebola: Mapping the Outbreak," BBC online, June 19, 2015).

There was this national sigh of collective relief, amid an atmosphere of subdued celebration for Liberians, when the WHO declared the country free of the Ebola virus disease. Optimism in Liberia was tempered by recognition of the fact that the deadly disease was still spreading in neighboring Guinea and Sierra Leone.

After eighteen months of battling the Ebola scourge in West Africa, Sierra Leone became the second of the worst-affected country to be officially declared Ebola-free by the WHO on Saturday, November 7, 2015. According to reports, thousands of people took to the streets of the capital, Freetown, to celebrate the end of the Ebola outbreak, which killed 3,955 people in Sierra Leone.

Thousands of Children Orphaned by Ebola

One of the tragedies of the Ebola outbreak in West Africa was that thousands of children were orphaned as a result of the pandemic, which killed their parents and others.

In her Annual Message (State of the Nation Address) on January 26, 2015, President Sirleaf said the Ebola scourge had left behind 3,000 orphans. The affected children had lost one or both parents to Ebola. President Sirleaf noted that the government was required to provide love and care for the orphans.

CHAPTER ELEVEN

Ebola Exposed Extreme Poverty
and Corruption in Liberia

The outbreak of the deadly Ebola virus in West Africa, especially the three worst-affected countries—Liberia, Sierra Leone, and Guinea—seriously exposed the level of extreme poverty in those countries. The state of poverty and underdevelopment in those countries are also reflective of the state of affairs in other parts of Africa. The pandemic exposed the inability of the governments in those countries to adequately provide basic services for their people, such as security, health, education, transportation, and economic opportunities, for example.

With the television, Internet, social media, and other mediums of mass communication saturated with images of depravation and destitution of people living in near-primitive conditions, the global community was exposed to the reality of those countries' poverty and underdevelopment. The world was faced with glaring images of people living in shacks and slums with no electricity, water, and sanitation, not to talk about the absence or limitation of other basic services such as medical and educational facilities. Images of areas cut off from modern society due to lack of roads and only accessible by trekking on foot or by canoe ride reflect how much some parts of Africa continue to exist in a primitive state in the twenty-first century.

Those images left many wondering: What is wrong with Africa? Why do many African countries continue to lag behind in poverty when most parts of the world are moving ahead and making progress?

As exemplified by countries worst affected by the Ebola pandemic, people in many parts of Africa have endured lack of access to such basic services as safe drinking water and sanitation, and they have been impoverished principally because of bad governance. Rampant corruption, weak public institutions, and a patronage system in which public resources are squandered by the unaccountable few in power are among the major challenges that have kept many parts of Africa underdeveloped.

Even though Africa is well endowed with abundance of natural resources, there has been an entrenched culture where a country is basically turned into a "cash cow," so to speak, to fatten those in power and their hangers-on. A general perception has prevailed in Africa, where a country is seen like an "elephant meat," from which anyone can carve out a big piece as they want without regards for how much is left for others. The bloody contest for power in parts of Africa, characterized by military coups, rebel insurgencies, and civil wars that have killed and maimed millions and left countries ruined, are waged for control over resources. As a result of this criminal and unacceptable practice, the general population, dispossessed and disempowered, is left to languish in poverty.

And while the general population suffer and die from preventable and curable diseases like malaria, diarrhea, and typhoid due to poor health care delivery systems in various parts of the continent, prominent public officials and their families would travel abroad to countries with advanced medical and other services. It is regarded as a status symbol to have the means to seek advanced medical treatment in the United States, Europe, or other parts of the developed world while at home the masses are stuck with hospitals and clinics that are nothing more than "death chambers."

From the glaring television and other media images of extreme poverty and human deprivation in the worst-affected countries, the Ebola epidemic called the world's attention to what is clearly seen to be subhuman living conditions of millions of people. It goes without saying that these near-primitive conditions are totally unacceptable in this twenty-first century of technological innovations and tremendous human progress.

Take, for example, West Point, a naturally beautiful piece of land situated between the Atlantic Ocean and the Mesurado River, with a population that was estimated to be between 50,000 to 75,000. Despite its natural beauty, West Point is Monrovia's most congested slum, with little or no general electricity, pipe-borne water, or other basic services.

At the time of the Ebola outbreak, living conditions in West Point were so terrible that in open broad day, residents used the riverbank and beach for toilet because they did not have latrine. Images of West Point residents squatting on the beach or riverbank easing themselves were captured by international reporters and others who traveled to Liberia during the Ebola crisis. Residents of West Point and other urban slum communities lived in shacks that were jam-packed with people.

At the same time, many parts of the country were only accessible by trekking on foot or by canoe due to deplorable road conditions or lack of motor road. The distance to some of the places, which lacked medical and educational facilities, would take hours and days of trekking. Imagine someone getting critically ill in those places and they have to be toted in hammocks carried on the heads of men for hours to get to the nearest health centers that were mostly ill-equipped to treat cases other than malaria, diarrhea, and other preventable diseases.

In the wake of the West Africa Ebola outbreak, the nauseating images of poverty, destitution, and death that inundated the international media shocked the world. As I heard many times during the Ebola crisis, there is a general perception around the world that Africa is underdeveloped compared to Europe, Asia, among others. But the images of people living in such extreme poverty were shocking, disturbing, and difficult to watch. For Africans, especially those of us with direct ties to the most affected countries, images of people so poor to have a latrine that they had to squat in open broad daylight to ease themselves in public view, caused a great deal of shame and embarrassment.

A focus of more international media coverage because of the US intervention, Liberia, worst hit by the Ebola pandemic, became the face of human suffering, with images that show the country to be one of the poorest in the world. Indeed, the Ebola crisis exposed the very serious underdevelopment of Africa's oldest independent republic since 1847 and the critical problems that must be addressed to improve human conditions and the country as a whole.

This chapter seeks to throw out ideas regarding what must be done to end human suffering in resource-rich Liberia. Some of the ideas herein can also help to accelerate the enhancement of human conditions not just in the other worst-affected countries but also other parts of Africa, given the similarities of our circumstances.

Imagine the abundance of natural resources within the Mano River Union (MRU), a subregional bloc whose members are neighboring Liberia, Sierra Leone, Guinea, and the Ivory Coast. Countries within the MRU are well endowed with natural resources that include iron ore, diamonds, gold, timber, rubber, cocoa, coffee, and other agricultural produce while oil is also a new discovery in the subregion.

With a combined population of less than 50 million as of the date of this publication, imagine what transformation could occur if the natural resources of the MRU subregion were to be properly managed, with a focus on human and infrastructural development, including advanced transportation and communications networks, enhanced cross-border trade and commerce.

Think about how bright Africa's future would be when programs are instituted to ensure access to quality education and training for young people—who constitute more than half the population in many African countries—as well as empowerment of the people through entrepreneurship, agricultural development, and job creation, among others.

It goes without saying that it is through proper utilization of resources that Africa would have sustainable progress, the living conditions of the African masses would improve, and Africans would be able to globally compete in various areas of human endeavors, including business, science, and technology.

Critical aspects of good governance like transparency and accountability to ensure that resources intended for public services are properly utilized must be instituted. Bad governance, characterized by corruption, looting of public resources, and other acts of abuse of power, are among problems responsible for underdevelopment and poverty in Africa and other parts of the world for that matter. It has been proven unequivocally that countries which are better governed have a larger percentage of their citizens above poverty. On the other hand, countries that are poorly governed experience the opposite, where the masses languish in abject poverty and destitution.

Therefore, it goes without saying also that there is a crisis of leadership in many parts of Africa, as shown by the level of abject poverty and underdevelopment in countries worst affected by the largest Ebola outbreak ever in the world. Although very rich in natural resources, the worst-affected countries are among the poorest in the world because of gross mismanagement of their resources. Lack of competent leadership and strong public institutions leave the people prey to those who often end up in power to enrich themselves while the general population is basically condemned to live in poor and derelict conditions.

Deep-rooted mistrust of and contempt for government and public officials came to global focus from the way the general populations in the worst-affected countries reacted to reports of the Ebola outbreak. Because the people did not believe or trust their governments when alarm was raised about the Ebola outbreak, there is general agreement that this clearly contributed to the spread of the disease and more human casualties.

In Guinea, public distrust of the government and disbelief that Ebola is real led to the murder of eight members of an Ebola awareness team by villagers in the southeastern part of the country in September 2014.

As reported in a previous chapter, in Liberia, for example, there were criticisms that the government was raising false alarm following the outbreak of Ebola in order to generate more international foreign financial aid that would end up in the bank accounts and pockets of government officials. And so the people refused to listen regarding a disease that nobody could see, except for watching individuals dressed like spacemen going around spraying and transporting bodies.

Liberia's then minister of finance, Mr. Amara Konneh, acknowledged that much when he said that the lack of trust in government by citizens was a key reason why the deadly Ebola outbreak escalated. According to the November 10, 2014, edition of *FrontPage Africa online*, speaking at a ceremony in Monrovia, Minister Konneh said the reason for the lack of citizens' trust was "widespread corruption of public funds by some officials trusted with the responsibility to perform" ("'Lack of Trust in Gov't. Escalated Ebola,' Says Finance Minister").

The finance minister said officials of government had created a gap between them and the ordinary people, as evidenced by "the flashy cars with tainted windshields they ride while people go to bed hungry." As a result of this state of affairs, he added, the citizens expressed anger and refused to trust the government, even if it was about saving their own lives.

What an admission by the Liberian finance minister, who is the chief custodian of state or public resources. A few weeks earlier, Mr. Konneh had warned that those misusing funds intended to fight the Ebola epidemic would be prosecuted and jailed. His warning came in the wake of reports that some of the funds disbursed by the government to fight the spread of the disease had been squandered by individuals entrusted with the responsibility to manage the funds. How unfortunate that while thousands of people were dying from the mysterious Ebola virus that left the general population traumatized, part of the funds intended to combat the disease were being stolen by some of those who were supposed to seek the public interest! How disgusting!

While some of the public funds disbursed to combat Ebola were squandered, there were also reports that some body-collection teams dispatched to collect the Ebola dead received bribes to issue falsified death certificates to family members stating that their dead relatives did not die from Ebola. The bodies would then be left with the families to undertake traditional burial. This was also intended to blunt stigma that family members suffered when a relative was known to have died from the deadly pandemic.

At the time of the Ebola outbreak, Liberia was literally drowned in widespread public outcry regarding corruption, which was found to be endemic at every level of the government. The country had been stigmatized in the eyes of the international community as one of the most corrupt in the world, as reflected by reports by the US Department of State Human Rights Reports and numerous international transparency bodies, including Transparency International.

Over the course of the last few years of President Ellen Johnson Sirleaf's first term and, especially, during the period of her second term leading to the Ebola pandemic, the local media was saturated with reports of widespread corruption in government. There were also increasingly disturbing reports in the international media regarding corruption in Liberia, which had become a matter of serious concern by the country's international partners.

Several media accounts of scandals involving the president's close family members and aides occurred with disturbing frequency, and there were talk and suspicion of the president's personal involvement in some of the scandals. Despite several dozens of audit reports implicating many government officials, especially close family and aides of the president, little or no legal action was taken to hold said individuals accountable.

It was as a result of a slew of national and international reports focusing on the endemic level of corruption in the Liberian government that Liberia was stigmatized as one of the most corrupt countries in the world.

Growing public disaffection with the government due to widespread corruption, very high unemployment particularly among the youth who constituted more than 60 percent of the population, coupled with increasing hardships endured by the general population, led to heightened tensions in the country.

Even though the country made significant progress over the years of sustainable peace following the end of the civil war, there was an emerging groundswell of public dissatisfaction and frustration due to economic hardship because many ordinary Liberians found it more difficult to make ends meet. The estimated US$16 billion foreign direct investment Liberia attracted during the administration of President Sirleaf had not generated the desired number of jobs for a population that had grown increasingly restless due to widespread unemployment and hardship.

Virtually all the areas of foreign investment focused on extraction and exportation of raw materials from the country with little progress made toward attracting businesses that would also operate on manufacturing or processing locally for added value to the raw materials. For example, Liberia is the world's second-largest producer of natural rubber next to Malaysia. Yet while Malaysia, the world's leading natural rubber producer, manufactured about 63 percent of the world's rubber gloves, there was not a single plant to manufacture latex gloves in Liberia up to the time of the Ebola outbreak.

Firestone Rubber plantation, operated by Firestone Tire and Rubber Company, headquartered in Akron, Ohio, USA, began operating in Liberia since 1926 on one million acres of fertile, arable land, which the Liberian government leased to Firestone for ninety-nine years at the price of a miserly six cents per acre. Liberia was the largest producer of natural rubber before being overtaken by Malaysia.

Despite Liberia's ranking as the world's second-leading producer of natural rubber, latex gloves were imported from Malaysia and other countries to combat Ebola. In September 2014, Malaysia's Prime Minister Najib Razak announced that his country was sending more than 20 million medical gloves to five West African countries battling the Ebola pandemic. There can be no question that many doctors, health care workers, and others contracted the virus and died because of the shortage of latex gloves, among the various challenges that overwhelmed the country's health care system.

The level of extreme poverty and deep-rooted distrust of government demonstrated by the Liberian public in the wake of the Ebola outbreak indicate how the country was faced with a crisis of leadership. Independent since 1847 as Africa's first republic, the country's progress has snail-paced for the most period of its existence while the mass of the Liberian population have mired in extreme poverty because of limited visionary and progressive leadership.

Liberia is ranked as one of the poorest and least developed countries in the world because of bad governance resulting from an entrenched culture of widespread misuse of resources intended for human and infrastructural development. Due to an age-old culture of poor governance in Liberia, there is a general perception that when you want to get rich, hustle for a position in government.

Like Liberia, other countries that are ranked in the "poorest and least developed" category share similar characteristics in corrupt and incompetent leadership, such as underdevelopment, poverty, civil unrest, misery, and human tragedy.

The magnitude of the weak health care systems in both Liberia and Sierra Leone, for example, is reflected by the following data compiled by the Afri-Dev.Info, a health and social development agency, quoted by BBC News. At the time of the Ebola outbreak, Liberia, with a population of 4.2 million, had only 51 doctors, 978 nurses and midwives, and 269 pharmacists. Also Sierra Leone, with a population of 6 million, had 136 doctors; 1,017 nurses and midwives; and 114 pharmacists. There was an average of 0.1 doctor per 10,000 people in Liberia while in Sierra Leone, the ratio of doctor to population was an average of 0.2 per 10,000 ("Ebola Drains Already Weak West African Health Systems," BBC online, September 24, 2014).

Faced with ineffective leadership, weak public institutions, mismanagement of public resources, and an impoverished population, a fragile country like Liberia and other countries in similar category do tend to become something like a powder keg waiting to explode in the wake of civil strife or disease epidemic such as the Ebola. The Ebola outbreak, which occurred at a time when the health care delivery systems in the worst-affected countries were very weak and ill-equipped, exemplify how it only takes a spark for an explosion that could spread with unbelievable consequences.

Without robust international intervention, there was a strong possibility that the three worst-affected countries could have collapsed under the attack of the mysterious disease. This is certainly true of Liberia, which had the lowest number of medical doctors and suffered the highest number of casualties from the Ebola pandemic. President Sirleaf and other senior officials of the Liberian government spoke of how the Ebola scourge threatened the very existence of the country.

The Liberian government's handling of the Ebola crisis was widely criticized by Liberians as a colossal failure. Just as Liberia became a failed state and virtually collapsed during the civil war, the threatened collapse of the country in the wake of the Ebola epidemic manifest a very serious crisis of leadership. Like the civil war when the Liberian population became a fair game at the mercy of marauding armed thugs, so it was that the general population was left unprotected in the wake of the Ebola outbreak.

What do you make of countries that claim national sovereignty but are not capable of providing even the bare necessities for their people, like adequate security to ensure protection for life and property? How can there be a government that is not capable of providing basic services for its people, such as water and sanitation, electricity, health, and education, among others? Liberia is seen to fit the mode of these questions. In the wake of the Ebola outbreak, many Liberians found themselves wondering, what kind of independent country do we have that is not able to protect its people or territory or provide the basic necessities? What a shame!

Going to about two decades now, the international community has been involved in bailing out Liberia from one crisis to another, such as the massive UN peacekeeping intervention in 2003 to end the nearly fifteen years of civil war. This was followed by the 2014 Ebola outbreak that required another massive international intervention, led by a US military deployment code named "Operation United Assistance," to contain the spread of the deadly pandemic. There can be no question that bad governance is the primary reason that Liberia has been underdeveloped and unable to fully function as a sovereign nation while the Liberian masses languish in poverty.

From the couple of examples that have been given, it could be said that Liberia runs the risk of becoming something like an "international problem child," constantly relying on the international community to come to its aid to solve one problem after another. Problems surrounding lack of effective leadership that has long undermined Liberia's progress and stability must be addressed through constructive engagement between Liberia and the international community to ensure that the rule of law and good governance prevail in the country.

To control the seemingly unending problem of corruption in government that has kept Liberia in a state of underdevelopment, the international community, including the United States, must push for another agreement with Liberia to put in place a framework under which Liberia's resources would be comanaged with international financial experts deployed in relevant government ministries and agencies to ensure proper accountability.

Such proposed economic management assistance program for Liberia could be similar to or should consider the positive results of the Governance and Economic Management Assistance Program (GEMAP). In 2005, the Liberian National Transitional Government (LNTG) reached an agreement with the international community, which included the UN and the United States, to restructure the fundamentally broken system of governance, such as widespread corruption and mismanagement, which contributed to decades of conflict and abject poverty in Liberia.

In their engagement with Liberia, the international community, led by the UN and the United States, must take cue from the successful examples of their relationship with Liberia to completely change the country's dysfunctional system of governance.

I make this recommendation mindful that there are Liberian officials and others who have argued that Liberia is a sovereign nation that does not need outside interference in its financial and other internal affairs. That point is well and understood. However, Liberians who propagate such argument must understand that they cannot be selective in invoking national sovereignty. The sovereignty argument rings hollow when we have a country that has been unable to fully protect and provide for its citizens and have to rely on the goodwill of the international community for survival. It certainly makes no sense to hide behind sovereignty to continue to sustain a dysfunctional system of governance in which corruption and mismanagement have thrived to the detriment of the country and its people.

CHAPTER TWELVE
Liberia's Role in Modern Africa

As the century of African independence ended, Liberia, modern Africa's first independent republic, was consumed by a vicious civil war from 1989 to 2003. Accordingly, rather than contributing to the continent's progress, Liberia became the sick man of Africa fomenting subregional instability, the aftereffects of which remain a continuing challenge.

Because of its destabilizing effects in the West African subregion during the regime of Charles Taylor, Liberia was internationally blacklisted as a pariah nation. Mr. Taylor, the rebel leader turned president of Liberia, has given the country and Africa the dubious distinction for being the first sitting African president to be indicted. He was subsequently arrested, tried, convicted, and given a fifty-year prison sentence by an international tribunal for war crimes and crimes against humanity.

Mr. Taylor's indictment was for sponsoring the civil war in neighboring Sierra Leone to loot diamonds. Taylor's sponsorship of Sierra Leone's brutal and barbaric civil war in exchange for looted diamonds popularized the expression "blood diamond," in reference to diamonds gotten from conflict areas, which are used to fuel instability.

Since African independence, many countries on the continent, especially in West Africa, have had their share of civil upheavals that have affected their neighbors. However, the destructive effects of Liberia's civil war in the subregion was unprecedented. Examples of such destructive activities include the civil wars that raged in neighboring Sierra Leone and Côte d'Ivoire, also known as the Ivory Coast; armed insurgency in Guinea; and the plundering of diamonds, timbers, and other resources. This is a manifestation of the historic, strategic, and economic importance of Liberia although a small country with a population a little less than five million, as of this publication.

Long before the civil war meltdown, which also profoundly affected the subregion, a peaceful and stable Liberia played a significant leadership role in the liberation struggle and progress of modern Africa. The point is that a peaceful, stable, and prosperous Liberia is a force for good while an unstable Liberia is a danger to regional and the continental stability and progress, as examples have shown.

As Liberia shows signs of recovery from the years of war devastation and has embarked upon a course of reclaiming its positive image and rightful place in the comity of nations, it is noted with disappointment that the country's historic role in the formation of the Organization of African Unity (OAU), now renamed the African Union (AU), among other contributions to the affairs of modern Africa, have been largely forgotten. While Liberia's historical role has been diminished or basically forgotten, other countries and their leaders are being exalted for their pioneering roles. In recent years, Liberia is hardly mentioned as a founding member of the continental body during AU programs or events related to the AU. There has even been attempts at misrepresentation and distortion of historical facts regarding what country is the oldest independent in Africa and the founding fathers of the OAU, for example.

The creation in May 1963 of the OAU was a culmination of collaborative effort by an emerging African leadership as the post–World War II political order was being negotiated. Liberia, Africa's oldest republic, not only played its part in the common effort, but also led in thought and action as Africa struggled to find its path in the modern world.

This chapter seeks to highlight the singular role of the Republic of Liberia in the process of organizing African unity. Much of the information contained in this chapter are gathered from an hitherto unpublished document on Liberia's role in the formation of the OAU, prepared by Dr. D. Elwood Dunn, eminent historian, author, and retired professor of political science at the University of South in Sewanee, Tennessee, USA. Dr. Dunn's document covers interviews with two legendary diplomats, now deceased, who were personally involved in the process to organize the OAU, during the administration of Liberian president William V. S. Tubman (1944–1971). As president of Africa's oldest independent republic, Tubman provided continental leadership to begin the process of creating a new African political order during the early period as more African countries gained independence from colonial subjugation.

The distinguished diplomats were Liberia's former secretary of state (now minister of foreign affairs) J. Rudolph Grimes and former undersecretary of state T. Ernest Eastman. Honorable Grimes, a graduate of the renowned Harvard and Columbia universities, respectively in the United States, who was an eminent lawyer and diplomat, is credited as the diplomatic architect who engineered the very precepts on which the OAU's foundations were laid. Ambassador Eastman, who later served as Liberia's minister of foreign affairs in the 1980s, along with two other young Liberian officials at the time, prepared the original draft which evolved into the charter of the OAU.

As I delved more into understanding Liberia's historical role in modern Africa, there were many discoveries of a proud national past. For example, it was a pleasant surprise to realize that there is a house in Monrovia, which was the late Eastman's residence, where Mr. Nelson Mandela resided when he visited Liberia incognito. According to historical accounts, Mr. Mandela was lodged at Mr. Eastman's residence because he could not be booked into a hotel to avoid being recognized and exposed. He is said to have also carried a Liberian passport under an alias to enable him to travel abroad. Liberia supported Mandela's African National Congress (ANC)'s struggle to end the racist exploitative minority regime in South Africa and also aided other liberation leaders and movements in various African countries in their struggles to end colonial domination.

The small residence where Ambassador Eastman lived until his death, which also contained the bed on which Mandela slept up to Liberia's civil crisis, deserves to be designated as a historical landmark to memorialize the legendary liberation fighter and global freedom icon.

Based on accounts provided by the two Liberian diplomats who were present at the OAU's creation—Secretary of State J. Rudolph Grimes (1960–72) and Ambassador T. Ernest Eastman (1960s through 2000)—as well as widely available records in the various theaters of diplomatic activity, Liberia was in the forefront of the effort to decolonize Africa. Records of the UN, the OAU/AU, and other international organizations, as well as national archives around the world corroborate the eyewitness accounts of Grimes and Eastman.

Highlights of Dr. Dunn's document regarding Liberia's role in the founding of the OAU include as follows:

Stoically struggling to maintain its independence in the face of the onslaught of colonialism, Liberia took pride in success of sorts as World War II ended. In short order, colonialism was delegitimized, and the stage was set for its systematic dismantling. One of only four African voices at the UN in the 1940s (others being Egypt, Ethiopia, and apartheid South Africa), the record shows a vocal Liberia advocating for African causes at UN headquarters in New York and its many agencies worldwide.

Though Libya, Tunisia, Morocco, and Sudan preceded Ghana into independent nationhood in 1957, it was the independence of the latter that set in motion Free Africa's quest for a framework for consultation. The road to a consensus was strewn with trials and tribulations as Free Africa sought both to direct the "wind of change" and to safeguard its interests in a complex international environment.

Perhaps the stage was first set in 1951 when upon the invitation of President Tubman, the newly appointed "Leader of Government Business" in the Gold Coast (later Ghana), Kwame Nkrumah, visited Liberia where the two leaders discussed "options available for obtaining full independence."

Subsequent African consultations eventuated in pioneering meetings of African heads of State such as the First Conference of Independent African States in Accra (Ghana) in 1958, the Sanniquellie (Liberia) Conference that hosted three heads of state in 1959, the Monrovia Conference of African heads of state in 1961, and the Lagos Summit in 1962. These gatherings set the stage and made possible the African Summit in Addis Ababa in May 1963 that brought about the birth of the OAU.

Presidents Ahmed Sekou Toure of Guinea, William V.S. Tubman of Liberia, and Kwame Nkrumah of Ghana sign a joint Communique after the Sanniquellie Conference

Guinea **Liberia** **Ghana**

OAU Seal

LIBERIA IS A FOUNDING MEMBER OF THE ORGANIZATION OF AFRICAN UNITY (O.A.U.). IN 1959, LIBERIA HOSTED A CONFERENCE IN SANNIQUELLIE, NIMBA COUNTY, TO DISCUSS MATTERS RELATING TO AFRICAN UNITY. ATTENDING THE MEETING WERE PRESIDENT SEKOU TOURE OF GUINEA, PRESIDENT KWAME NKRUMAH OF GHANA AND LIBERIA'S PRESIDENT, WILLIAM V.S. TUBMAN. IT WAS DURING THIS CONFERENCE (JULY 15TH TO 19TH) THAT THE FIRST PRINCIPLES OF AFRICAN UNITY WERE PREPARED.

THEREAFTER IN MAY, 1961, LIBERIA SPONSORED A CONFERENCE OF 21 AFRICAN HEAD OF STATES TO FURTHER EXPLORE THE POSSIBILITIES OF ESTABLISHING THE ORGANIZATION OF AFRICAN UNITY. THE ORGANIZATION WAS FINALLY ESTABLISHED WITH HEADQUARTERS IN ADIS ABABA, ETHIOPIA, AFTER MANY MEETINGS IN OTHER AFRICAN STATES.

WE MUST THANK THE O.A.U. FOR ESPECIALLY OVERSEEING THE DISMANTLING OF APARTHEID IN AFRICA. THE WORLD AT

In 1959, Pres. W.V.S. Tubman hosted a summit in Sanniquellie, Liberia, with Guinean Pres. Sekou Toure (L) and Ghanaian Prime Minister Kwame Nkrumah (R) on African unity. (Courtesy, Selena Horace, Liberian Embassy)

As the whirlwinds of self-determination swept across Africa in the early 1950s, it may be recalled that Liberia and Ethiopia were the only two sub-Saharan independent states at the time. With Ghana's accession to the *independence club* on 6 March 1957, and following intensive consultations among President Tubman, Emperor Haile Selassie of Ethiopia, and Prime Minister Nkrumah of Ghana, a *preliminary conference* of independent African states was convened in Accra on 15 April 1958.

On that momentous occasion, the far-reaching diplomatic vision enshrined in President Tubman's keynote speech that would serve as the bedrock of the OAU initiative had been crafted by his astute diplomatic adviser, J. Rudolph Grimes, prior to becoming secretary of state.

In it, President Tubman declared,

It is of great significance that this meeting has not been convoked to deliberate upon the possibility of partitioning or expropriating any portion of the earth's surface which inherently belongs to others. On the contrary, we have come here with the hope of advancing and promoting the interest and welfare of the independent states, as well as the dependent peoples of Africa. More than that, our interest should extend beyond nationalism into the broad arena of international affairs and seek to ameliorate and adjust, as far as possible, the strained relations which now harass and perturb the minds of men and nations.

As Guinea (Conakry) joined the now-expanding *independence club* on 2 October 1958, at the initiative of Liberia, the first *substantive conference* of the independent states of sub-Saharan Africa was held from July 15–19, 1959 at Sanniquellie, capital of the northern Liberian county (state) of Nimba. In his opening remarks, President Tubman highlighted respect for the ideals and sovereignty of each nation-state. He emphasized that the idea of African unity should only be *exploratory* inasmuch as a topic of such magnitude should ideally be pursued after the majority of African states had acquired independence. Nonetheless, a twin approach toward governing diplomatic relations among African states did come into focus: safeguarding newly acquired independence and achieving African unity. The final resolution of the conference adopted "independence and unity" as its watchword.

In January 1960, President Tubman appointed Grimes to head Liberia's diplomatic establishment. In the capacity of secretary of state, his diplomatic primacy enabled him to embark upon a new strategy that focused on strengthening Liberia's foreign policy consistent with its endowed status as doyen of African independence. Essentially, that entailed intensification of its lead role in promoting self-determination in favor of African states under colonial domination. Accordingly, on May 12, 1961, a second substantive conference convened by Liberia was held in Monrovia, bringing together some twenty independent African states to build on the achievements of two years earlier in July 1959. It was Secretary Grimes who set the conference agenda and astutely provided professional advice that helped steer its outcome successfully. The Monrovia Conference adopted a four-point resolution that would henceforth govern the relationships between African states.

Complementary to the moves toward African unity, at the Second Conference of Independent African States held in Addis Ababa June 1960, Secretary Grimes persuaded Ethiopia to join Liberia in instituting contentious proceedings against South Africa for its continued Mandate over South West Africa (now Namibia). The situations in Angola, South Africa, and Congo (Leopoldville/Kinshasa) were also just a few political hotspots that Secretary Grimes placed on his diplomatic agenda, steering them to successful conclusion within the international arena.

Liberia's Approach to Regionalism

Before the creation in 1963 of the Organization for African Unity (OAU), the first continental organization, the colonization, and Balkanization of Africa had yielded multiple regional arrangements such as the East African Community, French-inspired West African regionalism, including a common currency, even the British-inspired Federation of Rhodesia and Nyasaland. African decolonization was meant to recast all such arrangements, though the cold war context of decolonization itself would pose monumental challenges.

As Pan-Africanism returned home as it were in the years after the 1945 Manchester Pan-African Congress, it engendered an immediate debate about the nature of the political order desirable in a decolonized Africa. Ghana's Kwame Nkrumah led the advocacy for a union government or a pooling of African sovereignties. Liberia's William V. S. Tubman countered with a regionalism based on the Organization of American States (OAS) model. The cold war quickly emasculated whatever the original intentions of these pioneering leaders were, for the debate soon degenerated into pro-Western and pro-Communist African states. The crisis in the Congo in 1960 became the classic and tragic expression of this situation.

And yet in a more profound sense, the question remained regarding the nature of the African debate about regionalism's prospect in independent Africa. Professor Adebayo Adedeji, confining himself to West Africa's regional ambitions, has written about "literal thinkers who see everything only in orthodox and doctrinaire terms." The purpose of economic cooperation and integration for such people, he adds, "is trade liberalization, creating a customs union, and establishing a fund for compensation." Adedeji thinks that economic cooperation must instead fundamentally be about "socioeconomic transformation as well as forum for forging common strategies and policies."

The absence of such requisite political commitments was captured in a 2000 interim report by a former executive secretary of ECOWAS (Economic Community of West African States), Lansana Kouyate: "The integration process in West Africa has been such that attention has been focused on the choice of the institutions needed for integration, thus relegating the actual business of building the community to the background." "Instead of asking," he continues "with whom, in what context and under what conditions integration might be possible, attention has rather been on the institutions to be established and the measures to be promoted." Kouyate concludes, "Giving priority to identifying institutional arrangements completely diverts attention from the vital task of determining socioeconomic objectives and setting priorities."

Context of Liberia's Relations with Independent Africa

Though this brief profile is focused on relations since independence came to the nations of Africa, it may be useful to highlight antecedents to this period. The Liberian state was initiated amidst colonial settlement in the 1820s and an independence in 1847 precipitated by complications with her British colonial neighbor in Sierra Leone. Thereafter, tension remained the hallmark of the relationship between the sole black republic on the continent and Liberia's British and French colonial neighbors. In 1885, Britain forcibly annexed the Gallinas territory heretofore a part of Liberia. Following the Berlin African Congress, Liberia was obliged to follow the dictates of "effective occupation" of acquired African territory as determined in Europe. Though inconclusive, an 1892 treaty with colonial France demarcated the borders between Liberia and French possessions in neighboring Guinea and Côte d'Ivoire.

The dawn of the twentieth century witnessed an intensification of British-French rivalry over Liberian territory. A joint Liberian-French commission was busy at work negotiating outstanding border issues in the late 1950s when independence abruptly came to Guinea. Liberia withdrew from further engagement because, according to the government of the day, the issue had become moot, as the territory was now indisputably African.

As the Second World War drew to a close and African nationalism began consolidating in the decades that followed, Liberia, one of then only four independent African states, was challenged to consider a clearer Africa policy. Because the wave of decolonization would soon replace Liberia's European colonial neighbors with free states under African leadership, the administration of President Tubman deemed it necessary to formulate policies toward these new states within the broader framework of the challenge that loomed of creating a new African political order.

Over time, Tubman's Africa policy developed along two lines: one domestic, the other international, or more precisely the development of a domestic base for an external policy. Domestically, Tubman proffered a National Unification and Integration policy designed to address a historic divide between New World immigrants and indigenous peoples. Internationally, Tubman shared America's apprehension toward what they both considered as radical nationalism and its Pan-African derivative. He consequently joined the United States to contain what both parties perceived as radicalism tending toward socialism. Tubman aspired toward a moderate African political order and understood that his American cold war partner would assist him achieve that end.

Liberia sought thus to be attuned to African developments both as witness and participant in a period of birth, growth, and profound changes in the immediate postwar period. As an early advocate of the rights of African peoples to self-determination and independence, Liberia availed herself of the arenas of the UN. The status of non-self-governing territories and trust territories were not only reflected in UN Charter articles 11 and 12, but specific issues emanating from them soon claimed the attention of UN organs.

Liberia remained vocally engaged as the UN went on to address such colonial issues as the disposal of the former Italian colonies of Libya, Somaliland, and Eritrea; the question of Algeria; the question of South West Africa; and the policy of apartheid of the government of South Africa. On the South West Africa question, the Liberian role was large as she joined Ethiopia in filing before the International Court of Justice in 1960 application instituting contentious proceeding against South Africa for attempting to relinquish its international obligations by introducing apartheid into the territory.

In 1951, as Kwame Nkrumah bursts on to the African scene as first "leader of government business" in the Gold Coast (later Ghana), he was invited by President Tubman to discuss options available for obtaining full independence. The visit took on the character of a full-fledged state event with the attendant pomp and circumstance. Both Tubman and Nkrumah in their respective remarks spoke of the imperative for accelerated African independence. This Liberian invitation triggered a *Time* magazine feature story on the Gold Coast march to independence and may have added momentum to the African independence movement.

Notwithstanding his strong expression of support for African liberation, Tubman's approach to liberation contrasted sharply with Nkrumah's. The independence of Ghana in 1957 with its promise of radical nationalism Nkrumah espoused did not go unnoticed by Tubman. Rather than radical political transformations, Tubman envisaged formal legal sovereignty with pragmatic ties to the Western world.

Only months following Ghana's independence and in view of the radical rhetoric that emanated from Accra, Tubman addressed the question of the leadership of Africa and the form unity might take: "I have observed," he declared in his 1957 Independence Day message, "that there seem to be three schools of thought on the leadership question.

"There are those who feel that Liberia should assume leadership based on the fact that she is the oldest African Republic and is riper in political experience; but it will require more than age and political experience to assume leadership of Africa. There are others who hold that Ghana should assume that role because she is physically more developed and embraces larger territories. It will require more than development and larger territory to assume leadership of Africa. And there are yet those who opine that Egypt with its rich traditions dating back to the remotest antiquity should do so. It will require more than rich traditions of antiquity. It will require, in my opinion, the aggregate of all three of these and more besides. It will require the aggregate of the best of all that Liberia, Ghana, Egypt, Tunisia, Ethiopia, the Sudan, Morocco, and all other African

Territories and States possess, molded together, to assume the leadership of Africa, compounded in such a manner as to represent the divisibility of Africa indivisible."

Until the independence in October 1960 of the populous Nigeria, Liberia appeared the leader of African moderation. Nkrumah was riding a crest of radical nationalism as the situations in such disparate places as Guinea, the Congo, apartheid South Africa, and elsewhere on the continent tended to lend credence to this approach. Tubman consequently initiated, in reaction to the seemingly unstoppable developments, a crucial consultation in Sanniquellie, Liberia, in July 1959 involving Nkrumah and Toure. The substance of the Sanniquellie Declaration that resulted was that consultation and the patient hammering out of a consensus should be the African modus operandi. A fuller African consultation to involve a larger number of states whose independence was imminent was slated for Ethiopia the following year.

At the 1960 gathering in Addis, Free Africa had grown from eight to fifteen states, including populous Nigeria and a host of moderate Francophone states. Liberia was now in its comfort zone. And when African differences split the continent into three ways—the so-called Brazzaville, Casablanca, and "uncommitted" groups—Liberia felt it had positioned itself precisely where it wanted to be, a potential moderator, a facilitator of African affairs. According to Tubman's secretary of state, J. Rudolph Grimes, Liberia was soon urged by "quite a few" African leaders to take some initiative to bridge the existing African divisions.

Tubman's response to the suggestions that he convene a bridging conference was to propose that such a conference be sponsored by a number of carefully chosen states. He proposed two representatives each from the Brazzaville and Casablanca groups and three from the "uncommitted." Through consultations, Guinea and Mali represented Casablanca, Ghana having refused the invitation to serve a sponsor. Côte d'Ivoire and Cameroon represented Brazzaville. And Nigeria, Togo, and Liberia represented the uncommitted. It was therefore these seven African states that issued invitations to all independent African states to meet in Monrovia on May 8–12, 1961.

After the invitations had been issued and many had indicated acceptance, a meeting was held in Accra of the Casablanca group. Guinea and Mali soon announced withdrawal of their sponsorship. Tubman was not dissuaded. By May 7, fourteen delegations had arrived in Monrovia. Some six others would soon follow as the conference convened on schedule. Though Tubman held a commanding role at informal preconference exchange of views, a participant, Liberian economist Charles Dunbar Sherman, relates this interesting anecdote: "It was interesting to observe the attending Heads of States meet around the Conference table as equals, many for the first time. I recall distinctly a rather sharp exchange between Abubakar Tafawa Balewa, who was at that particular session said to President Tubman: 'You are wrong!' Mr. Tubman, forgetting who Ballewa was, for a moment, shouted back at him and said: 'What did you say?' Mr. Ballewa, who was the first Prime Minister of independent Nigeria, calmly repeated: 'I said, Mr. President, you are wrong.' Tubman smiled and the tension was broken."

The twenty states attending the conference marked the largest single gathering of African countries ever to that date. They reviewed the issues on the continental agenda, regretted the absence of the Casablanca powers, and expressed the hope that these powers would soon join the African consultative process. Awarded the chairmanship of the conference by his colleagues, Tubman stated that the objective was "to bring all African leaders to reason together." Only "tolerance, good faith, honor, good neighborliness" could lead Africa to the desired unity and solidarity.

In an overwhelming endorsement of Tubman's approach to unity and cooperation, the conference's communiqué faithfully reflected his views. Participants agreed that a summit meeting would convene in Nigeria in 1962 to develop processes for technical and cultural cooperation and carry forward the "unity of aspirations and action" of African states.

While a majority of the African and Western press hailed the Monrovia gathering as a success, the Ghanaian press issued scathing attacks on "the Monrovia slave-mentality." Tubman remained quiet, believing he had won a major battle. The Inter-African and Malagasy Union emerged from the January 1962 Lagos conference. It fixed a date of May 1963 for a summit conference in Ethiopia that would usher in what became the Organization of African Unity (OAU).

All seemed in order for a conference designed to organize African unity, when on January 13, 1963, the congenial Togolese president Sylvanus Olympio was assassinated under circumstances that evoked considerable concern among African leaders. The concern was acute for Liberia for several reasons. Olympio had attended Tubman's January 1960 inauguration, and the two leaders seemed temperamentally compatible. They had both closely collaborated as sponsors at the crucial 1961 Monrovia conference. Even more, the assassination had occurred only a day before Olympio's scheduled departure for a state visit to Liberia. The January 29, 1963, letter of the widow of the president to Tubman recounting the events leading to her husband's death and characterizing the brutal murder "as sinister non-Togolese design" fueled the concerns.

Shortly following the Olympio assassination, a dramatic meeting of the council of ministers of the Inter-African and Malagasy Organization (IAMO) convened in Lagos on January 24–26, 1963. Two rival Togolese delegations, one from the provisional Nicholas Grunitzky government and the other composed of members of Olympio's cabinet were present. The IAMO recognized that the murder of Olympio could not be condoned by automatic recognition of a successor government, thus establishing a dangerous precedent. The ministers called for an investigating mission of neighboring states to visit Togo, the prosecution of those responsible for the murder, and free elections at an early date. The group also agreed a draft Mutual Security Treaty for submission to the May meeting of African heads of state in Addis.

The Addis summit convened under the cloud of this assassination, as well as against the backdrop of the still outstanding differences between the two African political tendencies. At one early session, President Toure of Guinea openly accused President Nkrumah of complicity in the Olympio assassination. This accusation of one member of the erstwhile Casablanca group by another placed Nkrumah squarely on the defensive and weakened his moral authority and therefore his effectiveness in making the case for political union. Continuing what must have been a moment of personal delight, Tubman calmly implored his fellow conferees to "think like men of action and act like men of thought." The OAU that emerged from the 1963 Addis conference was precisely the traditional state-centric body Tubman had hoped for and Nkrumah had feared would materialize.

The functionalist imperative or the approach of socioeconomic, as opposed to exclusive political, development has been advanced with consistency, especially following Nkrumah's positing of his united states of Africa thesis. In a series of well-staged diplomatic offensives directed from Monrovia, a steady stream of working papers and strategic conversations were held across and beyond the continent. Some of these efforts culminated eventually in the establishment of such staple African institutions as the West African Rice Development Association (WARDA), the African Development Bank, the Mano River Union (MRU), and the Economic Community of West African States (ECOWAS).

Implicit in Tubman's association of African states idea has always been what he described as the need for Africans, long estranged from one another, to come to know each other through a variety of social and economic measures, not the least of which the need to promote intra-African trade and other forms of economic cooperation. Beyond the memoranda of conversations with African and Africa-interested players, Tubman underscored orthodox economic cooperation in all of his landmark statements, including the July 1959 Independence Day remarks, and speeches at the Sanniquellie conference and at the 1962 Monrovia conference.

Policy of Economic Regionalism

In pursuit of African economic regionalism, Liberia joined Sierra Leone, Guinea, and Côte d'Ivoire in February 1965 in initiating an interim West African Free Zone Area. In August of the same year, the West African Iron and Steel conference ended in Liberia with agreement in principle to establish an iron and steel authority to coordinate industrial development in West Africa. That this desire did not become reality is much discussed in the literature comparing the South Korean growth experience with those of West Africa, notably Ghana. The OAU and the UN Economic Commission for Africa endorsed this important initiative. In attendance were Diallo Telli, a Guinean diplomat and politician, who was the first secretary-general of the OAU, and Robert K. A. Gardiner, a Ghanaian professor and economist, who served as the second executive secretary of the UN Economic Commission for Africa (ECA).

It may be interesting to interject that following the end of his tenure as OAU Secretary-General, Telli, a Guinean diplomat and politician, returned to his home country, where he served as minister of justice during the regime of Ahmed Sekou Toure. Accused and imprisoned for plotting to overthrow Toure's government, Telli was starved to death in 1977. Under the guise of the provision of its charter of noninterference in the internal affairs of another country, there was no official protest from the OAU regarding the killing of this great son of Africa, not to speak of someone who was the OAU's own first secretary-general. Even though he was one of the prominent Pan-Africanist and socialist leaders in Africa during his days, Toure was also known to have ruled Guinea with an iron fist from independence until his death.

Crucial conferences prior to the 1975 establishment of ECOWAS occurred in Monrovia in November 1967 (fourteen countries and a draft articles of association) and in April 1968. The latter conference brought together nine of the fifteen West African heads of state with the object of evolving what they called appropriate measures to remove obstacles to economic cooperation in the subregion. These efforts awaited more propitious circumstances in the early 1970s to begin bearing fruit.

One organizational effort, however, the African Development Bank, was actually realized in 1962 with the organization's establishment of its first headquarters in Abidjan, the first presidency to Sudan, and Liberia serving on the first board of directors. This was result of a tortuous series of events that began with an idea from the Liberian banker, A. Romeo Horton. Possibly in reaction to President Tubman's earlier advocacy for African economic cooperation, Horton presented the president a concept paper for an African development bank that he conceived of as contributing to African unity "by financing and investing in multinational enterprises and projects." Horton has insisted that the original idea was not for financing national projects as has actually happened but transnational ones. At Tubman's behest, and following extensive consultations with African leaders, Horton and the Liberian economist P. Clarence Parker prepared a draft charter. An implementation committee of nine countries (Cameroon, Ethiopia, Guinea, Liberia, Mali, Nigeria, Sudan, Tanganyika, and Tunisia) was constituted; and the committee held its first meeting in Monrovia on June 1–22, 1962. It was this committee that husbanded the organization into existence following intensive and extensive consultations with African leaders. The multilateral agreement that brought the ADB into existence was signed by twenty-five African states in Khartoum in September 1964.

There were multiple motives for this Liberian advocacy of African regionalism. They included a desire to blunt Nkrumah's idea of an African Union government, a practical alternative for cooperation among African states, as well as a concomitant Liberian desire to show solidarity with the United States in the midst of the cold war. Whatever the primary motive, what followed was the majority acceptance of the furtherance of African cooperation in all domains, with any possible union government consigned to a distant future.

Until then, Liberia wanted the territorial integrity of Nigeria maintained, as she became a part of the OAU mediation committee on the Nigerian civil war of 1967–1970, even engaging Vice President William R. Tolbert Jr. in dangerous shuttle diplomacy in the Biafra war zone.

Following Tubman's death, the transfer of the mantle of leadership to his vice president, William R. Tolbert, Jr. in July 1971 promised some significant changes, while building on Tubman's legacy of a moderate African political order. The challenge at home of a more thorough Africanization of Liberia, or democratization of the political order, would move in tandem with Tolbert's engagement of solidarity with African "progressives" who were in the vanguard of completing African liberation, including terminating white minority rule on the continent. Crucially, the new administration endeavored to carry decidedly forward the measure of economic regionalism earlier initiated.

As Liberia hosted, at much sacrifice, the sixteenth OAU summit in 1979, the contours of its Africa policy were clearly in evidence given the country's now legendary advocacy for ending the vestiges of colonialism over the preceding years. Considering Liberia's role in the founding of the organization, some saw the OAU "returning home." Yet, one cannot escape observing that the OAU of 1979 was unlike the OAU of the founders. Where Tubman wished to heal the "wound of loneliness since [Liberia's] 1847 independence" and stamp on the organization a conservative imprimatur "with some Casablanca [representing African radical nationalism] coloring," Tolbert saw his task as one of deepening the dye of the Casablanca coloring, or more closely aligning policy with African progressives.

An early signal of Tolbert's regionalist thrust was the start of his presidency with a series of one-day visits to neighboring Guinea, Côte d'Ivoire, and Sierra Leone. An activist policy was pursued with frequent messages to African colleagues as well as the frequent dispatch of special envoys. Africa was clearly on Liberia's radar screen. A 1979 defense pact with Guinea signaled less dependence on the U.S.

At accelerated pace, African freedom fighters made their way to Liberia for material and moral support, as Liberia acquired for the first time membership on the OAU Liberation Committee. Peace efforts were undertaken as Liberia served on the OAU mediating committee on the Ethiopia-Somalia dispute. In addition,

Tolbert's efforts resulted in the "miracle of Monrovia" when in March 1978, along with the presidents of Togo and The Gambia, Tolbert facilitated an end to a long-standing acid relationship between President Toure of Guinea, and his colleagues, Presidents Felix Houphouët-boigny of Côte d'Ivoire, and Leopold Sedar Senghor of Senegal. Tolbert had used his lightening shuttle to good effect. The result was a solemn undertaking "to finally end all dissensions which have affected their relations." and to establish full diplomatic relations with the exchange of ambassadors.

Economic emancipation was Tolbert's way of advocating for and carrying forward the earlier OAU economic cooperation schemes. Such schemes took the form of specific cooperation agreements with Côte d'Ivoire, Guinea, and Sierra Leone, respectively. These agreements culminated in the 1973 creation of the MRU and the 1975 establishment of the ECOWAS.

In early 1979, Liberia hosted another "Monrovia conference," with OAU and ECA joint sponsorship of a colloquium. Its purpose was to suggest common patterns for African economic development up to the year 2000. A number of African experts assembled in Monrovia. They agreed to tackle the problem of first creating joint institutions toward an African common market and the development of a center to promote the continent's technological potentials. The sixteenth Summit built its economic resolutions on these foundations.

A series of other progressive resolutions emerged from the Summit, among them the Monrovia Strategy for the Development of Africa and a resolution to establish an Africa expert group to study and prepare a treaty for an African Economic Community; the first-of-its-kind resolution on human rights that called for a committee of experts to draft an African charter on human rights, an initiative that subsequently became the African Charter on Human and Peoples' Rights (Liberia's Supreme Court Associate Justice and former Ambassador to the UN, Angie Brooks Randolph, contributed significantly. Ambassador Randolph was the first black female President of the UN General Assembly); the renewal of the OAU Committee of Twelve on Afro-Arab Cooperation, which included Liberia; the unequivocal resolutions on southern Africa including support for OAU-recognized liberation movements in Namibia and South Africa, and the Lancaster House peace negotiations for Zimbabwe; as well as a prescient proposal for OAU charter amendment to create an ad hoc action machinery to include a Pan-African force that would enable the organization to "respond at all times to problems of varying dimensions."

The OAU chairmanship, which traditionally went to the host head of state, was to give Tolbert a platform to demonstrate Liberia's African commitments, as well as a challenge to convince a majority of leaders about the needed new path.

Despite Zambian President Kenneth Kaunda's experience of duplicity with South African Prime Minister John Vorster as revealed in an April 1971 Zambian publication of "Details of exchange between President Kaunda of Zambia and Prime Minister Vorster of South Africa," Tolbert decided to engage in dialogue with the apartheid regime. Where such countries as Côte d'Ivoire, Malawi, Madagascar, Ghana, Gabon, Kenya, Senegal, and Congo-Kinshasa had all conducted dialogue in secret with the apartheid regime, Liberia did not seem sanguine about taking precautionary measures.

Accordingly, at Tolbert's invitation Vorster and his foreign minister arrived in Liberia in secret on February 11, 1975 and departed the next day. No sooner had they departed than the Times of London headlined

"Mr. Vorster Pays Secret Visit to Liberian leader." Stunned by the early revelation, Liberian officials initially attempted to deny the story, but then they soon issued a statement of explanation. Such an explanation was necessary because of the widespread internal and external suspicion generated by the visit.

In the wake of the revelation the Liberian press headlined "Tolbert in Trouble with the OAU," the opposition movement Progressive Alliance of Liberia (PAL) pointed out "how seriously embarrassed the people of Liberia [felt] before the entire world," and the Tanzanian press exclaimed: "Liberia Welcomes Africa's Enemy!"

To address the public relations implications of the revelation, Tolbert dispatched his foreign minister on expensive briefing shuttles to 15 African states. While the Liberian minister reported general African understanding of the initiative, there was some African outrage. For example, Guinea's Sekou Toure tried unsuccessfully to contain his anger as he rejected any rationale for dialogue. Toure exclaimed twice to the Liberian envoy: "I am scared…scare not of Tolbert being bought, but of making moral mistakes because as leaders of our people our only true strength is our moral stature before our people and world opinion." And then, in what must have irked Tolbert, Toure added, "If (former President W.V.S.] Tubman was not dynamic leader as far as his internal policies for social development [were concerned], at the African level he was always an honest man, and all African leaders knew this and had confidence in him."

This occurrence notwithstanding, and given the fact that Tolbert was not alone in the advocacy of dialogue with South Africa as an attempt to end apartheid, Liberia remained faithful to what had become a tradition of solid support for African liberation.

African freedom fighters continued the tradition of beating their paths to Monrovia for diplomatic support and financial assistance. Angola's Jonas Savimbi of UNITA met with Tolbert in October 1975, receiving Liberian diplomatic passport and financial support. A year later, the Pan Africanist Congress's (PAC) Potlako Lebello of South Africa also received travel documents and financial support. The South West African People's Organization (SWAPO)'s Sam Njoma of Namibia benefitted from Liberian financial aid. Others making the journey to Liberia included National Cultural Liberation Movements' (INKATHA's) Mangosuthu Buthelezi, representatives of the African National Congress (ANC), Zimbabwe's nationalist and guerrilla leader Joshua NKomo, and PAC's David Sibokwe. PAC's Vusumzi Make resided in Liberia, lecturing at the University of Liberia while freely engaging in his liberation activities, often briefing government officials about the progress of the struggle in southern Africa.

In furtherance of economic regionalism, three landmark regional organizations emerged in the 1970s. The first was the West African Rice Development Association (WARDA), an agricultural research center constituted by 11 West African states including Liberia. Its constitution was signed in Dakar in 1970, with the first meeting in Liberia in September 1971 at which time the secretariat was established there as Liberia made the first financial contribution to the organization. This was the product of OAU/ECA cooperation in agriculture research. The first headquarters was located in Liberia, and Liberian agriculturist Nah Doe Bropleh became deputy executive secretary. In the 1980s WARDA became The Africa Rice Center (Africa Rice) with eventual expansion to 24 states of West, Central, East and North Africa. Now headquartered in Benin, the center is one of 15 specialized research outfits under the Future Harvest Centers of the Consultative Group on International Agricultural Research (CGIAR).

The Mano River Union (MRU), a customs union, originates from a series of bilateral cooperation arrangements – Côte d'Ivoire/Liberia, Guinea/Liberia, and Sierra Leone/Liberia. At a September 12, 1973 joint ministerial meeting on Liberian-Sierra Leone cooperation emerged the text of a document, The Mano River Declaration that in October was signed in Malema (Sierra Leone) by Sierra Leone's Siaka Stevens and Liberia's William R. Tolbert, Jr. Guinea and Côte d'Ivoire subsequently acceded to the treaty. Headquartered in Freetown three Liberians have served as Secretary-General, first the economist Cyril Bright, followed by the diplomat Ernest Eastman, and then the sociologist Augustus F. Caine.

As regards the Economic Community of West African States (ECOWAS), efforts were initiated in the early 1960s and credited to Liberian President Tubman who was an early advocate for a West African economic community. The idea was re-launched by Togo and Nigeria in 1972, following which a series of technical meetings culminated in a ministerial meeting in Monrovia, January 27-31, 1975. The Treaty of Lagos that brought into existence the organization was signed in Nigeria by 15 West African states, including Liberia, on May 28, 1975.

ECOWAS' initial mission was to promote economic integration across the subregion, but since expanded to address political and security issues as well. ECOWAS has been designated one of five regional pillars of the African Economic Community (AEC) that grew out of the preparations for the 16th OAU summit in Liberia and has since become a part of the continent's development and security architectures. Among institutions under which it functions are a Secretariat and a Fund for Cooperation, now the ECOWAS Bank for Investment and Development. Liberians Romeo Horton and Robert Tubman have served as executive directors of the bank. Another Liberian, Dr. J. Toga Gayewea McIntosh, an economist, joined the staff as Vice President of the ECOWAS Commission in early 2012.

Regional Impacts of Liberia's Instability

A few months into the Liberia-hosted sixteenth summit of the OAU, and while serving as the current chairman of the organization, President Tolbert was assassinated and his government overthrown in a bloody military coup d'état. Ten days following the April 12, 1980 event, thierteen senior officials of the regime, including his foreign minister, C. Cecil Dennis, Jr. who was well known across the continent, were publicly executed. Africa's immediate reaction to the bloody events was to twice rebuff the military regime that emerged from the coup, first at the second extraordinary session of the Heads of State and Government of the OAU on the Economic Development of Africa in Lagos, April 28, 1980, and then at the ECOWAS summit in Lome, Togo on May 28, 1980.

In reaction to these rebuffs, the size of the Nigerian mission in Liberia was reduced, and Liberian ambassadors were recalled from neighboring Sierra Leone, Côte d'Ivoire, and Nigeria.

Guinea opted to play a mediatory role, and communication channels were gradually opened enabling Head of State Samuel K. Doe to attend arranged summits in Yamoussoukro and Monrovia with four other West African leaders – Felix Houphouët-boigny of the Côte d'Ivoire, Sekou Toure of Guinea, Siaka Stevens of Sierra Leone, and Gnassingbe Eyadema of Togo. Houphouet's abrupt departure from the June 1980 one-day visit to Liberia during which he reportedly said that he would return only when Liberians were smiling again, did not bode well for the Côte d'Ivoire-Liberia relationship. Though normalcy was returned over time, it does not appear that the traditional relationship of mutual trust among regional neighbors was ever fully restored.

A war of words, several months later, ensued between Liberia and Sierra Leone. Then came the November 1985 foiled coup during which former Commanding General Thomas Quiwonkpa attempted to overthrow the Doe regime. Under the circumstances, Houphouet never returned to Liberia. Rather, he allowed liberal use of his territory when the Liberian insurgents, under the National Patriotic Front of Liberia (NPFL), led by Charles Taylor, initiated in December 1989 the Liberian civil war.

At this point Liberia quickly became a negative force on the continent rekindling such cleavages as the Francophone and Anglophone divide, involving Nigeria and a neo-colonial France. In addition to the Côte d'Ivoire from whence the Liberian insurgency had been launched, Libya and Burkina Faso were early allies of Taylor's NPFL. As well, the powerful Nigerian military leader, Ibrahim Babangida, remained faithful to his Liberian counterpart, Samuel Doe.

As the standoff between Taylor and Doe spiraled out of control, and the OAU seemed unable to do more than issue appeals seemingly paralyzed by its Charter provision of noninterference in members' domestic matters, ECOWAS deemed it necessary to attempt robust mediation.

Authorized by a five-member mediation committee an ECOWAS-created ECOMOG force of some 3,500 troops from Gambia, Guinea, Ghana, Nigeria, and Sierra Leone entered Liberia on August 24, 1990 in an attempt to enforce a cease-fire and otherwise facilitate resolution of the conflict through an "ECOWAS Peace Plan." ECOWAS had first taken note of the Liberian conflict at its annual summit in Gambia May 28-30, 1990.

A Standing Mediation Committee was established and the organization soon endorsed a Liberia-derived peace plan that essentially called for a cease-fire and the installation of interim political arrangements pending elections. Once the mediation committee established ECOMOG in August, and following the establishment of an interim government by Liberian politicians and civil society organizations, the committee decided to deploy to Liberia.

Given the context of the deployment or intervention, not to speak of the motives of the various internal and external players, Liberia soon found itself the proverbial cloth between the scissors. All of this was played out in seven years of war and mayhem amidst international conferences that finally culminated in a reluctant UN Security Council involvement in 1992 with the imposition of an arms embargo on the warring factions and the posting of a Secretary-General Special Representative to monitor the situation in Liberia.

Preceding UN action was widespread foreign involvement in the crisis. First came the African provision of training facilities for the rebellion. NPFL rebel recruited in Côte d'Ivoire were taken to Libya and Burkina Faso for training, and in time military personnel from both countries fought alongside NPFL rebels inside Liberia. In addition to the original ECOMOG contingent, Senegalese and East African soldiers saw service in the West African-led intervention force.

There was yet another dimension to the foreign involvement. As the conflict escalated as a result of Sierra Leone and Gambia dissidents aiding the NPFL in expectation of reciprocal assistance in future launching of similar rebellion in their respective countries, the NPFL invaded Sierra Leone 23 March 1991 and initiated there a brutal war. The Liberian involvement in the war in Sierra Leone led to Taylor's indictment for war crimes and crimes against humanity, as have been previously noted.

On April 26, 2012 former president Charles Taylor was found guilty of aiding and abetting war crimes committed in Sierra Leone during that country's civil war in the 1990s. He thus became the first African and the first world leader to be so convicted since the Nuremburg Trials in Germany following the Second World War.

Repositioning Postwar Liberia on the African Stage

In office as Liberia's and Africa's first democratically elected female president, Ellen Johnson Sirleaf (2006–2018) endeavored to restore "the years the locusts have eaten." Since her first inauguration in 2006, Liberia has been returned to good standing in the OAU/AU with the payment of all outstanding financial obligations to the organization, as well as fulfillment of financial obligations to other regional and international organizations. During her tenure, the Liberian leader's activities in African diplomacy enabled her to serve as third vice chairperson of the Assembly of the AU, and she also served as chairperson of ECOWAS and the MRU, respectively.

Sirleaf came to the Liberian presidency with strong African credentials though largely as a technocrat and development expert. Among her many international responsibilities in various parts of Africa, Madam Sirleaf served as Assistant Administrator and Regional Director for Africa, United Nations Development Program (UNDP) from 1992 to 1997. Her UNDP responsibility entailed the management of country programs in thirty-two sub-Saharan African states.

Given her intense engagement with Liberian and African affairs since the 1970s, Madam Sirleaf appeared to have fitted almost seamlessly into her role as an African leader. It is important, however, to frame her government's ties with Africa both in terms of building upon some solid historical foundations as well as responding to the positive and negative impact of the civil war on Liberia-Africa relations.

As a manifestation of the country's reemergence on the African stage, on June 4, 2017, Liberia hosted the largest gathering of African leaders since the 1979 OAU summit—the 51st Session of the Summit of ECOWAS Authority of Heads of State and Government—chaired by President Sirleaf. Among the special guests at the summit was Prime Minister Benyamin Netanyahu of Israel, who addressed the ECOWAS summit, calling for renewed partnership between Israel and African countries.

One of her major accomplishments as chairperson of ECOWAS was the forced removal from power of Gambian dictator Yahya Jammeh, who refused to hand over power despite having been defeated in the tiny West African nation's December 2016 presidential election by Adama Barrow, the main opposition candidate. Jammeh, who came to power in a 1994 coup, was forced to step down after twenty-two years in power, in the face of pressure from West African armies under the auspices of ECOWAS which were poised to enter The Gambia to force him to recognize that he had lost the mandate of the Gambian people by his defeat in the democratic presidential election. It was attributed to the credit of President Sirleaf's astute leadership that ECOWAS became deeply engaged in The Gambian crisis, which prevented the country from degenerating into violence, a development that could have aborted the first democratic transition of that country.

During her tenure, domestic policy of national reconstruction projected abroad meant returning Liberia to the African fold and respectability within the wider comity of nations. Madam Sirleaf's personal recognitions, including the Nobel Peace Prize, which she won in 2011 along with fellow Liberian Leymah Gbowee, a peace activist, and Yemeni women's rights activist Tawakkul Karman, contributed immensely to restoring Liberia's image on the continent and beyond. Liberia has been resuming activities reminiscent of the 1960s and 1970s in such flagship regional organizations as the AU, ECOWAS and MRU.

Ms. Gbowee received the Nobel Peace Prize for her work in leading a women's peace movement, which contributed immensely to the effort to bring an end to the Liberian civil war in 2002. In 1999, Ms. Gbowee made the courageous move to mobilize an interreligious coalition of Christian and Muslim women and to organize the Women of Liberia Mass Action for Peace movement. Through her leadership, thousands of women staged pray-ins and nonviolent protests demanding reconciliation and revival of peace talks to bring an end to the civil war, which started when she was said to be just seventeen years old.

After serving two terms in office, Madam Sirleaf was replaced in January 2018 as president of Liberia by Mr. George Manneh Weah, the retired international soccer legend turned politician. He has endeavored to build upon some of the positive gains of the Sirleaf administration. For example, President Weah has embraced the policy of good neighborliness espoused by his predecessor through close ties with neighboring countries, sustained engagements in regional and continental activities through the MRU, ECOWAS, and AU, as well as reaffirming Liberia's strong commitment to the principles and policies of the UN for global peace, security, and prosperity.

CHAPTER THIRTEEN
Misrepresentation and Distortion of Historical Facts

The highlights in chapter 12 reflecting Liberia's historical role in modern Africa, gathered mostly from eminent political scientist and historian, Dr. D. Elwood Dunn's hitherto unpublished work on the subject matter, is refreshing. This is in consideration that while Liberia is striving to resume its rightful place in the comity of nations, there have been attempts to misrepresent and distort historical facts regarding the country's place as modern Africa's oldest independent republic, which has provided continental leadership.

An example of what is a misrepresentation of historical facts regards information being peddled from some sources as to which country is the oldest independent in Africa as reflected in a BBC online article. In the article, which is part of a series of letters from African journalists published by the BBC, Ghanaian writer Elizabeth Ohene, a former BBC reporter and Ghanaian government minister, said that "Ghana was the first sub-Saharan country to gain independence." The subject of the article was "Africa's love of titles," with a focus on the practice of how African leaders acquire long list of titles ("Letter from Africa: Our Presidents Are Addicted to Titles," BBC online, June 30, 2015).

I have followed Ms. Ohene's work as a journalist over the years with deep respect and admiration. However, as I read her article under review, I was left to wonder, "Where in the world is Liberia located?" Her article, like many similar others promoting Ghana as Africa's oldest independent country, is factually incorrect. Ethiopia and Liberia are the two oldest countries in modern Africa, as have already been reported in this chapter. Ethiopia emerged as an empire during ancient times and long existed as a monarchy until the country was briefly occupied by the Italians from 1935 to 1941. Following the defeat of the Italian army, the deposed emperor of Ethiopia, Haile Selassie, was returned to the throne.

As also reported earlier, Liberia became a haven and a beacon of hope for people of color the world over during the colonial era. Besides the repatriated blacks from the United States and Africans from other parts of the continent, the country also become home to people of African descent from countries in the Caribbean or West Indies. For example, in 1864, President Daniel B. Warner issued a proclamation inviting people from the West Indies, the area where Granada, Jamaica, Trinidad, Barbados, and Guyana are found, to migrate to Liberia. Among the many who accepted the invitation from the various countries were more than 360 Barbadians ("Burleigh Holder Passes," *Liberian Observer* online, August 30, 2018).

The country's open-door (trade and investment) policy meant that not only large multinationals were given opportunities to enter into joint ventures with the Liberian government to exploit the country's natural resources, but its liberal immigration policies also allowed the country to be a haven for both political and economic refugees from around Africa and other parts of the world. The presence of large communities of Lebanese and Indians, among others who have settled in Liberia for generations, reflects the diversity of the country's population.

So was Liberia's support for the emancipation of the entire African continent from colonial subjugation, as have been in this chapter. In his memoir, *I Was There—Reflections of a Liberian Journalist,* legendary journalist Stanton B. Peabody recalls that in 1965, while he was on assignment as a reporter at the Executive Mansion, he met South African freedom fighter Nelson Mandela, who was in the presidential waiting room waiting to be ushered in to meet with President William V. S. Tubman. Mr. Peabody recalls that while he and Mr. Mandela began to talk when he entered the waiting room, then undersecretary of state T. Ernest Eastman called out to Mr. Mandela not to speak to Peabody because he was a reporter. Mr. Mandela was then whisked away into the president's office.

According to Mr. Peabody, Mr. Mandela was making his last visit to Monrovia incognito before returning to South Africa, where he was arrested, tried, and imprisoned for over twenty-seven years ("A Call to Journalism; Part One—The Awaking," page 7, *I Was There*).

It may also be interesting to note that Liberia and Ghana share a very special historical bond. Dr. Kwame Nkrumah, who led that country's independence struggle from British colonial rule and became the first president of the Republic of Ghana, is said to have had a very strong Liberian connection by blood. There are historical accounts that Nkrumah's father was a Liberian native from Maryland County in southeastern Liberia. He migrated to the Gold Coast, which was renamed Ghana during independence, where he married a Ghanaian woman who gave birth to a boy named Francis Weah. During the colonial era, many Liberians predominantly from the coastal areas migrated to the then Gold Coast in search of work.

In an apparent effort to be regarded as a bona fide Ghanaian, Francis Weah was renamed Kwame Nkrumah. Weah is a name native to Liberia, as the last name of Liberia's current president and retired international soccer legend, George Weah, indicates. Could it be a matter of mere historical coincidence that very little is recorded or known about Nkrumah's Liberian father or his Liberian family connection?

As of this publication, there are Liberians who are identified as close blood relatives of Dr. Nkrumah. For example, a nephew from his Liberian half-sister on his father's side, a Liberian engineer, served as a cabinet minister during the regime of military ruler Samuel K. Doe in the 1980s. He and other known Liberian family members of Dr. Nkrumah are in Liberia and abroad.

Because of that special bond regarding Nkrumah, Liberia, then one of the most influential countries on the global stage from the 1950s through the 1970s, was known to have generously supported Ghana's independence struggle. Liberia's president William V. S. Tubman, one of the prominent global leaders back then, was seen like a mentor to Nkrumah, who paid frequent visits to Liberia. History has it that the relationship between the two men was made more special because President Tubman, like Dr. Nkrumah's father, also hailed from Maryland County.

Nevertheless, both Tubman and Nkrumah espoused different ideological positions relative to the bipolar world order that existed. President Tubman was regarded as a pro-Western leader who was a staunch anticommunist or antisocialist while President Nkrumah was an avowed socialist, who became a leading crusader for Pan-Africanism and a united states of Africa. These differences would strain the relationship between the two men.

As he was distanced from Tubman, Dr. Nkrumah developed a kindred spirit with President Ahmed Sekou Toure of Guinea, a liberation fighter and staunch socialist, who also fought for his country's independence from France and became its first president. Like Dr. Nkrumah, President Toure was one of the leading advocates for a united states of Africa during the formation of the OAU. As a manifestation of the special relationship between the two men, when Nkrumah was deposed in Ghana, he went into exile in Guinea, where President Toure made him a co-president. And Tubman was among the first African leaders to pay a visit to the military leaders of Ghana who overthrew Nkrumah.

There are historical accounts that part of the reasons for Nkrumah's overthrow was that many of his key political opponents, who were also involved in the struggle for Ghana's independence, saw him as a foreigner who was dominating them.

In his memoir earlier cited in this chapter, Mr. Peabody, the legendary Liberian journalist, who died in 2013 at the age of eighty, also provided interesting accounts regarding Dr. Nkrumah's very close ties to Liberia, especially his relationship with President Tubman, as Mr. Peabody had the opportunity to interact with him back in those days. In one account, he narrates the story of Henry B. Cole, a Liberian who had migrated to Ghana, then known as the Gold Coast. While in Ghana, he founded and edited the newspaper, the *Daily Graphic*, which agitated for change in the Gold Coast, standing against colonialism and fought alongside such African nationalists as Dr. Nkrumah and other freedom fighters for self-determination and independence for Ghana.

According to Mr. Peabody, during his editorship of the *Graphic*, Cole was said to be a thorn in the flesh of the British colonial masters. They wanted him out of Ghana, but their allegiance to press freedom gained a better part of them and so Cole stayed on.

However, after Ghana became independent and Nkrumah was its President, he and Cole parted ways, as he became just as much a thorn in Nkrumah's flesh. Cole began to oppose, through his editorials, some of the political maneuverings of President Nkrumah. They were no longer allies, and Nkrumah wanted him out of Ghana too. During a state visit to Liberia, Nkrumah intimated to Tubman that Cole was "getting under his skin," but that he did not want to deport Cole because it would not be good for African relations. Tubman promised Nkrumah he would do something about it. His solution was to ask Cole to return home to Liberia to lead the *Liberian Age*, the main government-funded newspaper. After also falling out with Cole due to Cole's editorials that spoke truth to power, President Tubman revealed this incidence at one of his press conferences, during which he raved at Cole for being a troublemaker ("Liberian Journalism in the 1940s," Chapter 3, page 31, *I Was There—Reflections of a Liberian Journalist* by Stanton B. Peabody).

Nkrumah's origin bears similarity to that of former US president Barack Obama, whose father matriculated to the United States from his native Kenya in East Africa for advanced education. It was while in the United States that he married the young American woman that became young Barack's mother. Barack H. Obama

Jr. manifested a monumental event in history as the first African American president of the United States of America.

However, the similarity between the two men does not go any further than that as far as how their respective family background could shed light on the interconnectedness of people the world over is concerned. And here is why. Whereas President Obama's American Kenyan background is being celebrated globally as a reflection of the beauty of human diversity and connectedness, Dr. Nkrumah's Ghanaian Liberian background has continued to be shrouded in "hush-hush," obviously, as someone once put it, out of nationalistic considerations.

Dr. Nkrumah is today celebrated with honor and reverence as one of the great leaders in the history of modern Africa and the world. He was a visionary far ahead of his time. There can be little question that Africa would be a better place today if Dr. Nkrumah's vision for African unity and collective progress had been actualized.

It has been a reality in Africa, as I have endeavored to reflect through this book, that people would use anything within their power and means to suppress whatever situation with which they may not be in agreement. Some of them will actually fight against what is for the common good, to the detriment of general society, because it does not align with their personal desire or interest.

So it was that at the domestic and continental levels, Dr. Nkrumah encountered resistance to changes that were imperative to strengthen Ghana and Africa in general. At the continental and international level, not only was he obstructed in his effort to bring about a united Africa, he also encountered fierce resistance at home for some of his domestic policies and programs that were intended to accelerate Ghana's development. He was accused of putting on the cloak of dictatorship. Out of desperation to stop him in his tracks, there were attempts to assassinate him. Eventually, in February 1966, Dr. Nkrumah was overthrown while he was on a visit to Vietnam. He was forced to live in exile in Guinea, where President Toure made him co-president.

Mr. Ernest A. Jenkins, also known as GI, is a grandson of President Tubman. Mr. Jenkins has often narrated stories of his personal interactions with Dr. Nkrumah. As a young man, Mr. Jenkins said he had the opportunity to interact with Dr. Nkrumah, especially during the period of the former Ghanaian leader's exile in Guinea. Mr. Jenkins said that he had a good friendship with Mr. Stokely Carmichael, the West Indian–born civil rights activist and leader of Black Nationalism in the United States in the 1960s, who became a close aide to Dr. Nkrumah.

According to the *Encyclopedia Britannica*, among prominent roles in the civil rights movement in the United States, Mr. Carmichael served as chairman of the Student Non-violent Coordinating Committee (SNCC), and he and others associated with SNCC supported the nonviolence approach to desegregation espoused by Dr. Martin Luther King Jr. However, he got increasingly frustrated, having witnessed the beatings and murders of several civil rights activist. He was also arrested and jailed for about fifty days in Jackson, Mississippi, for his participation as one of several "Freedom Riders" who traveled through the American South challenging segregation laws in interstate transportation.

During a march in Mississippi, according to the *Encyclopedia Britannica*, Carmichael rallied demonstrators in founding the "black power" movement, which espoused self-defense tactics, self-determination, political and economic power, and racial pride. He became a leader of Black Nationalism in the United States in the

1960s and originator of its rallying slogan, "black power." This was a controversial split from King's ideology of nonviolence and racial integration in the United States.

Faced with growing security and political challenges, Carmichael left the United States in 1969 and moved to Guinea with his wife, now legendary singer Mariam Makeba. There, he changed his name to Kwame Toure, in honor of Dr. Kwame Nkrumah and President Sekou Toure, two leading proponents of Pan-Africanism during that period.

According to Mr. Jenkins, his activities with Mr. Kwame Toure included playing the game of checkers, which was a favorite pastime for Dr. Nkrumah and Mr. Toure. Mr. Jenkins recalled that while Dr. Nkrumah and Mr. Toure were once playing, Dr. Nkrumah asked Jenkins if he could also play. "I told him, 'well I can play but not anywhere good as someone like you, Sir.'" Mr. Jenkins said Dr. Nkrumah responded that he, Jenkins, should not limit his potentials, as there was nothing he could not do with a focused mind and hard work. Following that admonition, Mr. Jenkins said he competed against Dr. Nkrumah several times on the checkerboard, but he lost every match to the now revered African leader.

Mr. Jenkins said it was through his association with Mr. Toure that he began to develop more awareness regarding the African cause, such as the issues of injustice, poverty, and other conditions that affect people of African descent universally. For example, he said, it was through Toure that he got to know that the Catholic Church has had three black popes, something he did not even learn while attending Catholic school in Liberia.

Mr. Jenkins indicated that through his association with Mr. Toure, he also learned that during his tenure as president of Ghana, Dr. Nkrumah had proposed the creation of a joint security command for conflict intervention in Africa, but that such proposal was objected by President Tubman, who did not see the need for such arrangement during those days. However, it would turn out that Liberia would be one of the first countries to benefit from a similar African intervention force, such as the West African peacekeeping force ECOMOG, which intervened to end the civil wars in Liberia and Sierra Leone.

A former Liberian police officer, Mr. Jenkins said he was in active service in the US military when his grandfather, President Tubman, died, and he was given official permission to return to Liberia to attend the funeral. He also narrated accounts of an interesting development which occurred during the funeral of President Tubman. According to him, Dr. Nkrumah came to Liberia disguised to attend the funeral. As the bereaved family and distinguished guests surrounded the grave during the burial ceremony, standing directly across from the Ghanaian military leader on the opposite side of the grave was Dr. Nkrumah. At a point during the ceremony when the Ghanaian leader lifted his head, he found himself looking straight in the eyes of Dr. Nkrumah, who was staring at him. Apparently shocked upon recognizing Nkrumah, the Ghanaian military leader collapsed and was rushed away from the gravesite. Nkrumah's security also immediately whisked him away to his hotel.

Attired in his military outfit and permitted to join members of the Liberian armed forces who participated in the state funeral ceremonies in Monrovia, Mr. Jenkins said he and the group of Liberian soldiers bearing the flags were standing at attention when the Ghanaian leader collapsed a few yards away, and they all rushed over to render whatever assistance was necessary. It was in the midst of that drama that he heard that the Ghanaian leader collapsed after he saw Nkrumah at the gravesite. As the Ghanaian leader was being rushed from the gravesite, Jenkins said he saw another VIP vehicle with security, which was believed to be conveying Dr. Nkrumah, also leaving the scene on speed.

While he was in exile in Guinea, Dr. Nkrumah reportedly died after months of failing health with no family members at his side in April 1972, in a hospital in Bucharest, Romania. He was sixty-two. He is said to have spent almost a year in Romania seeking medical treatment after the government led by Dr. Kofi Busia rejected pleas from Guinea to have him return home to Ghana for medical treatment. Following Nkrumah's death, Guinea resisted the Ghanaian government's demand to turn over his body. The impasse was broken due to the intervention of Liberia's President William Tolbert and a couple of other African leaders who prevailed on President Toure to release the body to Ghana.

President Sekou Toure, who held a state funeral and interred the remains of Dr. Nkrumah, had reportedly demanded that Ghana's military regime drop all criminal charges brought against Nkrumah following his overthrow, and that Nkrumah's remains be accorded all the honors due to a deceased head of state. President Tolbert and Cuban president Fidel Castro were among world leaders at the state funeral in Conakry. Due to breakthrough in negotiation, Nkrumah's body was exhumed and finally flown to Ghana in July 1972 and buried in his home village. In July 1992, twenty years after his death, Nkrumah was reburied with military honors in a mausoleum, erected at the spot where he declared Ghana's independence in 1957.

As has also been a characteristic of the African reality, those who seized power and disrupted Ghana's forward march, proved to be incapable custodians of the public trust, consumed by greed and corruption, as well as the lack of leadership ability for the public good. Ghana would tailspin into years of instability and poverty, as one corrupt and incompetent regime took over from the other.

This is why Ghana was blessed by the ascendency of a patriotic son in the person of Flt Lt. Jerry John Rawlings. He first came to power as a flight lieutenant of the Ghana Air Force following a coup in 1979. After initially handing power over to a civilian government, Rawlings took back control of a country that was literally bleeding to death in 1981, instituted some radical and aggressive reforms and turned Ghana around in the right direction. Like Nkrumah, Rawlings demonstrated true love for his people and a desire to empower them and change their conditions for betterment. He is by no means a perfect individual, as he made his share of mistakes during his leadership of Ghana. However, it can be said without fear of contradiction that it was due to Rawlings's visionary and farsighted leadership that turned Ghana around from a dysfunctional state of governance.

A renewed Ghana under the inspiring leadership of President Rawlings was repositioned as a major player in regional and international affairs. As an example, Ghana played a critical role in the regional and international efforts to end Liberia's civil war. Ghanaian troops were among the original force organized under the auspices of ECOWAS which intervened during the early period of the Liberian civil war in 1990, and Ghanaian forces also helped keep the peace as a part of UNMIL, whose mandate in Liberia ended in March 2018.

During the years of the crises, many Ghanaians gave their lives for peace in Liberia. Ghana hosted the last peace conference in its capital of Accra, which brought together Liberia's warring factions, political parties, and other interest groups. This resulted to the signing of the Accra Comprehensive Peace Accord between the warring factions and the other parties to the conference in August 2003, bringing an end to the civil war. Ghana has also been a strong partner in Liberia's postwar reconstruction, among which was the effort to restore electricity to Liberia.

Ghanaians are an innovative and industrious people. What Ghanaians needed all along were leaders with the vision, such as Dr. Nkrumah and President Rawlings, to create the enabling environment for the people to manifest their potentials and capabilities to highest levels possible.

Take, for example, Ghana's current president Nana Addo Dankwa Akufo-Addo, who is clearly emerging as one of the most eloquent spokespersons for the entire African continent, articulating not just the cause of Ghana but the collective African cause. The Ghana reality, therefore, supports the premise and title of this book that Africa is not poor but poorly managed. Whereas, recalling that Ghana was mired in poverty and instability under leaders who lacked the vision and leadership ability to move the country forward, under the present dispensation of adherence to democracy, good governance, and accountability, the country is rapidly developing into a major regional and continental power.

Even though he was not assassinated in office, Nkrumah's situation bears similarity to President Tolbert of Liberia, as both men were leaders who were seen to be instituting programs and policies for the development of their respective countries and the entire African Continent when they were violently removed from power. As we have found also in Liberia, those who disrupted the order of progress of the country proved to be incapable custodians of the public trust, corrupt and consumed by greed for political power and wealth. I am not unmindful, though, that the settlers-indigenous divide that existed for over a century in which the indigenous population—an overwhelming majority of the population—was discriminated against, was presented as the main reason for the bloody overthrow of Tolbert's government. Although he was part of the old political establishment, Tolbert tried to institute necessary reforms for the betterment of the Liberian people but those reforms were not tangible enough to avert the takeover by noncommissioned soldiers of indigenous background.

Be that as it may, Ghanaians deserve commendation for the significant progress they have made toward healing the wounds of their national past by receiving the remains of Dr. Nkrumah, giving him a state funeral befitting a former head of state, and laying him to rest in a mausoleum that has become a national shrine. For us in Liberia, there has yet to be an official identification where the bodies of Tolbert and other officials killed after the coup were dumped in mass graves. The fact that there is yet no official grave site for the slain president is an indication of the challenges in healing the wounds of our national past.

Another example of what was a glaring attempt to distort historical facts was perpetrated by then Libyan leader, Col. Muammar Gaddafi. During his regime, Gaddafi erected in his hometown of Sirte a huge magnificent conference center called Ouagadougou International Conference Center, named for the capital of the West African nation of Burkina Faso. In the main lobby of the conference center were murals of the "Founding Fathers" of the OAU. However, missing among the founding fathers was the image of Liberia's president William V. S. Tubman, who played a critical leadership role in the founding of the OAU; neither was there any mention of Liberia.

In June 2007, I had the opportunity to accompany President Sirleaf to a summit of heads of state and government of the Community of Sahel-Saharan States, a regional bloc commonly known by the French acronym CENSAD, which was convened in Sirte by Col. Gaddafi. As we entered the main lobby of the

Ouagadougou Conference Center and I saw the murals, out of curiosity, I tried to inquire as to why President Tubman's image was not also included among the founding fathers. However, no one that I talked to could offer any reasonable explanation for Tubman's exclusion. That experience at Gaddafi's conference center became the motivation for this chapter, which is intended to highlight Liberia's role, gradually being buried by those who may not subscribe to Tubman's position regarding continental unity.

The argument has been proffered that Africa's weakness and underdevelopment are due in part to the fragmentation of the continent into different countries. That a united states of Africa would have been better positioned in dealing with collective African issues, as the saying goes, there is strength in unity. Considering the collective challenges across the divided continent, these arguments have gained more merits in recent years. The restructuring of the OAU into the African Union (AU) is along the lines of Africa's integration and prosperity. And some effort has continued to explore the possibility of a united states of Africa.

Colonel Gaddafi was one recent African leader who made a very strong push for the creation of a united states of Africa. With the blessing of Libya's oil wealth, he provided significant funding for the necessary restructuring to bring the AU into existence. This may explain why, in the conference hall, Gaddafi selected to display the images of only those African leaders who supported a united states of Africa as the "Founding Fathers" of the OAU, leaving out the others. However, choosing to cherry-pick historical accounts, so to speak, in order to serve a narrow interest amounts to a distortion of history. Even though one is not unmindful that the Libyan strongman was known to be an unconventional leader who flouted established norms as he wished.

His ambition was to become the first leader of a united states of Africa, a cause that was seen to have motivated him to spend hundreds of millions of dollars on various development projects in many parts of Africa.

Gaddafi also regarded himself as a champion in the liberation fight against imperialist domination of Africa by not only supporting anticolonial liberation movements in various parts of the continent but he supported military takeovers and insurgencies in countries that were seen to be pro-western.

Mr. Taylor's destructive activities also plunged neighboring Sierra Leone into a bloody civil war, followed by Côte d'Ivoire. Neighboring Guinea was also racked by Taylor supported armed insurgency. The Sierra Leone civil war, which took place from 1991 to 2002, caused the death of an estimated 50,000 people. As part of their method to terrorize the people, the rebels cut off the limbs of many of their victims.

Thanks to Nigeria's unyielding resolve to contain the spread of Taylor's destructive influence in the subregion, which had the full backing of Gaddafi, who saw the insurgencies as an opportunity to extend his sphere of influence in West Africa. This justifies my point earlier that a strong and prosperous Nigeria is a force for good in Africa and the world at large. Nigeria was one country in Africa Gaddafi could not bend to his will. This was because Nigeria did not need his money, the millions he threw at those poor struggling countries with their hands stretched, so to speak, beseeching the benevolence of the great leader of the Libyan Arab Jamahiriya, as the country was officially known during Gaddafi's regime.

During the course of his regime, Colonel Gaddafi, who was in power from 1969 to 2011, demonstrated a strong interest in building partnership with Liberia. For example, during the administration of Liberia's President William R. Tolbert, who succeeded President Tubman upon his death, the Libyan leader seemed to have hit it off with Tolbert, who, unlike Tubman, extended Liberia's relationship to communist and socialist countries through diplomatic ties and other areas of cooperation.

In the 1970s, economic joint ventures between both countries were established through the Liberian-Libyan Holding Companies, which contributed to Liberia's economic growth. One of the major landmarks in Monrovia is the nearly ten-story Pan-African Plaza building, constructed in the 1970s as the headquarters of the Liberian-Libyan Holding Companies. The Pan-African Plaza, which is within a quarter mile from the Executive Mansion, served as the headquarters of UNMIL during the UN peacekeeping operation in Liberia, which ended in March 2018.

However, Colonel Gaddafi's unpredictability became evident in 1980, when President Tolbert, who was the sitting chairman of the OAU, was assassinated in a bloody military coup that shocked the world and enraged many of the African leaders. So anguished was then Nigerian president Shehu Shagari that he was said to have expressed that he will not shake the hands of Master Sergeant Samuel Doe, who led the coup, because they were stained with blood.

While many of the African leaders were devastated by the tragic death of President Tolbert, seen to be a progressive leader who was instituting policies and programs for Liberia's and Africa's transformation, Gaddafi broke ranks with them by recognizing the new military rulers in Monrovia. Hoping to woo the young and inexperienced military ruler into his sphere of influence, Gaddafi also extended an invitation for Doe to visit Libya, along with offers of assistance to the new regime.

Concerned by the Libyan leader's diplomatic move toward Liberia, the United States quickly acted to ensure that Gaddafi did not establish a foothold in a country that some have dubbed America's backyard. US assistant secretary of state Richard Moose reportedly flew to Liberia in a chartered jet with US$10 million in cash after the coup to urge Doe not to turn to Libya for financial assistance ("Liberia-Libya Relations," Wikipedia).

Head of state Doe soon became suspicious of Gaddafi's motives, and relations between both countries were strained. Relations soured to a point where Doe closed down the Libyan embassy in Monrovia and expelled Libyan diplomats from Liberia. So hostile was the relationship that speaking upon his return from an OAU summit, Doe said that he almost got into a fistfight with Gaddafi for the Libyan leader's relentless criticism of the United States. Doe said he had to stand up for America out of deep respect for the historical ties subsisting between Liberia and the United States. He also accused Gaddafi of supporting terrorism and other acts of destabilization in Africa.

Doe became very closely aligned with Nigeria to the chagrin of Gaddafi, who saw Nigeria as a major obstacle to the extension of his sphere of influence in the West African subregion.

This is why, in view of the above, among other geopolitical considerations, Gaddafi decided to finance Taylor's insurgency to eject Doe from power by force of arms. No wonder why he was irate when Taylor was arrested in Nigeria and turned over to the international war crimes court for Sierra Leone for prosecution on war crimes and crimes against humanity.

Upon assuming office, Madam President was keen to cultivate a special bond with her "Brother Leader," cognizant of the potential danger Gaddafi represented to Liberia's peace and stability. She paid frequent visits to him, but he never visited Liberia, even though he once came as close as neighboring Sierra Leone.

On the other hand, Colonel Gaddafi badly needed Madam President to use the full measure of her influence to support his goal for the establishment of a united states of Africa, of which he had positioned himself to be its first president. However, President Sirleaf had to thread carefully so as not to upset Nigeria, one of Liberia's most strategic ally, which was lukewarm toward Gaddafi's united states of Africa crusade.

Liberian-Libyan relations took another dramatic turn when Monrovia broke diplomatic relations on June 14, 2011, at the height of the civil war that ignited in Libya, leading to Gaddafi's eventual overthrow and assassination by Libyan rebels. The announcement came as air raids by the North Atlantic Treaty Organization (NATO) continued to bombard that North African country in a bid to depose Colonel Gaddafi. Liberia said it decided to sever diplomatic relations with Libya as a result of reported atrocities perpetrated by the Libyan leader.

Liberia's move to sever ties with Libya came after then US secretary of state Hillary Rodham Clinton urged African leaders to abandon Col Gaddafi and embrace democratic reforms. Secretary Clinton made the call when she spoke at a summit of the AU in the Ethiopian capital of Addis Ababa in June 2011, the first US secretary of state to address the AU.

Clinton said, "It is true that Gaddafi has played a major role in providing financial support for many African nations and institutions, including the AU. But it has become clear that we have long past the time when he can remain in power" ("Clinton Urges Africa to Drop Gaddafi," Reuters online, June 13, 2011).

Immediately following the AU summit, Monrovia severed ties with Tripoli. The announcement also came on the eve of President Sirleaf's visit to Washington, during which a potential for retribution from Gaddafi as a result of Liberia's action against him was among matters of bilateral and multilateral concern discussed with high-level American officials. In 2012, however, Liberia restored relations with the internationally recognized Libyan government that took over from Col. Gaddafi

It was at the CEN-SAD summit in Sirte, where I accompanied Madam President, that I had the opportunity to be within close proximity of Col. Gaddafi and to have a handshake with him. He appeared to be an intense individual, who employed various means possible to bring the dream of a united states of Africa into reality. He verbally chastised his fellow African leaders, some of whom, he said, were dragging their feet in relations to the creation of a united Africa.

To attend that summit, the president and her delegation flew to Sirte on a small presidential jet, courtesy of the benevolent leader. As we descended and landed in Sirte around 8–9:00 PM, I was simply wowed by the lights and beauty of the place. They we were coming from a broken city that was in pitch darkness due to lack of electricity, and here we were in a place that was once a little desert village being transformed into a metropolis.

Author Gabriel Williams (R) seated at the magnificent Ouagadougou Conference Center in Sirte, Libya during a summit of African leaders hosted by Libyan leader Col. Muammar Gaddafi in 2007. (Courtesy, the Author)

Some members of the Liberian government delegation flying from Libya on a presidential plane owned by Libyan leader Col. Muammar Gaddafi in 2007. (Courtesy, the Author)

It is sad to note that since Gaddafi was captured and killed in Sirte, his hometown, which, like the rest of Libya, has been in total ruins, as the country has also been drowning in a state of instability, with different armed groups locked in a bloody contest for power, as was the case in Liberia during its civil war.

There can be little question that Gaddafi meant well for the progress of Africa, a cause to which he committed hundreds of millions of dollars. However, another disturbing side to this African benefactor was his propensity to resort to violence and destruction of human life, if that was what it took, to consolidate his political power and extend his sphere of influence.

CHAPTER FOURTEEN
Negative Image Undermines Liberia's and Africa's Progress

On September 20, 2018, the *New York Times* published an article titled "$100 Million in Cash Vanishes in Liberia, and Fingers Start Pointing." Part of the article is as follows:

Containers full of newly minted currency worth more than $100 million have gone missing in Liberia, setting off fingers pointing and travel bans as officials puzzle over the mystery in one of the poorest countries in the world.

The cash is said to have been shipped from Sweden late last year, in the midst of Liberia's elections to choose a successor to President Ellen Johnson Sirleaf, according to Front Page Africa, the country's leading investigative newspaper. Voters elected George Weah, an international soccer star.

Liberia does not have its own mint. Its currency, the Liberian dollar, is printed outside of the country with the approval of the Central Bank.

The disappearance has caused public outrage in a nation that has long been dogged by corruption scandals. Blame for the missing money is being passed around, with Mr. Weah's opponents accusing him and his supporters of blaming Ms. Sirleaf.

The plot thickened . . . when the Ministry of Information issued a list of 15 'persons of interest' who have been barred from travel. Among them was Milton Weeks, a former Central Bank governor who worked in Ms. Sirleaf's government and resigned in July. Also on the list was Charles Sirleaf, Ms. Sirleaf's son, who is a deputy governor of the Central Bank in the Weah administration. He held the same post during his mother's tenure.

The disappearance was first reported by the news outlet Hot Pepper, which specializes in covering political scandals. The government, which initially denied that the money was missing, eventually confirmed that it could not account for the currency, and ordered an investigation.

In the wake of this mysterious development, President Weah told the nation that the case will be fully investigated, and anyone found culpable for the alleged disappearance of the billions missing will bear the full weight of the law. The government also announced that international experts, including the US Federal Bureau of Investigation (FBI), had been invited to help with the investigation.

As Liberia grappled with the scandal came media reports that the US Federal Reserve had declared its severance of relationships with the Central Bank of Liberia until there was clarity to the state of confusion regarding the alleged "missing billions." The US dollar is legal tender in Liberia, and there were concerns that the disappearance of billions of Liberian dollar banknotes, which could be traded for US dollars on the open market currency could lead to situations in which money from illegal, drug, or terrorist-related sources, could be laundered in the Liberian economy.

The newly minted amount of Liberian dollar bills reported missing was L$16 billion, equivalent to US$104 million. As someone put it, the story of missing containers of billions of dollars is truly comical, if it was not deeply troubling, especially for a country that is rated as one of the poorest in the world, as the *New York Times* report indicates. This is a country with majority of the population unemployed and the people have endured extreme poverty.

On the heels of the scandal that had generated global media headlines, Mr. Weah made his first trip to the United States as president of Liberia to attend the Seventy-first Session of the UN General Assembly in New York. His stay in New York was characterized by protests from Liberian groups advocating for return of the "missing billions" and for the establishment of a war and economic crimes court in Liberia. There were also demonstrations back in Liberia by civil society organizations and others who demanded return of the "missing billions," and they submitted petitions to the US Embassy, missions of the UN, European Union, ECOWAS, among other partners, seeking international intervention regarding the money.

Upon his return to Liberia from the UN General Assembly, President Weah said he was embarrassed by questions from many of the world leaders he encountered regarding the "missing billions." Liberia's international partners and many people around the world were left wondering, how can this happen in a normal functioning country? Stories about the mysterious money disappearance also generated a comic relief of global proportions, with social media saturated by jokes and cartoons depicting the disappearance of containers full of money.

For example, while getting some groceries from a shop in my Washington DC neighborhood at the time news of the "missing billions" generated public interest, I encountered a mother and two children. The children had picked up more groceries than their mother was prepared to pay for. While telling them to take the items back, with laughter, she said something to the effect, "Do I look like I've got some of the billions of dollars gone missing in Africa?" Then another complete stranger near the lady who was also in the store doing his shopping, chimed in, laughing and naming Liberia as the African country.

And that set off an open conversation about the money, as I listened close by and pretended to be doing my shopping. In reference to Liberia, the man said it was a tragedy that one of the world's poorest countries, which the United States had recently rescued from being destroyed from the Ebola epidemic due to very poor health care system, can have billions of dollars missing when that money could do so much to improve the conditions of their people. He said their leaders always come with hands stretched begging for aid, which they would squander and leave their people poor and destitute. He wondered how the United States will use taxpayers' money to continue to assist countries whose leaders are so corrupt and greedy and they do not show any regard for the well-being of their own people. No wonder why, he furthered, President Donald Trump called those kinds of countries "shitholes" and that he supported President Trump's position to cut off US aid to countries that are not seeking to advance the interest of their own people.

Following weeks of uncertainty regarding the scandal, the governor of the Central Bank of Liberia (CBL), Mr. Nathaniel Patray, said in a statement that the money was secured and in the vault and not missing as speculated. According to Mr. Patray's statement, "There is no such record showing that such money has not been delivered to the CBL ("Case Closed – No Money Missing?" *Liberian Observer* online editorial, October 3, 2018).

The global media reports about the disappearance of billions of dollars in Liberia had a serious negative impact on the country's image internationally.

Like my experience in the store where those who were conversing did not even know me or recognize that I was listening, I departed the store feeling ashamed and demeaned due to the fact of being a Liberian. Many Liberians everywhere were also not only embarrassed but shaken as well by reports of the mysterious disappearance of billions of dollars. Especially at a time the country had been declared broke amid grave economic challenges and Liberians faced extreme hardship and depravation.

Less than a week before news broke about the "missing billions," I represented the Embassy of Liberia near Washington at the dedicatory ceremony of a historical marker at the St. David's Episcopal Church and School in Ashburn, Virginia, in memory of Ms. Margaret Mercer, an educator and abolitionist, who also arranged and financed the repatriation of many former slaves from the United States to Liberia in the 1830s.

During that well-attended and impressive event, which was also graced by the presence of many local and state officials, I recalled the long-standing historical ties subsisting between the Republic of Liberia and the state of Virginia dating from the founding of Liberia, as many of the country's founders from the United States originated from Virginia (see chapter 1).

In this light, I called for strong partnership between the Republic of Liberia and the state of Virginia, USA, especially in the area of education and in economic activities. I pointed out that an enhanced relationship between Liberia and Virginia with a focus on education and business would be mutually beneficial. I also noted that Liberia is well endowed with natural resources, and the country is also ideal for the establishment of light and heavy manufacturing industries in agriculture and other areas to add value to the resources, which could expand more Virginia business outreach into West Africa. On the other hand, I intoned, Liberians could benefit from the education and training for empowerment, as well as the employment and revenue that could be realized from such partnership with the state of Virginia.

Following my Virginia remarks and news reports about the "missing billions" in Liberia, I had a conversation with an American businessman who, for some time, had shown interest in investing in Liberia and was close to planning a trip there to explore business possibilities. He had visited Ghana a few times, where he had established business connections.

The businessman said to me, "Thank you for representing your country well, by so eloquently articulating the possibilities that are there for successful business ventures." However, he added that news out of Liberia did not show that the business atmosphere there was encouraging. Then he asked, "What protection is in your country for any business venture against illegal activities when billions of dollars are missing from the government itself and no one in authority appeared to know what happened to such astronomical amount of money?"

My only response to the businessman was that the Liberian government had opened an investigation to determine what happened regarding the reported "missing billions," as President Weah had promised to do. And following appeal to the United States for assistance to conduct the investigation, the US Agency for International Development (USAID) assisted by recommending the auditing firm Kroll Associates to undertake the task.

Following conclusion of the investigation, the former governor of the Central Bank of Liberia, Mr. Milton Weeks, and the deputy governor, Mr. Charles Sirleaf, son of former president Sirleaf, along with three other staff of the bank, were arrested and charged with economic sabotage in connection with the "missing billions."

The investigation found that the Central Bank of Liberia had acted unilaterally and unlawfully by printing and importing into the country three times the amount of banknotes it had been authorized to do ("Sirleaf's Son charged with Economic Crimes," BBC Africa Live, March 4, 2019).

The Weah administration was also criticized after the Kroll investigation and another investigation found there was lack of accountability for $25 million imported into the country in 2018 on orders of the Weah administration.

While Liberians were grappling with the mystery surrounding the "missing billions," *Forbes*, the internationally reputable American business magazine, ranked Liberia as the first on the list of the top 10 worst countries for business in Africa in 2018. Forbes, whose annual report is noted to be based on studies conducted of the business climate of various countries, is said to look at several key indicators. The magazine's ranking of each country covered by the survey is tallied after the evaluation of several factors including the following: property rights; innovation; taxes; technology; corruption; infrastructure; market size; political risk; freedom (personal, trade, and monetary); red tape; and investor protection. In 2018, *Forbes* determined the best countries for business by rating 153 nations on 15 different factors, including those identified ("Best Countries for Business 2018: Behind the Numbers," Forbes.com, October 14, 2018).

How disappointing that Liberia, which recorded an average growth rate of 7.53 percent between 2006 and 2013 and ranked as one of Africa's fastest-growing economies, was experiencing such economic decline that it had again to become one of the worst business destinations in Africa. Equally disheartening is the fact that the *Forbes* report placed Liberia behind the Democratic Republic of Congo, Mauritania, Togo, Zimbabwe, Burundi, Guinea, Libya, Gambia, and Chad. Most of the countries listed ahead of Liberia in the category of worst business destinations have recently been or are being faced with instability and poor governance. Therefore, the poor ranking of countries like Libya, DR Congo, and Burundi, for example, did not come as a total surprise, as compared to the rapid decline in Liberia's ranking.

The United Kingdom was ranked as the best country in the world for doing business in 2018. On the African front, South Africa clinched the first position on the index for best country to do business on the continent.

South Africa was ranked forty-eighth in the world as the best place on the index for business, followed by Morocco on fifty-fifth position, and Rwanda, third in Africa and seventy-ninth position on the global index.

No doubt, Liberia's image at home and abroad was injured by the widespread reports surrounding the "missing billions," as well as reports of troubling economic signs, as reflected by the Forbes 2018 report.

The Liberia/Africa Image Problem

It is owing to the kinds of developments, as reflected above, that whenever there has been discussion regarding countries like Liberia and Africa as a whole, people are often left scratching their heads pondering a question along the lines of, how can a country or a continent that is so well endowed with resources continue to be so poor and underdeveloped?

One answer that has remained constant, as reflected throughout the pages of this publication, is that poor governance, manifested by corruption and political misrule, are vices that have gravely undermined the stability and progress of Liberia and Africa in general and contributed to the continent's negative image abroad.

Africa has been poor because, as Kenyan legal luminary and very eloquent public speaker Professor Patrice L. O. Lumumba once noted, since independence, African leaders have demonstrated consistently that they are not working in the interest of their people. "We live in a continent where we celebrate thieves and vilify good men and women; that is the tragedy of Africa," he said at an anti-corruption convention ("Speech by Prof PLO Lumumba at the 3rd Anti-Corruption Convention," published on YouTube, January 7, 2014).

There can be no question that Africa will earn the respect it deserves from the rest of the world only when African countries begin to demonstrate the ability to effectively manage their own affairs to improve the conditions of the African people. The world will show Africa more respect when African leaders demonstrate more that they are putting the interest of Africa and the African people first by actions taken to ensure progress. Similarly, Africa will be treated with contempt by others as long as many African countries continue to remain poor and underdeveloped due to bad governance.

For example, on January 11, 2018, United States President Donald J. Trump ignited a firestorm that generated widespread national and international outrage and condemnation when he reportedly described Haiti, El Salvador, and African nations as "shithole countries." President Trump was meeting with members of the United States Congress to discuss a bipartisan immigration deal when he reportedly grew frustrated at the suggestion that immigrants with protected status in the United States would need that status restored. Immigrants from Haiti, El Salvador, and African countries—including Liberia—were beneficiaries of the temporary protected status (TPS), which enabled them to legally reside in the United States.

President Trump was said to have told the lawmakers that instead of granting temporary residency to citizens of countries affected by natural disasters, war, or epidemics, the United States must instead bring more people from countries like Norway. The population of Norway is Caucasian while the country is one of the most developed in Europe and the world.

"Why are we having all these people from shithole countries come here," President Trump inquired during the meeting with lawmakers at the White House, according to the *Washington Post* newspaper ("Trump Derides Protections for Immigrants from 'Shithole' Countries," *Washington Post*, January 12, 2018). He also suggested that he would be open more to immigrants from Asian countries because he felt that they help the United States economically.

According to the *Washington Post*, Mr. Trump's vulgar and racist outburst shocked and embarrassed many Americans. The American media, along with politicians and other leaders of diverse background, blasted Mr. Trump, recalling his defense of a group of white supremacists who on August 12, 2017, screamed racial, ethnic, misogynistic epithets at blacks and other protesters at a white supremacist and white nationalist rally, organized by the "Unite the Right" racist supremacist movement in Charlottesville, Virginia. Heather Heyer, a young lady who was among those protesting against the white supremacists, was killed when a vehicle driven by a supporter of the racist movement, plowed into a large crowd of protesters.

In his reaction to the Charlottesville violence, President Trump made the following comments, which generated the public backlash: "We condemn in the strongest terms this egregious display of hatred, bigotry, and violence on many sides, many sides" ("A Year after Charlottesville, Not Much Has Changed for Trump," NPR online, August 11, 2018).

While conversing with a Caucasian friend and media colleague amid the outrage generated by the president's comments, he asked me a question to which I did not respond but left me scratching my head. The question was something like, even though the comments were derogatory and unacceptable, but if conditions in Africa did not resemble that of a "shithole," then why are thousands of Africans from various countries running away from home in desperation, perishing in the Sahara Desert, and drowning in the Mediterranean to get to Europe?

My colleague and I are comfortable discussing sensitive racial matters without fear of provoking conflict, which has become a common experience at a time of heightened racial tensions in the United States, Europe, and other parts of the world due to the reported rise of nationalism and extreme right-wing political activities. The heightened tensions have led to attacks against minorities based on race and religion, such as the June 17, 2015, shooting death of nine black church members who were attending Bible study at a predominantly African American church in Charleston, South Carolina, by a twenty-two-year-old avowed white supremacist, who said he wanted the shootings to bring back segregation or perhaps start a race war ("Dylann Roof Sentenced to Death for Killing 9 Black Members in South Carolina, January 10, 2017").

Another human tragedy that was blamed on the heightened racial tensions was the October 27, 2018, attack on a Jewish synagogue in Pittsburgh, Pennsylvania. Armed with an AR-15 style assault rifle and at least three handguns, a man shouting anti-Semitic slurs opened fire inside the synagogue, killing at least 11 congregants and wounding four police officers and two others, authorities said ("11 Killed in Synagogue Massacre: Suspect Charged with 29 Counts," *New York Times* online, October 27, 2018).

Despite the confrontational racial environment, my colleague and I are able to hold the kinds of conversations where you are comfortable to express your honest feeling about given situations. We joke each other without fear of being accused of prejudice. As the saying goes, fact comes through joke, a reality which I think has been mutually beneficial in our understanding of the perspectives of another person on the other side of the equation. We also usually argue about how the world is backsliding into authoritarianism, while there is an alarming rise in right-wing nationalism in the United States, Europe, and other parts of the world.

As have been reflected in this book, the story of Liberia is similar to that of many countries in Africa and other parts of the world that are not functioning to their full potentials due to poor governance, to the detriment of the common good of society or country. Poor governance has fueled instability, bloodshed, and destruction in Africa and other parts of the world, leading to the progress of affected countries slowed or reversed.

An example of a country whose potentials are seen to be underutilized is resource-rich Nigeria, which surpassed South Africa as the continent's second-largest economy. In 2011, the Organization of Petroleum Exporting Countries (OPEC) ranked Nigeria its second biggest crude oil exporter by volume, next to Saudi Arabia. OPEC statistics revealed that Nigeria earned US$70.58 billion from the oil exports, according to the July 26, 2011, online publication of *Sweet Crude Reports*, a review of the Nigerian energy industry.

Nigeria reached this peak in the export of crude oil in 2011 even after the country's oil production had been disrupted by years of violent campaign by militants in the main producing region of Niger Delta. According to *Sweet Crude Reports*, attacks on oil-producing facilities between 2006 and 2009 cut the country's production around 1.3 million barrel a day until a government amnesty offered to the militants ended hostilities in the region.

A well-functioning and prosperous Nigeria, Africa's most populous country of 190 million people, is a force for good in Africa and the world as a whole. An example that a strong and vibrant Nigeria is necessary for Africa's peace, security, and progress was demonstrated during the brutal and barbaric civil wars in Liberia and Sierra Leone, respectively.

When chaos and bloodshed consumed both Liberia and Sierra Leone, Nigeria led the two intervention and peacekeeping forces under the auspices of the Economic Community of West African States (ECOWAS) subregional bloc. Nigeria committed hundreds of millions of dollars and thousands of troops during the course of the respective civil wars in Liberia and Sierra Leone. More importantly, thousands of Nigerians made the ultimate sacrifice with their lives for the restoration of peace to Liberia and Sierra Leone.

On the economic front, Nigerian businesses extending operations to Liberia and other parts of the subregion and beyond is a major move toward Africa's economic empowerment, integration, and development. On the personal level, Nigerians are a very warm and generous people, who were mostly wonderful hosts to tens of thousands of Liberian refugees during the civil war. Liberian refugees in Nigeria were not subjected to the kinds of abuse as was the case in a certain other African country, where Liberian refugees endured harassment, imprisonment, and deportation.

As someone rightly indicated, Nigeria is a sleeping giant, whose potentials have yet to be fully utilized due to the vestiges of corruption and poor governance. Otherwise, there is no reason why a Nigerian space program is not a world leader; otherwise, there is no reason Nigerian scientific and medical institutions are not on the cutting edge of global technology when there are numerous Nigerian scientists around the globe; otherwise, there is no reason why millions of Nigerians are impoverished; and there is no reason why Africa's leading oil exporter have continued to suffer fuel shortages and regular electric power outages.

Added to Nigeria's woes has been the ongoing campaign by Boko Haram, the terrorist group that have sought to terminate Western education and impose strict Islamic sharia laws in the country. Boko Haram escalated its murderous rampage, slaughtering thousands in a series of attacks, including some spectacular attacks in Abuja, the Nigerian capital. An audacious act by this terrorist group was the 2014 kidnap of 276 female students from the town of Chibok in Borno State, northern Nigeria, which awoke the world to the savagery of the extremist group.

There are some reports that point to poverty as a major root cause for Boko Haram's creation and its reign of terror. These reports are supported by experts on Nigeria who argue that many of these fighters were driven to join the murderous group mostly out of economic gain rather than the propagation of political or religious ideologies. Northern Nigeria, where Boko Haram originated and has perpetrated some of the worst carnages, is reported to be one of the poorest regions of that very rich and vast country. Poverty is a perfect ingredient for insecurity.

Applauding African Countries Making Progress Due to Good Governance

It is apparent that African countries that are adhering to practices of good governance and making efforts to improve conditions of their people are enjoying peace and stability and are making progress in economic and infrastructural development.

Prominent among the few progressive African countries is the southern African nation of Botswana, which has had the highest average economic growth rate in the world, averaging about 9 percent per year from 1966 to 1999, and the country's economic growth has been on par with some of Asia's largest economies, according to Wikipedia. Botswana's impressive economic record has been built on a foundation of diamond mining, prudent fiscal policies, international financial and technical assistance, and was rated the least corrupt country in Africa, according to an international corruption watchdog, Transparency International.

Another African country that is blazing the trail in technology, as well as achieving impressive gains in economic and infrastructural development, is Rwanda. After the Rwanda genocide in 1994 that killed an estimated 500,000 to 1 million people, the Tutsi-led government in the landlocked east African nation began a major program to improve the country's economy and reduce its dependence on subsistence farming. The failing economy had been a major factor behind the genocide, as was overpopulation and the resulting competition for scarce farmland and other resources.

Under what is clearly seen to be a visionary leadership, the government of President Paul Kagame focused primarily on building up Rwanda's manufacturing and service industries, as well as infrastructural development, according to Wikipedia.

The once war-ravaged country of Rwanda entered a high period of economic growth in 2006. The following year, it managed to register a growth rate of 8 percent, turning the country into one of the fastest-growing economies in Africa. This sustained growth has succeeded in reducing poverty, with growth between 2006 and 2011, reducing the percentage of the country's population living in poverty from 57 percent to 45 percent, according to Wikipedia online.

A major transformation that has taken place in Rwanda, which has few natural resources, is the empowerment of women. According to a May 28, 2010, report in the London-based the *Guardian* newspaper, women occupy some of the most important government ministries and make up 56 percent of the country's parliamentarians, including the speaker—giving Rwanda's parliament the distinction of having a higher percentage of women than any other parliament in the world.

As another example of Rwanda's progress, in June 2018, the global car manufacturing company Volkswagen (VW) launched a car assembly plant in the Rwandan capital of Kigali, which is regarded to be one of the cleanest cities in Africa. According to a Global Information Network report published by InDepth News (IDN)—a flagship agency of the International Press Syndicate—Volkswagen's new factory is the fourth of its kind in Africa after Nigeria, Kenya, and South Africa. Polo is the first model being made at the site to be followed by the Passat, Tiguan, Amarok, and Teramont models.

The IDN report stated that VW's US$20 million investment will create up to 1,000 jobs, and is an example of much-needed spending by overseas firms in the nation, which received US$1 billion in foreign aid and development assistance but was making business-friendly reforms.

Speaking at the launch of the VW assembly plant, President Kagame said, "Africa does not need to be a dumping ground for second hand cars or second hand anything. In the long run, you end up paying a higher price anyway." President Kagame said that Africa is not merely positioning itself as a new low-cost hub to manufacture goods for exports. "African consumers will also be among the biggest contributors to growth in global demand in the years ahead," he said ("Rwanda President Launches VW's Car Assembly Plant in Kigali," *IDN*, July 25, 2018).

Under President Kagame's visionary leadership, Rwanda has been striving to be an example of the transformation that Africa needs to empower its people and bring about sustainable progress. Rwanda's growing international appeal as a peaceful, prospering, and conducive business destination is because of the reforms and progress the country has made to be taken seriously by international investors. With more industries and investment opportunities opening up in Rwanda, the country's respect and international profile are growing.

In the West African subregion, Ghana has emerged as a model of political stability and economic progress. According to Wikipedia online, Ghana is the seventh best governed country, fifth-most stable country, and thirteenth most developed country in Africa. It has the continent's seventh-largest economy by purchasing power parity. The country has one of the fastest-growing economies in the world, with the highest per capita income in West Africa. Ghana has enjoyed steady progress since its return from military rule to democratic rule in 1992, enhancing a democratic environment that promotes transparency and accountability.

I am very impressed by the aggressive reforms Ghanaians instituted to turn around a country that was wallowing in a state of dysfunction in the 1970s and '80s. As a teenager in junior and senior high school during that period, I remember that a large number of Ghanaians, as was the case with Guineans, Sierra Leoneans, Nigerians, and other Africans, flocked to Liberia, where the United States dollar is legal tender. These Africans had immigrated to Liberia to experience better living conditions and opportunities, including the opportunity for easier travel to the United States. Many Ghanaians became teachers in Liberian schools while Ghanaian traders came to Liberia to purchase merchandize, including toiletries such as soap and toothpaste.

Considering that Ghana, which was very unstable and poor, has managed to reverse its losses and is now positioned as a regional power in Africa, is a testament to the resilience of the Ghanaian people and what a country can accomplish in a democratic environment where the government adheres to the principles of accountability and transparency.

The government of President Julius Maada Bio of Sierra Leone, which assumed power in 2018, must be highly applauded for undertaking aggressive economic reforms, especially the fight against corruption, which President Bio has described as a national security threat.

As a mark of appreciation for President Bio's economic reforms and the fight against corruption, in March 2019, the World Bank Group (WBG) announced that the WBG had committed US$325 million to increase financial support to Sierra Leone.

Making the announcement during a meeting with President Bio, who was on a visit to Washington, the interim president of the World Bank Group, Madam Kristalina Georgieva, commended President Bio for his bold economic reforms.

If the path of progress that Sierra Leone has embarked upon during the tenure of President Bio continues, that country, which is well endowed with natural resources, has the opportunity to rise from the pit where it has been stuck as one of the world's poorest countries. With proper management of the resources, there is no reason why resource-rich Sierra Leone cannot be a prosperous country.

The Global Refugee and Migrant Crises Caused by Instability and Poverty

Similar to Liberia, there are other countries that were even more developed or prosperous, such as Libya, Iraq, and Syria, which have been plunged in mindless bloodshed and destruction as a result of decades of bad governance or political misrule. The political upheavals in those countries were compounded by ill-conceived international interventions. Like Liberians, people in those countries, especially the poor, have suffered the most from starvation and displacement, and they have been terrorized by armed men.

Blessed with massive oil wealth, Iraq and Libya were major players on the global economic stage while Syria was a regional power in her own right with its military occupation of Lebanon for years. Fast-forward to this period, refugees from Syria and Iraq, terrorized and dispossessed, were reported to be generally middle class and well-educated people with diverse professional background before the onset of the upheavals that became human tragedies in the region.

Following decades of the rule of "Strong Men" in those countries—Saddam Hussein of Iraq, Muammar Gaddafi of Libya, Bashar al-Assad of Syria—the three countries have been engulfed in total chaos. Saddam and Gaddafi were captured and killed following the collapse of their respective regimes while Assad has continued to hang on to power as of the date of this publication, thanks to the very strong military and diplomatic backing of the Russian government of President Vladimir Putin. The presence of Russian troops in Syria has been credited for the survival of the Assad regime.

Attempts to remove each of these three regimes from power by force of arms generated an implosion that led to widespread instability in the Middle East and surrounding regions. Contending armed factions, prominent among them jihadist movements, have battled for control of territory and resources.

For example, large swathes of territory in Syria and Iraq were occupied by the jihadist group so-called Islamic State (IS), which declared its occupied territory a caliphate in 2014. Also known by its Arab name Daesh, the group's regular Internet postings of images of public beheading of victims, burning of people in cage, suicide bombings that killed large numbers indiscriminately and other unspeakable acts of brutality brought chills down the spine of global viewers.

IS has also spawned affiliates elsewhere in the Middle East, Asia, and Africa like the Nigerian terrorist group Boko Haram while some individuals who carried out terrorist acts in the Europe and the United States have claimed allegiance to IS.

Parts of Libya, Somalia, and the Sahel region in Africa were occupied by contending armed factions, the most dangerous of which were Islamist groups seeking to impose Islamic rules on the general population by perpetrating some of the most heinous crimes against humanity.

IS and other militant groups in Libya reportedly occupied territories containing major oil wealth to sustain their enterprise of death and destruction. These extremist groups have also resorted to extortion and kidnapping to fill their coffers. By the most unspeakable acts of barbarity and brutality committed against defenseless populations that include children, women, and the elderly, IS and the other jihadist groups have proved to be apocalyptic, as they glorified death and demonstrated a very strong willingness to die and kill others for their cause.

The security and economic meltdown in the Middle East and surrounding regions created what was regarded as the greatest wave of human migration since the Second World War. With millions of people violently uprooted from their homes, vast numbers of migrants and refugees fleeing into Europe plunged European countries into a crisis as they struggled to cope with the unprecedented influx.

Those fleeing to Europe included people from Afghanistan, which was faced with its own challenges of armed insurgency, as well as Yemen, whose government had collapsed in early 2015 amid an armed rebellion. The refugees and migrants also included influx from war-torn Somalia, Eritrea, and other parts of Africa, where people have been fleeing poverty and civil strife.

According to a November 9, 2015, BBC report quoting the International Organization for Migration (IMO), more than 750,000 migrants were estimated to have made their way across the sea and arrived in Europe in 2015 ("Migrant Crisis: Migration to Europe Explained in Graphics," BBC, November 9, 2015).

Thousands of the migrants, including women and children desperately trying to flee the violence and poverty, drowned while trying to make the perilous journey across the Mediterranean Sea to Europe. As the British national daily, the *Guardian*, reported in September 2015, the full horror of the human tragedy unfolding on the shores of Europe was brought home with the images of the lifeless body of a three-year-old boy found lying facedown on a beach in Turkey. The boy, whose five-year-old brother also met similar fate, was among at least twelve Syrians who drowned attempting to reach Greece while fleeing the carnage in Syria ("Shocking Images of Drowned Syrian Boy Show Tragic Plight of Refugees," *Guardian*, September 2, 2015).

Europe and, particularly, the Western world, stand accused of sharing responsibility for the Middle East's unresolved past, which is the foundation for the chaos and bloodshed that have now spread beyond the Arab world and spilled into the streets of Western cities and other parts of the world. From Nigeria to Kenya, Somalia to Mali, the world has witnessed an alarming spread of Islamic extremism that has led to mass killings of thousands from suicide bombings, public beheadings, and some of the most heinous acts against humanity imaginable.

Given the reality of the prevailing crises, it goes without saying that the demographic landscape of Europe—including European social, cultural, or religious life—will never be the same again. As the global community becomes increasingly interconnected due to advancement in travel and trade, we are witnessing the rise of insecurity and inequality around the world because it has become easy for a spark in one area to spread to other areas.

Global Spread of Infectious Diseases, Terrorism

It can be said without fear of contradiction that the international community is faced with the challenges of a new world order, as reflected by the following major developments: the rise in global Islamic terrorism; fast global spread of emerging infectious diseases as exemplified by the profound worldwide impacts of the SARS, Ebola, and Zika viruses; and the growing devastation around the world due to severe drought, fire, flood, erosion, among other natural calamities attributed to climate change and global warming.

As an example, between 2014 and 2015, three major events occurred that greatly impacted the global community and clearly demonstrate the reality of a new world order. These were the 2014 outbreak of the Ebola virus epidemic in West Africa that killed over 11,000 people and quickly spread to various parts of the world, including Europe and the United States and the 2015 European migrant and refugee crises involving millions of desperate people fleeing war and poverty, as well as the growing crisis of climate change with 2015 becoming the hottest year in recorded human history. Since then, there has been a steady rise in temperature, and the heat wave has intensified around the world.

Take the rapid worldwide spread of the infectious diseases mentioned to illustrate this point. Severe acute respiratory syndrome (SARS) was discovered as a respiratory illness that generated worldwide panic in 2002 and 2003 when the virus, which first infected people and spread in parts of Asia, also spread to Europe and North America, leaving nearly eight hundred dead and more than eight thousand cases of illness. The 2014 Ebola epidemic outbreak in West Africa, which also spread to Europe and North America, before the pandemic was brought under control. The mosquito-borne Zika virus outbreak that began and spread in 2015 in South America also spread to Central America and the Caribbean. Zika was linked to the upsurge of birth defects among babies born with smaller head, as well as other neurological diseases.

Advancement in air travel, characterized by robust and diverse global travel patterns, have brought people around the world closer together and made the world an increasingly smaller global community.

This is why it has become a regular occurrence, as confirmed by media reports and other mediums of information dissemination, regarding how a development in one part of the world is easily spread to other parts. With a growing number of people flying from one part of the world to the other along with the transportation of goods and products, the possibility of the spread of terrorism or disease, for example, has become a reality.

These are reality of a new world order, challenges of a world now closely linked by technology and through frequent air travel and shipped products as a result of the massive global trade. As people spread around the world with goods and products, so too are diseases or pathogens, examples being the SARS, Ebola, and Zika viruses, which spread like wildfire, so to speak.

In these days of technological advancement and accessibility of information technology anywhere in the world, a growing number of people in the global community, for example from the ancient African city of Timbuktu in Mali to the modern city of Paris, France, are able to interact with one another in real time.

Technology is no longer the exclusive domain of a certain race of people and countries in the world. The Internet has changed the flow of information around the world as an equal-opportunity medium for people around the globe. Powerful countries and entities that once controlled global information dissemination are losing their dominance as the use of the Internet and social media platforms have connected and empowered more people around the world. An example of this new global reality is how extremists have been able to increasingly use the Internet and social media to propagate their cause, brainwash, and recruit more followers, mostly young people, to their crusade of death and destruction.

Gone are the days when certain countries were only those that had scientists and some of the brightest minds that invented and produced bombs, guns, and other military devices for warfare. Today, we are seeing Internet-savvy young people belonging to extremist groups who are able to sit at home and create improvised bombs and other explosive devices that have been used to blow up airplanes in the skies and also kill thousands of people in crowded areas through suicide bombing by using children and young men and women to blow up themselves.

Among growing examples of how rudimentary devices are being used to wreak maximum havoc anywhere relates to reports that an affiliate of IS used a soft drink can to make an improvised bomb that brought down a Russian passenger airliner over Egypt's Sinai Peninsula, killing 224 on board on October 31, 2015. While the international community was grappling with the downing of the Russian airliner, a group of IS jihadists staged a daring attack in Paris on November 13, 2015, killing 130 people. The seven coordinated terror attacks in Paris that Friday night targeted crowded entertainment centers, a stadium where a soccer match between a German and French teams were playing, as well as random street shootings.

Those developments, along with an increasing number of brazen attacks in the streets of Western countries and other parts of the world, exemplify a dramatic shift in the global security order.

The need to restore stability to volatile regions and create the enabling environment for sustainable peace and economic progress, as a way to control the mass exodus of people, cannot be overemphasized. In the absence of personal safety and economic opportunities that would encourage people to stay in their respective countries, no amount of legal or physical barriers erected to control people fleeing to more peaceful and prosperous places would work.

The caravans of several thousands of migrants that have besieged the US-Mexico border seeking to enter the United States in recent years is an example of the challenges the United States has also been faced with in dealing with an alarming increase in the number of migrants and refugees. Thousands of these are reported to be unaccompanied minors, as well as mothers with their little children.

According to media reports, since 2012, thousands of unaccompanied minors seeking refuge from abject poverty and increasing violence from Central America have flooded the US-Mexico border seeking entry into the United States. The surge of mostly young migrants trekking north through Mexico created a humanitarian crisis and sparked debate about how the United States should handle the situation, which has continued as of this publication.

Applauding New Zealand for Gun Control Measures

On March 15, 2019, a gunman identified to be a white supremacist opened fire on two mosques in Christchurch, New Zealand, during Friday prayers, killing fifty people and injuring many more. Following the mass shootings, the government of New Zealand took swift action to ban semiautomatic weapons and assault rifles in the country.

The passage of New Zealand's law that banned most semiautomatic weapons in the country less than a month after the mass shooting had a global significance in terms of what actions countries around the world must take to ensure the safety and protection of every human life, especially defenseless people, who are the victims of mass shootings.

New Zealand prime minister Jacinda Ardern and her government were applauded around the globe for putting the safety of the people of New Zealand above the proliferation of guns, which is tied to business interests.

In an editorial highlighting the extraordinary measure New Zealand took to ensure gun control, the *Washington Post* states, "Fifty victims. Twenty-six days. That—along with common-sense leadership from government officials—is what it took for New Zealand to pass a law that bans most semiautomatic weapons in the country. The contrast with the United States is both inescapable and striking. Despite the loss of far more lives in far more mass shootings—more than 2,000 mass shootings since the slaughter of elementary school children in Newton, Conn., in 2012 – Congress has refused to make any significant change in federal gun law, including a needed reimposition of the ban on the assault rifles that are often the weapons of choice of mass murderers" ("It took New Zealand 26 days to act on gun control. Congress has been stalling for years," *Washington Post*, April 10, 2019).

The *Washington Post* editorial also highlighted another alarming situation, which was the frequency with which mass shooting and gun violence in the United States were becoming a new normal. Most distressing is the frequency in mass shooting on school and college campuses, which have cut down the lives of many innocent little children and promising young people and robbed them of the opportunity to live to the fullness of their lives.

For example, since the massacre at Columbine High School in Littleton, Colorado, in 1999 in which 13 students and teachers were killed and 24 injured, some of the school shootings that this author has gathered from records include the following: 2007 massacre at Virginia Tech in Blacksburg, Virginia, in which 33 people were killed and 23 injured; the 2012 massacre at Sandy Hook Elementary School in Newton, Connecticut, which left 27 killed and 2 injured; and the 2018 massacre at Marjory Stoneman Douglas High School in Parkland, Florida, which caused 17 fatalities and 14 injured.

On May 8, 2019, the *Washington Post* reported that more than 228,000 students in the United States had experienced gun violence during school hours since the Columbine High School massacre in 1999.

Although the right to bear arms is guaranteed by the US Constitution, Americans must find a balance between said constitutional rights and the very important need to control the proliferation of firearms, which has been responsible for the growing wave of gun-related violence and more innocent bystanders being killed in the United States. Gun violence will only be brought under control with effective gun control legislations and actions.

The Urgent Need to Tackle Climate Change

While the international community is struggling to cope with the rising tide of terrorism, extremism, and what is said to be the largest displacement of people since the Second World War, climate change or global warming is wreaking more havoc around the world. Flood, drought, storm, tornado, hurricanes, erosion, among other phenomena, are causing one disaster after another around the world. Thousands of people have been killed, and Pacific Island nations are in danger of being wiped off the global map as a result of what scientists attribute to climate change and global warming.

As global temperature heats up, causing streams and rivers to dry, the international community must brace itself for serious conflicts surrounding water rights. It is, therefore, a matter of extreme urgency for the international community to begin serious dialogue on how to mitigate water-related conflicts and save Pacific Island countries from being wiped away due to rising tides. In recent years, tensions have been rising in many parts of the world while there have been violence in some parts related to water rights.

Wherever one lives in the world, it does not take a rocket scientist to realize the changing pattern in the global climate. Massive flooding due to torrential rainfall, hurricanes, tornadoes, tsunamis, erosion, extreme drought, desertification, wildfires, as well as extreme heat waves and winter blizzards, are but a few examples of climate change that have caused widespread death and destruction around the world.

Scientists and experts have warned that some species are already in danger while others face extinction due to climate change and global warming. There can be no question that climate change and global warming will definitely exacerbate existing problems in the world, such as conflict, hunger, poverty, and population displacement. As has been the situation with many man-made and natural calamities, the poor will suffer the greatest impacts of climate change, and that will likely increase global instability.

At a meeting in October 2018 where the UN General Assembly Second Committee focused on agriculture, food security, and nutrition, speakers told the body that the destructive impacts of climate change like droughts, floods, and increasingly severe storms are the primary culprits behind decreased farming output and rising hunger worldwide. Experts have also warned that the impact of climate change in Africa regarding food shortage could be even more acute, given the fact that the continent has been unable to feed itself.

During the summer of 2018, scorching heat knocked out entire electrical grids, threatened food supplies, and killed hundreds of people in Greece, Canada, and Japan, for example. Prior to those tragedies, in 2017, mudslides in Freetown, capital of the West African nation of Sierra Leone, killed over 1,140 people and left widespread infrastructural destruction. Following several days of torrential rainfall, devastating floods and mudslides occurred in and around Freetown on August 14, 2017. According to reports, the destructive behavior of the mudslides was exacerbated by a number of factors, including poor infrastructure, cutting down of trees, and ineffective drainage system.

In March and April 2019, several East and Southern African countries were devastated by tropical cyclones that hit the region. For example, in March 2019, more than 1,000 people were killed and millions displaced after Cyclone Idai hit Mozambique, Madagascar, Malawi, and Zimbabwe. A month after Cyclone Idai, tropical Cyclone Kenneth also hit Mozambique, Tanzania, and other countries, wreaking more havoc in the region.

It is disturbing to note that natural disasters around the world are increasing in frequency and becoming more deadly and destructive.

The felling of forests, the plundering of seas and soils, and the pollution of air and water are together pushing the natural world to the brink. That was the warning of five hundred experts in fifty countries in a major UN-backed report released in May 2019, according to *BBC News*. The assessment highlighted the losses that have hit the natural world over the past fifty years and how the future is looking bleak for tens to hundreds of thousands of species.

According to the report, quoted by BBC, one million animal and plant species are now threatened with extinction. The report added that nature everywhere is declining at a speed never previously seen as humans' need for evermore food and energy are the main drivers.

These trend can be halted, according to the report, but it will take "transformative change" in every aspect of how humans interact with nature ("Nature Crisis: Humans 'Threaten 1m Species with Extinction,'" *BBC Science and Environment*, May 6, 2019).

From the bees that pollinate the crops to the forests that hold back flood waters, the report revealed how humans are ravaging the very ecosystems that support their societies.

According to reports also quoting the National Oceanic and Atmospheric Administration (NOAA), in the United States, storms, fires, floods, and heat caused at least US$306 billion in destruction in 2017. Other estimates put the total cost of destruction closer to US$400 billion.

Judging from the extreme climatic developments that have occurred, there can be no question that climate change is becoming harder to ignore in our own community and around the world. According to a *CNN* news article in November 2018 in the United States, a new US government report had delivered a dire warning about climate change and its devastating impacts. The report stated that the US economy could lose hundreds of billions of dollars—or, in the worst-case scenario, more than 10 percent of its GDP—by the end of the century ("Climate Change Will Shrink U.S. Economy and Kill Thousands, Government Report Warns," *CNN*, November 23, 2018).

As part of the effects of climate change in Africa, there has been coastal erosion due to rising sea levels, which has significantly altered many coastlines and led to the displacement of communities in many parts of the world, including West Africa. Liberia's coastline is among those in the subregion, which has been experiencing intense erosion to the level that livelihoods of some communities have been threatened, as well as the displacement of a growing number of people and loss of property.

In 2008, the Liberian government conducted a study titled, "Shoreline Erosion of the Liberian Coastline—An Initial Assessment," which was undertaken through support of the UN based on a request from the Liberian government. The study was conducted by the Dutch company, Royal Haskoning, reputed as a world-leading engineering and consultancy firm in many fields of expertise ranging from urban planning and waste management to architecture. Royal Haskoning is said to be most famous for its maritime and coastal and river engineering services. Around the world, engineers of the company have been working on port extensions, coastal defense, integrated coastal management plans, among others. In West Africa, Royal Haskoning has been in charge of coastal reconstruction works in The Gambia, a multimillion-dollar reclamation and reconstruction work, financed by the African Development Bank. Royal Haskoning was also involved in the deepening works in the Freeport of Monrovia, and it has also been advising various West African governments, including Nigeria, Ghana, and Senegal, according to a company introduction.

In recognition of Royal Haskoning's engineering expertise and knowledge of the regional physical and environmental systems, the company was selected to conduct the study.

During the survey, Royal Haskoning obtained photos and satellite imageries of Liberia's coastline to determine the rate of shoreline recession, undertook field visits and aerial survey to identify locations where erosion was seriously threatening or will threaten coastal communities, and also identified areas of accretion (deposition) and depletion (erosion). Among the places covered were the five urban areas located at the coast that are recognized to have major economic value to Liberia and high population concentration. They are Robertsport, capital of Grand Cape Mount County; Buchanan, Grand Bassa Greenville, Sinoe County; and Harper, Maryland County. Buchanan, Greenville, and Harper also respectively have commercial ports, which, like the Freeport of Monrovia, operate under the National Port Authority (NPA).

The Royal Haskoning report also included consultations with relevant stakeholders—Liberian government institutions, bilateral partners, and relevant international bodies and agencies—and it gathered necessary information to assess the impact and develop a term of reference for subsequent work required to develop an Integrated Coastal Area Management Plan (ICAMP), including strategy to minimize the effects of beach erosion.

During the course of the assessment, the Royal Haskoning team held consultations with leaders of relevant Liberian government ministries and agencies, such as the Ministry of Lands, Mines and Energy; Ministry of Public Works; the Environmental Protection Agency (EPA); and the Ministry of Information, Culture Affairs and Tourism (MICAT), among others. They also met with President Ellen Johnson Sirleaf and the special representatives of the UN secretary-general to Liberia, Ambassador Allen Doss. The team undertook helicopter flyovers of the coastline and site visitations.

The problem of sand mining was highlighted during the consultations. The Minister of Lands, Mines and Energy, Dr. Eugene Shannon, a veteran geologist, stressed that the problem of sand mining was a major contributing factor for erosion. He spoke of regulations that were being instituted by the government to control the problem of sand mining. At the EPA, the team was informed that part of the environmental problems being confronted were due to pollution and degradation of the mangrove and wetlands.

The technical team also visited MICAT to discuss the impacts of coastal erosion on cultural, historic, and potential tourism sites. The team was received by yours truly, deputy minister for public affairs and then acting minister in the absence of the minister proper. Also at the meeting was Ms. Scholastica Y. Doe, assistant minister for tourism. Among the issues discussed included the challenges regarding creating public awareness, through information and education, about the danger of sand mining, pollution, cutting down trees, and other activities that are harmful to the environment and public health. We also discussed the location of the historic Providence Island, which was also in great danger due to erosion. Located on the Mesurado River close to where the river meets the ocean, what is now named Providence Island was where the settlers from the United States first landed in the early 1800s to found Liberia, Africa's first independent republic.

MICAT also attached a photographer, Mr. Foley S. Siryon, with the technical team to cover the survey. Tall, slender, easygoing, and always cracking funny jokes, Siryon—whom I call by the nickname Rastafo—and I worked together in the 1980s at the *Daily Observer* newspaper, where he was a photographer when I started my journalism career as an intern. He was one of the best photographers around with extensive national and international media experience. He was a photo editor at MICAT's photo department when I began my tenure at the ministry. Siryon and other colleagues from my *Observer* days call me by the nickname Bill Green.

Following the conclusion of their work, In March 2008, Royal Haskoning released copies of its draft report, "Shoreline Erosion of the Liberian Coastline—An Initial Assessment." The report covered the areas or terms of reference identified above and proffered recommendations as to how to mitigate the problems of erosion in Liberia. The report found that widespread sand mining was one of the major contributing factors for erosion. The report contains recommendation for beach nourishment or coastal reconstruction works, which would restore the coastline or ensure beach reclamation.

The report made a number of recommendations, including for the government to set up a coastal protection unit under the Ministry of Lands, Mines and Energy, initially focusing on technical issues related to coastal engineering and morphological processes and that the unit can consist of engineers from relevant ministries and the EPA. It also recommended for the government to contract a capable international consultant to carry out feasibility studies for the interventions required in Monrovia and optionally Buchanan and that the coastal protection unit should participate in the studies.

Residents of New Kru Town, a Monrovia suburb, witness launch of the Coastal Defense Project in New Kru Town behind D. Twe Memorial High School, which is almost destroyed by rising sea level. (Courtesy, Liberian Embassy)

The start of the Coastal Defense project in the densely populated Monrovia suburb of New Kru Town, which has been seriously threatened by rising sea level. (Courtesy, Liberian Embassy Public Affairs)

This pile of garbage in a section of Monrovia is an example of the danger to public health and the environment. (Courtesy, West African Journal Magazine)

I never heard anything about this report again since its release in 2008, but I have kept a personal copy. Meanwhile, the problems of erosion have increased in Liberia, as more coastal residents and infrastructure are being negatively impacted.

In the ongoing reconstruction process of Liberia, it is very important that thorough environmental impact assessments are made to ensure that the country is not exposed to environmental degradation that could cause disasters in the future.

For example, under the Ramsar Convention on Wetlands, the intergovernmental treaty that provides the framework for the conservation and wise use of wetlands and their resources, Liberia, which is a signatory to the convention, has five sites designated as wetlands of international importance. Liberia's Ramsar-designated wetlands sites, which provide a favorable habitat for a variety of plant, animal, and marine species, include the following: Mesurado Wetlands in Monrovia, Marshall Wetlands in Margibi County, Kpatawee Wetlands in Bong County, and Gbedin Wetlands in Nimba County. ("Building the 'New Monrovia:' The Need to Plan Well and Protect the Environment," *West African Journal Magazine* online, May 12, 2018).

According to the Ramsar report quoted by the *West African Journal Magazine*, the Mesurado Wetlands is already facing environmental degradation as a result of being used for firewood collection, as a dumping site, for car washing, as well as threat from pollution.

There are also reports that other wetlands and mangrove in Monrovia and its environs are being destroyed rapidly due to poor urban planning. Widespread unregulated construction in wetlands and water channels, cutting down mangrove forests for firewood, and turning drainage into dump sites are some of the challenges threatening the future well-being of the environment and biodiversity in Liberia.

More wetlands and mangrove forests across Liberia are reported to be increasingly impacted negatively by human activities. Even more disturbing are reports of the continued use of dynamite, which is exploded in the water to kill fish and other marine species. There is an urgent need in Liberia to regulate the use of dynamite, which is clearly seen to have a destructive impact on the environment and biodiversity.

Indiscriminate logging and the slash-and-burn traditional method of farming where portions of the forest are cut down and burned by farmers during every farming season have continued to cause rapid depletion of Liberia's rain forests. Unregulated mining activities, such as what is occurring in many rural parts of Liberia where people are digging for minerals, also present environmental dangers like landslide and erosion, among others.

On March 26, 2018, barely two months following his inauguration, President Weah took a boat ride to Bali Island in the middle of the Mesurado River in Monrovia, where he revealed plans to transform the island into a modern city. Speaking during his visit on the island, President Weah said he intends to transform Bali Island into the "New Monrovia," commencing with the construction of a state-of-the-art international conference center and other standardized structures. The 4,000-seat state-of-the-art international conference center planned to be constructed is expected to be funded by the Indian government as part of its bilateral support to Liberia.

Bali Island is located in the Mesurado Wetlands in Monrovia, which, according to a Ramsar report, provides a favorable habitat and feeding grounds for several species of birds; and it also hosts vulnerable marine species and mangrove already being devastated due to human activities ("Building the 'New Monrovia': The Need to Plan Well and Protect the Environment", *West African Journal Magazine* online, May 12, 2018).

The island and its surrounding areas are naturally beautiful and picturesque. Unfortunately, the breathtaking view of the island and the entire Mesurado River waterfront have been overshadowed by heaps of garbage and stench.

Speaking on the island, President Weah said that while he was a child "growing up in Clara Town, Bushrod Island, playing just across the shores of the Stockton Creek, I often looked into the direction of the Bali Island, viewed an undeveloped tourist attraction." Although located on a naturally beautiful riverfront, Clara Town is a slum community. Whenever he gazed from his community toward the Bali Island, President Weah said, "I wondered what was going on there. I did not know anyone who knew what was going on there. There was no road, no bridge, or ferry to get over here (there)," according to the *West African Journal*.

The Liberian leader noted that his dream to see the island develop began from that moment. He noted, "From here I began to see a New City of Monrovia emerging from the ashes of the Old City of Monrovia," the *West African Journal* quoted the press release from the Executive Mansion in Monrovia. He explained how he envisioned skyscrapers, office buildings, shopping malls, banks, among others, on the island.

President Weah's vision and plan to build a "New Monrovia" are notable. However, in the process of national development, the Liberian government and people must focus on what is called "smart growth," which is an approach that covers a range of development and conservation strategies that protect the health of the people and natural environment and make the communities more attractive, economically stronger, and more socially diverse.

The transformation of Bali Island into a modern city community must reflect a well-developed plan to ensure sustainable development and environmental protection to enhance the quality of life of the people. Equally important, a thorough environmental impact assessment must be made to ensure that the area is not exposed to environmental degradation that could cause disaster in the future.

Both Bali Island and the historic Providence Island are in the same vicinity on the Mesurado River. The sceneries and location of the two islands make them ideal as potential business and tourism hotspots.

It is hoped that the government would back words with actions through increased support to empower Liberia's Environmental Protection Agency (EPA) and other relevant agencies to enforce environmental regulations, as well as institute public awareness programs on environmental conservation.

Meanwhile, in late 2018, prominent Liberian geologist, Dr. Eugene Shannon, published a book titled, *Safeguarding the Environment in Mining Development Projects*, which gives a description of the role the extractive industry plays in the economic sector of most developing countries, such as Liberia. The book is expected to be part of the environmental science studies at the University of Liberia and other institutions of higher learning in Liberia.

It may also be interesting to note that on the March 26, 2018, before President Weah took a boat ride to Bali Island, he broke grounds for the construction of Liberia's first military hospital, which is expected to be well equipped with modern facilities and a highly trained medical staff to cater to military and paramilitary personnel and their families.

While mostly personnel of the Armed Forces of Liberia (AFL) and their dependents looked on and cheered, President Weah broke grounds for a 200-room military hospital, which will be located at the Edward Benyan Kesselly Military Barracks in Schiefflin, Margibi County.

The site of the proposed hospital is on the main highway from the Roberts International Airport (RIA) to Monrovia, directly opposite the main Schiefflin Barracks. A large billboard containing a photo of the architectural design of what is set to be a teaching hospital to train men and women in arms in various medical disciplines give motorists and passersby a view of a beautiful structure that would enhance the modern architectural outlook of the rapidly developing Monrovia-RIA corridor.

More importantly, given the urgency to develop Liberia's broken health system, the need to construct the military hospital could not be more pressing. A military hospital, well equipped and funded, with qualified staff, would greatly help to enhance the quality of life of the men and women in arms and their families, as well as the Liberian population in general.

Even though the cost of the proposed military hospital was yet to be made public, its establishment provides an opportunity to plan well toward the future in terms of the human, financial, and material resources being harnessed to ensure that Liberians have access to first-rate medical services.

As have been noted numerous times in this publication, since the end of Liberia's civil crises, the country has struggled with a health care system so dysfunctional that many people have died from preventable and curable diseases, such as malaria, diarrhea, typhoid, pressure, heart attack, among others. Due to the dire state of the country's health care system, many Liberians who can afford the cost travel to Ghana or to other parts of the world for better medical treatment.

The Ebola epidemic that began in 2014, which caused 4,810 deaths and collapse of Liberia's health system, underscore the pressing need to plan and institute a modern health care system that would ensure accessible and affordable high-quality treatment for the people and effectively respond to any possible future epidemic outbreak.

CHAPTER FIFTEEN
Liberians and Africans Don't Have to Continue Being Object of Pity

Have you ever listened to the radio and the news on Africa that is mostly about wars, killings, and starvation? Have you ever seen on television nauseating images of malnourished African children and adults reduced to skeleton, many of the victims so weak that they can barely lift their hands to drive the flies that swamp their faces due to hunger and starvation? Perhaps you have also seen publications and videos with photos or images of desperate-looking African women and children, which are often used to solicit financial and other assistance or relief aid supposedly on their behalf.

And this is not to forget the thousands of so-called illegal African migrants that have drowned at sea when boats used to smuggle them to Europe capsize, leaving survivors traumatized and dispossessed, as reports and images from some of the boat tragedies have shown.

Even though the displacement of Africans from across the continent due to civil unrest, persecution and poverty had continued for decades without strong concerted international efforts to address the root causes, Europe found itself plunged in migrant and refugee crises of unprecedented proportions in 2015. Added to the desperate Africans voting with their feet for freedom and economic opportunity are hundreds of thousands of migrants and refugees fleeing war and poverty in the Middle East and parts adjacent including Syria, Iraq, Afghanistan, and Yemen.

Another major human tragedy in Africa that recently placed the entire global community on edge was the outbreak of the deadly Ebola epidemic in West Africa in February 2014. The World Health Organization (WHO) declared it as the world's deadliest Ebola epidemic recorded to date.

Widespread television images of health care workers dressed like astronauts in protective coveralls and gears, transporting body bags of Ebola victims, sent shock waves of panic and fear around the world. The level of pandemonium regarding this deadly virus was understandable for a disease about which little was known and for which there was no cure. The WHO declared an international health emergency for the Ebola outbreak, from which more than 11,300 people died, especially in the worst-affected countries of Guinea, Liberia, and Sierra Leone. There were also more than 28,600 confirmed or probable cases of infection from the virus, the WHO reported.

The West Africa Ebola outbreak, which was the thirty-fourth outbreak since the virus was discovered in 1976 in Zaire, renamed the Democratic Republic of Congo, manifested in a manner that posed a more serious existential threat to humans than previous outbreaks. According to the WHO, there were 318 cases of Ebola infection, 280 deaths, and only 38 serologically confirmed survivors from the first outbreak. Since the first outbreak, the number of deaths from each of the various known cases and outbreaks besides the West Africa outbreak were lower.

According to the US Centers for Disease Control and Prevention (CDC), "Ebola virus is the cause of a viral hemorrhagic fever disease. Symptoms include: fever, headache, joint and muscle aches, weakness, diarrhea, vomiting, stomach pain, lack of appetite, and abnormal bleeding. Symptoms may appear anywhere from 2 to 21 days after exposure to Ebola virus though 8-10 days is most common."

According to the WHO, this West Africa outbreak recorded 70 percent death rate of those infected, higher than the 50 percent initially reported during the early period of the pandemic.

Since the first incidence of infections experienced in Nzerekore, an area in southeastern Guinea, the virus spread to the capital, Conakry, and then on to neighboring Liberia and Sierra Leone, wreaking havoc along the way. A Liberian American who flew from Liberia to Lagos, Nigeria, was quarantined and later died of Ebola, which was the first case of the virus in Africa's most populous country of more than 168 million people. In Nigeria, the effects of the disease in terms of human casualties were very minimum in comparison to the devastations caused in the worst-affected countries, due in part by an aggressive containment approach, buttressed by a much-advanced health system.

Poverty and ignorance are the combustible fuel that fanned the flames, so to speak, regarding the spread and very devastating impact of the Ebola epidemic. Guinea, Liberia, and Sierra Leone, which are classified among the poorest countries in the world, have very weak health care delivery systems. The irony is that as with most parts of Africa, the Almighty God richly endowed each of these countries with abundance of natural resources. It is clear that if these resources were properly managed, this would yield strong economic and social development and alleviate poverty.

The rapid spread of the Ebola epidemic, which caused in its wake fear, panic, death, trauma, and anguish, has exposed how fragile most African countries are, as well as their limited capacity or lack thereof to provide basic quality social services for their people. While much has been articulated regarding the limited or lack of accessible and affordable quality health care and education, the provision of safe drinking water and sanitation, electricity, as well as conducive housing and transportation services have also been very inadequate.

On a continent where a large number of people have died from preventable diseases such as malaria and diarrhea, and where, according to the WHO, malnutrition is a factor in 45 percent of child deaths, any infectious epidemic can spread quickly with devastating consequences. It is exactly the types of conditions that precipitated the outbreak of the Ebola pandemic.

The portrait of human suffering and tragedies that this book has attempted to present is something that has left people often wondering, what is wrong with Africa. Experts and ordinary people have debated about how the continent is cursed or not. For how can a continent so rich in natural resources remain so poor that a mass of its populations live in conditions of deprivation and poverty that are unjustifiable and unacceptable in the twenty-first century?

There are countless reports and images of tragedies at sea involving people voting with their feet, attempting to illegally enter Europe, risking their lives in desperation to free themselves from poverty and misrule. These disturbing reports and images of human suffering have often left people wondering why. Africa has continued to suffer brain drain, and progress has been at a snail's pace due to the corrupt nature of governance on the continent. For what else can one attribute to the lack of progress in any given African country?

A 2014 report of the UN High Commission for Refugees (UNHCR) published by BBC online on June 18, 2015, states that at least fifteen conflicts erupted or reignited globally in the past five years. Eight of these conflicts were in Africa and three in the Middle East. This led to 59.9 million displaced people by the end of 2014 and 19.5 million refugees. The UNHCR report also states that more than 50 percent of these refugees were children ("Number Displaced Worldwide Hit Record High," 2014 UN report).

According to the UNHCR, with 59.5 million people displaced from their homes worldwide, there were now more refugees than at any time in history. Among the worst of these conflicts were the civil upheavals in Syria and Iraq, characterized by the invasion and brutal occupation of territory in that part of the Middle East by the barbaric terrorist group so-called the Islamic State (IS). The IS terrorist outfit even dared to declare its occupied territory a caliphate.

The civil war in Africa's newest independent nation called South Sudan, where political leaders with the biggest guns have fanned tribal flames to hang on to power, has killed an estimated 383,000 people and more than four people displaced, according to Wikipedia.

Of similar concern has been the situation in parts of Nigeria, where thousands have been killed and millions displaced as a result of the onslaught of the terrorist group Boko Haram, which claimed that its campaign of death and destruction is in the name of the Islamic faith.

During a visit to a UN refugee camp in Turkey for Syrian and Iraqi refugees around the time the UNHCR report was released, famed international actress Angelina Jolie pointed out, "There is an explosion of human suffering and displacement on a level that has never been seen before." Ms. Jolie visited the refugee camp in her capacity as a UN special envoy for refugees ("Jolie Decries 'Explosion of Suffering' after Visiting Refugee Camp," Reuters, June 20, 2015).

According to the Economic and Social Council of the United Nations, as of 2014, 34 out of 50 countries classified as "least developed countries" were in Africa. The one nagging question, which has been something like a refrain throughout this publication, has been: Why is it that many African countries, although endowed with abundant natural resources, continue to be poor?

Because several African governments are unaccountable to their people, progress has been slow or stagnant in many parts of the continent, which accounts for the largest number of countries that are designated as the poorest or least developed countries in the world. The least developed countries (LDC) are a group of countries that have been classified by the UN as "least developed" in terms of their low gross national income (GNI), their weak human assets, and their high degree of vulnerability. It was based on these factors that 34 of the 50 countries categorized as least developed in the world were designated to be in Africa, which has a population of 1.1 billion as of this writing.

Interestingly, only 10 countries were categorized as LDC in Asia, which has the world's largest population, estimated to be 4.4 billion as of 2014. Many Asian countries are making sustainable progress because they are investing more in their people and concentrating on infrastructural development to enhance productivity and the living conditions of their people.

In Africa on the contrary, despite billions of dollars in bilateral and multilateral aid from the so-called developed world, along with growing investment in the private sectors, many African countries are still struggling to provide basic services for their people because of failure to invest more in the people and infrastructural development.

My native country Liberia, although endowed with abundant natural resources, including iron ore, diamonds, gold, rubber, timber, and a recent prospect of oil discovery, is also classified as one of the poorest countries in the world, ranking 174th out of 186 countries on the Human Development Index (HDI). This data was contained in the Liberia Constraints Analysis, published in 2013 by the government of Liberia in partnership with the US government's Millennium Challenge Corporation (MCC).

This unacceptable state of affairs has obtained in Liberia despite the fact that the country was once a symbol of stability and economic progress in Africa. Liberia was recorded to be one of the world's leading iron ore exporters in the 1950s and '60s, and its per capita income was equivalent to that of Japan in the 1970s.

President George Manneh Weah and First Lady Clar Weah are in a delightful mood dedicating a new market structure, which is intended to improve the conditions of marketers. (Courtesy, Liberian Embassy Public Affairs)

As of this writing, Liberia was next to Malaysia as home to the world's second-largest rubber plantation, the Firestone rubber plantation. The country retains more than 43 percent of the tropical rain forest in the West African subregion, with unique plants and endangered animal species. While Malaysia has many industrial facilities to manufacture rubber-related products, including tires, Liberia has yet to boast of a single manufacturing plant to produce rubber gloves. Despite abundance of land for agriculture, the country has yet to be able to produce enough food for its population. The problem of food shortage and hunger, as well as lack of access to safe drinking water, are reported to affect hundreds of millions of people in sub-Sahara Africa.

It has been emphasized through these pages that Liberia's and Africa's progress have been undermined as a consequence of political misrule, weak governance institutions, lack of sustainable economic growth and empowerment of the people, and the poor management of public resources and services. As a result of these challenges as highlighted in this book, Liberia witnessed nearly three decades of instability, punctuated by fourteen years of a brutal civil war that left the once-beautiful country broken. In addition to the virtual collapse of the economy, Liberia's infrastructure, including medical and educational facilities, roads, bridges, power plants, factories, farms, telecommunications, and transport facilities, etc., were almost completely destroyed.

The country also suffered a massive brain drain as hundreds of thousands of people, including trained and skilled workers, left the country because of the instability and violence.

Given the similarity of circumstances, there can be no question that the challenges affecting Liberia's progress are similar in countries across Africa, as reflected by the fact that thirty-two of the fifty-two countries on the African continent are classified as least developed.

It also goes without saying that there is a crisis of governance in many parts of Africa. From war-torn Central African Republic to South Sudan, Democratic Republic of Congo, Cameroon, Burundi, Libya, you name them, millions of Africans are languishing under the yoke of rule of the jungle. And this is why the poverty rate on the continent has continued to remain very high.

Institute systems of good governance, such as the proper management of public resources and adequate provision of basic services, and the livelihood of the masses would improve. Empower the people through education, skills training, and the necessary financial support, and you can be assured of a continent with high prospects for double-digit economic growth for decades. The only thing that separates Africans from people in other parts of the world like America, Europe, or Asia is opportunity—the opportunity for an individual to enjoy the basic necessities of life and aspire to the best of their potentials.

Overcoming Poverty through Citizen Empowerment

There is an old adage, "Give a man a fish and you feed him for a day; teach a man to fish, and you feed him for a lifetime." A youth from an underprivileged background, I was given an opportunity out of poverty by Mr. Kenneth Yakpawolo Best, a legendary journalist and fearless warrior with the pen, who trained and mentored me to be a professional journalist at the *Daily Observer* newspaper, then one of West Africa's leading dailies. Mr. Best, who earned a master's degree from Columbia University Graduate

School of Journalism in New York, USA, in 1968, retired in 2018 after laboring for more than fifty years as a practicing journalist.

He truly exemplifies the old adage quoted above. Over the years, he taught, mentored, empowered, and employed many young people, especially in Liberia and The Gambia—where he relocated with his family in 1990 during Liberia's civil crises and founded that country's first independent daily newspaper, also known as the *Daily Observer*. His influence speaks to the conscience of the Liberian society in particular and to humanity in general.

Mr. and Mrs. Kenneth Y. and Mae Gene Best (front left in African attires and head-gears), were among the large turnout at a Liberian embassy event in Washington DC. (Courtesy, Liberian Embassy Public Affairs)

Here is an account of how Mr. Best's intervention in my life was a turning point from the conditions of poverty, as it opened doors of opportunity for me to excel and prosper.

While preparing to graduate from the D. Twe Memorial High School in Monrovia, in December 1982, I took a letter I had drafted to Mrs. Rachel A. B. Cox-George, then D. Twe's vice principal for administration, to proofread for me. The draft was one of several letters of appeal I had been sending to prominent individuals in the Liberian society seeking financial aid for college enrollment. Without financial support or a job, my prospect for college enrollment did not look promising.

A beautiful school campus built near the Atlantic beach, D. Twe is located in one of the poorest and most densely populated suburbs of Monrovia, called the Borough of New Kru Town. The school, which was earlier named William R. Tolbert Jr. High School, was constructed in the 1970s by President Tolbert to provide quality public education to young people in that low-income community. The school was renamed D. Twe Memorial High School following the assassination and overthrow of President Tolbert and his government. The D. Twe High School campus, like many infrastructure close to the ocean, are being threatened and damaged by erosion.

As Mrs. Cox-George (may her soul rest in peace) handed me back the proofread letter, she offered to sponsor me to pursue professional study in journalism at the Ghana Institute of Journalism (GIJ) in Accra, Ghana. Concerned that many young people who graduate from public schools like D. Twe are often stuck in their poor communities due to lack of support and opportunities for advancement, Mrs. Cox-George said she did not want me to fall through similar cracks because I had distinguished myself to be a studious and respectful youth.

When I enrolled at D. Twe in the tenth grade in 1980, there were many organizations, including the science club, drama and debate club, Bible club, press club, as well as the choir and sports. I joined the press club and became the reporter for my class. Upon promotion to the twelfth grade, I was elevated as chairman and editor in chief of the press club.

In 1980, I was one of the original reporters of "School Special," a popular weekly program that aired every Saturday on national radio ELBC, during which reporters from various high schools in Monrovia and parts adjacent filed reports from their respective schools. Some of School Special's notable reporters were Patrick Manjoe of Boatswain High School, now late Gabriel Gworlekaju of the William V. S. Tubman High School and then Monrovia Central High, and James Gbesie Nimene of the Assemblies of God High School (AGM). Both Manjoe and Gworlekaju, who was one of my best friends ever, went on to successful journalism careers while Nimene became an eloquent minister of the gospel and was the best man in my wedding in Sacramento, California. During my high school senior years, I also served as foreign minister of D. Twe High's student government and chairman of the Inter-High School Journalistic Association, which was under auspices of the Ministry of Information as a means of nurturing the practice of journalism in the schools.

It was having closely followed my activities as a student journalist and leader at D. Twe that Mrs. Cox-George offered to sponsor my study at the Ghana Institute of Journalism. While gathering information about GIJ, we learned that a critical requirement for enrollment was that an applicant must have no less than six months working experience with a recognized media entity.

And this is why after graduation, Mrs. Cox-George sent me with a note to Mr. Best, managing director of the Liberian Observer Corporation, publisher of the *Daily Observer* newspaper. The note was a request for Mr. Best to kindly take me in as a cub reporter at the *Daily Observer*, then one of West Africa's leading independent daily.

As God would have it, Mr. Best was in office when I arrived at the *Daily Observer* offices to deliver the note. The secretary requested me to be seated when she took the note in to him. When she came back out, I was informed that Mr. Best was waiting to see me.

I was almost a nervous wreck when ushered into Mr. Best's office. "Sit down, young man. I heard from your principal that you want to be a journalist?" he asked.

"Yes, sir," I responded.

"Do you know what it means to be a journalist in Africa, especially here in Liberia?"

With those two questions, Mr. Best gave me a pep talk about the importance of the role of a journalist in society. As the watchdogs of society, he said, journalists are obligated to serve the common good of society by being the voice of the voiceless and to advocate for equal justice and good governance, among others. Nevertheless, he added, being a journalist in Africa or Liberia for that matter was fraught with personal risks and dangers. This is because freedom of speech and of the press was basically criminalized, as journalists suffered arbitrary arrest and detention and independent media entities were banned for alleged antigovernment reporting. Some journalists who were not so fortunate were killed simply for performing their reportorial duties, he added.

Following his pep talk, Mr. Best had me accompany him to the newsroom, where he introduced me to Mr. T. Maxson Teah, then news editor of the *Daily Observer*. "This young man says he wants to be a journalist. Test him and let me know whether he has a foundation for development," Mr. Best instructed.

This is how I began my career as a journalist at the *Daily Observer*, which was also a training institution, where the editorial staff benefitted from regular training programs at home and abroad to upgrade their professional skills. At the time I was brought on board, *Observer* staff were undergoing a training program conducted by a lecturer from the London-based Thompson Foundation, which enjoys global recognition as a leader in journalism training.

My skills were sharpened while working under the tutelage of Mr. Best, along with the now late T-Max, as Mr. Teah was commonly known, as well as some of the best journalists in Liberia during that period.

Those included legendary Stanton B. Peabody, editor in chief of the *Observer*, whose imprisonment in the 1960s by the government led to journalists coming together to organize the Press Union of Liberia (PUL) in order to seek their collective interests in the discharge of their professional duties. He started his journalism career in 1952 as a reporter for the government-funded the *Liberian Age* newspaper, of which he later became editor in chief for over a decade until after the 1980 military coup. Following the coup, he was transferred from the *Age* to serve as editor in chief of the *New Liberian* newspaper, published under the auspices of the Ministry of Information, Cultural Affairs and Tourism. It was after he left the *New Liberian* that he joined the *Observer* as editor in chief in 1983.

A man of few spoken words, Mr. Peabody was noted as one of Liberia's best editorial writers, in terms of the articulation of the subject matter and impact on readers. For example, one of the editorials he penned for the *Observer*, which was titled, "Go, Mr. President, Go!" was a courageous call for President Samuel Doe to relinquish power to save Liberia from descending into total anarchy after rebels seeking to overthrow his government were on the outskirts of Monrovia. Following that editorial, the *Observer's* offices were attacked and destroyed, reportedly by government agents. In 2011, Mr. Peabody, regarded as a pillar of the Liberian press and mentor to generations of visiting foreign correspondents, died in Monrovia at the age of eighty.

Another veteran journalist who has contributed significantly to my professional growth is Mr. Joe S. Kappia, who was features editor at the *Observer*. A veteran classroom teacher, Mr. Kappia wrote and edited a series of articles during the process of drafting the Constitution of Liberia for the Second Republic and the public awareness campaign to educate Liberians about the constitution, which came into effect in 1986.

A graduate of Teachers College at the University of Liberia, Mr. Kappia holds a master of science degree in mass communication (1989) and a master of arts degree in school administration and supervision (2008) from San Jose State University in San Jose, California.

A prolific writer who was strongly critical of the Doe regime, Joe, as he is popularly known, fled Liberia in 1986 due to death threats. He resettled in San Jose, California, where he founded the *West African Journal Magazine*. The magazine became a major publication in the United States with a focus on the Mano River region and West Africa during the civil crises in Liberia and neighboring countries during the decades of the 1990s. This was the period when many Liberians and others in the subregion were fleeing their homeland due to conflicts, and the magazine was a reliable source of information covering developments in the region and in the Diaspora.

However, the *West African Journal Magazine* suspended publication in 1997 after publishing a news report about the brutal murder of politician Samuel S. Dokie, a former close ally of Charles Taylor who became a leading opposition figure to the rebel leader turned president of Liberia.

Dokie was one of the founding leaders and close allies of Taylor within the hierarchy of the NPFL during the launch and early years of the NPFL armed insurgency. However, he and others with the NPFL hierarchy broke away from Taylor due to political differences. Dokie and his breakaway faction instigated an abortive armed rebellion within the NPFL in an attempt to dislodge Taylor.

At the time he was tortured and murdered along with three family members allegedly by security forces loyal to Taylor, Dokie had served as deputy speaker of Liberia's Transitional Assembly, the parliament of the power-sharing government during the civil war. While traveling to attend the wedding of a relative in the northern Liberian county of Nimba, he was arrested at a checkpoint on the highway and taken to a police station in central Liberian city of Gbarnga along with his wife, sister, and cousin. According to media reports, Dokie was detained for "security reasons," and he and his family members were held at the police station until the arrival of officers of the Special Security Serviced (SSS), the equivalent of the US Secret Service, who took the detainees away. It was while in custody that Dokie, his wife Janet, sister Serrina, and cousin Emmanuel Voker were tortured to death and killed. Their bodies were found bound and half burned in 1997.

Liberians of all walks of life, as well as supporters of democratic governance and the rule of law around the world vehemently condemned the diabolical and heinous crimes of abduction and cold-blooded murder of Dokie and his family members. Through its coverage of this unspeakable act of brutality, the *West African*

Journal Magazine reflected the resounding condemnation of the Taylor regime for the murder of Dokie and his family. As a result, Mr. Kappia's family in Liberia reportedly endured serious threat by agents of the regime, who warned sternly that the family would suffer the consequences for what was regarded to be Kappia's antigovernment reporting in the United States.

Meanwhile, having been off the newsstands for several years, efforts began for the *West African Journal* to resume publishing with the launch of a website online in 2017. Plans are also under way to launch the print edition of the magazine, which is expected to circulate in Liberia and other parts of the West Africa and beyond, as well as in the United States and Europe, among others.

From my days at the *Daily Observer* to the publication of this book, I have been blessed to benefit from Mr. Joe Kappia's mentorship and friendship.

Among those on the *Observer* editorial staff who also helped to build my professional foundation was sub-editor Isaac Thompson, a progressive-oriented thinker and prolific writer. He is now more widely known as Dr. Nii Moi Thompson. Dr. Thompson is today an eminent economist and a highly influential political figure in Ghana. He is former director general of the National Development Planning Commission (NDPC), a Ghanaian government agency.

Dr. Thompson's life is a reflection of the triumph of the human spirit over adversity. Born in Ghana, he was compelled at age sixteen, to leave his home in Kumasi, Ghana, for Liberia, and later Sierra Leone, in order to fulfill his dream of obtaining a secondary and higher education, as well as to explore avenues for self-improvement.

According to a profile of the noted economist published by the Ghanaian news outlet, *Graphic Online*, the young Thompson was penniless when he traveled to Liberia through the assistance of another Ghanaian traveling to Liberia, who offered to assist him. In Liberia, he lived with his brother for a while before moving in with a friend. But the friend was soon evicted by his landlord, and young Thompson soon found himself homeless.

Dr. Thompson narrated to the *Graphic* that while he was in Liberia, a friend informed him of educational opportunities in Sierra Leone and so he left for that country. While in the Sierra Leonean capital Freetown, he gained employment as a "reporter in training" with a newspaper called *We Yone*, which means "Our Own" in Krio. He returned to Liberia and continued to work as a journalist while attending school at night. It was while Thompson was serving as deputy to the editor in chief at the *Observer* that I began my journalism career at the paper as a "reporter in training."

After four years in journalism, Thompson left Liberia for the United States, where he successfully obtained his first degree in general economics from City University of New York–Brooklyn College, a master's in international economics from the State University of New York, Albany, New York, as well as a doctorate in development economics and public policy from the University of Pittsburgh in Pennsylvania, United States ("Dr. Nii Moi Thompson Attained Education the Hard Way," *Graphic Online*, February 8, 2017).

Dr. Thompson's story in relation to Liberia is yet another example of how Liberia was something like a "melting pot," where everyone from everywhere could come and achieve their dreams depending on how hard they were prepared to work.

Among those who also positively impacted my early career were world news editor Mlanju Reeves, a veteran musician; photo editor Sando Moore, who has been one of Africa's well-known photojournalists; and layout and art editor Harrison Jiedueh, commonly known as Black Baby. It was through Black Baby's "Country Cartoon," published daily in the *Observer* that I learned the importance of cartoon as a medium of communication. Besides Mr. Peabody and T-Max, who are deceased, the distinguished individuals named have ascended to various careers.

At the conclusion of my six-month journalistic internship at the *Observer* after which I was expected to enroll at the GIJ, there came a major stumbling block. Ghana, then an unstable country due to successive military misrule, had been plunged into yet another bloody crisis that resulted to the closure of institutions of higher learning, including the GIJ.

The economy and living conditions in Ghana had deteriorated in those days that Ghanaian merchants and others came to Liberia to purchase basic commodities, such as toothpaste, tissue, and bath soap. Today, Ghana is one of the most democratically peaceful and prosperous countries in Africa.

As God would have it, Mr. Best decided to retain me as a reporter at the *Observer* because, he said, I had performed satisfactorily and that he saw in me the potential for growth. He also asked if I could go to New Kru Town and find one of my former schoolmates and colleagues of the press club, who was serious minded and dedicated to duty as I was, who would be trained and deployed in New Kru Town as a *Daily Observer* correspondent.

I went to New Kru Town and contacted Philip Wesseh, who graduated a year as my senior. I succeeded him as editor in chief of the D. Twe High School Press Club, following his graduation. Even though Wesseh graduated as the valedictorian of his class, he was unable to go to college and was without a job. When I contacted him about the *Observer* job prospect, which was to transform his life, he was basically idle, as has been the lot of many young people in such poor environment. He was also an example of the many students in public schools who are unable to transition from high school to college due to their economically disadvantaged background.

With the opportunity afforded him to excel, Wesseh soon became one of the best reporters at the *Daily Observer*, and he was later promoted to news editor, a very critical position in a newsroom. Before Wesseh's promotion, I was a higher-ranking reporter over him in the newsroom. With his elevation to lead the newsroom, he became my immediate boss.

Wesseh's appointment over other senior reporters ruffled some feathers in the newsroom, notable of which was a senior reporter who angrily expressed that he will neither take instruction from Wesseh nor report to him. As for me, I congratulated him and expressed the hope that our working relationship would continue to be good, and we did work together well.

However, little did we know that in a few years ahead, circumstances would change and I was to be elevated to a higher position to also become Wesseh's boss. The change came during the early period of the civil war, when fighting erupted between government and rebel forces for control of the capital Monrovia in 1990. Besides the alarming death rate, the infrastructure of the city, including the offices and printing facilities of the *Daily Observer*, sustained massive destruction. Mr. Best and his family resettled in The Gambia, where he established the first independent daily newspaper of that country, the *Daily Observer*, also known as the *Gambian Observer*.

Following the intervention of the Nigerian-led West African peacekeeping force, which pushed the rebel forces out of the city and created the atmosphere for Monrovia residents to enjoy a sense of normalcy, the only radio stations and newspapers that existed during that period were operated by parties to the conflict, including the armed factions. Charles Taylor's NPFL occupied about 90 percent of the country outside of Monrovia, Prince Johnson and his INPFL faction occupied an area on the outskirts of Monrovia, while the West African–backed interim government held control over Monrovia and surrounding areas under the control of the ECOMOG peacekeeping force.

There was a huge void in terms of the dissemination of information from an independent perspective, as each party was driven by the desire to articulate their respective positions in the conflict. In an effort to give the Liberian people an alternative source of independent information, T-Max Teah, who was a senior editor at the *Daily Observer*, arranged a meeting for former staff of the *Observer* to come together and determine how we could produce a newspaper that would chart an independent course in terms of information dissemination.

During that meeting, T-Max, who was a mentor to all of us in attendance, endorsed me over himself to lead the effort for the establishment of the independent newspaper. I first took it as a joke when T-Max mentioned me as the person he desired to lead the venture instead of himself. And I initially declined my selection for two very important reasons: (1) We did not have one cent to start such a very important venture, as everyone was displaced and there was devastation everywhere; and (2) it was very dangerous to operate an independent newspaper when the country was consumed by violence and destruction. A few months earlier, I was almost killed when gunmen arrested me in the downtown district of Monrovia, several blocks from where we were meeting to establish the newspaper. The armed men put a gun to my head and almost killed me when they discovered that I was a journalist.

Still deeply traumatized by such an attempt on my life, I had absolutely no desire to get myself involved in any undertaking that was to place me in further danger. However, with the insistence of T-Max, who expressed strong confidence in my ability to lead such enterprise, and with the concurrence of the other former coworkers who attended the meeting, I reluctantly accepted the challenge, assuming the post of managing editor of the *Inquirer* newspaper. Wesseh, who was one of those in the meeting, became assistant editor in chief. With the change in circumstances, I was now not only Wesseh's boss but also head of an entire media entity.

We started operation by cleaning up a space in an abandoned dilapidated public building, and a few of the organizing members brought in a couple of typewriters and some reams of paper for production. We were able to beg and convince the manager of a printing house to print our first edition, with the promise to pay off the printing cost from the sale of the paper. On January 15, 1991, the maiden edition of the *Inquirer* hit the newsstands. And that's how we got into business. From the first edition going forward, the *Inquirer* sold like hotcakes. There was no question that the people were very hungry for balanced and independent information regarding prevailing developments, at a time when the airwaves and the print media were inundated with propaganda from parties to the brutal armed conflict. Because of its independent orientation and aggressive pursuit of the news, the *Inquirer* soon became the leading and most reliable newspaper in Liberia, playing a very critical role as Liberia's window to the world during the years of the civil crises.

The progress made with the *Inquirer* did not come without tremendous sacrifices and personal risks, as the newspaper and its staff faced regular threats from warlords and armed combatants displeased with the reportage. In one incident, the building housing the offices of the *Inquirer* was set ablaze and destroyed by fire ignited by antimedia elements. Despite the setback due to destruction of its offices, the paper relocated to a different area, reorganized, and resumed publishing.

In the wake of my departure from Liberia due to constant death threats for my journalistic activities, I chose Wesseh to replace me as the managing editor of the *Inquirer* newspaper. Our relationship is a testimony that folks do not have to fight, crush, or destroy one another in the pursuit of personal ambitions. We must recognize that each of us are endowed with unique qualities, and we will benefit from favors as destined by God, not by the dictate of another human. When our efforts are harnessed in a purpose of unity, the sky is the limit to what can be accomplished in our collective.

As of this publication, Attorney Philip Wesseh, who is a graduate of the Louis Arthur Grimes School of Law at the University of Liberia, has continued to serve as the managing editor of the *Inquirer* newspaper, and he is also a university lecturer. He has emerged as one of the prominent and well-respected journalists in Liberia.

I have decided to share the story narrated above for three important reasons: Firstly, Wesseh and I are with poor family backgrounds and are examples of how education and skill training are important means of empowerment to lift people out of poverty. This is why I am a strong advocate for youth empowerment because without empowerment, I would have been stuck in poverty and my life would have been unfulfilled.

Secondly, the story regarding how Wesseh and I exchanged positions without acrimony is an indication that you do not have to envy, fight, and seek to destroy another person because that person got a promotion or because he or she was blessed with a favor. You never know what God has in store for you. In Liberia, as has also been the case in some parts of Africa, there is a common awareness that many good and promising individuals have had their careers or jobs terminated, and many have also lost their lives simply because they were envied by those who felt threatened by them.

And thirdly, Mr. Best is an example of what Liberia and Africa need to ensure sustainable growth through capacity building and empowerment. Take, for example, the professional and institution-building knowledge that we, founders of the *Inquirer,* received from the mentorship of Mr. Best, which we utilized to create Liberia's leading newspaper for the nearly one and the half decades of civil upheavals. Today, the *Inquirer,* which, over the years also served as a training ground for many aspiring journalists who are now making their marks in journalism and other professions, has continued to serve as a credible source of information dissemination.

During the years he mentored us, Mr. Best maintained a culture of hard work at the *Observer* and did not have tolerance for mediocrity. He often reminded us that journalists are part of the intelligentsia of the society, always stressing that you must be the best of whatever you are. He strived to ensure that the media is positioned to play its role as part of the main foundations on which rest a democratic society.

The *Daily Observer* newspaper was launched by Kenneth and his wife Mae Gene Best in February 1981, less than a year following the military takeover of the government in Liberia. In the succeeding years leading to the civil crises, the *Observer* suffered five closures, including one that lasted nearly two years, for alleged antigovernment reporting. There were several government imprisonment of the *Observer* staff, including Mr. Best and his wife, as well as several arson attacks, the last of which completely destroyed the building housing the newspaper's offices and facilities during the early stage of the civil upheaval.

During the prolonged period of the *Observer*'s closure in 1984, I landed a reporter job with then newly established *Suntimes* newspaper, led by legendary journalist Rufus M. Darpoh, following his release from the notorious Belle Yallah prison, where he was incarcerated for alleged antigovernment reporting.

While at *Suntimes*, I applied for an international journalism fellowship, the Daj Hammarskjöld Memorial Fellowship, through which about three to five journalists are brought to the United Nations Headquarters in New York annually for learning and mentoring in international affairs and to cover the annual session of the UN General Assembly. From the essay submissions, I became number one out of more than 380 journalists around the world, competing for only four spots in 1986. By winning the fellowship, I became the first Liberian to serve as a Daj Hammarskjöld scholar, one of the most prestigious awards in international journalism since its establishment in 1961. In 2012, Ms. Wade Williams became the second Liberian journalist to win the prestigious Daj Hammarskjöld Memorial Fellowship.

Upon return from my studies in the United States, I became assistant secretary-general and secretary-general, respectively, of the Press Union of Liberia, and during the civil war, acting president of the PUL. After I fled to the United States because of death threats during the civil war, I served as staff writer of the *Sacramento Observer* newspaper in Sacramento, California. While resident in California, I published the book, *Liberia: The Heart of Darkness—Accounts of Liberia's Civil War and Its Destabilizing Effects in West Africa* (www. google.com).

When I returned to Liberia to serve in the government, I was able to apply the knowledge acquired from the benefit of higher education and work experience in the United States, the greatest country in the world, to help promote freedom of speech and of the press in Liberia. I have come to deeply admire the strength of the American political system and the institutions of government, which are grounded in democratic traditions. Invaluable were the experiences I also obtained as a journalist working with a couple of media entities, such as the *Sacramento Observer* newspaper, a leading African American publication that advocates for the cause of African Americans and minorities. My stay at the *Observer* gave me a better understanding of the issues of civil rights, racism, and the continued struggle of African Americans for total equality in America.

Former US president Barack Obama, left, poses with Honorable Gabriel Williams following a 2017 meeting in Washington DC. (Courtesy, Liberian Embassy Public Affairs)

The doors to opportunities were open to someone like me, and I can say the same for Wesseh, as well as for many young people in Liberia and The Gambia, because of Mr. Best's tutorship and mentoring, which empowered us out of economic deprivation and poverty.

Despite the trials and tribulations, the *Daily Observer* celebrated its thirty-seventh anniversary in February 2018, becoming Liberia's oldest surviving newspaper. At thirty-seven, the *Observer* has surpassed the *Liberian Herald*, founded in 1826, which lasted for thirty-six years. As for The Gambia *Daily Observer*, Mr. Best was arrested and deported from The Gambia in 1994 by the then military regime in the country after the *Observer* published articles that were critical of the regime.

The point is that in order for Africa to catch up and compete with the rest of the developed world, the need to build capacity and empower the people cannot be overemphasized. This why throughout this book, part of the emphasis has been education and empowerment of the people as critical to the elimination of poverty and to ensure sustainable progress.

Indeed, Africa will truly rise when young Africans have access to quality education with a focus on science and technological innovations. As President Obama indicated in his 2010 State of the Union address, "In the 21st Century, the best anti-poverty program around is a world-class education." There is a need for an education program that would also focus on entrepreneurship, as well as apprenticeship training for the less educated. That is what will empower the people and create the momentum for Africa to leap and jump ahead.

Africans do not necessarily need aid and handouts, but they need opportunity to aspire to the best of their human potentials or possibilities. Limited opportunities is a major reason why many Africans are stuck in conditions of poverty. Mentoring and transfer of knowledge are critical to ensure sustainable progress in any society. As a wise saying goes in Liberia, "One has to sit on an old mat to plait a new mat." To understand the future, one has to understand the past, which comes through transfer of knowledge.

I first heard this traditional maxim quoted supra, which has profoundly impacted my conscience, from the Reverend J. Emmanuel Z. Bowier, who has distinguished himself in postwar Liberia as a leading voice of reason and a source of inspiration and motivation. Eloquent, handsome, and intellectually stimulating, the Reverend Bowier has been known as a walking library for his vast knowledge of the history of Liberia and the Liberia people. He has also been a leader in many national reconciliation endeavors, aimed at ensuring that Liberia enjoys sustainable peace.

For example, numerous protests, some violent, staged by ex-soldiers of the disbanded Armed Forces of Liberia to demand financial benefits from the government, were peacefully ended through negotiations between the government and the aggrieved ex-soldiers conducted by Reverend Bowier and other negotiators. This is highly significant, considering the fact that in some of the countries near Liberia that are also emerging from war and instability, protests by soldiers demanding financial benefits have led to resurgence of war.

Reverend Bowier's radio programs and other public engagements to educate the public about the history of Liberia and the Liberian people have been informative and instructive. As another example, following the inauguration of George Manneh Weah as president, there was a public debate as to whether Weah was the twenty-fourth or twenty-fifth president of the Republic of Liberia, in the order of presidential ranking. Weighing in on the debate on a live radio show, Reverend Bowier, a former minister of information in the government of President Samuel K. Doe, noted that Weah was the twenty-fifth president of Liberia and not the twenty-fourth, as was being debated. Also a former speech writer to two former presidents, Reverend Bowier said when one checks Liberia's presidents, it is correct to include the late president James F. Smith, who succeeded President Edward James Roye in 1871, and President Moses Blah, who succeeded President Charles Taylor in 2003.

President Roye was succeeded by Smith, his vice president, after he was violently removed from power by an angry mob. He died under mysterious circumstances, including an account that he reportedly drowned at sea while trying to escape by canoe to a ship. Roye, who was born in the state of Ohio and immigrated to Liberia before it gained independence in 1847, was elected the fifth president of Liberia in 1870. Charged with misuse of loan funds and with unconstitutional actions concerning the extension of the presidential term, Roye was forcibly removed from office in 1871. Following Roye's removal, Smith, a medical doctor who was born in Charleston, South Carolina, and also immigrated to Liberia, served as president for two months, from November 1871 to January 1872 (*Historical Dictionary of Liberia*, Second Edition; pages 305 and 384).

Charles Taylor was also succeeded by Blah, his vice president, after he was forced out of power and into exile when rebels fighting to overthrow his government invaded Monrovia. Mr. Taylor had also been indicted for war crimes for his role in Sierra Leone's civil war, and the international community had offered for him to relinquish power and go into exile as a condition for not seeking his prosecution. Mr. Blah, who was a senior member of Taylor's NPFL rebel movement before becoming vice president, also served for two months as president from August to October 2003.

There are historical accounts that Roye was the first dark-skinned president of Liberia, which up to that time was led by people who were light complexioned or mulatto. And the color of his skin was attributed to be one of the reasons for his downfall. In those days, the lighter the skin and the stronger the family and social ties within the ruling establishment, the closer one was to the proximity of power. History have it that powerful elements within the mulatto ruling class were bitter over losing power to a dark-skinned individual after Roye won a hard-fought presidential election. How sad that even though Roye was one of the most accomplished leaders in the country during that era, there were those who used the color of his skin as a reason to oppose him.

According to the *Historical Dictionary of Liberia*, before the presidency, Roye was already a successful politician, having served as newspaper editor, senator, Speaker of the House of Representatives, and chief justice of the Supreme Court of Liberia. He was also a wealthy businessman who owned the first ships to display the Liberian flag in the ports of Liverpool and New York. In today's world, can you imagine Liberians being successful enough to own planes or ships?

Roye's forced removal from power and death due to division and infighting within the tiny minority Americo-Liberian ruling class shed lights on the ills of the ruling class, which instituted policies and practices of discrimination against the majority indigenous Liberians, who were treated as primitive and inferior to the settler class. Although Liberia became an independent nation in 1847, suffrage was not extended to indigenous Liberians until 1946. It took ninety-nine years following Liberia's independence for indigenous Liberians to be extended suffrage in a country where they were the original inhabitants. Consequently, it was due to the cleavages from the unresolved past that weight the country down to collapse and implode, as the civil upheavals exemplify.

Reverend Bowier's testimony at the TRC hearings was one of the longest, but it was very informative and instructive in terms of the historical background as to how Liberia drifted into a state of instability and it was eventually consumed by war and devastation.

Bowier, who started his career in journalism as a cadet at the Ministry of Information in the 1970s, rose through the ranks, including serving in a diplomatic post as minister counselor for Press and Public Affairs at the Embassy of Liberia in Washington DC. It was while serving in Washington that President Doe appointed him as Minister of Information, a position he held until the civil war erupted, leading to Doe's assassination and collapse of the Doe regime. While in exile in the United States during the civil upheaval, Bowier studied theology and became a minister of the gospel and a psychosocial counselor.

Since his return to Liberia, Reverend Bowier has been a crisis counselor helping to peacefully resolve various crises that have erupted in the country. Notable among those crises were public disturbances involving thousands of former soldiers of the disbanded Armed Forces of Liberia. In order to demand financial benefits from the government, the ex-soldiers often carried out violent protests or threats of violence during major holiday seasons such as Christmas and the July 26 Independence Day. Some of those disturbances had the potential to get the fragile country to relapse into armed violence. A quick reminder to the reader is that Liberia's nearly fifteen-year civil war started on Christmas Eve (December 24, 1989) from an incursion by a small band of armed dissidents led by Mr. Charles Taylor.

In 2008, the Reverend Bowier also played a very critical role in bringing about a peaceful end to what could have exploded into a serious diplomatic row between Liberia and Ghana regarding the treatment of Liberian refugees in Ghana. Even though hundreds of thousands of Liberian refugees from around West Africa had been repatriated to Liberia under the internationally sponsored repatriation and resettlement programs, some 26,000 Liberian refugees still resided in Ghana during that period.

In February 2008, Liberian refugees in Ghana started a monthlong protest, during which they delivered a petition to the United Nations High Commission for Refugees (UNHCR) and the Ghana Refugee Board— the state agency responsible for refugee matters—expressing strong opposition to integration into Ghanaian society. The petition called for resettlement to a third country, or US$1,000 per person to help them return to Liberia. The UNHCR was offering only US$100 per person. During the course of the protest, some of the refugees were accused of obstructing food distribution in the Buduburam Refugee Settlement outside the Ghanaian capital of Accra.

On March 17, 2008, Ghanaian police and other security forces from the Ministry of the Interior conducted a crackdown in the refugee settlement and arrested 630 Liberians, mostly women and child refugees for involvement in the protest. The detained refugees were accused of disrupting the peace and violating Ghanaian laws. Dozens of Liberian male refugees were imprisoned while the women were taken to a remote camp miles away from Accra. While detained at that deserted camp, the women had to cover the bare cement floor or ground with their *lappas* (pieces of cloths) and mats to sit and sleep.

According to IRIN News quoting a statement from Ghana's Ministry of the Interior, the refugees' refusal to be integrated into Ghanaian society after some of them had spent eighteen years in the country was "very insulting." Ghanaian minister of the interior Kwamena Bartels said in the statement that the arrested Liberians would be stripped of their refugee status and forcibly deported to Liberia.

The Ministry of the Interior is the government agency responsible to ensure internal security, as well as maintenance of law and order in Ghana. Other branches of the ministry include the Refugee Board, the Ghana Police Service, and the Ghana Immigration Service.

In his handling of the Liberian refugee crisis, Mr. Bartels demonstrated heavy-handedness, and he proved to be very inflammatory and hawkish in his public pronouncements and actions.

Amid the heightened anti-Liberian refugee public sentiments, particularly in the media, the minister of the Interior Bartels announced at a press conference that the Ghanaian government had invoked the clause of the 1951 Refugee Convention to force the UNHCR to close operation for Liberian refugees in Ghana. He said the government had also requested for the invocation of the Cessation Clause under Articles 1 (4)e of the 1969 Organization of African Unity (OAU) Refugee Convention because the ground on which the refugees remained in Ghana was no longer valid, noting that Liberia was now safe for the refugees to return home.

According to the Ghana News Agency, the minister said this had become necessary as the refugees themselves had stated that they did not want to be integrated into the Ghanaian society and that "they would resist local integration with all their might."

Underlying the tensions between the refugees and the Ghanaian authorities were fears within the Ghanaian establishment that some of the thousands of young Liberian ex-combatants residing in the refugee camp could be used by disgruntled Ghanaian politicians for subversive activities. The Ghanaian presidential election was approaching, and there were reports of politically motivated violence in certain parts of the country.

Speaking to the media, the minister of the Interior Bartels revealed that demonstrations by Liberian refugees were orchestrated by some people with the objective of destabilizing the rather peaceful and democratic atmosphere prevailing in Ghana. Said Bartels, "It may surprise you to know that the seemingly innocent demonstration by women and children was part of a wider plot by a number of persons to cause mayhem on the settlement as well as threaten the security of the country" ("Kwamena Bartels Reveals . . . Liberian Refugees' Demo Was Meant to Destabilize Ghana," *Modern Ghana* online, April 2, 2008).

Mr. Bartels said the government was aware of the presence of a number of ex-combatants at the refugee camp, and it was not going to sit unconcerned for Ghana's national security to be jeopardized. He reminded the refugees that they had a responsibility to respect Ghana's laws, as well as refrain from subversive activities against the country.

He also disclosed to the media that based on intelligence report, the government operated a swoop on some ring leaders and others whose activities posed threats to Ghana's security, and arrests were made. Some of those arrested were hastily deported to Liberia upon being declared a national security risk while some structures housing refugees were torn down at the settlement.

News of the crisis first reached Monrovia via cellphone calls aired live on a local radio station by refugees who called from the Buduburam Refugee Settlement to report the security crackdown. As news spread regarding developments on the settlement, many Liberians expressed anger while some advocated for reciprocal actions against Ghanaians, tens of thousands of who were residents in Liberia. The Liberian government was confronted with increased anti-Ghanaian sentiments and demand for retaliation.

President Sirleaf convened a meeting involving select members of her cabinet to map out strategy as to how to successfully deal with the crisis that would safeguard the interest of the refugees without damaging the ties subsisting between both countries. During that period, there were Ghanaian peacekeepers serving in the UNMIL, who were deployed in various parts of Liberia to help ensure peace and security. Ghana was also assisting in other areas of Liberia's postwar rebuilding, including the restoration of electricity to Monrovia, and the restructuring of the Liberian Immigration Service—under the Security Sector Reform to reorganize Liberia's military and paramilitary forces, which were disbanded at the end of the civil war.

There were also Ghanaians occupying various critical positions within the leadership of UNMIL and other international organizations, who contributed well to the rebuilding process of postwar Liberia. Among them was Madam Henrietta Joy Mensa-Bonsu, a Ghanaian law professor, who served for four years as the Deputy Special Representative of the Secretary-General (DSRSG) and Head of the Rule of Law Sector of the UN Mission to Liberia. Deputy SRSG Mensa-Bonsu contributed significantly to efforts to reconstruct the law-enforcement, legal and judicial sectors of postwar Liberia. I travelled with her to various parts of Liberia on public awareness campaigns against domestic violence and rape, as well as public awareness events to promote the rule of law.

In a move that reduced rising tensions, the Liberian government announced in a statement that an official delegation was being dispatched to Ghana with immediacy to engage with the Ghanaian government for a peaceful resolution to the refugee crisis. Meanwhile, the government urged all Liberians to remain calm and law-abiding and that no acts of violence against Ghanaian residents in Liberia would be tolerated by the government. The Ministry of Information was proactive in taking to the airwaves to keep the general public assured of government's commitment to fully addressing problems facing the refugees while also highlighting the significance of the relationship between Liberia and Ghana.

Pres. Sirleaf (R) at a Capitol Hill meeting during a 2011 U.S. visit. Next to her is Amb. William V.S. Bull, then Deputy Foreign Minister and Acting Chief of Mission of the Liberian Embassy and author Gabriel Williams.

President Sirleaf appointed then Foreign Minister Olubanke King-Akerele, a well-seasoned diplomat, to head the Liberian government delegation, with a mandate to constructively engage the government of Ghana to ensure a peaceful resolution of the crisis. A workaholic and very innovative person, Minister Akerele took over the Foreign Ministry after she was engaged for some twenty-four years in international development at senior level with the UN system. The official Liberian delegation included then justice minister Philip A. Z. Banks; internal affairs minister Ambulai B. Johnson (now late); deputy immigration commissioner Abla Gadegbeku-Williams; and Gabriel I. H. Williams, deputy minister of information.

The Reverend Bowier was a leader of the advanced technical team that included security personnel and others dispatched by the Liberian government to Buduburam Refugee Settlement to assess situation on the ground and begin to engage protest leaders pending the arrival of the official delegation. The advanced technical team was very instrumental in getting the refugees to end their protest actions.

On the first day following our arrival in Accra, the Liberian government delegation met with a delegation of Ghanaian officials, led by then Minister of the Interior Kwamena Bartels. The delegation was briefed by their Ghanaian hosts regarding what transpired relative to the Liberian refugees.

Thereafter, the Liberian delegation visited the remote camp where the hundreds of Liberian women and child refugees were detained. Conditions at the center was so terrible, with women and children sitting and lying on the bare cement floor or dirt ground with only pieces of cloths and mats to sit and lie on. Seeing the conditions of the place when the convoy arrived, Minister Akerele broke down and openly wept, as she dropped to the ground among a group of weeping women and children. Every member of the delegation, including the two male ministers and myself, was also in tears.

Members of the Liberian delegation were deeply disappointed about the very poor conditions in which the women and children were detained, and some of them did not hesitate to express their displeasure during the meeting held the next morning with our Ghanaian hosts. The diplomatic niceties that usually characterized such meetings was replaced by some very strong words, as Liberia's Justice Minister Banks and Internal Affairs Minister Johnson told the Ghanaian officials that the conditions under which the Liberian woman and children were being detained were deplorable and totally unacceptable. The two Liberian officials told the Ghanaian hosts that conditions under which the refugees were being held amounted to a violation of their basic human rights and international humanitarian laws, and also that it contravened the spirit of African unity.

Verbal sparks flew with table pounding as the Ghanaian side, led by Minister Bartels, fired back, noting that the Ghanaian government was left with no alternative but to take appropriate actions in the interest of peace and stability when Liberian refugees abused the goodwill of the Ghanaian people and violated the laws of the country.

Emotions were so high during the meeting that the talks between the both sides almost broke down, had it not been for the skillful leadership of Foreign Minister Akerele, who was able to get both sides to calm down and return to the negotiating table. Although other Ghanaian officials seemed reasonable, Minister Bartels insisted that he wanted for all the Liberian refugees to leave Ghana with immediate effect. The Liberian delegation requested for a reasonable timeline to be agreed upon for the repatriation of the refugees, as the war-torn country did not have the capacity to absorb some 26,000 refugees at once due to lack of resources and basic infrastructure such as housing.

While negotiations were ongoing, the Liberian government received a diplomatic note from the government of Ghana requesting for landing authorization for its military aircrafts within a given period of time. We learned that once given the landing right, the Ghanaian government had intended to proceed with airlifting the refugees to Liberia whether or not a timetable for refugee repatriation was agreed. Such plan could not be executed without a landing authorization. Accordingly, Liberia hedged on its response to the diplomatic note from Ghana, while Minister Akerele and her delegation were engaged in a series of meetings and brainstorming sessions with a focus on a peaceful resolution of the crisis.

Every now and then, she was on a call to President Sirleaf in Monrovia and leaders of some of the major international entities in New York, Geneva, Abuja, Nairobi, or wherever she knew someone or any agency that could provide assistance toward the repatriation program. Minister Akerele was able to use her personal and official connections to help harness the international resources and support required to implement a successful repatriation program for Liberian refugees in Ghana. Addressing many of the international personalities she called by their first name, she was able to identify the necessary support intended to ensure that the repatriation process was conducted in an orderly and dignified manner, and for the refugees to be given some resettlement aid upon arrival in Liberia. The program also catered to Liberian refugees who were approved for resettlement in a third country.

Even though it was initially a focus of the refugees' protests, the UNHCR came through as a very critical partner, working with both countries to put in place a repatriation program that was generally successful. As a result of the negotiations, the UNHCR entered into a tripartite agreement with Liberia and Ghana for the repatriation of the Liberian refugees from Ghana to Liberia. Heading the UNHCR delegation to Accra for the negotiations was Ambassador Marjon V. Kamara, director of UNHCR for Africa from 2005 to 2009. Following her retirement from the UNHCR, Ms. Kamara, a Liberian, served as Liberia's ambassador to the United Nations in New York. She was the last minister of foreign affairs during the administration of President Sirleaf from 2016 to the end of the government's tenure in January 2018.

While the Liberian delegation was frantically seeking to find a resolution to the crisis, tensions remained high in the refugee settlement, which was basically on lockdown. Ghanaian security forces were fully deployed to clamp down on any confusion by the refugees, who demanded the release of their protest leaders from further detention. There was growing anger within the refugee settlement that the Liberian government had not taken an aggressive stand against Ghana, and also that the Liberian embassy in Accra had not sought their interest since the onset of the crisis.

In the wake of their pent-up anger and frustrations, some of the more radical protesters threatened to disrupt any meeting on the settlement if the Foreign Minister and her official delegation visited there. Any outbreak of violence at the Budunburam Refugee Settlement during the visit of the foreign minister in the full glare of the local and international media, which widely covered the refugee crisis, could have further poisoned the anti-Liberian refugee sentiments in the larger Ghanaian society.

In view of the foregoing, Ghanaian officials advised Madam Foreign Minister during a meeting that she should consider not visiting the Budunburam refugee settlement on this trip for security reason and that she could make a visit there the next time when the atmosphere was conducive. Minister Akerele responded that there was no way she could return to Monrovia without visiting the settlement to meet with the aggrieved people whose interest she was seeking.

Thanks to the wisdom of dispatching an advanced technical team, led by the Reverend Bowier, directly to the refugee settlement to personally engage the leaders and residents. Through the constructive engagement of Reverend Bowier and his team, leaders of the refugee community who were not in detention, including those who had planned disruption, agreed to call of their protest actions and meet with the official government delegation.

Immediately upon arrival at the refugee settlement that beautiful sunny afternoon, the official delegation and leaders of the refugee community held a closed-door meeting. Various leaders of the community, including those who had planned to cause disruption during the delegation's visit, spoke during the meeting. That quick meeting provided an opportunity for the community leaders to vent their anger and frustrations.

After leaders of the refugees spoke, Minister Akerele briefed them on the mission of the Liberian government delegation, and the agreement that was being concluded between Liberia, Ghana and the UNHCR to ensure that they were repatriated through an orderly and a dignified process. That was the beginning of the easing of the tensions, when those people heard that something was being done to address their plight as refugees in a strange land. Their frowned faces melted into smiles and harsh words were replaced by more conciliatory tones after the minister's briefing.

Thousands of Liberian refugees were already assembled in an open area on the settlement when we emerged from the meeting. In their remarks and introduction of Minister Akerele and her delegation at the beginning of the mass meeting, the refugee leaders were nonconfrontational, and they sternly warned against any disturbance. This set the stage for a mass meeting that ended on a peaceful and hopeful note. A copious note-taker and a prolific writer, Minister Akerele took the microphone and gave the refugees a detailed report on the agreement Liberia was concluding with Ghana and the UNHCR to ensure their safety and welfare. The agreement included a timeline for the orderly repatriation and resettlement of Liberian refugees from Ghana.

A straight shooter and no-nonsense person, Minister Akerele then admonished the refugees to be law-abiding at all times. She emphasized that it is very important for the refugees to respect the laws of the country which had offered them sanctuary for nearly two decades. She added that Liberia was once a leader in Africa, therefore, irrespective of the prevailing circumstances, it behooved Liberians to conduct themselves in a respectful and dignified manner whatever or wherever the challenges may be at this point in time. A forceful and passionate speaker, Minister Akerele declared that Liberia shall rise again, and that Liberians must exercise discipline and commit to hard work and honesty in the cause of the country.

Punctuated by applause from an increasingly approving crowd as she exhorted her fellow country men and women to forge ahead despite the prevailing challenges, Minister Akerele concluded by leading the crowd in the singing of Liberia's national anthem. And that was the beginning of the end of serious problems at the refugee settlement until it was finally closed down.

Earlier in the day before the visit to the settlement, Minister Akerele and her delegation, including members of our technical team, were received in audience at the official presidential residence by then president John Agyekum Kufuor, during which Minister Akerele briefed the president about the Liberian delegation and presented a special message from President Sirleaf to her Ghanaian counterpart. The special message underscored President Sirleaf's desire for an amicable resolution of the refugee situation.

In response, President Kufuor demonstrated a commendable act of statesmanship when he emphasized that Ghana will work with Liberia to ensure that the refugee problems were amicably resolved. He assured that the refugee situation will not interfere with the overall very amicable relationship between the two countries.

Following remarks for the media, President Kufuor held a closed-door meeting with the Liberian delegation. During that meeting, he provided us insights into the security challenges in Ghana leading to the pending general and presidential elections. He indicated that there were concerns and fear within the general Ghanaian society that some disgruntled politicians, who were agitating violence, could use idle and disaffected Liberian ex-combatants at the refugee settlement to disrupt the peace and destabilize the country. He also indicated that Ghanaians felt insulted by the refugees that they did not want to integrate into Ghanaian society but rather that they should be repatriated preferably to the United States or to Europe.

Nevertheless, he assured that Ghana, which was a contributor to the UN peacekeeping forces deployed in Liberia and was also involved in its postwar reconstruction, will not take any action that would disrupt the peace and stability of that country. The Ghanaian leader understood the grave security challenges and a humanitarian crisis which could develop in Liberia if there was to be a forced repatriation of the tens of thousands of refugees from Ghana to Liberia. It may be interesting to note that President Kufuor was chair of the ECOWAS subregional body who presided over the internationally backed peace negotiations in Accra, which ended Liberia's fourteen-year civil war.

The Liberian delegation's meeting with President Kufuor, as well as the meeting with the refugees at the Buduburam refugee resettlement, were covered by the Ghanaian and international media, many of which maintained regular coverage of developments since the crisis started on the refugee settlement.

Following our meeting with President Kufuor, I was left with the impression of him as an attentive and engaging leader. For example, during the period of informal interaction and refreshment, the president went around the room personally interacting with delegation members and Ghanaian officials present. As we chatted when he got to me, I recommended to His Excellency for the establishment of a channel for the Ministries of Information in both Ghana and Liberia to coordinate information to be disseminated to the media and public regarding the refugee situation. This was intended to control the release of information from both countries that may be conflicting due to lack of coordination.

In order to ease public anxiety in both countries regarding the refugee situation, it was my professional determination that there was a need to coordinate information released by the two governments to the media, and particularly to control the rhetoric's of Minister Bartels, who appeared to be having a blissful media season with his inflammatory antirefugee sentiments.

The president commended me for what he said was a great idea, and he immediately motioned his minister of information to come over. He told the minister what I had recommended, and he instructed that we both should meet to establish a channel that would enable both governments to contain the flow of misinformation, which contributed to the intensification of the refugee crisis.

Another striking development that left a lasting memory was when the Liberian delegation was being received upon arrival at the presidential residence. President Kufuor shook hands with Minister Akerele and went down the greeting line when he came to a member of the delegation's technical team. As the president shook the gentleman's hand when he was introduced, the Ghanaian leader jokingly said, "So you are the alligator in my water." And there was a burst of laughter by the gathering.

The president had apparently received intelligence report that the gentleman, a six foot plus, handsome, and dashing cigar-smoking member of the Liberian delegation, had been flirting with a female official of the Ghana Immigration Service. The female immigration official, a tall, dark, and well-proportioned beauty, was a major player in the bilateral partnership under which Ghana aided in the reorganization of Liberia's immigration service. During the course of our visit, other Ghanaian officials had notice the pair flirting and joked about it. Be that as it may, to the extent that President Kufuor was in the know about the interactions between the Liberian male guest and the Ghanaian female host was a demonstration that presidents or leaders have many eyes and ears.

It may be interesting to note that in May 2008, Mr. Bartels, who had served in several previous cabinet positions of the government since 2001, including minister of Information and Orientation, was fired by President Kufuor. According to Ghanaweb online quoting the *Enquirer*, Minister Bartels was fired in the wake of a scandal in which police apprehended sixty-seven cartons or parcels of cocaine weighing 1,900 kilograms, but forty-two of the cartons were reported stolen while locked away at the headquarters of Ghana's Criminal Investigations Division.

Even though no official reason was given for his dismissal, Ghanaian media quoted analysts as saying that Bartels's mishandling of the Liberian refugee crisis was one of the reasons for his dismissal. There were reports that the president was dissatisfied with the manner in which Minister Bartels handled the refugee crisis, at a time Ghana was playing a major regional and international role in the postwar reconstruction of Liberia.

According to Ghanaian media reports, in the wake of speculations surrounding his abrupt dismissal, Bartels wept openly as he turned over the affairs of the Ministry of the Interior, citing betrayals within the ruling establishment.

Regarding President Kufuor's directive for the Ministries of Information in both countries to coordinate, a good relationship was developed between my Ghanaian deputy minister counterpart and me. As a result, I used the opportunity to seek the support of the Ghana News Agency (GNA) in the process of reorganizing the Liberia News Agency (LINA), a semiautonomous agency under the Information Ministry, which, like virtually the entire country, collapsed during the civil war.

On another visit to Ghana to attend a meeting of the tripartite committee related to the refugee situation, I was pleased to have a working meeting with the leaders of GNA—Africa's oldest news agency created to fully articulate Ghanaian or African issues from the African perspectives. The meeting provided me more information and insights regarding the role GNA played in the establishment of LINA in the 1970s, including the training of the first group of LINA reporters in Ghana. My interest regarded how GNA could assist in the reorganization of LINA to make it economically viable and effective in information dissemination in the twenty-first-century media environment.

I returned to Monrovia hopeful with a promise that GNA would be disposed to assist LINA again, especially in the area of training, once the Liberia government made such request through the usual diplomatic channels. However, such request was never made as the minister of information, who was my immediate boss, decided not to take any actions on the report I submitted to him regarding the offer from the Ghanaians to assist in the reorganization of LINA.

Embroiled in a number of financial scandals, one of which eventually led to his dismissal and prosecution, the minister was seen to have begun to suppress programs or activities in which he was not the main player. There were deliberate actions taken to suppress the activities of other officials of the ministry who were not deemed to be reliable lieutenants of the minister, whose mismanagement of the tiny budget of the MICAT undermined the ministry's operations. Policy and administrative differences with the minister would lead to the president having me transferred from the ministry. Thereafter, the Ministry of Finance reported to the president serious financial mismanagement at the MICAT. Following an audit report finding the minister culpable of financial crimes, he was dismissed and forwarded to court for prosecution.

Before leaving office at the end of his tenure, President Kufuor visited Liberia, during which he was honored with one of the country's highest distinctions for his leadership role in bringing an end to Liberia's civil war and for supporting the country's postwar reconstruction.

The developments highlighted supra underscore the leadership qualities of individuals, whose actions or engagements, despite public awareness or not, have helped to make our part of the world a better place. The Reverend Bowier has been one of such individuals striving to make a difference in postwar Liberia through imparting of knowledge and constantly imploring Liberians to seek a peaceful resolution to differences.

During the early years of the government of President Sirleaf, which included my tenure at the MICAT, Reverend Bowier served as a consultant at the ministry, to help mentor the ministry's cabinet, which comprised mostly young people, regarding the functions of the ministry and how to successfully disseminate government information to the public. The mentorship programs, from which many government ministries and agencies benefitted, was aimed at building institutional capacity. Whatever I accomplished during my tenure at MICAT was due in part to the wise counsel of the Reverend Bowier. He has been a blessing not just to me, but most of all a blessing to war-weary Liberians seeking to understand the past as we forge ahead in our struggle to rebuild a truly wholesome functioning society.

It is, therefore, imperative that the Liberian government creates the enabling environment that would support more retired leaders and professionals, who are recognized to have distinguished themselves during the course of their respective services so that they would continue to serve in various areas of mentorship. For example, in the United States, retired leaders and professionals are usually absorbed by think tanks, policy-oriented advocacy entities, institutions of higher learning, consultancy agencies, corporate boards, you name it. Through these mediums, the United States is enriched, and the entire world as a whole is also enriched due to the invaluable contributions people who have been there and done that, as the saying goes, continue to make. They are helping to shape the future of the world, being an example of the old mat that we sit on to plait the new mat.

It is of significance that retired Liberian officials or leaders are given the necessary support to live comfortably and honorably in retirement. It is equally important that those who have labored enjoy the benefits of a comfortable retirement, which is a manifestation of a wholesome functioning society.

In order to adequately cater to the needs of senior citizens and those who are disabled or physically challenged, it is imperative for the government to set up some kind of a department of aging and the physically challenged, for example. This section of the population, along with the children, are the most vulnerable of any society.

Poverty reduction or poverty eradication can only be successful if programs are instituted to also support women and children, the aged, and the physically challenged.

There are many Liberians in the United States, for example, with the requisite education and expertise in various areas of social work, who can be encouraged to return home to contribute to the establishment of first-class social service programs to care for the vulnerable members of society, once the government demonstrates the political will and provides the necessary resources.

Don't tell me it cannot be done. We must resolve to make a difference for our generation and the generations to come. The question is, how do you want to be remembered? I'd rather be remembered for trying to make a difference in the lives of others, especially those who are less fortunate than I am.

CHAPTER SIXTEEN

Entrenched Corruption Is a Threat to Liberia's Stability

As have already been reflected in this book, during her inauguration in 2006 as Liberia and Africa's first democratically elected president, Madam Ellen Johnson Sirleaf declared corruption as public enemy number one. "Fellow Liberians, we know that if we are to achieve our economic and income goals, we must take on forcibly and effectively the debilitating cancer of corruption. Corruption erodes faith in government because of the mismanagement and misapplication of public resources. It weakens accountability, transparency and justice. Corruption short changes and undermines key decision and policy-making processes. It stifles private investments which create jobs and assures support from our partners. Corruption is a national cancer that creates hostility, distrust, and anger," the president said her in inaugural address.

President Sirleaf stated further that during the campaign, she assured Liberians that if elected, she would wage war against corruption regardless of where it exists or by whom it is practiced. "Corruption, under my Administration, will be the major public enemy. We will confront it. We will fight it. Any member of my Administration who sees this affirmation as mere posturing, or yet another attempt by yet another Liberian leader to play to the gallery on this grave issue should think twice. Anyone who desires to challenge us in this regard will do so at his or her personal disadvantage," the Liberian leader strongly warned upon taking the oath of office.

Nevertheless, as the president began her second term in 2012, a popular joke among Liberians was that corruption had now become "public friend number one" instead of "public enemy number one." This public mockery of the government was the result of a slew of corruption scandals that had engulfed the Sirleaf administration.

With numerous investigations, audit reports, indictments, and cases on court dockets reflecting widespread corruption within the government, the chair of the Liberia Anti-Corruption Commission (LACC), Madam Frances Johnson-Allison, issued a dire warning that "unless the Liberian nation takes a different approach in the fight against corruption, the whole legitimacy of this government may be undermined."

As reported in chapter 7, the *New Democrat* newspaper published an interview on December 5, 2012, in which Johnson-Allison, a former minister of justice and attorney general of Liberia, said that despite the government's achievements in the fight against corruption, the "limited success scored could be weakened by the uncooperative tendencies on the part of government institutions that stand accused of acts of corruption."

Counselor Johnson-Allison said, "People who manage various resources of the government, including those who make decisions are themselves corrupt. There's corruption in the management of revenue, and that people are stealing and doing all kinds of things. This is an open secret. Everybody knows that there's corruption. People are plundering and siphoning government's money out of the coffers."

A glaring example of how individuals in the Liberian government were plundering and siphoning government's money occurred in 2012, when Liberia was plunged in yet another major corruption scandal, this time around with serious international implications due to its negative consequences for the global environment. This was the discovery that more than 60 percent of Liberia's virgin rain forests had been granted to logging companies to plunder since President Ellen Johnson came to power in 2006.

A report released on September 4, 2012, by the London-based international watchdog organization Global Witness, which has also been cited in chapter 7, raised alarm about the plundering of Liberia's rain forests as stated below:

Then Liberian Ambassador to the U.S., Jeremiah Sulunteh, with Embassy staff DeContee Clements and author Gabriel Williams at a diplomatic event in Washington, D.C. in 2013(Courtesy, Liberian Embassy Public Affairs.)

"A quarter of Liberia's total landmass has been granted to logging companies in just two years, following an explosion in the use of secretive and often illegal logging permits, an investigation by Global Witness, Save My Future Foundation (SAMFU) and Sustainable Development Institute (SDI) shows. Unless this crisis is tackled immediately, the country's forests could suffer widespread devastation, leaving the people who depend upon them stranded and undoing the country's fragile progress following the resource-fueled conflicts of 1989-2003."

The report stated that the new logging contracts, termed "private use permit," covered 40 percent of Liberia's forest and almost half of the country's best intact forests. This gave companies linked to Malaysian logging giant Samling unparalleled access to some of Liberia's most pristine forests.

Global Witness reported that the private use permit (PUP), which was designed to allow private land owners to cut trees on their property, was being used by companies to avoid Liberia's carefully crafted forest laws and regulations. The report added that companies holding the permits were not required to log sustainably, and they paid little in compensation to either the Liberian government or the people who owned the forests for the right to export valuable tropical timbers.

The tragedy and deep sadness about this major scandal was that those implicated were mostly officials of government, including the then managing director of the state-owned Forestry Development Authority (FDA) and a former prominent official of the Sirleaf government, who has been a confidant of the president, as well as other officials of the Ministry of Agriculture, FDA, and the Ministry of Lands, Mines and Energy.

The PUP was designed to allow private landowners to cut trees on their property. Unfortunately, the communities in the forest areas did not benefit from the wholesale looting of their forests.

The scandal came to light after Global Witness, Save My Future, and the Liberia-based Sustainable Development Institute sent a letter to President Sirleaf calling for urgent action to address widespread illegality, abuse of forest communities, and the blatant disregard for governance structure that characterized Liberia's PPUPs, according to FrontPage Africa newspaper, which is also a leading Liberia-based online publication.

When the scandal was unearthed, President Sirleaf suspended the managing director of the FDA and commissioned a Special Independent Investigating Body (SIIB) to conduct a comprehensive review regarding the issuance of PUPs.

After the SIIB published its reports, the president issued Executive Order No. 44 on January 4, 2013, expanding a moratorium on logging under PUPs. Citing the reasons for declaring the moratorium, the president stated in the executive order that while the forests are part of Liberia's natural heritage that exist for the benefit of its people, there had been allegations of misrepresentations and abuses in implementing the National Forestry Reform Law of 2006, in which provision is made for private use permits that allow landowners who have forest resources on their land to apply for such permits.

The president noted that the report issued by the Special Independent Investigating Body revealed that there had been "massive fraud, misrepresentations, abuses and violations of the National Forestry Reform Law in the issuance of PUPs," according to an Executive Mansion press release.

President Sirleaf also announced the establishment of a Special Prosecution Team within the Ministry of Justice "to prosecute all violations of the law in relation to PUPs by government officials, PUP holders, community leaders, logging companies and others."

The Liberian leader also ordered a full review of the legal and regulatory framework governing the management of community forest and private user permits to assure intended reforms of the forestry sector, as embodied in the National Forestry Reform Law and the Community Rights Law.

The Special Independent Investigative Body found that the logging companies evaded payment of government taxes and requisite compensation to communities that owned the rain forests. The logging companies were able to defraud the government and the largely impoverished Liberian masses who own the forests with the support of those fat cats in the government.

At the time the scandal became public, sixty-six logging companies were in operation in the country, according to the Global Witness report.

UN Panel of Experts Report

On the heels of the report by Global Witness and the other organizations, the UN Panel of Experts on Liberia, under the mandate of the UN Security Council, also issued a report dated December 4, 2012. Among other things, the Panel of Experts report states, "Weak natural resource governance jeopardizes the government of Liberia's post-conflict reconstruction efforts, while simultaneous undermining the rule of law, hampering development, weakening the fragile social compact between the government and its citizens, and threatening stability."

The UN Panel of Experts report indicated that what was particularly worrisome was the Forestry Development Authority's procedurally flawed and—in most, if not all cases, in the context of violations of the community rights law—apparently illegal issuance of PUPs as an alternative largely unregulated route to substantial concession holdings, bypassing a formal concessions process.

According to the Panel of Experts report, "The status of private use permits in Liberia is a symptom of the ailing forestry sector; analyzing the permits provides a window on the broader sectoral challenges and reveals that the deeper, persistent root problems are uncertain land tenure and poor natural resource governance. Moreover, the Forestry Development Authority's focus on Private Use Permits has come at the expense of more sustainable forestry concessions, principally forest management contracts and timber sales contracts."

For example, no new forest management contracts and timber sales contracts were issued since 2010, whereas the Panel found that 99 percent of the PUPs granted for a total 2,327,352 hectares of land, 24 percent of Liberia's total land area, were issued in 2010 and 2011, with 89 percent issued in 2011 alone.

Following their investigations, the Panel of Experts established that the actual number of private use permits issued by the government of Liberia was uncertain. Although the Forestry Development Authority reported that 65 PUPs were issued, the FDA was only able to provide documentary evidence for 37 PUPs. The Panel's report also noted that the Ministry of Agriculture was unable to provide documentation to support the FDA's figures, despite the fact that the Minister of Agriculture, as Chair of the FDA Board, should approve and sign every PUP contract.

The Panel of Experts also reported that during its investigation, it "obtained documents that reflect troubling irregularities, apparent instances of fraud, forgery, alteration and inconsistencies, in addition to the problematic misapplication of Liberia's legal code related to forestry. For example, two Private Use Permits—one relating to Doedian District, Rivercess County, and one relating to District No. 3, Grand Bassa County—appear to be based on a single, clearly fraudulent deed."

The fraudulent deed in question "is dated 1924 and is signed by President Edwin Barclay. However Edwin Barclay did not become President of Liberia until 1930," according to the Panel of Experts' investigation. The then acting assistant minister of Lands, Mines and Energy authenticated this fraudulent deed for both permits, an act that one finds unbelievable.

In the wake of the disgusting acts of fraud, forgery, and other criminal activities perpetrated by government officials and their collaborators regarding the forestry industry, the Panel of Experts report also draws attention to the fact that the PUP saga has grave security implications for the fragile country, which is emerging from a brutal civil war that was fueled by the exploitation of timber and other natural resources to enrich a few fat cats in authority while the masses languished in abject poverty. The unfortunate fact or potential danger to peace and stability is that the masses are still impoverished while the well connected enrich themselves.

The Panel of Experts report states that PUPs often pertain to areas that are vulnerable and outside the effective control of government. "Areas covered by the Private Use Permits overlap with locations that mercenaries and Ivorian militia members use as staging grounds and support bases for cross-border attacks into the Ivory Coast, particularly in Grand Gedeh County. Moreover, these areas also contain many artisanal gold and diamond mining claims that the mercenary and militia groups use to sustain themselves." According to the Panel report, "This makes the lack of government oversight and regulation more worrisome in the current environment and a destabilizing factor for the future."

The serious international implication regarding this scandal is that Liberia retains 40 percent of the remaining rain forests in the West African subregion, one of the most important remaining biodiversity areas in the world, with unique plant and animal species like the pygmy hippo.

During Liberia's fourteen-year bloody civil war, the country's forests were plundered and timber used to finance arms sales. At the height of the civil upheavals, Liberia's logging companies were responsible for widespread abuses of forest inhabitants and destructive logging in concession areas covering nearly half of the country.

Under the dictatorship of Charles Taylor, villagers in many of the logging concession areas were reduced to nothing more than slaves on their own land. Those who resisted the exploitation of their forests were terrorized and murdered by logging companies, which had ties to higher-ups in the government, including Mr. Taylor himself. Many of the logging companies deployed private armed militias to ensure that villagers did not interrupt their indiscriminate plunder of the forests.

For example, Mr. Abbas Fawaz, a prominent Lebanese business tycoon in Liberia, who was a close business partner of Charles Taylor in several timber logging companies and other businesses, was linked to the massacre in River Gee County by the Independent National Commission on Human Rights, although he denied the allegation.

In February 2008, witnesses appearing before Liberia's Truth and Reconciliation (TRC) Public Hearings in Fishtown, River Gee, gave chilling accounts of the massacre of 369 inhabitants of a place called Glaro in River Gee County. The witnesses who survived the massacre said weapons used by the militia that committed the massacre were transported there by Mr. Fawaz, who managed a timber logging company, Maryland Wood Processing Industries, in River Gee and Maryland Counties.

As reported in chapter 3, Mr. Fawaz was suspected of supplying arms and ammunition to the Taylor regime to attack neighboring Ivory Coast. He and other members of his family were also involved with Taylor in the diamond trade, importation of arms and ammunition to the regime, among other business partnerships.

Despite his known criminal activities and collaboration with Charles Taylor, the business tycoon was not placed on the UN sanctions list as was the case with many close Taylor family members and associates. It was revealed in 2005 that a niece of Mr. Fawaz, who was reportedly involved in a sexual relationship with a senior UN official in Liberia, used her relationship with the official to secretly pass information to Charles Taylor while the former dictator was in exile in Nigeria.

Could it be that despite his known criminal activities in Liberia as a partner of Charles Taylor, Fawaz escaped the UN sanctions because of an alleged sexual relationship involving his niece and a senior UN official in Liberia at the time?

It was because of the widespread abuse of forest inhabitants and destructive logging operations that in 2003, the UN Security Council, which recognized the role logging played in Liberia's ongoing conflict, imposed sanctions, banning import of Liberian timber.

Following the end of Liberia's civil war in late 2003, the Liberian government, with support from Liberian civil society, international nongovernmental organizations, and key international partners, particularly the United States, World Bank, and European Commission, embarked on a major effort to reform the forest sector.

In 2006, the Liberia National Forestry Reform Law was enacted. The reform law was intended to address reform requirements of the UN Security Council sanctions on timber, especially focused on the improvement of timber revenue management and accountability, as well as sustainable forest management programs based on commercial conservation and community forestry. As a result of the reform of the forestry sector, the UN Security Council lifted sanctions on Liberia's timber export in June 2006.

This is why it was worrisome, as the Panel of Experts report indicated, that Liberia's forestry industry could be criminalized again by government officials in collaboration with foreign companies with past records as plunderers. More worrisome is the destabilizing effects the criminalization of the forests represent.

As the plunder of Liberia's forests has continued unabated, one of the country's leading human rights activists, Atty. Samuel Kofi Woods II, said Liberians had failed to realize that the abuse of the forest was an abuse of human civilization and a threat to the environment.

Speaking in Monrovia at the launch of a strategy of the nongovernmental organization (NGO) Coalition on Forest Governance in Liberia in October 2018, Attorney Woods expressed fear about the reported unabated loss of forests in the country to illegal logging, which, he said, has become common and may increase because measures are not being instituted to curb such criminal activities. He added that the strategy was geared toward helping Liberians to appreciate the connectivity between human survival, use of the forests and the environment in general, as well as the overall impact related to change in the climate and weather patterns.

The NGO Coalition of Liberia is a conglomeration of local nongovernmental organizations working alongside government and international partners to ensure the prudent management of Liberia's natural resources, including its forests.

The lawyer and activist indicated that researchers and forest advocates have warned that Liberians should not sit reluctantly and wait for the government to take action to reverse the situation or else the forests will be depleted. "The bleeding of our forest must come to an end, and I know it is a cliché," but "our unique species of wildlife, flora, and fauna are being destroyed and it is now time to act for the good of posterity" ("Abuse of Our Forest, Abuse of Human Civilization, Threat to Environment," *Liberian Observer*, October 24, 2018).

He recalled that for many years, communities in rural Liberia have remained hapless as they faced depravations associated with conditions imposed on them by the exploitative nature of forest management. He observed that whether it was through the looting of the 1990s during the civil war, corruption, or the private use permit, the complicity of government officials and the onslaught of greedy individuals on the forests have become a proverbial resource curse that stared the country in the face.

A human rights activist who worked tirelessly to expose human rights abuses, including child labor in Liberia, Atty. Woods was appointed as the first minister of labor in the administration of President Sirleaf, during which he instituted aggressive labor reforms to protect the rights of workers and improve their working conditions. He also served as minister of public works in the Sirleaf administration before resigning from the government to return to human rights advocacy. During the 1980s and 1990s, Woods suffered imprisonment and death threats for his relentless efforts to expose injustice in Liberia.

More than a week before Atty. Wood's remarks, Global Witness released yet another disturbing report, which shed light on how Liberia's forests were being plundered through certain shady activities. According to FrontPage Africa, On October 7, 2018, the international anti-corruption NGO issued a report, titled "Power to the People," which revealed how progressive community forestry in Liberia was being undermined by logging companies.

Liberia's reformed forestry laws include specific provisions, such as the provision titled Community Rights Laws for Forest Lands, which give communities the right to manage their own forests, empowering the people to protect and nurture their customary lands and to call the shots when negotiating with companies such as logging firms.

However, according to the Global Witness report quoted by FrontPage Africa, logging companies had hijacked the new process, disempowering communities and undermining rules intended to place control of the forests back in the hands of the Liberian people. The report noted that investigation showed that instead of working with communities to give them space for negotiations, logging companies were dodging the legal process, forming secret pacts with local elites, and making decisions that serve their own interests rather than those of the communities as a whole.

Global Witness called on the Liberian government to take immediate action to investigate and cancel any unlawful company-community agreements and ensure that its own rules are followed when new community forest agreements are approved. It also called on donors and partners for the sustainable maintenance of Liberia's forests, such as Norway, the European Union, and the United Kingdom, to press Liberia to implement the promised independent investigation into the legality of each existing permit, and ensure that any illegally logged timber was not traded for profit by those exploitative companies.

The London-based international watchdog organization also warned that the failure by logging companies to respect communities creates a serious risk for future conflict.

Under the reformed forestry laws, there are three prerequisites for a logging company to operate in a community forest in Liberia. They are the following:

First, under Chapter 6 of the Community Rights Law for Forest Lands, commercial logging companies require a contract between the community and the logging operator. Second, under Section 4.2 of the same law, the only group that may sign a contract in the name of the community is the Community Forestry Management Board. And third, under Section 6.4 of the law, and repeated in Section 10.1 of the Associated Regulations (2017), commercial logging (and therefore the contract to do so) is not permitted unless five conditions relating to the establishment of community governance structures and a forest management plan have been met ("Liberia: Community Forestry Hijacked by Logging Companies, Risk of Future Conflict Heightens," *FrontPage Africa*, October 10, 2018).

The Global Witness report was released after two years of research, and it exposed the ways many logging companies attempted to loot the forests for their own profits rather negotiate fairly with the communities who own the land.

Many of the logging companies involved reportedly showed opaque or unclear ownership. Some show apparent links to the Malaysian logging giant, Samling, raising alarm bells that the notorious company, previously linked to the private use permits scandal of 2012, as well as to committing widespread illegal logging, was seeking once again to expand its domination over Liberia's forests.

The increasingly brazen illegal activities by logging companies also claimed the attention of the leadership of the Union of Liberia Community Forests (ULCF), which issued a press statement in October 2018. The statement called on heads of logging companies in Liberia to desist from using the names of politicians and government officials to take over community forests. This, according to the ULCF, was undermining the development of rural communities and their people. The situation was also fueling conflict in the local communities, especially among leaders, according to the statement published by the *Liberian Observer*.

In the press statement, signed by the union's secretary-general Jefferson Z. Zoegbeh and approved by its president, Arthur K. Gbabow, the union said it was founded to work collaboratively with the Forestry Development Authority (FDA) and foreign partners for the protection, education, and guidance of all community forests. The FDA is the state agency established for the management of Liberia's forests.

Another Global Witness report in 2016 alleged that the then Speaker of the House of Representatives, J. Alex Tyler, as well as some prominent senators and other top officials of the government, changed Liberia's Public Procurement Commission Committee (PPCC) law in favor of a London-based company, Sable Mining, to exploit iron in a mountain in Liberia.

As a bribe to secretly carry out the illegal change in the law, Sable Mining allegedly paid out more than US$900,000 to Speaker Tyler and the other officials of government. In the wake of the outbreak of the scandal, Mr. Tyler was forced to resign from the speakership. He was subsequently defeated in the 2017 elections as an incumbent member of the House of Representatives. He and the other officials of government, as well as leaders of Sable Mining involved in the alleged economic crimes, were indicted and are facing prosecution as of this publication.

Concluding Recommendations

In order to control the seemingly unending problem of corruption in Liberia, which in the recent past contributed to the country's instability and has kept it in a state of underdevelopment and poverty, the urgent need for direct international involvement in the management of Liberia's economy cannot be overemphasized.

Accordingly, I would respectfully propose that Liberia's international partners, led by the United States, including the UN and EU, engage the Liberian government for the purpose of reaching another agreement under which the international community would assist in the management of Liberia's resources. This would require international financial experts being deployed in relevant government ministries and agencies under an arrangement with international partners, to ensure transparency and proper accountability in the management of public resources.

Such proposed economic management assistance program for Liberia could be similar to or should take into consideration lessons learned and positive results from the Governance and Economic Management Assistance Program (GEMAP). In 2005, the Liberian transitional government, which presided over the affairs of Liberia following the civil war's end, reached an agreement with the international community to establish GEMAP, a partnership between the government and the international community, to promote accountability and transparency in the country. As part of the effort to revive the broken economy of the failed Liberian state, the GEMAP intervention, which was in effect for a few years, was intended to restructure the fundamentally broken system of governance, such as widespread corruption and mismanagement, which contributed to decades of conflict and abject poverty in Liberia.

As highlighted in this book, the international involvement in the management of Liberia's resources through GEMAP immediately following the end of the civil war, led to the establishment of systems and processes for accountability and transparency. The programs that were instituted put the country on a course of rapid economic recovery, which was undermined by widespread corruption and the outbreak of the Ebola epidemic.

Because the institutions were not strong enough to sustain the systems of good governance put in place due to the limited period GEMAP was effective, the systems broke down after GEMAP ended in Liberia.

In their engagement with Liberia, the international community, led by the United States, UN, and other international partners, must insist that aid-dependent Liberia must fulfill certain conditions to ensure accountability and transparency in order to receive such foreign assistance. One of the conditions must be an agreement for international partners to comanage the Liberian economy for several more years to enable the public financial institutions and integrity agencies to be further strengthened and empowered with the requisite financial, human, and material resources.

I make this recommendation mindful that there are Liberian officials and others who have argued that Liberia is a sovereign nation that does not need outside interference in its financial and other internal affairs. That point is well and understood. However, Liberians who propagate such argument must understand that they cannot be selective in invoking national sovereignty. The sovereignty argument rings hollow when we have a country that has been unable to fully protect and provide for its own citizens and have to rely on the goodwill of the international community for survival. It certainly makes no sense to hide behind sovereignty to continue to sustain a dysfunctional system of governance in which corruption and mismanagement have thrived to the detriment of the country and its people.

The peace and progress of the fragile country are being undermined by widespread corruption and mismanagement of public resources, emboldened by the culture of impunity.

On January 29, 2018, in his first state of the nation address upon assuming office, President Weah announced that his government inherited a country that was broke. He said the economy was broken, the government was broke, the currency was in freefall, and inflation was rising. He also noted that unemployment was at an unprecedented high, and Liberia's foreign reserves were at an all-time low.

It is in view of President Weah's pronouncements regarding a broke country and broken economy that I have respectfully appealed to the international community to engage the Liberian government to assist in instituting the necessary measures to ensure accountability and transparency and economic recovery. It therefore goes without saying that due to lack of proper utilization of the country's resources, Liberia's progress has been gravely hindered and the government's efforts to ensure poverty reduction have yet to achieve the desired results.

There is also a need for the international community to lend full, if the Liberia people, in their collective, call for the establishment of war and economic crimes courts, as a measure to help end the culture of impunity in Liberia, which have emboldened war and economic criminals.

As Liberians grapple with the very delicate issues of national reconciliation, I would also respectfully recommend that the Liberian people appeal to and prevail on the government of the day to exhume and officially rebury the remains of President William R. Tolbert, who was assassinated in the bloody military coup in 1980, and accord him all the honors befitting a former president of the Republic of Liberia.

A monument should also be erected at the mass grave where the thirteen former government officials publicly executed were buried, following the putsch, with each of their names and titles engraved on the tombstones.

That all charges brought against Tolbert and his officials by the PRC be dropped, and the affected officials' convictions pronounced by the kangaroo military tribunal that tried them be overturned posthumously. This, I believe, is in the spirit of national reconciliation and unity.

It can be said without fear of contradiction that there is a growing awareness among majority of Liberians that Tolbert was one of the best presidents Liberia ever had, especially during the course of the past several decades. Simply put, ask any Liberian who lived before the outbreak of violence in the 1980s this question: "Is Liberia better off now than it was during Tolbert's administration?" I can guarantee that the answer will be a near-unanimous *No*, if not completely unanimous. While Tolbert had his failures and weaknesses, there is increasing recognition among more Liberians that the country's progress was aborted by the military takeover.

Corruption, nepotism, and other charges for which Tolbert and his officials were brutally killed have worsened. As a result of poor governance, Liberia has been rated as one of the poorest and most corrupt countries in the world. There can be no question that the painful state of affairs of Liberia will not change until Liberians are able to end the culture of impunity and create the enabling conditions for reconciliation in the country.

As then president Sirleaf noted in her 2017 annual state of the nation address, the coup d'état and years of civil conflict exacerbated long-standing divides that have left deep wounds in Liberia. This is why I respectfully submit that Liberians undertake the reconciliation process, beginning with the posthumous pardon of President Tolbert and all those who were executed following the military takeover.

In order to ensure that the historical role of President William V. S. Tubman and Liberia in the establishment of the Organization of African Unity (OAU), renamed the African Union (AU), is not distorted and forgotten, I also respectfully recommend that the AU institute measures to give the late president Tubman similar recognition that has been accorded the late Ghanaian president Kwame Nkrumah and Ethiopian emperor Haile Selassie, who were also founders of the OAU.

At the end of an AU summit in the Ethiopian capital of Addis Ababa in February 2019, a statue of Emperor Selassie was unveiled outside the $200 million magnificent AU headquarters in Addis Ababa, for his and Ethiopia's role in the formation of the OAU. Prior to that, a statue of the late president Nkrumah was also unveiled at the AU's headquarters, intended to honor his and Ghana's contributions to the establishment of the OAU.

Accordingly, I respectfully propose that a similar honor be bestowed upon Liberia by the erection of a statue of the late president Tubman on the grounds of the AU headquarters. President Tubman and Liberia's role in the establishment of the AU is well documented in chapter 12 of this book while chapter 13 also provides additional historical highlights.

As part of the advocacy, Liberians must begin a public awareness campaign, including the collection of signatures for a petition to the AU, demanding that Liberia be given the recognition it well deserves for its leadership role in the establishment of the OAU. The distortion of historical facts related to the OAU will not be ended until Liberians counter by setting the record straight, as in the case of this book.

There is a very urgent need for the AU to reform its charter and policies to reflect the realities of the prevailing global necessity for good governance and the rule of law to be sustainable in Africa. Hence, the reformed AU charter and policies must affirm that the AU will not recognize any seizure of power in African countries through military takeover or armed insurgency.

Soldiers are not trained to be politicians or political leaders. As a result, violent takeovers have deprived affected African countries of quality leadership, leaving the affairs of those countries in the hands of misfits and criminals.

Finally, to President Weah: As a manifestation that Liberians are a deeply religious people, it has been pronounced that you were appointed by God to lead his people at this time, as reflected by the support from the mass of the population, resulting in your landslide election as president of the Republic of Liberia. There is a popular Latin phrase, "Vox populi, vox Dei," which means "the voice of the people is the voice of God."

It is my prayer and hope that you would seize upon the popular mandate the Liberian people have given you to bring about the desired change Liberia needs to make a difference in the lives of the people and transform the country. We pray for your success, mindful that your success as president of Liberia is our collective success as a country and people.

May the Lord bless Liberia and Africa with more leaders with the wisdom and vision to make a difference in the lives of a vast mass of the people, who have been stuck in poverty because of poor governance.

Printed in the United States
By Bookmasters